DATE DUE

NOV 2 4 1994		

Brodart Co. Cat. # 55 137 001 Printed in USA

WITHOUT FORCE OR LIES

WITHOUT FORCE OR LIES

Voices from the Revolution of Central Europe in 1989-90

Essays, Speeches, and Eyewitness Accounts

edited by
William M. Brinton and Alan Rinzler

Mercury House, Incorporated, San Francisco
Mercury House Books, U.K., Ltd.

Published in the United States by
Mercury House
San Francisco, California

Distributed to the trade by
Consortium Book Sales & Distribution, Inc.
St. Paul, Minnesota

Library of Congress Cataloging-in-Publication Data

Without force or lies : voices from the revolution of Central Europe
  in 1989-90 : essays, speeches, and eyewitness accounts / edited by
  William M. Brinton and Alan Rinzler.
      p. cm.
  ISBN 0-916515-78-8 : $15.95
  ISBN 0-916515-92-3 (pbk.) : $10.95
1. Europe, Eastern — Politics and government — 1989— I. Brinton,
William M. II. Rinzler, Alan.
DJK51.W58   1990
943 — dc20   90-31716
                                                           CIP

Acknowledgments

The editors gratefully acknowledge the following sources for permission to publish the chapters included in this anthology:

Andrei Sakharov, "Thoughts on Progress, Peaceful Coexistence, and Intellectual Freedom," from the *New York Times,* July 22, 1968. Copyright © 1968 by The New York Times Company. Reprinted by permission.

Václav Havel, "The Power of the Powerless," extract taken from *The Power of the Powerless,* by Václav Havel, reproduced by kind permission of Unwin Hyman Ltd., London, England © 1985 Unwin Hyman, Ltd.

Alfred Herrhausen, "New Horizons in Europe," the third Arthur Burns Memorial Lecture, New York, December 4, 1989, reprinted courtesy of Deutsche Bank, Frankfurt am Main, Federal Republic of Germany.

Reiner Kunze, "Tales from *The Wonderful Years,*" from *The Wonderful Years* (New York: George Braziller, 1977), originally published in West Germany as *Die wunderbaren Jahre,* © 1976 by S. Fischer Verlag, translation copyright © 1977 by Joachim Neugroschel. Reprinted by permission.

Reiner Kunze, "Life and Consequences," from Reiner Kunze, "Konsequenz Leben — Schriftsteller Sein Im Geteilten Deutschland," pages 89–113, taken from *Das Weisse Gedicht,* © 1989 S. Fischer Verlag GmbH, Frankfurt.

Edith Anderson, "Town Mice and Country Mice," written for this anthology.

Eric Gabriel, "November in Berlin," written for this anthology.

Günter Grass, "Don't Reunify Germany," from the *New York Times,* January 7, 1990. Copyright © 1990 by The New York Times Company. Reprinted by permission.

Ewa Kuryluk, "Poland — the World's Guinea Pig," written for this anthology.

Leszek Balcerowicz, "The Price of Polish Economic Reform," speech by the Polish Minister of Finance at a meeting of the Polish Sejm in Warsaw, December 17, 1989, translation courtesy of the United States Department of State.

Adam Michnik, "The Moral and Spiritual Origins of Solidarity," written for this anthology.

Josef Škvorecký, "Czech Writers: Politicians in Spite of Themselves," from the *New York Times,* December 10, 1989. Copyright © 1989 by The New York Times Company. Reprinted by permission.

Václav Havel, "Meeting with Gorbachev," from *Granta,* spring 1988, pp. 13–15. Reprinted by permission. Originally "Treffen mit Gorbatschoff/Setkani S Gorbacovem," published by permission of Rowohlt Taschenbuch Verlag GmbH, Reinbek bei Hamburg, copyright © 1987 by Václav Havel.

Václav Havel, "Cards on the Table"("Vylozene Karty"), from *Lidové noviny,* Prague, December 1, 1988. Copyright © 1988 by Václav Havel.

Václav Havel, "Address to the Court," Václav Havel's concluding statement at the appeal tribunal of the Prague Municipal Court on March 21, 1989, and Václav Havel's final statement at the court hearing on February 21, 1989, distributed by the Documentation Centre for the Promotion of Independent Czechoslovak Literature (Dokumentationszentrum, Schwarzenberg). Copyright © 1989 by Václav Havel.

Václav Havel, "Excerpts from New Year's Day Address by the President of Czechoslovakia, Václav Havel," from the *New York Times,* January 2, 1990. Copyright © 1990 by The New York Times Company. Reprinted by permission.

Tamas Aczel, "Hungary Hearts," from the *New Republic,* December 25, 1989, pp. 13–15. Reprinted by permission of the author.

George Paul Csicsery, "The Siege on Nógrádi Street, Budapest, 1989," written for this anthology.

Norman Manea, "Romania: Three Lines with Commentary," written for this anthology.

Thomas A. Oleszczuk, "The Peaceful Revolution in Lithuania," written for this anthology.

John Jekabson, "Economic Independence Is Not Enough for Lithuania, Estonia, and Latvia," written for this anthology.

William M. Brinton, "Gorbachev and the Revolution of 1989," written for this anthology.

"Z" (anonymous), "To the Stalin Mausoleum," from "Eastern Europe . . . Central Europe . . . Europe," Proceedings of the American Academy of Arts and Sciences, in the winter 1990 issue of *Daedalus,* volume 119, number 1.

Mikhail Gorbachev, "Address to the Soviet Communist Party Central Committee's Plenary Meeting, February 5, 1990," courtesy of the Soviet embassy, Ottawa, Canada.

William M. Brinton, "The Role of the Media in a Telerevolution," written for this anthology.

William M. Brinton, "The Helsinki Final Act and Other International Covenants Supporting Freedom and Human Rights," written for this anthology.

Václav Havel, "Address to the United States Congress, February 1990," from the *Congressional Record — House,* February 21, 1990, pp. H392–H395.

Contents

Epilogue

Introduction

The expression "without force or lies" was first used by Anton P. Chekhov in his book, *Russian Silhouette,* published in 1915. We have chosen it as the title for this anthology in appreciation of the miraculous transformation that swept through Central Europe in 1989. In one country after another — Poland, Czechoslovakia, Hungary, East Germany — the oppressive ruling power of the Communist Party was overthrown . . . without violence, without campaigns of deceit or military coups, without outside interventions or invasion. Only in Romania, where an especially draconian regime more stubbornly resisted, was there extended bloodshed.

This decent, relatively peaceful revolution was all the more extraordinary for being unexpected. Who would have predicted just one year ago that within such a short, dramatic period of time, these cataclysmic upheavals could occur? Certainly their success owes much to the policies of Mikhail Gorbachev's *perestroika,* his hands-off permissive attitude toward the internal affairs of what had once been satellite countries in the so-called eastern bloc. And certainly such upheavals would not have been necessary had not the entrenched totalitarian regimes been so unyielding, stagnant, and oppressive.

But more significant than those factors, the breathtaking events of 1989 bear witness to what Václav Havel calls "the power of the powerless," the indomitable moral strength of the people, outside the political process. Years ago, Havel called for an existential revolution, a moral reconstitution of society, a radical renewal of the relationship of human beings, which no political order can replace. He described this radical change of attitude as a sense of "higher responsibility," a new-found inner relationship to other people and to the human community, which would create "post-totalitarian" democratic organizations.

"These structures should naturally arise from below as a consequence of authentic social self-organization; they should derive vital energy from a living dialogue with the genuine needs from which they arise . . . " Today, as president of Czechoslovakia, Havel is seeing this too come to pass.

Our anthology is not meant to be a complete, comprehensive, or definitive history of the revolution in Central Europe in 1989. There will likely be many lengthy volumes on that, yet to be written — since so much is still happening and it is too soon for all to be digested and understood.

What we offer instead in these pages is a very immediate inside report on recent crucial events — key speeches by leading spiritual and political figures such as Andrei Sakharov and Mikhail Gorbachev of the Soviet Union, Alfred Herrhausen of Germany, and Leszek Balcerowicz of Poland; eyewitness accounts of dramatic incidents by writers and journalists who were on the spot, such as Edith Anderson and Eric Gabriel in Germany, Ewa Kuryluk in Poland, Tamas Aczel and George Csicsery in Hungary; knowledgeable political and historical analyses by activist writers, intellectuals, and academics who have both studied and significantly participated in the revolutionary process, such as Václav Havel and Josef Škvorecký of Czechoslovakia, Reiner Kunze and Günter Grass of Germany, Norman Manea of Romania, and Thomas Oleszczuk and John Jekabson of the Baltic states of Estonia, Lithuania, and Latvia; and insightful observation and exegesis by the international lawyer, environmentalist, and publisher of Mercury House books, William M. Brinton.

The result is, we hope, a kaleidoscopic, impressionistic portrait of Central Europe at a crucial moment: a sense of how it reached this point, some dramatic views of what it has been like during the intense revolutionary moments themselves — in the streets, behind the scenes — plus a general feeling of the emotional atmosphere, the turbulent changes that continue, and the prospects for the future.

A note on our use of the term *Central Europe* in the subtitle and throughout the book: since the end of World War II and during the long dark years of the cold war, the term *Eastern Europe* has been used to describe the area that includes Poland, East Germany, Czechoslovakia, Hungary, Romania, and the other nations in the Warsaw Pact. More recently, however, progressive, revolutionary writers such as Václav Havel, Gyorgy Konrad, and others have used the term *Eastern European* when the context is neutral or negative and they are describing something in that same region that is positive, affirmative, and forward looking—as if to escape the dark shadow of the Soviet colossus of the East and to lean more toward the democratic progressive traditions of the West. So it is to this spirit and use of the term *Central Europe* that we also subscribe.

Alan Rinzler
Berkeley, California
February 1990

PART I

The Great Issues

Andrei Sakharov

Thoughts on Progress, Peaceful Coexistence, and Intellectual Freedom

The late Andrei Sakharov was not only a brilliant nuclear physicist and winner of the Nobel Prize for Peace in 1975 but also one of the most powerful and effective voices for democracy, personal freedom, and human rights in the Soviet Union. In historical terms his impact upon Russian society is equivalent to that of both Albert Einstein *and* Martin Luther King. For his courageous and outspoken views, Sakharov was stripped of his position in the scientific community and banished to Gorky for five years of internal exile. Brought home to Moscow only with the personal intervention of Mikhail Gorbachev in 1986, he died in 1989 at the age of sixty-eight.

The essay below is Sakharov's historic proposal for international peace and freedom, which was originally smuggled from the Soviet Union, translated, and published in *The New York Times* on July 22, 1968. We are proud to place it at the beginning of this book because it is one of the most important seminal documents contributing to subsequent revolutionary movements in Central Europe and the Soviet Union.

In this essay, advanced for discussion by its readers, the author has set himself the goal to present, with the greatest conviction and frankness, two theses that are supported by many people in the world. The theses are:

3

1. The division of mankind threatens it with destruction. Civilization is imperiled by: a universal thermonuclear war, catastrophic hunger for most of mankind, stupefaction from the narcotic of "mass culture" and bureaucratized dogmatism, a spreading of mass myths that put entire peoples and continents under the power of cruel and treacherous demagogues, and destruction or degeneration from the unforeseeable consequences of swift changes in the conditions of life on our planet.

In the face of these perils, any action increasing the division of mankind, any preaching of the incompatibility of world ideologies and nations is madness and a crime. Only universal cooperation under conditions of intellectual freedom and the lofty moral ideals of socialism and labor, accompanied by the elimination of dogmatism and pressures of the concealed interests of ruling classes, will preserve civilization.

The reader will understand that ideological collaboration cannot apply to those fanatical, sectarian and extremist ideologies that reject all possibility of rapprochement, discussion and compromise, for example, the ideologies of Fascist, racist, militaristic and Maoist demagogy.

Millions of people throughout the world are striving to put an end to poverty. They despise oppression, dogmatism and demagogy (and their more extreme manifestations — racism, Fascism, Stalinism and Maoism). They believe in progress based on the use, under conditions of social justice and intellectual freedom, of all the positive experience accumulated by mankind.

2. The second basic thesis is that intellectual freedom is essential to human society — freedom to obtain and distribute information, freedom for open-minded and unfearing debate and freedom from pressure by officialdom and prejudices. Such a trinity of freedom of thought is the only guarantee against an infection of people by mass myths, which, in the hands of treacherous hypocrites and demagogues, can be transformed into bloody dictatorship. Freedom of thought is the only guarantee of the feasibility of a scientific democratic approach to politics, economy and culture.

But freedom of thought is under a triple threat in modern society — from the opium of mass culture, from cowardly, egotistic and narrow-minded ideologies and from the ossified dogmatism of a bureaucratic oligarchy and its favorite weapon, ideological censorship. Therefore, freedom of thought requires the defense of all thinking and honest people. This is a mission not only for the intelligentsia but for all strata of society, particularly its most active and organized stratum, the working class. The worldwide dangers of war, famine, cults of personality and bureaucracy — these are perils for all of mankind.

Recognition by the working class and the intelligentsia of their common interests has been a striking phenomenon of the present day. The most progressive, internationalist and dedicated element of the intelligentsia is, in essence, part of the working class, and the most advanced, educated, internationalist, and broad-minded part of the working class is part of the intelligentsia.

This position of the intelligentsia in society renders senseless any loud demands that the intelligentsia subordinate its strivings to the will and interests of the working class (in the Soviet Union, Poland and other socialist countries). What these demands really mean is subordination to the will of the party or, even more specifically, to the party's central apparatus and its officials. Who will guarantee that these officials always express the genuine interests of the working class as a whole and the genuine interests of progress rather than their own caste interests?

We will divide this essay into three parts: Dangers, The Basis for Hope and A Four-Stage Plan for Cooperation.

Dangers

The Threat of Nuclear War

Three technical aspects of thermonuclear weapons have made thermonuclear war a peril to the very existence of humanity. These aspects are: the enormous destructive power of a thermonuclear explosion, the relative cheapness of rocket-thermonuclear weapons and the practical impossibility of an effective defense against a massive rocket-nuclear attack.

1. Today one can consider a three-megaton nuclear warhead as "typical" (this is somewhere between the warhead of a Minuteman and of a Titan II). The area of fires from the explosion of such a warhead is 150 times greater than from the Hiroshima bomb and the area of destruction is 30 times greater. The detonation of such a warhead over a city would create a 100-square-kilometer [40-square-mile] area of total destruction and fire.

Tens of millions of square meters of living space would be destroyed. No fewer than a million people would perish under the ruins of buildings, from fire and radiation, suffocate in the dust and smoke or die in shelters buried under debris. In the event of a ground-level explosion, the fallout of radioactive dust would create a danger of fatal exposure in an area of tens of thousands of square kilometers.

2. A few words about the cost and the possible number of explosions.

After the stage of research and development has been passed, mass production of thermonuclear weapons and carrier rockets is no more complex and expensive than, for example, the production of military aircraft, which were produced by the tens of thousands during the war.

The annual production of plutonium in the world now is in the tens of thousands of tons. If one assumes that half this output goes for military purposes and that an average of several kilograms of plutonium goes into one warhead, then enough warheads have already been accumulated to destroy mankind many times over.

3. The third aspect of thermonuclear peril (along with the power and cheapness of warheads) is what we term the practical impossibility of preventing a massive rocket attack. This situation is well known to specialists. In the popular scientific literature, for example, one can read this in an article by Richard L. Garwin and Hans A. Bethe in the *Scientific American* of March 1968.

The technology and tactics of attack have now far surpassed the technology of defense despite the development of highly maneuverable and powerful antimissiles with nuclear warheads and despite other technical ideas, such as the use of laser rays and so forth.

Improvements in the resistance of warheads to shock waves and to the radiation effects of neutron and x-ray exposure, the possibility of mass use of relatively light and inexpensive decoys that are virtually indistinguishable from warheads and exhaust the capabilities of an antimissile defense system, a perfection of tactics of massed and concentrated attacks, in time and space, that overstrain the defense detection centers, the use of orbital and fractional-orbital attacks, the use of active and passive jamming and other methods not disclosed in the press — all this has created technical and economic obstacles to an effective missile defense that, at the present time, are virtually insurmountable.

The experience of past wars shows that the first use of a new technical or tactical method of attack is usually highly effective even if a simple antidote can soon be developed. But in a thermonuclear war the first blow may be the decisive one and render null and void years of work and billions spent on creation of an antimissile system.

An exception to this would be the case of a great technical and economic difference in the potentials of two enemies. In such a case, the stronger side, creating an antimissile defense system with a multiple reserve, would face the temptation of ending the dangerous and unstable balance once and for all by embarking on a pre-emptive adventure, expending part of its attack potential on destruction of most of the enemy's launching bases and counting on impunity for the last stage of escalation, i.e., the destruction of the cities and industry of the enemy.

Fortunately for the stability of the world, the difference between the technical-economic potentials of the Soviet Union and the United States is not so great that one of the sides could undertake a "preventive aggression" without an almost inevitable risk of a destructive retaliatory blow. This situation would not be changed by a broadening of the arms race through the development of antimissile defenses.

In the opinion of many people, an opinion shared by the author, a diplomatic formulation of this mutually comprehended situation, for example, in the form of a moratorium on the construction of antimissile systems, would be a useful demonstration of a desire of the Soviet Union and the United States to preserve the status quo and not to widen the arms race for senselessly expensive antimissile systems. It would be a demonstration of a desire to cooperate, not to fight.

Two Doctrines Decried

A thermonuclear war cannot be considered a continuation of politics by other means (according to the formula of Clausewitz). It would be a means of universal suicide.

Two kinds of attempts are being made to portray thermonuclear war as an "ordinary" political act in the eyes of public opinion. One is the concept of the "paper tiger," the concept of the irresponsible Maoist adventurists. The other is the strategic doctrine of escalation, worked out by scientific and militarist circles in the United States. Without minimizing the seriousness of the challenge inherent in that doctrine, we will just note that the political strategy of peaceful coexistence is an effective counterweight to the doctrine.

A complete destruction of cities, industry, transport and systems of education, a poisoning of fields, water and air by radioactivity, a physical destruction of the larger part of mankind, poverty, barbarism, a return to savagery and a genetic degeneracy of the survivors under the impact of radiation, a destruction of the material and information basis of civilization—this is a measure of the peril that threatens the world as a result of the estrangement of the world's two superpowers.

Every rational creature, finding itself on the brink of a disaster, first tries to get away from the brink and only then does it think about the satisfaction of its other needs. If mankind is to get away from the brink, it must overcome its divisions.

A vital step would be a review of the traditional method of international affairs, which may be termed "empirical-competitive." In the simplest definition, this is a method aiming at maximum improvement of one's position everywhere possible and, simultaneously, a method of causing maximum unpleasantness to opposing forces without consideration of common welfare and common interests.

If politics were a game of two gamblers, then this would be the only possible method. But where does such a method lead in the present unprecedented situation?

The War in Vietnam

In Vietnam, the forces of reaction, lacking hope for an expression of national will in their favor, are using the force of military pressure. They are violating all legal and moral norms and are carrying out flagrant crimes against humanity. An entire people is being sacrificed to the proclaimed goal of stopping the "Communist tide."

They strive to conceal from the American people considerations of personal and party prestige, the cynicism and and cruelty, the hopelessness and ineffectiveness of the anti-Communist tasks of American policy in Vietnam, as well as the harm this war is doing to the true goals of the American people, which coincide with the universal tasks of bolstering peaceful coexistence.

To end the war in Vietnam would first of all save the people perishing there. But it also is a matter of saving peace in all the world. Nothing undermines the possibilities of peaceful coexistence more than a continuation of the war in Vietnam.

The Middle East

Another tragic example is the Middle East. If direct responsibility on Vietnam rests with the United States, in the Middle East direct responsibility rests not with the United States but with the Soviet Union (and with Britain in 1948 and 1956).

On one hand, there was an irresponsible encouragement of so-called Arab unity (which in no way had a socialist character — look at Jordan — but was purely nationalist and anti-Israel). It was said that the struggle of the Arabs had an essentially anti-imperialist character. On the other hand, there was an equally irresponsible encouragement of Israeli extremists.

We cannot here analyze the entire contradictory and tragic history of the events of the last 20 years, in the course of which the Arabs and Israel, along with historically justified actions, carried out reprehensible deeds, often brought about by the actions of external forces.

Thus in 1948, Israel waged a defensive war. But in 1956, the actions of Israel appeared reprehensible. The preventive six-day war in the face of threats of destruction by merciless, numerically vastly superior forces of the Arab coalition could have been justifiable. But the cruelty to refugees and prisoners of war and the striving to settle territorial questions by military means must be condemned. Despite this condemnation, the breaking of relations with Israel appears a mistake, complicating a peaceful settlement in this region and complicating a necessary diplomatic recognition of Israel by the Arab governments.

In our opinion, certain changes must be made in the conduct of international affairs, systematically subordinating all concrete aims and local tasks to the basic task of actively preventing an aggravation of the international situation, of actively pursuing and expanding peaceful coexistence to the level of cooperation, of making policy in such a way that its immediate and long-range effects will in no way sharpen international tensions and will not create difficulties for either side that would strengthen the forces of reaction, militarism, nationalism, Fascism and revanchism.

International affairs must be completely permeated with scientific methodology and a democratic spirit, with a fearless weighing of all facts, views and theories, with maximum publicity of ultimate and intermediate goals and with a consistency of principles.

New Principles Proposed

The international policies of the world's two leading superpowers (the United States and the Soviet Union) must be based on a universal acceptance of unified and general principles, which we initially would formulate as follows:

1. All peoples have the right to decide their own fate with a free expression of will. This right is guaranteed by international control over observance by all governments of the "Declaration of the Rights of Man." International control presupposes the use of economic sanctions as well as the use of military forces of the United Nations in defense of "the rights of man."

2. All military and military-economic forms of export of revolution and counterrevolution are illegal and are tantamount to aggression.

3. All countries strive toward mutual help in economic, cultural and general-organizational problems with the aim of eliminating painlessly all domestic and international difficulties and preventing a sharpening of international tensions and a strengthening of the forces of reaction.

4. International policy does not aim at exploiting local, specific conditions to widen zones of influence and create difficulties for another country. The goal of international policy is to insure universal fulfillment of the "Declaration of the Rights of Man" and to prevent a sharpening of international tensions and a strengthening of militarist and nationalist tendencies.

Such a set of principles would in no way be a betrayal of the revolutionary and national liberation struggle, the struggle against reaction and counterrevolution. On the contrary, with the elimination of all doubtful cases, it would be easier to take decisive action in those extreme cases of reaction, racism and militarism that allow no course other than armed struggle. A strengthening of peaceful coexistence would create an opportunity to avert such tragic events as those in Greece and Indonesia.

Such a set of principles would present the Soviet armed forces with a precisely defined defensive mission, a mission of defending our country and our allies from aggression. As history has shown, our people and their armed forces are unconquerable when they are defending their homeland and its great social and cultural movements.

Hunger and Overpopulation

Specialists are paying attention to a growing threat of hunger in the poorer half of the world. Although the 50 per cent increase of the world's population in the last 30 years has been accompanied by a 70 per cent increase in food production, the balance in the poorer half of the world has been unfavorable. The situation in India, Indonesia, in a number of countries of Latin America and in a large number of other underdeveloped countries — the absence of technical-economic reserves, competent officials and cultural skills, social backwardness, a high birth rate — all this systematically worsens the food balance and without doubt will continue to worsen it in the coming years.

The answer would be a wide application of fertilizers, an improvement of irrigation systems, better farm technology, wider use of the resources of the oceans and a gradual perfection of the production, already technically feasible, of synthetic foods, primarily amino acids. However, this is all fine for the rich nations. In the more backward countries, it is apparent from an analysis of the situation and existing trends that an improvement cannot be achieved in the near future, before the expected date of tragedy, 1975–80.

What is involved is a prognosticated deterioration of the average food balance in which localized food crises merge into a sea of hunger, intolerable suffering and desperation, the grief and fury of millions of people. This is a tragic threat to all mankind. A catastrophe of such dimension cannot but have profound consequences for the entire world and for every human being. It will provoke a wave of wars and hatred, a decline of standards of living throughout the world and will leave a tragic, cynical and anti-Communist mark on the life of future generations.

The first reaction of a Philistine in hearing about the problem is that "they" are responsible for their plight because "they" reproduce so rapidly. Unquestionably, control of the birth rate is important and the people in India, for example, are taking steps in this direction. But these steps remain largely ineffective under social and economic backwardness, surviving traditions of large families, an absence of old-age benefits, a high infant mortality rate until quite recently, and a continuing threat of death from starvation.

It is apparently futile only to insist that the more backward countries restrict their birth rates. What is needed most of all is economic and technical assistance to these countries. This assistance must be of such scale and generosity that it is absolutely impossible before the estrangement in the world and the egotistical, narrow-minded approach to relations between nations and races is eliminated. It is impossible as long as the United States and the Soviet Union, the world's two great superpowers, look upon each other as rivals and opponents.

Social factors play an important role in the tragic present situation and the still more tragic future of the poor regions. It must be clearly understood that if a threat of hunger is, along with a striving toward national independence, the main cause of "agrarian" revolution, the "agrarian" revolution in itself will not eliminate the threat of hunger, at least not in the immediate future. The threat of hunger cannot be eliminated without the assistance of the developed countries, and this requires significant changes in their foreign and domestic policies.

Inequality of American Negroes

At this time, the white citizens of the United States are unwilling to accept even minimum sacrifices to eliminate the unequal economic and cultural position of the country's black citizens, who make up 10 per cent of the population.

It is necessary to change the psychology of the American citizens so that they will voluntarily and generously support their government and worldwide efforts to change the economy, technology and level of living of billions of people. This, of course, would entail a serious decline in the United States rate of economic growth. The Americans should be willing to do this solely for the sake of lofty and distant goals, for the sake of preserving civilization and mankind on our planet.

Similar changes in the psychology of people and practical activities of governments must be achieved in the Soviet Union and other developed countries.

In the opinion of the author, a 15-year tax equal to 20 per cent of national incomes must be imposed on developed nations. The imposition of such a tax would automatically lead to a significant reduction in expeditures for weapons. Such common assistance would have an important effect of stabilizing and improving the situation in the most underdeveloped countries, restricting the influence of extremists of all types.

Changes in the economic situation of underdeveloped countries would solve the problem of high birth rates with relative ease, as has been shown by the experience of developed countries, without the barbaric method of sterilization.

Certain changes in the policies, viewpoints and traditions on this delicate question are inescapable in the advanced countries as well. Mankind can develop smoothly only if it looks upon itself in a demographic sense as a unit, a single family without divisions into nations other than in matters of history and traditions.

Therefore, government policy, legislation on the family and marriage and propaganda should not encourage an increase in the birth rates of advanced countries while demanding that it be curtailed in underdeveloped countries that are receiving assistance. Such a two-faced game would produce nothing but bitterness and nationalism.

In conclusion on that point, I want to emphasize that the question of regulating birth rates is highly complex and that any standardized, dogmatic solution "for all time and all peoples" would be wrong. All the foregoing, incidentally, should be accepted with the reservation that it is somewhat of a simplification.

Pollution of Environment

We live in a swiftly changing world. Industrial and water-engineering projects, cutting of forests, plowing up of virgin lands, the use of poisonous chemicals — all this is changing the face of the earth, our "habitat."

Scientific study of all the interrelationships in nature and the consequences of our interference clearly lag behind the changes. Large amounts of harmful wastes of industry and transport are being dumped into the air and water, including cancer-inducing substances. Will the safe limit be passed everywhere, as has already happened in a number of places?

Carbon dioxide from the burning of coal is altering the heat-reflecting qualities of the atmosphere. Sooner or later, this will reach a dangerous level. But we do not know when. Poisonous chemicals used in agriculture are penetrating into the body of man and animals directly and in more dangerous modified compounds, causing serious damage to the brain, the nervous sytem, blood-forming organs, the liver and other organs. Here, too, the safe limit can be easily crossed, but the question has not been fully studied and it is difficult to control all these processes.

The use of antibiotics in poultry raising has led to the development of new disease-causing microbes that are resistant to antibiotics.

I could also mention the problems of dumping detergents and radioactive wastes, erosion and salinization of soils, the flooding of meadows, the cutting of forests on mountain slopes and in watersheds, the destruction of birds and other useful wildlife like toads and frogs and many other examples of senseless despoliation caused by local, temporary, bureaucratic and egotistical interest and sometimes simply by questions of bureaucratic prestige, as in the sad fate of Lake Baikal.

The problem of geohygiene (earth hygiene) is highly complex and closely tied to economic and social problems. This problem can therefore not be solved on a national and especially not on a local basis. The salvation of our environment requires that we overcome our divisions and the pressure of temporary, local interests. Otherwise, the Soviet Union will poison the United States with its wastes and vice versa. At present, this is a hyperbole. But with a 10 per cent annual increase of wastes, the increase over 100 years will be 20,000 times.

Police Dictatorship

An extreme reflection of the dangers confronting modern social development is the growth of racism, nationalism and militarism and, in particular, the rise of demagogic, hypocritical and monstrously cruel dictatorial police regimes. Foremost are the regimes of Stalin, Hitler and Mao Tse-tung, and a number of extremely reactionary regimes in smaller countries, Spain, Portugal, South Africa, Greece, Albania, Haiti and other Latin-American countries.

These tragic developments have always derived from the struggle of egotistical and group interests, the struggle for unlimited power, suppression of intellectual freedom, a spread of intellectually simplified, narrow-minded mass myths (the myth of race, of land and blood, the myth about the Jewish danger, anti-intellectualism, the concept of lebensraum in Germany, the myth about the sharpening of the class struggle and proletarian infallibility bolstered by the cult of Stalin and by exaggeration of the contradictions with capitalism in the Soviet Union, the myth about Mao Tse-tung, extreme Chinese nationalism and the resurrection of the lebensraum concept, of anti-intellectualism, extreme antihumanism and certain prejudices of peasant socialism in China).

The usual practice is the use of demagogy, storm troopers and Red Guards in the first stage and terrorist bureaucracy with reliable cadres of the type of Eichmann, Himmler, Yezhov and Beria at the summit of the deification of unlimited power.

The Rule of Hitler

The world will never forget the burning of books in the squares of German cities, the hysterical, cannibalistic speeches of the Fascist "fuehrers" and their even more cannibalistic plans for the destruction of entire peoples, including the Russians. Fascism began a partial realization of these plans during the war it unleashed, annihilating prisoners of war and hostages, burning villages, carrying out a criminal policy of genocide (during the war, the main blow of genocide was aimed at the Jews, a policy that apparently was also meant to be provocative, especially in the Ukraine and Poland).

We shall never forget the kilometer-long trenches filled with bodies, the gas chambers, the SS dogs, the fanatical doctors, the piles of women's hair, suitcases with gold teeth and fertilizer from the factories of death.

Analyzing the causes of Hitler's coming to power, we will never forget the role of German and international monopolist capital. We also will not forget the criminally sectarian and dogmatically narrow policies of Stalin and his associates, setting Socialists and Communists against one another (this has been well related in the famous letter to Ilya Ehrenburg by Ernst Henri).

The Stalinist Period

Fascism lasted 12 years in Germany. Stalinism lasted twice as long in the Soviet Union. There are many common features but also certain differences. Stalinism exhibited a much more subtle kind of hypocrisy and demagogy, with reliance not on an openly cannibalistic program like Hitler's but on a progressive, scientific and popular socialist ideology.

This served as a convenient screen for deceiving the working class, for weakening the vigilance of the intellectuals and other rivals in the struggle for power, with the treacherous and sudden use of the machinery of torture, execution and informants, intimidating and making fools of millions of people, the majority of whom were neither cowards nor fools. As a consequence of this "specific feature" of Stalinism, it was the Soviet people, its most active, talented and honest representatives, who suffered the most terrible blow.

At least 10 to 15 million people perished in the torture chambers of the N.K.V.D. [secret police] from torture and execution, in camps for exiled kulaks [rich peasants] and so-called semikulaks and members of their families and in camps "without the right of correspondence" (which were in fact the prototypes of the Fascist death camps where, for example, thousands of prisoners were machine-gunned because of "overcrowding" or as a result of "special orders").

People perished in the mines of Norilsk and Vorkuta from freezing, starvation and exhausting labor, at countless construction projects, in timber cutting, building of canals or simply during transportation in prison trains, in the overcrowded holds of "death ships" in the Sea of Okhotsk and during the resettlement of entire peoples, the Crimean Tatars, the Volga Germans, the Kalmyks and other Caucasus peoples. Readers of the literary journal *Novy Mir* recently could read for themselves a description of the "road of death" between Norilsk and Igarka [in northern Siberia].

Temporary masters were replaced (Yagoda, Molotov, Yezhov, Zhdanov, Malenkov, Beria), but the antipeople's regime of Stalin remained equally cruel and at the same time dogmatically narrow and blind in its cruelty. The killing of military and engineering officials before the war, the blind faith in the "reasonableness" of the colleague in crime, Hitler, and the other reasons for the national tragedy of 1941 have been well described in the book by Nekrich, in the notes of Maj. Gen. Grigorenko and other publications — these are far from the only examples of the combination of crime, narrow-mindedness and short-sightedness.

Stalinist dogmatism and isolation from real life was demonstrated particularly in the countryside, in the policy of unlimited exploitation and the predatory forced deliveries at "symbolic" prices, in the almost serf-like enslavement of the peasantry, the depriving of peasants of the most simple means of mechanization and the appointment of collective-farm chairmen on the basis of their cunning and obsequiousness. The results are evident — a profound and hard-to-correct destruction of the economy and way of life in the countryside, which, by the law of interconnected vessels, damaged industry as well.

The inhuman character of Stalinism was demonstrated by the repressions of prisoners of war who survived Fascist camps and then were thrown into Stalinist camps, the antiworker "decrees," the criminal exile of entire peoples condemned to slow death, the unenlightened zoological kind of anti-semitism that was characterisitic of Stalinist bureaurcracy and the N.K.V.D. (and Stalin personally), the Ukrainophobia characteristic of Stalin and the draconian laws for the protection of socialist property (five years' imprisonment for stealing some grain from the fields and so forth) that served mainly as a means of fulfilling the demands of the "slave market."

An Unpublished History

A profound analysis of the origin and development of Stalinism is contained in the 1,000-page monograph of R. Medvedev. This was written from a socialist, Marxist point of view and is a successful work, but unfortunately it has not yet been published. The present author is not likely to receive such a compliment from Comrade Medvedev, who finds elements of "Westernism" in his views. Well, there is nothing like controversy! Actually the views of the present author are profoundly socialist and he hopes that the attentive reader will understand this.

The author is quite aware of the monstrous relations in human and international affairs brought forth by the egotistical principle of capital when it is not under pressure from socialist and progressive forces. He also thinks however, that progressives in the West understand this better than he does and are waging a struggle against these manifestations. The author is concentrating his attention on what is before his eyes and on what is obstructing, from his point of view, a worldwide overcoming of estrangement, obstructing the struggle for democracy, social progress and intellectual freedom.

Our country has started on the path of cleansing away the foulness of Stalinism. "We are squeezing the slave out of ourselves drop by drop" (an expression of Anton Chekhov). We are learning to express our opinions, without taking the lead from the bosses and without fearing for our lives.

Khrushchev Is Credited

The beginning of this arduous and far from straight path evidently dates from the report of Nikita S. Khrushchev to the 20th congress of the soviet Communist party. This bold speech, which came as a surprise to Stalin's accomplices in crime, and a number of associated measures — the release of hundreds of thousands of political prisoners and their rehabilitation, steps toward a revival of the principles of peaceful coexistence and toward a revival of democracy — oblige us to value highly the historic role of Khrushchev despite his regrettable mistakes of a voluntarist character in subsequent years and despite the fact that Khrushchev, while Stalin was alive, was one of his collaborators in crime, occupying a number of influential posts.

The exposure of Stalinism in our country still has a long way to go. It is imperative, of course, that we publish all authentic documents, including the archives of the N.K.V.D., and conduct nationwide investigations. It would be highly useful for the international authority of the Soviet Communtist party and the ideals of socialism if, as was planned in 1964 but never carried out, the party were to announce the "symbolic" expulsion of Stalin, murderer of millions of party members, and at the same time the political rehabilitation of the victims of Stalinism.

In 1936–39 alone more than 1.2 million party members, half of the total membership, were arrested. Only 50,000 regained freedom; the others were tortured during interrogation or were shot (600,000) or died in camps. Only in isolated cases were the rehabilitated allowed to assume responsible posts, even fewer were permitted to take part in the investigation of crimes of which they had been witnesses or victims.

We are often told lately not to "rub salt into wounds." This is usually being said by people who suffered no wounds. Actually only the most meticulous analysis of the past and of its consequences will now enable us to wash off the blood and dirt that befouled our banner.

It is sometimes suggested in the literature that the political manifestations of Stalinism represented a sort of superstructure over the economic basis of an anti-Leninist pseudosocialism that led to the formation in the Soviet Union of a distinct class — a bureaucratic elite from which all key positions are filled and which is rewarded for its work through open and concealed privileges. I cannot deny that there is some (but not the whole) truth in such an interpretation, which would help explain the vitality of neo-Stalinism, but a full analysis of this issue would go beyond the scope of this article, which focuses on another aspect of the problem.

It is imperative that we restrict in every possible way the influence of neo-Stalinists in our political life. Here we are compelled to mention a specific person. One of the most influential representatives of neo-Stalinism at the present time is the director of the Science Department of the Communist party's Central Committee, Sergei P. Trapeznikov. The leadership of our country and our people should know that the views of this unquestionably intelligent, shrewd and highly consistent man are basically Stalinist (from our point of view, they reflect the interests of the bureaucratic elite).

His views differ fundamentally from the dreams and aspirations of the majority and most active section of the intelligentsia, which, in our opinion, reflect the true interests of all our people and progressive mankind. The leadership of our country should understand that as long as such a man (if I correctly understand the nature of his views) exercises influence, it is impossible to hope for a strengthening of the party's position among scientific and artistic intellectuals. An indication of this was given at the last elections in the Academy of Sciences when S.P. Trapeznikov was rejeced by a substantial majority of votes, but this hint was not "understood" by the leadership.

The issue does not involve the professional or personal qualities of Trapeznikov, about which I know little. The issue involves his political views. I have based the foregoing on word-of-mouth evidence. Therefore, I cannot in principle exclude the possibility (although it is unlikely) that in reality everything is quite the opposite. In that pleasant event, I would beg forgiveness and retract what I have written.

The Cult of Maoism

In recent years, demagogy, violence, cruelty and vileness have seized a great country that had embarked on the path of socialist development. I refer, of course, to China. It is impossible without horror and pain to read about the mass contagion of antihumanism being spread by "the great helmsman" and his accomplices, about the Red Guards who, according to the Chinese radio, "jumped with joy" during public executions of "ideological enemies" of Chairman Mao.

The idiocy of the cult of personality has assumed in China monstrous, grotesquely tragicomic forms, carrying to the point of absurdity many of the traits of Stalinism and Hitlerism. But this absurdity has proved effective in making fools of tens of millions of people and in destroying and humiliating millions of more honest and more intelligent people.

The full picture of the tragedy in China is unclear. But in any case, it is impossible to look at it in isolation from the internal economic difficulties of China after the collapse of the adventure of "the great leap forward," in isolation from the struggle by various groups for power, or in isolation from the foreign political situation — the war in Vietnam, the estrangement in the world and the inadequate and lagging struggle against Stalinism in the Soviet Union.

The greatest damage from Maoism is often seen in the split of the world Communist movement. That is, of course, not so. The split is the result of a disease and to some extent represents the way to treat that disease. In the presence of the disease a formal unity would have been a dangerous, unprincipled compromise that would have led the world Communist movement into a blind alley once and for all.

Actually the crimes of the Maoists against human rights have gone much too far, and the Chinese people are now in much greater need of help from the world's democratic forces to defend their rights than in need of the unity of the world's

Communist forces, in the Maoist sense, for the purpose of combatting the so-called imperialist peril somewhere in Africa or in Latin America or in the Middle East.

The Threat to Intellectual Freedom

This is a threat to the independence and worth of the human personality, a threat to the meaning of human life.

Nothing threatens freedom of the personality and the meaning of life like war, poverty, terror. But there are also indirect and only slightly more remote dangers.

One of these is the stupefaction of man (the "gray mass," to use the cynical term of bourgeois prognosticators) by mass culture with its intentional or commercially motivated lowering of intellectual level and content, with its stress on entertainment or utilitarianism, and with its carefully protective censorship.

Another example is related to the question of education. A system of education under government control, separation of school and church, universal free education — all these are great achievements of social progress. But everything has a reverse side. In this case it is excessive standardization, extending to the teaching process itself, to the curriculum, especially in literature, history, civics, geography, and to the system of examinations.

One cannot but see a danger in excessive reference to authority and in the limitation of discussion and intellectual boldness at an age when personal convictions are beginning to be formed. In the old China, the system of examinations for official positions led to mental stagnation and to the canonizing of the reactionary aspects of Confucianism. It is highly undesirable to have anything like that in a modern society.

Modern technology and mass psychology constantly suggest new possibilities of managing the norms of behavior, the strivings and convictions of masses of people. This involves not only management through information based on the theory of advertising and mass psychology, but also more technical methods that are widely discussed in the press abroad. Examples are biochemical control of the birth rate, biochemical control of psychic processes and electronic control of such processes.

Warning on Experiments

It seems to me that we cannot completely ignore these new methods or prohibit the progress of science and technology, but we must be clearly aware of the awesome danger to basic human values and to the meaning of life that may be concealed in the misuse of technical and biochemical methods and the methods of mass psychology.

Man must not be turned into a chicken or a rat as in the well known experiments in which elation is induced electrically through electrodes inserted into the brain. Related to this is the question of the ever increasing use of tranquilizers and anti-depressants, legal and illegal narcotics, and so forth.

We also must not forget the very real danger mentioned by Norbert Wiener in his book *Cybernetics,* namely the absence in cybernetic machines of stable human norms of behavior. The tempting, unprecedented power that mankind, or, even worse, a particular group in a divided mankind, may derive from the wise counsels of its future intellectual aides, the artificial "thinking" automata, may, as Wiener warned, become a fatal trap; the counsels may turn out to be incredibly insidious and, instead of pursuing human objectives, may pursue completely abstract problems that had been transformed in an unforeseen manner in the artificial brain.

Such a danger will become quite real in a few decades if human values, particularly freedom of thought, will not be strengthened, if alienation will not be eliminated.

Let us now return to the dangers of today, to the need for intellectual freedom, which will enable the public at large and the intelligentsia to control and assess all acts, designs and decisions of the ruling group.

Marx and Lenin Quoted

Marx once wrote that the illusion that the "bosses know everything best" and "only the higher circles familiar with the official nature of things can pass judgment" was held by officials who equate the public weal with governmental authority.

Both Marx and Lenin always stressed the viciousness of a bureaucratic system as the opposite of a democratic system. Lenin used to say that every cook should learn how to govern. Now the diversity and complexity of social phenomena and the dangers facing mankind have become immeasurably greater; and it is therefore all the more important that mankind be protected against the danger of dogmatic and voluntaristic errors, which are inevitable when decisions are reached in a closed circle of secret advisers or shadow cabinets.

It is no wonder that the problem of censorship (in the broadest sense of the word) has been one of the central issues in the ideological struggle of the last few years. Here is what a progressive American sociologist, Lewis A. Coser, has to say on this point:

> It would be absurd to attribute the alienation of many avant-garde authors solely to the battle with the censors; yet one may well maintain that those battles contributed in no mean measure to such alienation. To these authors, the censor came to be the very symbol of the Philistinism, hypocrisy and meanness of bourgeois society.
>
> Many an author who was initially apolitical was drawn to the political left in the United States because the left was in the forefront of the battle against censorship. The close alliance of avant-garde art with avant-garde political and social radicalism can be accounted for, at least in part, by the fact that they came to be merged in the mind of many as a single battle for freedom against all repression. [I quote from an article by Igor Kon, published in *Novy Mir* in January 1968.]

We are all familiar with the passionate and closely argued appeal against censorship by the outstanding Soviet writer A. Solzhenitsyn. He as well as G. Vladimov, G. Svirsky and other writers who have spoken out on the subject have clearly shown how incompetent censorship destroys the living soul of Soviet literature; but the same applies, of course, to all other manifestations of social thought, causing stagnation and dullness and preventing fresh and deep ideas.

Such ideas, after all, can arise only in discussion, in the face of objections, only if there is a potential possibility of expressing not only true, but also dubious ideas. This was clear to the philosophers of ancient Greece and hardly anyone nowadays would have any doubts on that score. But after 50 years of complete domination over the minds of an entire nation, our leaders seem to fear even allusions to such a discussion.

At this point we must touch on some disgraceful tendencies that have become evident in the last few years. We will cite only a few isolated examples without trying to create a whole picture. The crippling censorship of Soviet artistic and political literature has again been intensified. Dozens of brilliant writings cannot see the light of day. They include some of the best of Solzhenitsyn's works, executed with great artistic and moral force and containing profound artistic and philosophical generalizations. Is this not a disgrace?

Wide indignation has been aroused by the recent decree adopted by the Supreme Soviet of the Russian Republic, amending the Criminal Code in direct contravention of the civil rights proclaimed by our Constitution. [The decree included literary protests among acts punishable under Article 190, which deals with failure to report crimes.]

Literary Trials Assailed

The Daniel-Sinyavsky trial, which has been condemned by the progressive public in the Soviet Union and abroad (from Louis Aragon to Graham Greene) and has compromised the Communist system, has still not been reviewed. The two writers languish in a camp with a strict regime and are being subjected (especially Daniel) to harsh humiliations and ordeals.

Most political prisoners are now kept in a group of camps in the Mordvinian Republic, where the total number of prisoners, including criminals, is about 50,000. According to available information, the regime has become increasingly severe in these camps, with personnel left over from Stalinist times playing an increasing role. It should be said, in all fairness, that a certain improvement has been noted very recently; it is to be hoped that this turn of events will continue.

The restoration of Leninist principles of public control over places of imprisonment would undoubtedly be a healthy development. Equally important would be a complete amnesty of political prisoners, and not just the recent limited amnesty, which was proclaimed on the 50th anniversary of the October Revolution as a result of a temporary victory of rightist tendencies in our leadership. There should also be a review of all political trials that are still raising doubts among the progressive public.

Was it not disgraceful to allow the arrest, 12-month detention without trial and then the conviction and sentencing to terms of five to seven years of Ginzburg, Galanskov and others for activities that actually amounted to a defense of civil liberties and (partly, as an example) of Daniel and Sinyavsky personally? The author of these lines sent an appeal to the party's Central Committee on Feb. 11, 1967, asking that the Ginzburg-Galanskov case be closed. He received no reply and no explanations on the substance of the case. It was only later that he heard that there had been an attempt (apparently inspired by Semichastny, the former chairman of the K.G.B.) to slander the present writer and several other persons on the basis of inspired false testimony by one of the accused in the Galanskov-Ginzburg case. Subsequently the testimony of that person — Dobrovolsky — was used at the trial as evidence to show that Ginzburg and Galanskov had ties with a foreign anti-Soviet organization, which one cannot help but doubt.

[The reference here is to evidence given by Dobrovolsky in the pretrial investigation of the case of Vladimir Bukovsky, Vadim Delone and Yevgeny Kushev in early 1967. Dobrovolsky said there allegedly existed "a single anti-Communist front ranging from Academicians Sakharov and Leontovich to SMOG," an illegal group of young writers and artists.]

Persecution Is Charged

Was it not disgraceful to permit the conviction and sentencing (to three years in camps) of Khaustov and Bukovsky for participation in a meeting in defense of their comrades? Was it not disgraceful to allow persecution, in the best witchhunt tradition, of dozens of members of the Soviet intelligentsia who spoke out against the arbitrariness of judicial and psychiatric agencies, to attempt to force honorable people to sign false, hypocritical "retractions," to dismiss and blacklist people, to deprive young writers, editors and other members of the intelligentsia of all means of existence?

Here is a typical example of this kind of activity.

Comrade B., a woman editor of books on motion pictures, was summoned to the party's district committee. The first question was, Who gave you the letter in defense of Ginzburg to sign? Allow me not to reply to that question, she answered. All right, you can go, we want to talk this over, she was told. The decision was to expel the woman from the party and to recommend that she be dismissed from her job and barred from working anywhere else in the field of culture.

With such methods of persuasion and indoctrination the party can hardly expect to claim the role of spiritual leader of mankind.

Was it not disgraceful to have the speech at the Moscow party conference by the president of the Academy of Sciences [Mstislav V. Keldysh], who is evidently either too intimidated or too dogmatic in his views? Is it not disgraceful to allow another backsliding into anti-Semitism in our appointments policy (incidentally, in the highest bureaucratic elite of our government, the spirit of anti-Semitism was never fully dispelled after the nineteen thirties).

Was it not disgraceful to continue to restrict the civil rights of the Crimean Tatars, who lost about 46 per cent of their numbers (mainly children and old people) in the Stalinist repressions? Nationality problems will continue to be a reason for unrest and dissatisfaction unless all departures from Leninist principles are acknowledged and analyzed and firm steps are taken to correct mistakes.

Is it not highly disgraceful and dangerous to make increasingly frequent attempts, either directly or indirectly (through silence), to publicly rehabilitate Stalin, his associates and his policy, his pseudosocialism of terroristic bureaucracy, a socialism of hypocrisy and ostentatious growth that was at best a quantitative and one-sided growth involving the loss of many qualitative features? (This is a reference to the basic tendencies and consequences of Stalin's policy, or Stalinism, rather than a comprehensive assessment of the entire diversified situation in a huge country with 200 million people.)

Although all these disgraceful phenomena are still far from the monstrous scale of the crimes of Stalinism and rather resemble in scope the sadly famous McCarthyism of the cold war era, the Soviet public cannot but be highly disturbed and indignant and display vigilance even in the face of insignificant manifestations of neo-Stalinism in our country.

Effect on Other Parties

We are convinced that the world's Communists will also view negatively any attempts to revive Stalinism in our country, which would, after all, be an awful blow to the attractive force of Communist ideas throughout the world.

Today the key to a progressive restructuring of the system of government in the interests of mankind lies in intellectual freedom. This has been understood, in particular, by the Czechoslovaks and there can be no doubt that we should support their bold initiative, which is so valuable for the future of socialism and all mankind. That support should be political and, in the early stages, include increased economic aid.

The situation involving censorship (Glavlit) in our country is such that it can hardly be corrected for any length of time simply by "liberalized" directives. Major organizational and legislative measures are required, for example, adoption of a special law on press and information that would clearly and convincingly define what can and what cannot be printed and would place the responsibility on competent people who would be under public control. It is essential that the' exchange of information on an international scale (press, tourism and so forth) be expanded in every way, that we get to know ourselves better, that we not try to save on sociological, political and economic research and surveys, which should be conducted not only according to government-controlled programs (otherwise we might be tempted to avoid "unpleasant" subjects and questions).

The Basis for Hope

The prospects of socialism now depend on whether socialism can be made attractive, whether the moral attractiveness of the ideas of socialism and the glorification of labor, compared with the egotistical ideas of private ownership and the glorification of capital, will be the decisive factors that people will bear in mind when comparing socialism and capitalism, or whether people will remember mainly the limitations of intellectual freedom under socialism or, even worse, the fascistic regime of the cult [of personality].

I am placing the accent on the moral aspect because, when it comes to achieving a high productivity of social labor or developing all productive forces or insuring a high standard of living for most of the population, capitalism and socialism seem to have "played to a tie." Let us examine this question in detail.

The U.S.–Soviet Ski Race

Imagine two skiers racing through deep snow. At the start of the race, one of them, in striped jacket, was many kilometers ahead, but now the skier in the red jacket is catching up to the leader. What can we say about their relative strength? Not very much, since each skier is racing under different conditions. The striped one broke the snow, and the red one did not have to. (The reader will understand that this ski race symbolizes the burden of research and development costs that the country leading in technology has to bear.) All one can say about the race is that there is not much difference in strength between the two skiers.

The parable does not, of course, reflect the whole complexity of comparing economic and technological progress in the United States and the Soviet Union, the relative vitality of RRS and AME (Russian Revolutionary Sweep and American Efficiency).

We cannot forget that during much of the period in question the Soviet Union waged a hard war and then healed its wounds; we cannot forget that some absurdities in our development were not an inherent aspect of the socialist course of development, but a tragic accident, a serious, though not inevitable, disease.

On the other hand, any comparison must take account of the fact that we are now catching up with the United States only in some of the old, traditional industries, which are no longer as important as they used to be for the United States (for example, coal and steel). In some of the newer fields, for example, automation, computers, petrochemicals and especially in industrial research and deveopment, we are not only lagging behind but are also growing more slowly, so that a complete victory of our economy in the next few decades is unlikely.

It must also be borne in mind that our nation is endowed with vast natural resources, from fertile black earth to coal and forest, from oil to manganese and diamonds. It must be borne in mind that during the period under review our people worked to the limit of its capacity, which resulted in a certain depletion of resources.

We must also bear in mind the ski-track effect, in which the Soviet Union adopted principles of industrial organization and technological development previously tested in the United States. Examples are the method of calculating the national fuel budget, assembly-line techniques, antibiotics, nuclear power, oxygen converters in steel-making, hybrid corn, self-propelled harvester combines, strip mining of coal, rotary excavators, semiconductors in electronics, the shift from steam to diesel locomotives, and much more.

There is only one justifiable conclusion and it can be formulated cautiously as follows:

1. We have demonstrated the vitality of the socialist course, which has done a great deal for the people materially, culturally and socially and, like no other system, has glorified the moral significance of labor.

2. There are no grounds for asserting, as is often done in the dogmatic vein, that the capitalist mode of production leads the economy into a blind alley or that it is obviously inferior to the socialist mode in labor productivity, and there are certainly no grounds for asserting that capitalism always leads to absolute impoverishment of the working class.

Progress by Capitalism

The continuing economic progress being achieved under capitalism should be a fact of great theoretical significance for any nondogmatic Marxist. It is precisely this fact that lies at the basis of peaceful coexistence and it suggests, in principle, that if capitalism ever runs into an economic blind alley it will not necessarily have to leap into a desperate military adventure. Both capitalism and socialism are capable of long-term development, borrowing positive elements from each other and actually coming closer to each other in a number of essential aspects.

I can just hear the outcries about revisionism and blunting of the class approach to this issue; I can just see the smirks about political naiveté and immaturity. But the facts suggest that there is real economic progress in the United States and other capitalist countries, that the capitalists are actually using the social principles of socialism, and that there has been real improvement of the position of the working people. More important, the facts suggest that on any other course except ever-increasing coexistence and collaboration between the two systems and the two superpowers, with a smoothing of contradictions and with mutual assistance, on any other course annihilation awaits mankind. There is no other way out.

Two Systems Compared

We will now compare the distribution of personal income and consumption for various social groups in the United States and the Soviet Union. Our propaganda materials usually assert that there is crying inequality in the United States, while the Soviet Union has something entirely just, entirely in the interests of the working people. Actually both statements contain half-truths and a fair amount of hypocritical evasion.

I have no intention of minimizing the tragic aspects of the poverty, lack of rights and humiliation of the 22 million American Negroes. But we must clearly understand that this problem is not primarily a class problem, but a racial problem, involving the racism and egotism of white workers, and that the ruling group in the United States is interested in solving this problem. To be sure the government has not been as active as it should be; this may be related to fears of an electoral character and to fears of upsetting the unstable equilibrium in the country and thus activate extreme leftist and especially extreme rightist parties. It seems to me that we in the socialist camp should be interested in letting the ruling group in the United States settle the Negro problem without aggravating the situation in the country.

At the other extreme, the presence of millionaires in the United States is not a serious economic burden in view of their small number. The total consumption of the rich is less than 20 per cent, that is, less than the total rise of national consumption over a five-year period. From this point of view, a revolution, which would be likely to halt economic progress for more than five years, does not appear to be an economically advantageous move for the working people. And I am not even talking of the blood-letting that is inevitable in a revolution. And I am not talking of the danger of the "irony of history," about which Friedrich Engels wrote so well in his famous letter to V. Zasulich, the "irony" that took the form of Stalinism in our country.

There are, of course, situations where revolution is the only way out. This applies especially to national uprisings. But that is not the case in the United States and other developed capitalist countries, as suggested, incidentally, in the programs of the Communist parties of these countries.

As far as our country is concerned, here, too, we should avoid painting an idyllic picture. There is still great inequality in wealth between the city and the countryside, especially in rural areas that lack a transport outlet to the private market or do not produce any goods in demand in private trade. There are great differences between cities with some of the new, privileged industries and those with older, antiquated industries. As a result 40 per cent of the Soviet population is in difficult economic circumstances. In the United States about 25 per cent of the population is on the verge of poverty. On the other hand the 5 per cent of the Soviet population that belong to the managerial group is as privileged as its counterpart in the United States.

The Managerial Group

The development of modern society in both the Soviet Union and the United States is now following the same course of increasing complexity of structure and of industrial management, giving rise in both countries to managerial groups that are similar in social character.

We must therefore acknowledge that there is no qualitative difference in the structure of society of the two countries in terms of distribution of consumption. Unfortunately the effectiveness of the managerial group in the Soviet Union (and, to a lesser extent, in the United States) is measured not only in purely economic or productive terms. This group also performs a concealed protective funtion that is rewarded in the sphere of consumption by concealed privileges.

Few people are aware of the practice under Stalin of paying salaries in sealed envelopes, of the constantly recurring concealed distribution of scarce foods and goods for various services, privileges in vacation resorts, and so forth.

I want to emphasize that I am not opposed to the socialist principle of payment based on the amount and quality of labor. Relatively higher wages for better administrators, for highly skilled workers, teachers and physicians, for workers in dangerous or harmful occupations, for workers in science, culture and the arts, all of whom account for a relatively small part of the total wage bill, do not threaten society if they are not accompanied by concealed privileges; moreover, higher wages benefit society if they are deserved.

The point is that every wasted minute of a leading administrator represents major material loss for the economy and every wasted minute of a leading figure in the arts means a loss in the emotional, philosophical and artistic wealth of society. But when something is done in secret, the suspicion inevitably arises that things are not clean, that loyal servants of the existing system are being bribed.

It seems to me that the rational way of solving this touchy problem would be not the setting of income ceilings for party members or some such measure, but simply the prohibition of all privileges and the establishment of unified wage rates based on the social value of labor and an economic market approach to the wage problem.

I consider that further advances in our economic reform and a greater role for economic and market factors accompanied by increased public control over the managerial group (which, incidentally, is also essential in capitalist countries) will help eliminate all the roughness in our present distribution pattern.

An even more important aspect of the economic reform for the regulation and stimulation of production is the establishment of a correct system of market prices, proper allocation and rapid utilization of investment funds and proper use of natural and human resources based on appropriate rents in the interest of our society.

A number of socialist countries, including the Soviet Union, Yugoslavia and Czechoslovakia are now experimenting with basic economic problems of the role of planning and of the market, government and cooperative ownership, and so forth. These experiments are of great significance.

Andrei Sakharov

Rapprochement Advocated

Summing up, we now come to our basic conclusion about the moral and ethical character of the advantages of the socialist course of development of human society. In our view, this does not in any way minimize the significance of socialism. Without socialism, bourgeois practicism and the egotistical principle of private ownership gave rise to the "people of the abyss" described by Jack London and earlier by Engels.

Only the competition with socialism and the pressure of the working class made possible the social progress of the 20th century and, all the more, will insure the now inevitable process of rapprochement of the two systems. It took socialism to raise the meaning of labor to the heights of a moral feat. Before the advent of socialism, national egotism gave rise to colonial oppression, nationalism and racism. By now it has become clear that victory is on the side of the humanistic, international approach.

The capitalist world could not help giving birth to the socialist, but now the socialist world should not seek to destroy by force the ground from which it grew. Under the present conditions this would be tantamount to suicide of mankind. Socialism should ennoble that ground by its example and other indirect forms of pressure and then merge with it.

The rapprochement with the capitalist world should not be an unprincipled, antipopular plot between ruling groups, as happened in the extreme case [of the Soviet-Nazi rapprochement] of 1939–40. Such a rapprochement must rest not only on a socialist, but on a popular, democratic foundation, under the control of public opinion, as expressed through publicity, elections and so forth.

Such a rapprochement implies not only wide social reforms in the capitalist countries, but also substantial changes in the structure of ownership, with a greater role played by government and cooperative ownership, and the preservation of the basic present features of ownership of the means of production in the socialist countries.

Our allies along this road are not only the working class and the progressive intelligentsia, which are interested in peaceful coexistence and social progress and in a democratic, peaceful transition to socialism (as reflected in the programs of the Communist parties of the developed countries), but also the reformist part of the bourgeoisie, which supports such a program of "convergence." (Although I am using this term, taken from the Western literature, it is clear from the foregoing that I have given it a socialist and democratic meaning.)

Typical representatives of the reformist bourgeoisie are Cyrus Eaton, President Franklin D. Roosevelt and, especially, President John F. Kennedy. Without wishing to cast a stone in the direction of Comrade N. S. Khrushchev (our high esteem of his services was expressed earlier), I cannot help recalling one of his statements, which may have been more typical of his entourage than of him personally.

On July 10, 1961, in speaking at a reception of specialists about his meeting with Kennedy in Vienna, Comrade Khrushchev recalled Kennedy's request that the Soviet Union, in conducting policy and making demands, consider the actual possibilities and the difficulties of the new Kennedy Administration and refrain from demanding more than it could grant without courting the danger of being defeated in elections and being replaced by rightist forces. At that time, Khrushchev did not give Kennedy's unprecedented request the proper attention, to put it mildly, and began to rail. And now, after the shots in Dallas, who can say what auspicious opportunities in world history have been, if not destroyed, but, at any rate, set back because of a lack of understanding.

Bertrand Russell once told a peace congress in Moscow that "the world will be saved from thermonuclear annihilation if the leaders of each of the two systems prefer complete victory of the other system to a thermonuclear war" (I am quoting from memory). It seems to me that such a solution would be acceptable to the majority of people in any country, whether capitalist or socialist. I consider that the leaders of the capitalist and socialist systems by the very nature of things will gradually be forced to adopt the point of view of the majority of mankind.

Intellectual freedom of society will facilitate and smooth the way for this trend toward patience, flexibility and a security from dogmatism, fear and adventurism. All mankind, including its best organized and active forces, the working class and the intelligentsia, is interested in freedom and security.

A Four-Stage Plan for Cooperation

Having examined in the first part of this essay the development of mankind according to the worse alternative, leading to annihilation, we must now attempt, even schematically, to suggest the better alternative. (The author concedes the primitiveness of his attempts at prognostication, which requires the joint efforts of many specialists, and here, even more than elsewhere, invites positive criticism.)

1. In the first stage, a growing ideological struggle in the socialist countries between Stalinist and Maoist forces, on the one hand, and the realistic forces of leftist Leninist Communists (and leftist Westerners), on the other, will lead to a deep ideological split on an international, national and intraparty scale.

In the Soviet Union and other socialist countries, this process will lead first to a multiparty system (here and there) and to acute ideological struggle and discussions, and then to the ideological victory of the realists, affirming the policy of increasing peaceful coexistence, strengthening democracy and expanding economic reforms (1960–80). The dates reflect the most optimistic unrolling of events.

The author, incidentally, is not one of those who consider the multiparty system to be an essential stage in the development of the socialist system or, even less, a panacea for all ills, but he assumes that in some cases a multiparty system may be an inevitable consequence of the course of events when a ruling Communist party refuses for one reason or another to rule by the scientific democratic method required by history.

2. In the second stage, persistent demands for social progress and peaceful coexistence in the United States and other capitalist countries, and pressure exerted by the example of the socialist countries and by internal progressive forces (the working class and the intelligentsia) will lead to the victory of the leftist reformist wing of the bourgeoisie, which will begin to implement a program of rapprochement (convergence) with socialism, i.e. social progress, peaceful coexistence and collaboration with socialism on a world scale and changes in the structure of ownership. This phase includes an expanded role for the intelligentsia and an attack on the forces of racism and militarism (1972–85). (The various stages overlap.)

3. In the third stage, the Soviet Union and the United States, having overcome their alienation, solve the problem of saving the poorer half of the world. The above-mentioned 20 per cent tax on the national income of developed countries is applied. Gigantic fertilizer factories and irrigations systems using atomic power will be built, the resources of the sea will be used to a vastly greater extent, indigenous personnel will be trained, and industrialization will be carried out. Gigantic factories will produce synthetic amino acids, and synthesize proteins, fats and carbohydrates. At the same time disarmament will proceed (1972–90).

4. In the fourth stage, the socialist convergence will reduce differences in social structure, promote intellectual freedom, science and economic progress and lead to creation of a world government and the smoothing of national contradictions (1980–2000). During this period decisive progress can be expected in the field of nuclear power, both on the basis of uranium and thorium and, probably, deuterium and lithium.

Some authors consider it likely that explosive breeding (the reproduction of fertile materials such as plutonium, uranium 233 and tritium) may be used in subterranean or other enclosed explosions.

During this period the expansion of space exploration will require thousands of people to work and live continuously on other planets and on the moon, on artificial satellites and on asteroids whose orbits will have been changed by nuclear explosions.

The synthesis of materials that are superconductors at room temperature may completely revolutionize electrical technology, cybernetics, transportation and communications. Progress in biology (in this and subsequent periods) will make possible effective control and direction of all life processes at the levels of the cell, organism, ecology and society, from fertility and aging to psychic processes and heredity.

If such an all-encompassing scientific and technological revolution, promising uncounted benefits for mankind, is to be possible and safe, it will require the greatest possible scientific foresight and care and concern for human values of a moral, ethical and personal character. (I touched briefly on the danger of a thoughtless bureaucratic use of the scientific and technological revolution in a divided world in the section on "Dangers," but could add a great deal more.) Such a revolution will be possible and safe only under highly intelligent worldwide guidance.

The foregoing program presumes:

(a) worldwide interest in overcoming the present divisions;

(b) the expectation that modifications in both the socialist and capitalist countries will tend to reduce contradictions and differences;

(c) worldwide interest of the intelligentsia, the working class and other progressive forces in a scientific democratic approach to politics, economics and culture;

(d) the absence of unsurmountable obstacles to economic development in both world economic systems that might otherwise lead inevitably into a blind alley, despair and adventurism.

Every honorable and thinking person who has not been poisoned by narrow-minded indifference will seek to insure that future development will be along the lines of the better alternative. However only broad, open discussion, without the pressure of fear and prejudice, will help the majority to adopt the correct and best course of action.

Proposals Summarized

In conclusion, I will sum up some of the concrete proposals of varying degrees of importance that have been discussed in the text. These proposals, addressed to the leadership of the country, do not exhaust the content of the article.

1. The strategy of peaceful coexistence and collaboration must be deepened in every way. Scientific methods and principles of international policy will have to be worked out, based on scientific prediction of the immediate and more distant consequences.

2. The initiative must be seized in working out a broad program of struggle against hunger.

3. A law on press and information must be drafted, widely discussed and adopted, with the aim not only of ending irresponsible and irrational censorship, but of encouraging self-study in our society, fearless discussion and the search for truth. The law must provide for the material resources of freedom of thought.

4. All anticonstitutional laws and decrees violating human rights must be abrogated.

5. Political prisoners must be amnestied and some of the recent political trials must be reviewed (for example, the Daniel-Sinyavsky and Galanskov-Ginzburg cases). The camp regime of political prisoners must be promptly relaxed.

6. The exposure of Stalin must be carried through to the end, to the complete truth, and not just to the carefully weighed half-truth dictated by caste considerations. The influence of neo-Stalinists in our political life must be restricted in every way (the text mentioned, as an example, the case of S. Trapeznikov, who enjoys too much influence).

7. The economic reform must be deepened in every way and the area of experimentation expanded, with conclusions based on the results.

8. A law on geohygiene must be adopted after broad discussion, and ultimately become part of world efforts in this area.

With this essay the author addresses the leadership of our country and all its citizens as well as all people of goodwill throughout the world. The author is aware of the controversial character of many of his statements. His purpose is open, frank discussion under conditions of publicity.

In conclusion a textological comment. In the process of discussion of previous drafts of this essay, some incomplete and in some respects one-sided texts have been circulated. Some of them contained certain passages that were inept in form and tact and were included through oversight. The author asks readers to bear this in mind. The author is deeply grateful to readers of preliminary drafts who communicated their friendly comments and thus helped improve the essay and refine a number of basic statements.

Translated by the New York Times

Václav Havel

The Power of the Powerless

To the memory of Jan Patočka

Václav Havel is one of the most important European writers and intellectuals of our time. Born in Czechoslovakia in 1936, he is best known in the West for his plays *The Garden Party, The Increased Difficulty of Concentration, The Memorandum, Largo Desolato,* and three one-act plays: *Audience, Private View,* and *Protest.* A founding spokesman of the Charter 77 Declaration and member of the Committee to Defend the Unjustly Prosecuted, he was sentenced to four and a half years of hard labor for these human rights activities in Czechoslovakia.

In the following essay, written in 1978, Havel calls for an existential revolution, a new spirit of higher responsibility to arise *from below,* to create plurality, diversity, self-organization, and independent self-constitution – despite the oppression of an apparently entrenched totalitarian dictatorship in his own country and elsewhere in Central and Eastern Europe.

In 1989 such a revolution did occur, and Václav Havel was elected unopposed as President of Czechoslovakia.

I

A spectre is haunting eastern Europe: the spectre of what in the West is called 'dissent'. This spectre has not appeared out of thin air. It is a natural and inevitable consequence of the present historical phase of the system it is haunting. It was born at a time when this system, for a thousand reasons, can no longer base itself on the unadulterated, brutal, and arbitrary application of power, eliminating all expressions of nonconformity. What is more, the system has become so ossified politically that there is practically no way for such nonconformity to be implemented within its official structures.

Who are these so-called 'dissidents'? Where does their point of view come from, and what importance does it have? What is the significance of the 'independent initiatives' in which 'dissidents' collaborate, and what real chances do such initiatives have of success? Is it appropriate to refer to 'dissidents' as an opposition? If so, what exactly is such an opposition within the framework of this system? What does it do? What role does it play in society? What are its hopes and on what are they based? Is it within the power of the 'dissidents' — as a category of subcitizen outside the power establishment — to have any influence at all on society and the social system? Can they actually change anything?

I think that an examination of these questions — an examination of the potential of the 'powerless' — can only begin with an examination of the nature of power in the circumstances in which these powerless people operate.

II

Our system is most frequently characterized as a dictatorship or, more precisely, as the dictatorship of a political bureaucracy over a society which has undergone economic and social levelling. I am afraid that the term 'dictatorship', regardless of how intelligible it may otherwise be, tends to obscure rather than clarify the real nature of power in this system. We usually associate the term with the notion of a small group of people who take over the government of a given country by force; their power is wielded openly, using the direct instruments of power at their disposal, and they are easily distinguished socially from the majority over whom they rule. One of the essential aspects of this traditional or classical notion of dictatorship is the assumption that it is temporary, ephemeral, lacking historical roots. Its existence seems to be bound up with the lives of those who established it. It is usually local in extent and significance, and regardless of the ideology it utilizes to grant itself legitimacy, its power derives ultimately from the numbers and the armed might of its soldiers and police. The principal threat to its existence is felt to be the possibility that someone better equipped in this sense might appear and overthrow it.

Even this very superficial overview should make it clear that the system in which we live has very little in common with a classical dictatorship. In the first place, our system is not limited in a local, geographical sense; rather it holds sway over a huge power bloc controlled by one of the two superpowers. And although it quite naturally exhibits a number of local and historical variations, the range of these variations is fundamentally circumscribed by a single, unifying framework throughout the power bloc. Not only is the dictatorship everywhere based on the same principles and structured in the same way (that is, in the way evolved by the ruling superpower), but each country has been completely penetrated by a network of manipulatory instruments controlled by the superpower centre and totally subordinated to its interests. In the stalemated world of nuclear parity, of course, that circumstance endows the system with an unprecedented degree of external stability compared with classical dictatorships. Many local crises which, in an isolated state, would lead to a change in the system, can be resolved through direct intervention by the armed forces of the rest of the bloc.

In the second place, if a feature of classical dictatorships is their lack of historical roots (frequently they appear to be no more than historical freaks, the fortuitous consequence of fortuitous social processes or of human and mob tendencies), the same cannot be said so facilely about our system. For even though our dictatorship has long since alienated itself completely from the social movements that gave birth to it, the authenticity of these movements (and I am thinking of the proletarian and socialist movements of the nineteenth century) give it undeniable historicity. These origins provided a solid foundation of sorts on which it could build until it became the utterly new social and political reality it is today, which has become so inextricably a part of the structure of the modern world. A feature of those historical

origins was the 'correct understanding' of social conflicts in the
period from which those original movements emerged. The fact
that at the very core of this 'correct understanding' there was a
genetic disposition toward the monstrous alienation characteristic of its subsequent development is not essential here. And in
any case, this element also grew organically from the climate of
that time and therefore can be said to have its origin there as well.

One legacy of that original 'correct understanding' is a third
peculiarity that makes our system different from other modern
dictatorships: it commands an incomparably more precise, logically structured, generally comprehensible and, in essence,
extremely flexible ideology that, in its elaborateness and com-
pleteness, is almost a secularized religion. It offers a ready answer
to any question whatsoever; it can scarcely be accepted only in
part, and accepting it has profound implications for human life.
In an era when metaphysical and existential certainties are in a
state of crisis, when people are being uprooted and alienated and
are losing their sense of what this world means, this ideology
inevitably has a certain hypnotic charm. To wandering humankind it offers an immediately available home: all one has to do is
accept it, and suddenly everything becomes clear once more, life
takes on new meaning, and all mysteries, unanswered questions,
anxiety, and loneliness vanish. Of course, one pays dearly for this
low-rent home: the price is abdication of one's own reason,
conscience, and responsibility, for an essential aspect of this
ideology is the consignment of reason and conscience to a higher
authority. The principle involved here is that the centre of power
is identical with the centre of truth. (In our case, the connection
with Byzantine theocracy is direct: the highest secular authority
is identical with the highest spiritual authority.) It is true of
course that, all this aside, ideology no longer has any great
influence on people, at least within our bloc (with the possible
exception of Russia, where the serf mentality, with its blind,
fatalistic respect for rulers and its automatic acceptance of all
their claims, is still dominant and combined with a superpower
patriotism which traditionally places the interests of empire
higher than the interests of humanity). But this is not important,

because ideology plays its role in our system very well (an issue to which I will return) precisely because it is what it is.

Fourth, the technique of exercising power in traditional dictatorships contains a necessary element of improvisation. The mechanisms for wielding power are for the most part not established firmly, and there is considerable room for accident and for the arbitrary and unregulated application of power. Socially, psychologically, and physically conditions still exist for the expression of some form of opposition. In short, there are many seams on the surface which can split apart before the entire power structure has managed to stabilize. Our system, on the other hand, has been developing in the Soviet Union for over sixty years, and for approximately thirty years in eastern Europe; moreover, several of its long-established structural features are derived from Czarist absolutism. In terms of the physical aspects of power, this has led to the creation of such intricate and well-developed mechanisms for the direct and indirect manipulation of the entire population that, as a physical power base, it represents something radically new. At the same time, let us not forget that the system is made significantly more effective by state ownership and central direction of all the means of production. This gives the power structure an unprecedented and uncontrollable capacity to invest in itself (in the areas of the bureaucracy and the police, for example) and makes it easier for that structure, as the sole employer, to manipulate the day-to-day existence of all citizens.

Finally, if an atmosphere of revolutionary excitement, heroism, dedication, and boisterous violence on all sides characterizes classical dictatorships, then the last traces of such an atmosphere have vanished from the Soviet bloc. For some time now this bloc has ceased to be a kind of enclave, isolated from the rest of the developed world and immune to processes occurring in it. To the contrary, the Soviet bloc is an integral part of that larger world, and it shares and shapes the world's destiny. This means in concrete terms that the hierarchy of values existing in the developed countries of the West has, in essence, appeared in our society (the long period of coexistence with the West has only hastened this process). In other words, what we have here is simply another form of the consumer and industrial society, with all its concomitant social, intellectual, and psychological consequences. It is impossible to understand the nature of power in our system properly without taking this into account.

The profound difference between our system — in terms of the nature of power — and what we traditionally understand by dictatorship, a difference I hope is clear even from this quite superficial comparison, has caused me to search for some term appropriate for our system, purely for the purposes of this essay. If I refer to it henceforth as a *post-totalitarian* system, I am fully aware that this is perhaps not the most precise term, but I am unable to think of a better one. I do not wish to imply by the prefix 'post-' that the system is no longer totalitarian; on the contrary, I mean that it is totalitarian in a way fundamentally different from classical dictatorships, different from totalitarianism as we usually understand it.

The circumstances I have mentioned, however, form only a circle of conditional factors and a kind of phenomenal framework for the actual composition of power in the post-totalitarian system, several aspects of which I shall now attempt to identify.

III

The manager of a fruit and vegetable shop places in his window, among the onions and carrots, the slogan: 'Workers of the World, Unite!' Why does he do it? What is he trying to communicate to the world? Is he genuinely enthusiastic about the idea of unity among the workers of the world? Is his enthusiasm so great that he feels an irrepressible impulse to acquaint the public with his ideals? Has he really given more than a moment's thought to how such a unification might occur and what it would mean?

I think it can safely be assumed that the overwhelming majority of shopkeepers never think about the slogans they put in their windows, nor do they use them to express their real opinions. That poster was delivered to our greengrocer from the enterprise headquarters along with the onions and carrots. He put them all into the window simply because it has been done that way for years, because everyone does it, and because that is the way it has to be. If he were to refuse, there could be trouble. He could be reproached for not having the proper 'decoration' in his window; someone might even accuse him of disloyalty. He does it because these things must be done if one is to get along in life. It is one of the thousands of details that guarantee him a relatively tranquil life 'in harmony with society', as they say.

Obviously the greengrocer is indifferent to the semantic content of the slogan on exhibit; he does not put the slogan in his window from any personal desire to acquaint the public with the ideal it expresses. This, of course, does not mean that his action has no motive or significance at all, or that the slogan communicates nothing to anyone. The slogan is really a *sign,* and as such it contains a subliminal but very definite message. Verbally, it might be expressed this way: 'I, the greengrocer XY, live here and I know what I must do. I behave in the manner expected of me. I can be depended upon and am beyond reproach. I am obedient and therefore I have the right to be left in peace.' This message, of course, has an addressee: it is directed above, to the greengrocer's superior, and at the same time it is a shield that protects the greengrocer from potential informers. The slogan's real meaning, therefore, is rooted firmly in the greengrocer's existence. It reflects his vital interests. But what are those vital interests?

Let us take note: if the greengrocer had been instructed to display the slogan, 'I am afraid and therefore unquestioningly obedient', he would not be nearly as indifferent to its semantics, even though the statement would reflect the truth. The greengrocer would be embarrassed and ashamed to put such an unequivocal statement of his own degradation in the shop window, and quite naturally so, for he is a human being and thus has a sense of his own dignity. To overcome this complication, his expression of loyalty must take the form of a sign which, at least on its textual surface, indicates a level of disinterested conviction. It must allow the greengrocer to say, 'What's wrong with the workers of the world uniting?' Thus the sign helps the greengrocer to conceal from himself the low foundations of his obedience, at the same time concealing the low foundations of power. It hides them behind the façade of something high. And that something is *ideology*.

Ideology is a specious way of relating to the world. It offers human beings the illusion of an identity, of dignity, and of morality while making it easier for them to *part* with them. As the repository of something 'supra-personal' and objective, it enables people to deceive their conscience and conceal their true position and their inglorious *modus vivendi,* both from the world and from themselves. It is a very pragmatic, but at the same time an apparently dignified, way of legitimizing what is above, below, and on either side. It is directed towards people and towards God. It is a veil behind which human beings can hide their own 'fallen existence', their trivialization, and their adaptation to the status quo. It is an excuse that everyone can use, from the greengrocer, who conceals his fear of losing his job behind an alleged interest in the unification of the workers of the world, to the highest functionary, whose interest in staying in power can be cloaked in phrases about service to the working class. The primary excusatory function of ideology, therefore, is to provide people, both as victims and pillars of the post-totalitarian system, with the illusion that the system is in harmony with the human order and the order of the universe.

The smaller a dictatorship and the less stratified by modernization the society under it, the more directly the will of the dictator can be exercised. In other words, the dictator can employ more or less naked discipline, avoiding the complex processes of relating to the world and of self-justification which ideology involves. But the more complex the mechanisms of power become, the larger and more stratified the society they embrace, and the longer they have operated historically, the more individuals must be connected to them from outside, and the greater the importance attached to the ideological excuse. It acts as a kind of bridge between the regime and the people, across which the regime approaches the people and the people approach the regime. This explains why ideology plays such an important role in the post-totalitarian system: that complex machinery of units, hierarchies, transmission belts, and indirect instruments of manipulation which insure in countless ways the integrity of the regime, leaving nothing to chance, would be quite simply unthinkable without ideology acting as its all-embracing excuse and as the excuse for each of its parts.

IV

Between the aims of the post-totalitarian system and the aims of life there is a yawning abyss: while life, in its essence, moves towards plurality, diversity, independent self-constitution and self-organization, in short, towards the fulfilment of its own freedom, the post-totalitarian system demands conformity, uniformity, and discipline. While life ever strives to create new and 'improbable' structures, the post-totalitarian system contrives to force life into its most probable states. The aims of the system reveal its most essential characteristic to be introversion, a movement towards being ever more completely and unreservedly *itself,* which means that the radius of its influence is continually widening as well. This system serves people only to the extent necessary to ensure that people will serve it. Anything beyond this, that is to say, anything which leads people to overstep their predetermined roles is regarded by the system as an attack upon itself. And in this respect it is correct: every instance of such transgression is a genuine denial of the system. It can be said, therefore, that the inner aim of the post-totalitarian system is not mere preservation of power in the hands of a ruling clique, as appears to be the case at first sight. Rather, the social phenomenon of self-preservation is subordinated to something higher, to a kind of blind *automatism* which drives the system. No matter what position individuals hold in the hierarchy of power, they are not considered by the system to be worth anything in themselves, but only as things intended to fuel and serve this automatism. For this reason, an individual's desire for power is admissible only in so far as its direction coincides with the direction of the automatism of the system.

Ideology, in creating a bridge of excuses between the system and the individual, spans the abyss between the aims of the

system and the aims of life. It pretends that the requirements of
the system derive from the requirements of life. It is a world of
appearances trying to pass for reality.

The post-totalitarian system touches people at every step, but it
does so with its ideological gloves on. This is why life in the
system is so thoroughly permeated with hypocrisy and lies:
government by bureaucracy is called popular government; the
working class is enslaved in the name of the working class; the
complete degradation of the individual is presented as his or her
ultimate liberation; depriving people of information is called
making it available; the use of power to manipulate is called the
public control of power, and the arbitrary abuse of power is called
observing the legal code; the repression of culture is called its
development; the expansion of imperial influence is presented as
support for the oppressed; the lack of free expression becomes
the highest form of freedom; farcical elections become the
highest form of democracy; banning independent thought
becomes the most scientific of world views; military occupation
becomes fraternal assistance. Because the regime is captive to its
own lies, it must falsify everything. It falsifies the past. It falsifies
the present, and it falsifies the future. It falsifies statistics. It
pretends not to possess an omnipotent and unprincipled police
apparatus. It pretends to respect human rights. It pretends to
persecute no one. It pretends to fear nothing. It pretends to
pretend nothing.

Individuals need not believe all these mystifications, but they
must behave as though they did, or they must at least tolerate
them in silence, or get along well with those who work with
them. For this reason, however, they must *live within a lie*. They
need not accept the lie. It is enough for them to have accepted
their life with it and in it. For by this very fact, individuals
confirm the system, fulfil the system, make the system, *are* the
system.

V

We have seen that the real meaning of the greengrocer's slogan has nothing to do with what the text of the slogan

actually says. Even so, this real meaning is quite clear and generally comprehensible because the code is so familiar: the greengrocer declares his loyalty (and he can do no other if his declaration is to be accepted) in the only way the regime is capable of hearing; that is, by accepting the prescribed *ritual,* by accepting appearances as reality, by accepting the given rules of the game. In doing so, however, he has himself become a player in the game, thus making it possible for the game to go on, for it to exist in the first place.

If ideology was originally a bridge between the system and the individual as an individual, then the moment he or she steps on to this bridge it becomes at the same time a bridge between the system and the individual as a component of the system. That is, if ideology originally facilitated (by acting outwardly) the constitution of power by serving as a psychological excuse, then from the moment that excuse is accepted, it constitutes power inwardly, becoming an active component of that power. It begins to function as the principal instrument of ritual communication *within* the system of power.

The whole power structure (and we have already discussed its physical articulation) could not exist at all if there were not a certain 'metaphysical' order binding all its components together, interconnecting them and subordinating them to a uniform method of accountability, supplying the combined operation of all these components with rules of the game, that is, with certain regulations, limitations, and legalities. This metaphysical order is fundamental to, and standard throughout, the entire power structure; it integrates its communication system and makes possible the internal exchange and transfer of information and instructions. It is rather like a collection of traffic signals and directional signs, giving the process shape and structure. This metaphysical order guarantees the inner coherence of the totalitarian power structure. It is the glue holding it together, its binding principle, the instrument of its discipline. Without this glue the structure as a totalitarian structure would vanish; it would disintegrate into individual atoms chaotically colliding with one another in their unregulated particular interests and inclinations. The entire pyramid of totalitarian power, deprived of the element that binds it together, would collapse in upon itself, as it were, in a kind of material implosion.

As the interpretation of reality by the power structure, ideology is always subordinated ultimately to the interests of the structure. Therefore, it has a natural tendency to disengage itself from reality, to create a world of appearances, to become ritual. In societies where there is public competition for power and therefore public control of that power, there also exists quite naturally public control of the way that power legitimates itself ideologically. Consequently, in such conditions there are always certain correctives that effectively prevent ideology from abandoning reality altogether. Under totalitarianism, however, these correctives disappear, and thus there is nothing to prevent ideology from becoming more and more removed from reality, gradually turning into what it has already become in the post-totalitarian system: a world of appearances, a mere ritual, a formalized language deprived of semantic contact with reality and transformed into a system of ritual signs that replace reality with pseudo-reality.

Yet, as we have seen, ideology becomes at the same time an increasingly important component of power, a pillar providing it with both excusatory legitimacy and an inner coherence. As this aspect grows in importance, and as it gradually loses touch with reality, it acquires a peculiar but very real strength. It becomes reality itself, albeit a reality altogether self-contained, one that on certain levels (chiefly inside the power structure) may have even greater weight than reality as such. Increasingly, the virtuosity of the ritual becomes more important than the reality hidden behind it. The significance of phenomena no longer derives from the phenomena themselves, but from their locus as concepts in the ideological context. Reality does not shape theory, but rather the reverse. Thus power gradually draws closer to ideology than it does to reality; it draws its strength from theory and becomes entirely dependent on it. This inevitably leads, of course, to a paradoxical result: rather than theory, or rather ideology, serving power, power begins to serve ideology. It is as though ideology had appropriated power from power, as though it had become dictator itself. It then appears that theory itself, ritual itself, ideology itself, makes decisions that affect people, and not the other way around.

If ideology is the principal guarantee of the inner consistency of power, it becomes at the same time an increasingly important guarantee of its *continuity*. Whereas succession to power in classical dictatorships is always a rather complicated affair (the pretenders having nothing to give their claims reasonable legitimacy, thereby forcing them always to resort to confrontations of naked power), in the post-totalitarian system power is passed on from person to person, from clique to clique, and from generation to generation in an essentially more regular fashion. In the selection of pretenders, a new 'king-maker' takes part: it is ritual legitimation, the ability to rely on ritual, to fulfil it and use it, to allow oneself, as it were, to be borne aloft by it. Naturally, power struggles exist in the post-totalitarian system as well, and most of them are far more brutal than in an open society, for the struggle is not open, regulated by democratic rules, and subject to public control, but hidden behind the scenes. (It is difficult to recall a single instance in which the First Secretary of a ruling Communist Party has been replaced without the various military and security forces being placed at least on alert.) This struggle, however, can never (as it can in classical dictatorships) threaten the very essence of the system and its continuity. At most it will shake up the power structure, which will recover quickly, precisely because the binding substance — ideology — remains undisturbed. No matter who is replaced by whom, succession is only possible against the backdrop and within the framework of a common ritual. It can never take place by denying that ritual.

Because of this dictatorship of the ritual, however, power becomes clearly *anonymous*. Individuals are almost dissolved in the ritual. They allow themselves to be swept along by it and frequently it seems as though ritual alone carries people from obscurity into the light of power. Is it not characteristic of the post-totalitarian system that, on all levels of the power hierarchy, individuals are increasingly being pushed aside by faceless people, puppets, those uniformed flunkies of the rituals and routines of power?

The automatic operation of a power structure thus de-humanized and made anonymous is a feature of the fundamental automatism of this system. It would seem that it is precisely the *diktats* of this automatism which select people lacking individual will for the power structure, that it is precisely the *diktat* of the empty phrase which summons to power people who use empty phrases as the best guarantee that the automatism of the post-totalitarian system will continue.

Western Sovietologists often exaggerate the role of individuals in the post-totalitarian system and overlook the fact that the ruling figures, despite the immense power they possess through the centralized structure of power, are often no more than blind executors of the system's own internal laws — laws they them-selves never can, and never do, reflect upon. In any case, experi-ence has taught us again and again that this automatism is far more powerful than the will of any individual; and should someone possess a more independent will, he or she must conceal it behind a ritually anonymous mask in order to have an opportunity to enter the power hierarchy at all. And when the individual finally gains a place there and tries to make his or her will felt within it, that automatism, with its enormous inertia, will triumph sooner or later, and either the individual will be ejected by the power structure like a foreign organism, or he or she will be compelled to resign his or her individuality gradually, once again blending with the automatism and becoming its servant, almost indistinguishable from those who preceded him or her and those who will follow. (Let us recall, for instance, the development of Husák or Gomulka.) The necessity of con-tinually hiding behind and relating to ritual means that even the more enlightened members of the power structure are often obsessed with ideology. They are never able to plunge straight to the bottom of naked reality, and they always confuse it, in the final analysis, with ideological pseudo-reality. (In my opinion, one of the reasons the Dubček leadership lost control of the situation in 1968 was precisely because, in extreme situations and in final questions, its members were never capable of extricating themselves completely from the world of appearances.)

It can be said, therefore, that ideology, as that instrument of internal communication which assures the power structure of inner cohesion is, in the post-totalitarian system, something that transcends the physical aspects of power, something that dominates it to a considerable degree and, therefore, tends to assure its continuity as well. It is one of the pillars of the system's external stability. This pillar, however, is built on a very unstable foundation. It is built on lies. It works only as long as people are willing to live within the lie.

VI

Why in fact did our greengrocer have to put his loyalty on display in the shop window? Had he not already displayed it sufficiently in various internal or semi-public ways? At trade-union meetings, after all, he had always voted as he should. He had always taken part in various competitions. He voted in elections like a good citizen. He had even signed the 'anti-Charter'. Why, on top of all that, should he have to declare his loyalty publicly? After all, the people who walk past his window will certainly not stop to read that, in the greengrocer's opinion, the workers of the world ought to unite. The fact of the matter is, they don't read the slogan at all, and it can be fairly assumed they don't even see it. If you were to ask a woman who had stopped in front of his shop what she saw in the window, she could certainly tell you whether or not they had tomatoes today, but it is highly unlikely that she noticed the slogan at all, let alone what it said.

It seems senseless to require the greengrocer to declare his loyalty publicly. But it makes sense nevertheless. People ignore his slogan, but they do so because such slogans are also found in other shop windows, on lamp posts, bulletin boards, in apartment windows, and on buildings; they are everywhere, in fact. They form part of the panorama of everyday life. Of course, while they ignore the details, people are very aware of that panorama as a whole. And what else is the greengrocer's slogan but a small component in that huge backdrop to daily life?

The greengrocer had to put the slogan in his window, therefore, not in the hope that someone might read it or be persuaded
by it, but to contribute, along with thousands of other slogans, to
the panorama that everyone is very much aware of. This panorama, of course, has a subliminal meaning as well: it reminds
people where they are living and what is expected of them. It tells
them what everyone else is doing, and indicates to them what
they must do as well, if they don't want to be excluded, to fall into
isolation, alienate themselves from society, break the rules of the
game, and risk the loss of their peace and tranquillity and
security.

The woman who ignored the greengrocer's slogan may well
have hung a similar slogan just an hour before in the corridor of
the office where she works. She did it more or less without
thinking, just as our greengrocer did, and she could do so
precisely because she was doing it against the background of the
general panorama and with some awareness of it, that is, against
the background of the panorama of which the greengrocer's shop
window forms a part. When the greengrocer visits her office, he
will not notice her slogan either, just as she failed to notice his.
Nevertheless their slogans are mutually dependent: both were
displayed with some awareness of the general panorama and, we
might say, under its *diktat*. Both, however, assist in the creation of
that panorama, and therefore they assist in the creation of that
diktat as well. The greengrocer and the office worker have both
adapted to the conditions in which they live, but in doing so, they
help to create those conditions. They do what is done, what is to
be done, what must be done, but at the same time — by that very
token — they confirm that it must be done in fact. They conform
to a particular requirement and in so doing they themselves
perpetuate that requirement. Metaphorically speaking, without
the greengrocer's slogan the office worker's slogan could not
exist, and, vice versa. Each proposes to the other that something
be repeated and each accepts the other's proposal. Their mutual
indifference to each other's slogans is only an illusion: in reality,
by exhibiting their slogans, each compels the other to accept the
rules of the game and to confirm thereby the power that requires

the slogans in the first place. Quite simply, each helps the other to be obedient. Both are objects in a system of control, but at the same time they are its subjects as well. They are both victims of the system and its instruments.

If an entire district town is plastered with slogans that no one reads, it is on the one hand a message from the district secretary to the regional secretary, but it is also something more: a small example of the principle of social *auto-totality* at work. Part of the essence of the post-totalitarian system is that it draws everyone into its sphere of power, not so they may realize themselves as human beings, but so they may surrender their human identity in favour of the identity of the system, that is, so they may become agents of the system's general automatism and servants of its self-determined goals, so they may participate in the common responsibility for it, so they may be pulled into and ensnared by it, like Faust with Mephistopheles. More than this: so they may create through their involvement a general norm and, thus, bring pressure to bear on their fellow citizens. And further: so they may learn to be comfortable with their involvement, to identify with it as though it were something natural and inevitable and, ultimately, so they may — with no external urging — come to treat any non-involvement as an abnormality, as arrogance, as an attack on themselves, as a form of dropping out of society. By pulling everyone into its power structure, the post-totalitarian system makes everyone instruments of a mutual totality, the auto-totality of society.

Everyone, however, is in fact involved and enslaved, not only the greengrocers but also the prime ministers. Differing positions in the hierarchy merely establish differing degrees of involvement: the greengrocer is involved only to a minor extent, but he also has very little power. The prime minister, naturally, has greater power, but in return he is far more deeply involved. Both, however, are unfree, each merely in a somewhat different way. The real accomplice in this involvement, therefore, is not another person, but the system itself. Position in the power hierarchy determines the degree of responsibility and guilt, but it gives no one unlimited responsibility and guilt, nor does it completely absolve anyone. Thus the conflict between the aims of life and the aims of the system is not a conflict between two socially defined and separate communities; and only a very generalized view (and even that only approximative) permits us to divide society into the rulers and the ruled. Here, by the way, is one of the most important differences between the post-totalitarian system and classical dictatorships, in which this line of conflict can still be drawn according to social class. In the post-totalitarian system, this line runs *de facto* through each person, for everyone in his or her own way is both a victim and a supporter of the system. What we understand by the system is not, therefore, a social order imposed by one group upon another, but rather something which permeates the entire society and is a factor in shaping it, something which may seem impossible to grasp or define (for it is in the nature of a mere principle), but which is expressed by the entire society as an important feature of its life.

The fact that human beings have created, and daily create, this self-directed system through which they divest themselves of their innermost identity, is not therefore the result of some incomprehensible misunderstanding of history, nor is it history somehow gone off its rails. Neither is it the product of some diabolical higher will which has decided, for reasons unknown, to torment a portion of humanity in this way. It can happen and did happen only because there is obviously in modern humanity a certain tendency towards the creation, or at least the toleration, of such a system. There is obviously something in human beings which responds to this system, something they reflect and accommodate, something within them which paralyses every effort of their better selves to revolt. Human beings are compelled to live within a lie, but they can be compelled to do so only because they are in fact capable of living in this way. Therefore not only does the system alienate humanity, but at the same time alienated humanity supports this system as its own involuntary masterplan, as a degenerate image of its own degeneration, as a record of people's own failure as individuals.

The essential aims of life are present naturally in every person. In everyone there is some longing for humanity's rightful dignity, for moral integrity, for free expression of being and a sense of transcendence over the world of existences. Yet, at the same time, each person is capable, to a greater or lesser degree, of coming to terms with living within the lie. Each person somehow succumbs to a profane trivialization of his or her inherent humanity, and to utilitarianism. In everyone there is some willingness to merge with the anonymous crowd and to flow comfortably along with it down the river of pseudo-life. This is much more than a simple conflict between two identities. It is something far worse: it is a challenge to the very notion of identity itself.

In highly simplified terms, it could be said that the post-totalitarian system has been built on foundations laid by the historical encounter between dictatorship and the consumer society. Is it not true that the far-reaching adaptability to living a lie and the effortless spread of social auto-totality have some connection with the general unwillingness of consumption-oriented people to sacrifice some material certainties for the sake of their own spiritual and moral integrity? With their willingness to surrender higher values when faced with the trivializing temptations of modern civilization? With their vulnerability to the attractions of mass indifference? And in the end, is not the greyness and the emptiness of life in the post-totalitarian system only an inflated caricature of modern life in general? And do we not in fact stand (although in the external measures of civilization, we are far behind) as a kind of warning to the West, revealing to it its own latent tendencies?

VII

Let us now imagine that one day something in our greengrocer snaps and he stops putting up the slogans merely to ingratiate himself. He stops voting in elections he knows are a farce. He begins to say what he really thinks at political meetings. And he even finds the strength in himself to express solidarity with those whom his conscience commands him to support. In this revolt the greengrocer steps out of living within the lie. He rejects the ritual and breaks the rules of the game. He discovers once more his suppressed identity and dignity. He gives his freedom a concrete significance. His revolt is an attempt to *live within the truth.*

The bill is not long in coming. He will be relieved of his post as manager of the shop and transferred to the warehouse. His pay will be reduced. His hopes for a holiday in Bulgaria will evaporate. His children's access to higher education will be threatened. His superiors will harass him and his fellow workers will wonder about him. Most of those who apply these sanctions, however, will not do so from any authentic inner conviction but simply under pressure from conditions, the same conditions that once pressured the greengrocer to display the official slogans. They will persecute the greengrocer either because it is expected of them, or to demonstrate their loyalty, or simply as part of the general panorama, to which belongs an awareness that this is how situations of this sort are dealt with, that this, in fact, is how things are always done, particularly if one is not to become suspect oneself. The executors, therefore, behave essentially like everyone else, to a greater or lesser degree: as components of the post-totalitarian system, as agents of its automatism, as petty instruments of the social auto-totality.

Thus the power structure, through the agency of those who carry out the sanctions, those anonymous components of the system, will spew the greengrocer from its mouth. The system, through its alienating presence in people, will punish him for his rebellion. It must do so because the logic of its automatism and self-defence dictate it. The greengrocer has not committed a simple, individual offence, isolated in its own uniqueness, but something incomparably more serious. By breaking the rules of the game, he has disrupted the game as such. He has exposed it as a mere game. He has shattered the world of appearances, the fundamental pillar of the system. He has upset the power structure by tearing apart what holds it together. He has demonstrated that living a lie is living a lie. He has broken through the exalted façade of the system and exposed the real, base foundations of power. He has said that the emperor is naked. And because the emperor is in fact naked, something extremely dangerous has happened: by his action, the greengrocer has addressed the world. He has enabled everyone to peer behind the curtain. He has shown everyone that it *is* possible to live within the truth. Living within the lie can constitute the system only if it is universal. The principle must embrace and permeate everything. There are no terms whatsoever on which it can coexist with living within the truth, and therefore everyone who steps out of line *denies it in principle and threatens it in its entirety.*

This is understandable: as long as appearance is not confronted with reality, it does not seem to be appearance. As long as living a lie is not confronted with living the truth, the perspective needed to expose its mendacity is lacking. As soon as the alternative appears, however, it threatens the very existence of appearance and living a lie in terms of what they are, both their essence and their all-inclusiveness. And at the same time, it is utterly unimportant how large a space this alternative occupies: its power does not consist in its physical attributes but in the light it casts on those pillars of the system and on its unstable foundations. After all, the greengrocer was a threat to the system not because of any physical or actual power he had, but because his action went beyond itself, because it illuminated its surroundings and, of course, because of the incalculable consequences of that illumination. In the post-totalitarian system, therefore, living within the truth has more than a mere existential dimension (returning humanity to its inherent nature), or a noetic dimension (revealing reality as it is), or a moral dimension (setting an example for others). It also has an unambiguous *political* dimension. If the main pillar of the system is living a lie, then it is not surprising that the fundamental threat to it is living the truth. This is why it must be suppressed more severely than anything else.

In the post-totalitarian system, truth in the widest sense of the word has a very special import, one unknown in other contexts. In this system, truth plays a far greater (and above all, a far different) role as a factor of power, or as an outright political force. How does the power of truth operate? How does truth as a factor of power work? How can its power — as power — be realized?

VIII

Individuals can be alienated from themselves only because there is *something* in them to alienate. The terrain of this violation is their authentic existence. Living the truth is thus woven directly into the texture of living a lie. It is the repressed alternative, the authentic aim to which living a lie is an inauthentic response. Only against this background does living a lie make any sense: it exists *because* of that background. In its excusatory, chimerical rootedness in the human order, it is a response to nothing other than the human predisposition to truth. Under the orderly surface of the life of lies, therefore, there slumbers the hidden sphere of life in its real aims, of its hidden openness to truth.

The singular, explosive, incalculable political power of living within the truth resides in the fact that living openly within the truth has an ally, invisible to be sure, but omnipresent: this hidden sphere. It is from this sphere that life lived openly in the truth grows; it is to this sphere that it speaks, and in it that it finds understanding. This is where the potential for communication exists. But this place is hidden and therefore, from the perspective of power, very dangerous. The complex ferment that takes place within it goes on in semi-darkness, and by the time it finally surfaces into the light of day as an assortment of shocking surprises to the system, it is usually too late to cover them up in the usual fashion. Thus they create a situation in which the regime is confounded, invariably causing panic and driving it to react in inappropriate ways.

It seems that the primary breeding ground for what might, in the widest possible sense of the word, be understood as an opposition in the post-totalitarian system is living within the truth. The confrontation between these opposition forces and the powers that be, of course, will obviously take a form essentially different from that typical of an open society or a classical dictatorship. Initially, this confrontation does not take place on the level of real, institutionalized, quantifiable power which relies on the various instruments of power, but on a different

level altogether: the level of human consciousness and conscience, the existential level. The effective range of this special
power cannot be measured in terms of disciples, voters, or
soldiers, because it lies spread out in the fifth column of social
consciousness, in the hidden aims of life, in human beings'
repressed longing for dignity and fundamental rights, for the
realization of their real social and political interests. Its power,
therefore, does not reside in the strength of definable political or
social groups, but chiefly in the strength of a potential, which is
hidden throughout the whole of society, including the official
power structures of that society. Therefore this power does not
rely on soldiers of its own, but on the soldiers of the enemy as it
were — that is to say, on everyone who is living within the lie and
who may be struck at any moment (in theory, at least) by the
force of truth (or who, out of an instinctive desire to protect their
position, may at least adapt to that force). It is a bacteriological
weapon, so to speak, utilized when conditions are ripe by a single
civilian to disarm an entire division. This power does not participate in any direct struggle for power; rather it makes its influence
felt in the obscure arena of being itself. The hidden movements it
gives rise to there, however, can issue forth (when, where, under
what circumstances, and to what extent are difficult to predict) in
something visible: a real political act or event, a social movement,
a sudden explosion of civil unrest, a sharp conflict inside an
apparently monolithic power structure, or simply an irrepressible transformation in the social and intellectual climate. And
since all genuine problems and matters of critical importance are
hidden beneath a thick crust of lies, it is never quite clear when
the proverbial last straw will fall, or what that straw will be. This,
too, is why the regime prosecutes, almost as a reflex action
preventively, even the most modest attempts to live within the
truth.

Why was Solzhenitsyn driven out of his own country? Certainly not because he represented a unit of real power, that is, not
because any of the regime's representatives felt he might unseat
them and take their place in government. Solzhenitsyn's expulsion was something else: a desperate attempt to plug up the

dreadful wellspring of truth, a truth which might cause incalculable transformations in social consciousness, which in turn might one day produce political debacles unpredictable in their consequences. And so the post-totalitarian system behaved in a characteristic way: it defended the integrity of the world of appearances in order to defend itself. For the crust presented by the life of lies is made of strange stuff. As long as it seals off hermetically the entire society, it appears to be made of stone. But the moment someone breaks through in one place, when one person cries out, 'The emperor is naked!' – when a single person breaks the rules of the game, thus exposing it as a game – everything suddenly appears in another light and the whole crust seems then to be made of a tissue on the point of tearing and disintegrating uncontrollably.

When I speak of living within the truth, I naturally do not have in mind only products of conceptual thought, such as a protest or a letter written by a group of intellectuals. It can be any means by which a person or a group revolts against manipulation: anything from a letter by intellectuals to a workers' strike, from a rock concert to a student demonstration, from refusing to vote in the farcical elections, to making an open speech at some official congress, or even a hunger strike, for instance. If the suppression of the aims of life is a complex process, and if it is based on the multifaceted manipulation of all expressions of life then, by the same token, every free expression of life indirectly threatens the post-totalitarian system politically, including forms of expression to which, in other social systems, no one would attribute any potential political significance, not to mention explosive power.

The Prague Spring is usually understood as a clash between two groups on the level of real power: those who wanted to maintain the system as it was and those who wanted to reform it. It is frequently forgotten, however, that this encounter was merely the final act and the inevitable consequence of a long drama originally played out chiefly in the theatre of the spirit and the conscience of society. And that somewhere at the beginning of this drama, there were individuals who were willing to live within the truth, even when things were at their worst. These people had no access to real power, nor did they aspire to it. The sphere in which they were living the truth was not necessarily even that of political thought. They could equally have been poets, painters, musicians, or simply ordinary citizens who were able to maintain their human dignity. Today it is naturally difficult to pinpoint when and through which hidden, winding channel a certain action or attitude influenced a given milieu, and to trace the virus of truth as it slowly spread through the tissue of the life of lies, gradually causing it to disintegrate. One thing, however, seems clear: the attempt at political reform was not the cause of society's reawakening, but rather the final outcome of that reawakening.

I think the present also can be better understood in the light of this experience. The confrontation between 1000 Chartists and the post-totalitarian system would appear to be politically hopeless. This is true, of course, if we look at it through the traditional lens of the open political system, in which, quite naturally, every political force is measured chiefly in terms of the positions it holds on the level of real power. Given that perspective, a mini-party like the Charter would certainly not stand a chance. If, however, this confrontation is seen against the background of what we know about power in the post-totalitarian system, it appears in a fundamentally different light. For the time being, it is impossible to say with any precision what impact the appearance of Charter 77, its existence, and its work has had in the hidden sphere, and how the Charter's attempt to rekindle civic self-awareness and confidence is regarded there. Whether, when, and how this investment will eventually produce dividends in the form of specific political changes is even less possible to predict. But that, of course, is all part of living within the truth. As an existential solution, it takes individuals back to the solid ground of their own identity; as politics it throws them into a game of chance where the stakes are all or nothing. For this reason it is undertaken only by those for whom the former is worth risking the latter, or who have come to the conclusion that there is no other way to conduct real politics in Czechoslovakia today. Which, by the way, is the same thing: this conclusion can be reached only by someone who is unwilling to sacrifice his or her own human identity to politics, or rather who does not believe in a politics that requires such a sacrifice.

The more thoroughly the post-totalitarian system frustrates any rival alternative on the level of real power, as well as any form of politics independent of the laws of its own automatism, the more definitively the centre of gravity of any potential political threat shifts to the area of the existential and the pre-political: usually without any conscious effort, living within the truth becomes the one natural point of departure for all activities that work against the automatism of the system. And even if such activities ultimately grow beyond the area of living within the truth (which means they are transformed into various parallel structures, movements, institutions, they begin to be regarded as political activity, they bring real pressure to bear on the official structures and begin in fact to have a certain influence on the level of real power), they always carry with them the specific hallmark of their origins. Therefore it seems to me that not even the so-called dissident movements can be properly understood without constantly bearing in mind this special background from which they emerge.

IX

The profound crisis of human identity brought on by living within a lie, a crisis which in turn makes such a life possible, certainly possesses a moral dimension as well; it appears, among other things, as *a deep moral crisis in society*. A person who has been seduced by the consumer value system, whose identity is dissolved in an amalgam of the accoutrements of mass civilization, and who has no roots in the order of being, no sense of responsibility for anything higher than his or her own personal survival, is a *demoralized* person. The system depends on this demoralization, deepens it, is in fact a projection of it into society.

Living within the truth, as humanity's revolt against an enforced position, is, on the contrary, an attempt to regain control over one's own sense of responsibility. In other words, it is clearly a moral act, not only because one must pay so dearly for it, but principally because it is not self-serving: the risk may bring rewards in the form of a general amelioration in the situation, or it may not. In this regard, as I stated previously, it is an all-or-nothing gamble, and it is difficult to imagine a reasonable person embarking on such a course merely because he or she reckons that sacrifice today will bring rewards tomorrow, be it only in the form of general gratitude. (By the way, the representatives of power invariably come to terms with those who live within the truth by persistently ascribing utilitarian motivations to them — a lust for power or fame or wealth — and thus they try, at least, to implicate them in their own world, the world of general demoralization.)

If living within the truth in the post-totalitarian system becomes the chief breeding ground for independent, alternative political ideas, then all considerations about the nature and future prospects of these ideas must necessarily reflect this moral dimension as a political phenomenon. (And if the revolutionary Marxist belief about morality as a product of the 'superstructure' inhibits any of our friends from realizing the full significance of this dimension and, in one way or another, from including it in their view of the world, it is to their own detriment: an anxious fidelity to the postulates of that world view prevents them from properly understanding the mechanisms of their own political influence, thus paradoxically making them precisely what they, as Marxists, so often suspect others of being — victims of 'false consciousness'.) The very special political significance of morality in the post-totalitarian system is a phenomenon that is at the very least unusual in modern political history, a phenomenon that might well have — as I shall soon attempt to show — far-reaching consequences.

X

Undeniably, the most important political event in Czechoslovakia after the advent of the Husák leadership in 1969 was the appearance of Charter 77. The spiritual and intellectual climate surrounding its appearance, however, was not the product

of any immediate political event. That climate was created by the
trial of some young musicians associated with a rock group
called 'The Plastic People of the Universe'. Their trial was not a
confrontation of two differing political forces or conceptions, but
two differing conceptions of life. On the one hand, there was the
sterile puritanism of the post-totalitarian establishment and, on
the other hand, unknown young people who wanted no more
than to be able to live within the truth, to play the music they
enjoyed, to sing songs that were relevant to their lives, and to live
freely in dignity and partnership. These people had no past
history of political activity. They were not highly motivated
members of the opposition with political ambitions, nor were
they former politicians expelled from the power structures. They
had been given every opportunity to adapt to the status quo, to
accept the principles of living within a lie and thus to enjoy life
undisturbed by the authorities. Yet they decided on a different
course. Despite this, or perhaps precisely because of it, their case
had a very special impact on everyone who had not yet given up
hope. Moreover, when the trial took place, a new mood had
begun to surface after the years of waiting, of apathy and of
scepticism towards various forms of resistance. People were 'tired
of being tired'; they were fed up with the stagnation, the
inactivity, barely hanging on in the hope that things might
improve after all. In some ways the trial was the final straw. Many
groups of differing tendencies which until then had remained
isolated from each other, reluctant to co-operate, or which were
committed to forms of action that made co-operation difficult,
were suddenly struck with the powerful realization that freedom
is indivisible. Everyone understood that an attack on the Czech
musical underground was an attack on a most elementary and
important thing, something that in fact bound everyone together:
it was an attack on the very notion of 'living within the truth', on
the real aims of life. The freedom to play rock music was
understood as a human freedom and thus as essentially the same
as the freedom to engage in philosophical and political reflection, the freedom to write, the freedom to express and defend the
various social and political interests of society. People were

inspired to feel a genuine sense of solidarity with the young musicians and they came to realize that not standing up for the freedom of others, regardless of how remote their means of creativity or their attitude to life, meant surrendering one's own freedom. (There is no freedom without equality before the law, and there is no equality before the law without freedom; Charter 77 has given this ancient notion a new and characteristic dimension, which has immensely important implications for modern Czech history. What Slábeček, the author of the book *Sixty-eight,* in a brilliant analysis, calls the 'principle of exclusion', lies at the root of all our present-day moral and political misery. This principle was born at the end of the Second World War in that strange collusion of democrats and communists and was subsequently developed further and further, right to the 'bitter end'. For the first time in decades this principle has been overcome, by Charter 77: all those united in the Charter have, for the first time, become equal partners. Charter 77 is not merely a coalition of communists and non-communists — that would be nothing historically new and, from the moral and political point of view, nothing revolutionary — but it is a community that is *a priori* open to anyone, and no one in it is *a priori* assigned an inferior position.) This was the climate, then, in which Charter 77 was created. Who could have foreseen that the prosecution of one or two obscure rock groups would have such far-reaching consequences?

I think that the origins of Charter 77 illustrate very well what I have already suggested above: that in the post-totalitarian system, the real background to the movements that gradually assume political significance does not usually consist of overtly political events of confrontations between different forces or concepts that are openly political. These movements for the most part originate elsewhere, in the far broader area of the 'pre-political', where 'living within a lie' confronts 'living within the truth', that is, where the demands of the post-totalitarian system conflict with the real aims of life. These real aims can naturally assume a great many forms. Sometimes they appear as the basic material or social interests of a group or an individual; at other times, they may appear as certain intellectual and spiritual interests; at still other times, they may be the most fundamental of existential demands, such as the simple longing of people to live their own lives in dignity. Such a conflict acquires a political character, then, not because of the elementary political nature of the aims demanding to be heard but simply because, given the complex system of manipulation on which the post-totalitarian system is founded and on which it is also dependent, every free human act or expression, every attempt to live within the truth, must necessarily appear as a threat to the system and, thus, as something which is political *par excellence*. Any eventual political articulation of the movements that grow out of this 'pre-political' hinterland is secondary. It develops and matures as a result of a subsequent confrontation with the system, and not because it started off as a political programme, project or impulse.

Once again, the events of 1968 confirm this. The communist politicians who were trying to reform the system came forward with their programme not because they had suddenly experienced a mystical enlightenment, but because they were led to do so by continued and increasing pressure from areas of life that had nothing to do with politics in the traditional sense of the word. In fact they were trying in political ways to solve the social conflicts (which in fact were confrontations between the aims of the system and the aims of life) that almost every level of society had been experiencing daily, and had been thinking about with increasing openness for years. Backed by this living resonance throughout society, scholars and artists had defined the problem in a wide variety of ways and students were demanding solutions.

The genesis of Charter 77 also illustrates the special political significance of the moral aspect of things that I have mentioned. Charter 77 would have been unimaginable without that powerful sense of solidarity among widely differing groups, and without the sudden realization that it was impossible to go on waiting any longer, and that the truth had to be spoken loudly and collectively, regardless of the virtual certainty of sanctions and the uncertainty of any tangible results in the immediate future. 'There are some things worth suffering for', Jan Patočka wrote shortly before his death.* I think that Chartists understand this not only as Patočka's legacy, but also as the best explanation of why they do what they do.

Seen from the outside, and chiefly from the vantage point of the system and its power structure, Charter 77 came as a surprise, as a bolt out of the blue. It was not a bolt out of the blue, of course, but that impression is understandable, since the ferment that led to it took place in the 'hidden sphere', in that semi-darkness where things are difficult to chart or analyse. The chances of predicting the appearance of the Charter were just as slight as the chances are now of predicting where it will lead. Once again, it was that shock, so typical of moments when something from the hidden sphere suddenly bursts through the moribund surface of 'living within a lie'. The more one is trapped in the world of appearances, the more surprising it is when something like that happens.

XI

In societies under the post-totalitarian system, all political life in the traditional sense has been eliminated. People have no opportunity to express themselves politically in public, let alone to organize politically. The gap that results is filled by ideological ritual. In such a situation, people's interest in political matters naturally dwindles and independent political thought, in so far as it exists at all, is seen by the majority as unrealistic, far-fetched, a kind of self-indulgent game, hopelessly distant from their everyday concerns; something admirable, perhaps, but quite pointless, because it is on the one hand entirely utopian and on the other hand extraordinarily dangerous, in view of the unusual vigour with which any move in that direction is per-secuted by the regime.

Editor's note [in Unwin Hyman edition]: a highly influential philosopher and disciple of Edmund Husserl, Jan Patočka was also one of the three founding spokespersons for Charter 77. He was severely harassed by the police, subjected to lengthy interrogations, and literally hounded by the police to his hospital death bed. The quotation above is taken from his final public state-ment, translated as 'Political testament', *Telos*, **31** (spring 1977), pp. 151–2.

Yet even in such societies, individuals and groups of people exist who do not abandon politics as a vocation and who, in one way or another, strive to think independently, to express themselves and in some cases even to organize politically, because that is a part of their attempt to live within the truth.

The fact that these people exist and work is in itself immensely important and worthwhile. Even in the worst of times, they maintain the continuity of political thought. If some genuine political impulse emerges from this or that 'pre-political' confrontation and is properly articulated early enough, thus increasing its chances of relative success, then this is frequently due to these isolated 'generals without an army' who, because they have maintained the continuity of political thought in the face of enormous difficulties, can at the right moment enrich the new impulse with the fruits of their own political thinking. Once again, there is ample evidence for this process in Czechoslovakia. Almost all those who were political prisoners in the early 1970s, who had apparently been made to suffer in vain because of their quixotic efforts to work politically among an utterly apathetic and demoralized society, belong today – inevitably – among the most active Chartists. In Charter 77, the moral legacy of their earlier sacrifices is valued, and they have enriched this movement with their experience and that element of political thinking.

And yet it seems to me that the thought and activity of those friends who have never given up direct political work and who are always ready to assume direct political responsibility very often suffer from one chronic fault: an insufficient understanding of the historical uniqueness of the post-totalitarian system as a social and political reality. They have little understanding of the specific nature of power that is typical for this system and therefore they overestimate the importance of direct political work in the traditional sense. Moreover, they fail to appreciate the political significance of those 'pre-political' events and processes that provide the living humus from which genuine political change usually springs. As political actors – or, rather, as people with political ambitions – they frequently try to pick up where natural political life left off. They maintain models of behaviour that may have been appropriate in more normal political circumstances and thus, without really being aware of it, they bring an outmoded way of thinking, old habits, conceptions, categories and notions to bear on circumstances that are quite new and radically different, without first giving adequate thought to the meaning and substance of such things in the new circumstances, to what politics as such means now, to what sort of thing can have political impact and potential, and in what way. Because such people have been excluded from the structures of power and are no longer able to influence those structures directly (and because they remain faithful to traditional notions of politics established in more or less democratic societies or in classical dictatorships) they frequently, in a sense, lose touch with reality. Why make compromises with reality, they say, when none of our proposals will ever be accepted anyway? Thus they find themselves in a world of genuinely utopian thinking.

As I have already tried to indicate, however, genuinely far-reaching political events do not emerge from the same sources and in the same way in the post-totalitarian system as they do in a democracy. And if a large portion of the public is indifferent to, even sceptical of, alternative political models and programmes and the private establishment of opposition political parties, this is not merely because there is a general feeling of apathy towards public affairs and a loss of that sense of 'higher responsibility'; in other words, it is not just a consequence of the general demoralization. There is also a bit of healthy social instinct at work in this attitude. It is as if people sensed intuitively that 'nothing is what it seems any longer', as the saying goes, and that from now on, therefore, things must be done entirely differently as well.

If some of the most important political impulses in Soviet bloc countries in recent years have come initially — that is, before being felt on the level of actual power — from mathematicians, philosophers, physicians, writers, historians, ordinary workers and so on, more frequently than from politicians, and if the driving force behind the various 'dissident movements' comes from so many people in 'non-political' professions, this is not because these people are more clever than those who see themselves primarily as politicians. It is because those who are not politicians are also not so bound by traditional political thinking and political habits and therefore, paradoxically, they are more aware of genuine political reality and more sensitive to what can and should be done under the circumstances.

There is no way around it: no matter how beautiful an alternative political model may be, it can no longer speak to the 'hidden sphere', inspire people and society, call for real political ferment. The real sphere of potential politics in the post-totalitarian system is elsewhere: in the continuing and cruel tension between the complex demands of that system and the aims of life, that is, the elementary need of human beings to live, to a certain extent at least, in harmony with themselves, that is, to live in a bearable way, not to be humiliated by their superiors and officials, not to be continually watched by the police, to be able to express themselves freely, to find an outlet for their creativity, to enjoy legal security, and so on. Anything that touches this field concretely, anything that relates to this fundamental, omnipresent and living tension, will inevitably speak to people. Abstract projects for an ideal political or economic order do not interest them to anything like the same extent — and rightly so — not only because everyone knows how little chance they have of succeeding, but also because today people feel that the less political policies are derived from a concrete and human 'here and now' and the more they fix their sights on an abstract 'some day', the more easily they can degenerate into new forms of human enslavement. People who live in the post-totalitarian system know only too well that the question of whether one or several political parties are in power, and how these parties define and label themselves, is of far less importance than the question of whether or not it is possible to live like a human being.

To shed the burden of traditional political categories and habits and open oneself up fully to the world of human existence and then to draw political conclusions only after having analysed it: this is not only politically more realistic but at the same time, from the point of view of an 'ideal state of affairs', politically more promising as well. A genuine, profound and lasting change for the better — as I shall attempt to show elsewhere — can no longer result from the victory (were such a victory possible) of any particular traditional political conception, which can ultimately be only external, that is, a structural or systemic conception. More than ever before, such a change will have to derive from human existence, from the fundamental reconstitution of the position of people in the world, their relationships to themselves and to each other, and to the universe. If a better economic and political model is to be created, then perhaps more than ever before it must derive from profound existential and moral changes in society. This is not something that can be designed and introduced like a new car. If it is to be more than just a new variation on the old degeneration, it must above all be an expression of life in the process of transforming itself. A better system will not automatically ensure a better life. In fact the opposite is true: only by creating a better life can a better system be developed.

Once more I repeat that I am not underestimating the importance of political thought and conceptual political work. On the contrary, I think that genuine political thought and genuinely political work is precisely what we continually fail to achieve. If I say 'genuine', however, I have in mind the kind of thought and conceptual work that has freed itself of all the traditional political schemata that have been imported into our circumstances from a world that will never return (and whose return, even were it possible, would provide no permanent solution to the most important problems).

The Second and Fourth Internationals, like many other political powers and organizations, may naturally provide significant political support for various efforts of ours, but neither of them can solve our problems for us. They operate in a different world and are a product of different circumstances. Their theoretical concepts can be interesting and instructive to us but one thing is certain: we cannot solve our problems simply by identifying with these organizations. And the attempt in our country to place what we do in the context of some of the discussions that dominate political life in democratic societies often seems like sheer folly. For example, is it possible to talk seriously about whether we want to change the system or merely reform it? In the circumstances under which we live, this is a pseudo-problem, since for the time being there is simply no way we can accomplish either goal. We are not even clear about where reform ends and change begins. We know from a number of harsh experiences that neither reform nor change is in itself a guarantee of anything. We know that ultimately it is all the same to us whether or not the system in which we live, in the light of a particular doctrine, appears 'changed' or 'reformed'. Our concern is whether we can live with dignity in such a system, whether it serves people rather than people serving it. We are struggling to achieve this with the means available to us, and the means it makes sense to employ. Western journalists, submerged in the political banalities in which they live, may label our approach as overly legalistic, as too risky, revisionist, counter-revolutionary, bourgeois, communist, or as too right-wing or left-wing. But this is the very last thing that interests us.

XII

One concept that is a constant source of confusion chiefly because it has been imported into our circumstances from circumstances that are entirely different, is the concept of an opposition. What exactly is an opposition in the post-totalitarian system?

In democratic societies with a traditional parliamentary system of government, political opposition is understood as a political force on the level of actual power (most frequently a party or coalition of parties) which is not a part of the government. It offers an alternative political programme, it has ambitions to govern, and it is recognized and respected by the government in power as a natural element in the political life of the country. It seeks to spread its influence by political means, and competes for power on the basis of agreed-upon legal regulations.

In addition to this form of opposition, there exists the phenomenon of the 'extra-parliamentary opposition', which again consists of forces organized more or less on the level of actual power, but which operate outside the rules created by the system, and which employ different means than are usual within that framework.

In classical dictatorships, the term 'opposition' is understood to mean the political forces which have also come out with an alternative political programme. They operate either legally or on the outer limits of legality, but in any case they cannot compete for power within the limits of some agreed-upon regulations. Or the term 'opposition' may be applied to forces preparing for a violent confrontation with the ruling power, or who feel themselves to be in this state of confrontation already, such as various guerrilla groups or liberation movements.

An opposition in the post-totalitarian system does not exist in any of these senses. In what way, then, can the term be used?

1. Occasionally the term 'opposition' is applied, mainly by western journalists, to persons or groups inside the power structure who find themselves in a state of *hidden* conflict with the highest authorities. The reasons for this conflict may be certain differences (not very sharp differences, naturally) of a conceptual nature, but more frequently it is quite simply a longing for power or a personal antipathy to others who represent that power.

2. Opposition here can also be understood as everything that does or can have an indirect political effect in the sense already mentioned, that is, everything the post-totalitarian system feels threatened by, which in fact means everything it *is* threatened by. In this sense, the opposition is every attempt to live within the truth, from the greengrocer's refusal to put the slogan in his window to a freely written poem; in other words, everything in which the genuine aims of life go beyond the limits placed on them by the aims of the system.

3. More frequently, however, the opposition is usually understood (again, largely by western journalists) as groups of people who make public their non-conformist stances and critical opinions, who make no secret of their independent thinking and who, to a greater or lesser degree, consider themselves a political force. In this sense, the notion of an 'opposition' more or less overlaps with the notion of 'dissent', although, of course, there are great differences in the degree to which that label is accepted or rejected. It depends not only on the extent to which these people understand their power as a directly political force, and on whether they have ambitions to participate in actual power, but also on how each of them understands the notion of an 'opposition'.

Again, here is an example: in its original declaration, Charter 77 emphasized that it was not an opposition because it had no intention of presenting an alternative political programme. It sees its mission as something quite different, for it has not presented such programmes. In fact, if the presenting of an alternative programme defines the nature of an opposition in post-totalitarian states, then the Charter cannot be considered an opposition.

The Czechoslovak government, however, has considered Charter 77 as an expressly oppositional association from the very beginning, and has treated it accordingly. This means that the government — and this is only natural — understands the term 'opposition' more or less as I defined it in point 2, that is, as everything that manages to avoid total manipulation and which therefore denies the principle that the system has an absolute claim on the individual.

If we accept this definition of opposition, then of course we must, along with the government, consider the Charter a genuine opposition, because it represents a serious challenge to the integrity of post-totalitarian power, founded as it is on the universality of 'living with a lie'.

It is a different matter, however, when we look at the extent to which individual signatories of Charter 77 think of themselves as an opposition. My impression is that most base their understanding of the term 'opposition' on the traditional meaning of the word as it became established in democratic societies (or in classical dictatorships); therefore, they understand 'opposition', even in Czechoslovakia, as a politically defined force which, although it does not operate on the level of actual power, and even less within the framework of certain rules respected by the government, would still not reject the opportunity to participate in actual power because it has, in a sense, an alternative political programme whose proponents are prepared to accept direct political responsibility for it. Given this notion of an opposition, some Chartists — the great majority — do not see themselves in this way. Others — a minority — do, even though they fully respect the fact that there is no room within Charter 77 for 'oppositional' activity in this sense. At the same time, however, perhaps every Chartist is familiar enough with the specific nature of conditions in the post-totalitarian system to realize that it is not only the struggle for human rights that has its own peculiar political power, but incomparably more 'innocent' activities as well, and therefore they can be understood as an aspect of opposition. No Chartist can really object to being considered in 'opposition' in this sense.

There is another circumstance, however, that considerably complicates matters. For many decades, the power ruling society in the Soviet bloc has used the label 'opposition' as the blackest of indictments, as synonymous with the word 'enemy'. To brand someone 'a member of the opposition' is tantamount to saying he or she is trying to overthrow the government and put an end to socialism (naturally in the pay of the imperialists). There have been times when this label led straight to the gallows, and of course this does not encourage people to apply the same label to themselves. Moreover, it is only a word, and what is actually done is more important than how it is labelled.

The final reason why many reject such a term is because there is something negative about the notion of an 'opposition'. People who so define themselves do so in relation to a prior 'position'. In other words, they relate themselves specifically to the power that rules society and through it, define themselves, deriving their own 'position' from the position of the regime. For people who have simply decided to live within the truth, to say aloud what they think, to express their solidarity with their fellow citizens, to create as they want and simply to live in harmony with their better 'self', it is naturally disagreeable to feel required to define their own, original and positive 'position' negatively, in terms of something else, and to think of themselves primarily as people who are against something, not simply as people who *are* what they are.

Obviously, the only way to avoid misunderstanding is to say clearly — before one starts using them — in what sense the terms 'opposition' and 'member of the opposition' are being used and how they are in fact to be understood in our circumstances.

XIII

If the term 'opposition' has been imported from democratic societies into the post-totalitarian system without general agreement on what the word means in conditions that are so different, then the term 'dissident' was, on the contrary, chosen by western journalists and is now generally accepted as the label for a phenomenon peculiar to the post-totalitarian system and almost never occurring — at least not in that form — in democratic societies.

Who are these 'dissidents'?

It seems that the term is applied primarily to citizens of the Soviet bloc who have decided to live within the truth and who, in addition, meet the following criteria:

1. They express their non-conformist positions and critical opinions publicly and systematically, within the very strict limits available to them, and because of this, they are known in the West.

2. Despite being unable to publish at home and despite every possible form of persecution by their governments, they have, by virtue of their attitudes, managed to win a certain esteem, both from the public and from their government, and thus they actually enjoy a very limited and very strange degree of indirect, actual power in their own milieu as well. This either protects them from the worst forms of persecution, or at least it ensures that if they are persecuted, it will mean certain political complications for their governments.

3. The horizon of their critical attention and their commitment reaches beyond the narrow context of their immediate surroundings or special interests to embrace more general causes and, thus, their work becomes political in nature, although the degree to which they think of themselves as a directly political force may vary a great deal.

4. They are people who lean towards intellectual pursuits, that is, they are 'writing' people, people for whom the written word is the primary — and often the only — political medium they command, and that can gain them attention, particularly from abroad. Other ways in which they seek to live within the truth are either lost to the foreign observer in the elusive local milieu or — if they reach beyond this local framework — they appear to be only somewhat less visible complements to what they have written.

5. Regardless of their actual vocations, these people are talked about in the West more frequently in terms of their activities as committed citizens, or in terms of the critical, political aspects of their work, than in terms of the 'real' work they do in their own fields. From personal experience, I know that there is an invisible line you cross — without even wanting to or becoming aware of it — beyond which they cease to treat you as a writer who happens to be a concerned citizen and begin talking of you as a 'dissident' who almost incidentally (in his or her spare time, perhaps?) happens to write plays as well.

Unquestionably, there are people who meet all of these criteria. What is debatable is whether we should be using a special term for a group defined in such an essentially accidental way, and specifically, whether they should be called 'dissidents'. It does happen, however, and there is clearly nothing we can do about it. Sometimes, to facilitate communication, we even use the label ourselves, although it is done with distaste, rather ironically, and almost always in quotations marks.

Perhaps it is now appropriate to outline some of the reasons why 'dissidents' themselves are not very happy to be referred to in this way. In the first place, the word is problematic from an etymological point of view. A 'dissident', we are told in our press, means something like 'renegade' or 'backslider'. But dissidents do not consider themselves renegades for the simple reason that they are not primarily denying or rejecting anything. On the contrary, they have tried to affirm their own human identity, and if they reject anything at all, then it is merely what was false and alienating in their lives, that aspect of 'living within a lie'.*

But that is not the most important thing. The term 'dissident' frequently implies a special profession, as if, along with the more normal vocations, there was another special one — grumbling about the state of things. In fact, a 'dissident' is simply a physicist, a sociologist, a worker, a poet, individuals who are merely doing what they feel they must and, consequently, who find themselves in open conflict with the regime. This conflict has not come about through any conscious intention on their part, but simply through the inner logic of their thinking, behaviour or work (often confronted with external circumstances more or less beyond their control). They have not, in other words, consciously decided to be professional malcontents, rather as one decides to be a tailor or a blacksmith.

In fact, of course, they do not usually discover they are 'dissidents' until long after they have actually become one. 'Dissent' springs from motivations far different from the desire for titles or fame. In short, they do not decide to become 'dissidents', and even if they were to devote twenty-four hours a day to it, it would still not be a profession, but primarily an existential attitude. Moreover, it is an attitude that is in no way the exclusive property of those who have earned themselves the title of 'dissident' just because they happen to fulfil those accidental external conditions already mentioned. There are thousands of nameless people who try to live within the truth and millions who want to but cannot, perhaps only because to do so in the circumstances in which they

---

Editor's note [in Unwin Hyman edition]: In this paragraph, Havel is in effect replying to the official Czechoslovak newspapers, in which 'dissident' is sometimes rendered as *odpadlík,* which means literally 'one who has fallen out', hence 'renegade' or 'backslider'.

live, they would need ten times the courage of those who have already taken the first step. If several dozen are randomly chosen from among all these people and put into a special category, this can utterly distort the general picture. It does so in two different ways. Either it suggests that 'dissidents' are a group of prominent people, a 'protected species' who are permitted to do things others are not and whom the government may even be cultivating as living proof of its generosity; or it lends support to the illusion that since there is no more than a handful of malcontents to whom not very much is really being done, all the rest are therefore content, for were they not so, they would be 'dissidents' too.

But that is not all. This categorization also unintentionally supports the impression that the primary concern of these 'dissidents' is some vested interest that they share as a group, as though their entire argument with the government were no more than a rather abstruse conflict between two opposed groups, a conflict that leaves society out of it altogether. But such an impression profoundly contradicts the real importance of the 'dissident' attitude, which stands or falls on its interest in others, in what ails society as a whole, in other words, on an interest in all those who do not speak up. If 'dissidents' have any kind of authority at all and if they have not been exterminated long ago like exotic insects that have appeared where they have no business being, then this is not because the government holds this exclusive group and their exclusive ideas in such awe, but because it is perfectly aware of the potential political power of 'living within the truth' rooted in the hidden sphere, and well aware too of the kind of world 'dissent' grows out of and the world it addresses: the everyday human world, the world of daily tension between the aims of life and the aims of the system. (Can there be any better evidence of this than the government's action after Charter 77 appeared, when it launched a campaign to compel the entire nation to declare that Charter 77 was wrong? Those millions of signatures proved, among other things, that just the opposite was true.) The political organs and the police do not lavish such enormous attention on 'dissidents' — which may give the impression that the government fears them as they might fear an alternative power clique — because they actually are such a power clique, but because they are ordinary people with ordinary cares, differing from the rest only in that they say aloud what the rest cannot say or are afraid to say. I have already mentioned Solzhenitsyn's political influence: it does not reside in some exclusive political power he possesses as an individual, but in the experience of those millions of Gulag victims which he simply amplified and communicated to millions of other people of good will.

To institutionalize a select category of well-known or prominent 'dissidents' means in fact to deny the most intrinsic moral aspect of their activity. As we have seen, the 'dissident movement' grows out of the principle of equality, founded on the notion that human rights and freedoms are indivisible. After all, did not 'well-known dissidents' unite in *KOR★* to defend unknown workers? And was it not precisely for this reason that they became 'well-known dissidents'? And did not the 'well-known dissidents' unite in Charter 77 after they had been brought together in defence of those unknown musicians, and did they not unite in the Charter precisely *with them,* and did they not become 'well-known dissidents' precisely because of that? It is truly a cruel paradox that the more some citizens stand up in defence of other citizens, the more they are labelled with a word that in effect separates them from those 'other citizens'.

This explanation, I hope, will make clear the significance of the quotation marks I have put around the word 'dissident' throughout this essay.

XIV

At the time when the Czech lands and Slovakia were an integral part of the Austro-Hungarian Empire, and when

---

★Editor's note [in Unwin Hyman edition]: The Workers' Defence Committee, a Polish organization that preceded the birth of Solidarity in August, 1980. It was later renamed *KSS-KOR* (Committee for Social Self-Defense — KOR) to indicate its commitment to defending civil rights as well as its support of all social initiatives against the institutions of the totalitarian state.

there existed neither the historical nor the political, psychological or social conditions that would have enabled the Czechs and Slovaks to seek their identity outside the framework of this empire, T. G. Masaryk established a Czechoslovak national programme based on the notion of 'small-scale work' (*drobná práce*). By that he meant honest and responsible work in widely different areas of life but within the existing social order, work that would stimulate national creativity and national self-confidence. Naturally he placed particular emphasis on intelligent and enlightened upbringing and education, and on the moral and humanitarian aspects of life. Masaryk believed that the only possible starting point for a more dignified national destiny was humanity itself. Humanity's first task was to create the conditions for a more human life; and in Masaryk's view, the task of transforming the stature of the nation began with the transformation of human beings.

This notion of 'working for the good of the nation' took root in Czechoslovak society and in many ways it was successful and is still alive today. Along with those who exploit the notion as a sophisticated excuse for collaborating with the regime, there are still many, even today, who genuinely uphold the ideal and, in some areas at least, can point to indisputable achievements. It is hard to say how much worse things would be if there were not many hard working people who simply refused to give up and try constantly to do the best they can, paying an unavoidable minimum to 'living within a lie' so that they might give their utmost to the authentic needs of society. These people assume, correctly, that every piece of good work is an indirect criticism of bad politics, and that there are situations where it is worthwhile going this route, even though it means surrendering one's natural right to make direct criticisms.

Today, however, there are very clear limitations to this attitude, even compared to the situation in the 1960s. More and more frequently, those who attempt to practise the principle of 'small-scale work' come up against the post-totalitarian system and find themselves facing a dilemma: either one retreats from that position, dilutes the honesty, responsibility and consistency on which it is based and simply adapts to circumstances (the approach taken by the majority), or one continues on the way begun and inevitably comes into conflict with the regime (the approach taken by a minority).

If the notion of small-scale work was never intended as an imperative to survive in the existing social and political structure *at any cost* (in which case individuals who allowed themselves to be excluded from that structure would necessarily appear to have given up 'working for the nation') then today it is even less significant. There is no general model of behaviour, that is, no neat, universally valid way of determining the point at which small-scale work ceases to be 'for the good of the nation' and becomes 'detrimental to the nation'. It is more than clear, however, that the danger of such a reversal is becoming more and more acute and that small-scale work, with increasing frequency, is coming up against that limit beyond which avoiding conflict means compromising its very essence.

In 1974, when I was employed in a brewery, my immediate superior was a certain Š., a person well-versed in the art of making beer. He was proud of his profession and he wanted our brewery to brew good beer. He spent almost all his time at work, continually thinking up improvements and he frequently made the rest of us feel uncomfortable because he assumed that we loved brewing as much as he did. In the midst of the slovenly indifference to work that socialism encourages, a more constructive worker would be difficult to imagine.

The brewery itself was managed by people who understood their work less and were less fond of it, but who were politically more influential. They were bringing the brewery to ruin and not only did they fail to react to any of Š.'s suggestions, but they actually became increasingly hostile towards him and tried in every way to thwart his efforts to do a good job. Eventually the situation became so bad that Š. felt compelled to write a lengthy letter to the manager's superior, in which he attempted to analyse the brewery's difficulties. He explained why it was the worst in the district and pointed to those responsible.

His voice might have been heard. The manager, who was politically powerful but otherwise ignorant of beer, a man who loathed workers and was given to intrigue, might have been replaced and conditions in the brewery might have been improved on the basis of Š.'s suggestions. Had this happened, it would have been a perfect example of small-scale work in action. Unfortunately the precise opposite occurred: the manager of the brewery, who was a member of the Communist Party's district committee, had friends in higher places and he saw to it that the situation was resolved in his favour. Š.'s analysis was described as a 'defamatory document' and Š. himself was labelled a 'political saboteur'. He was thrown out of the brewery and shifted to another one where he was given a job requiring no skill. Here the notion of small-scale work had come up against the wall of the post-totalitarian system. By speaking the truth, Š. had stepped out of line, broken the rules, cast himself out, and he ended up as a sub-citizen, stigmatized as an enemy. He could now say anything he wanted, but he could never, as a matter of principle, expect to be heard. He had become the 'dissident' of the Eastern Bohemian Brewery.

I think this is a model case which, from another point of view, illustrates what I have already said in the preceding section: you do not become a 'dissident' just because you decide one day to take up this most unusual career. You are thrown into it by your personal sense of responsibility, combined with a complex set of external circumstances. You are cast out of the existing structures and placed in a position of conflict with them. It begins as an attempt to do your work well, and ends with being branded an enemy of society. This is why our situation is not comparable to the Austro-Hungarian Empire, when the Czech nation, in the worst period of Bach's absolutism,* had only one real 'dissident',

---

*Editor's note [in Unwin Hyman edition]: Alexander Bach was Minister of the Interior for a decade — 1849–59 — in Vienna. His name has entered the Czech language and is synonymous with police rule. Karel Havlíček Borovský (1821–56) was a poet, literary critic and publicist. He is widely considered as the classical writer in the tradition of Czech political satire, and was involved

Karel Havlíček, who was imprisoned in Brixen. Today, if we are not to be snobbish about it, we must admit that 'dissidents' can be found on every streetcorner.

To rebuke 'dissidents' for having abandoned 'small-scale work' is simply absurd. 'Dissent' is not an alternative to Masaryk's notion, it is frequently its only possible outcome. I say 'frequently' in order to emphasize that this is not always the case. I am far from believing that the only decent and responsible people are those who find themselves at odds with the existing social and political structures. After all, the brewmaster Š. might have won his battle. To condemn those who have kept their positions simply because they have kept them, in other words, for not being 'dissidents', would be just as absurd as to hold them up as an example to the 'dissidents'. In any case, it contradicts the whole 'dissident' attitude — seen as an attempt to live within the truth — if one judges human behaviour not according to what it is and whether it is good or not, but according to the personal circumstances such an attempt has brought one to.

XV

Our greengrocer's attempt to live within the truth may be confined to not doing certain things. He decides not to put flags in his window when his only motive for putting them there in the first place would have been to avoid being reported by the house warden; he does not vote in elections that he considers false; he does not hide his opinions from his superiors. In other words, he may go no further than 'merely' refusing to comply with certain demands made on him by the system (which of course is not an insignificant step to take). This may, however, grow into something more. The greengrocer may begin to do something concrete, something that goes beyond an immediately personal self-defensive reaction against manipulation, something that will manifest his new-found sense of higher

directly in the Czech movement for nationhood and democracy during the 1840s and 1850s.

responsibility. He may, for example, organize his fellow green-grocers to act together in defence of their interests. He may write letters to various institutions, drawing their attention to instances of disorder and injustice around him. He may seek out unofficial literature, copy it and lend it to his friends.

If what I have called living within the truth is a basic existential (and of course potentially political) starting point for all those 'independent citizens' initiatives' and 'dissident' or 'opposition' movements dealt with in the essays to follow, this does not mean that every attempt to live within the truth automatically belongs in this category. On the contrary, in its most original and broad-est sense, living within the truth covers a vast territory whose outer limits are vague and difficult to map, a territory full of modest expressions of human volition, the vast majority of which will remain anonymous and whose political impact will probably never be felt or described any more concretely than simply as a part of a social climate or mood. Most of these expressions remain elementary revolts against manipulation: you simply straighten your backbone and live in greater dignity as an individual.

Here and there—thanks to the nature, the assumptions and the professions of some people, but also thanks to a number of accidental circumstances such as the specific nature of the local milieu, friends, and so on—a more coherent and visible initiative may emerge from this wide and anonymous hinterland, an initiative that transcends 'merely' individual revolt and is trans-formed into more conscious, structured and purposeful work. The point where living within the truth ceases to be a mere negation of living with a lie and becomes articulate in a particular way, is the point at which something is born that might be called 'the independent spiritual, social and political life of society'. This independent life is not separated from the rest of life ('dependent life') by some sharply defined line. Both types frequently coexist in the same people. Nevertheless, its most important focus is marked by a relatively high degree of inner emancipation. It sails upon the vast ocean of the manipulated life like little boats, tossed by the waves but always bobbing back as visible messengers of living within the truth, articulating the suppressed aims of life.

What is this independent life of society? The spectrum of its expressions and activities is naturally very wide. It includes everything from self-education and thinking about the world, through free creative activity and its communication to others, to the most varied free, civic attitudes, including instances of independent social self-organization. In short, it is an area in which living within the truth becomes articulate and materializes in a visible way.

Thus what will later be referred to as 'citizens' initiatives', 'dissident movements' or even 'oppositions', emerge, like the proverbial one-tenth of the iceberg visible above the water, from that area, from the independent life of society. In other words, just as the independent life of society develops out of living within the truth in the widest sense of the word, as the distinct, articulated expression of that life, so 'dissent' gradually emerges from the 'independent life of society'. Yet there is a marked difference: if the independent life of society, externally at least, can be understood as a higher form of living within the truth, it is far less certain that 'dissident movements' are necessarily a higher form of the 'independent life of society'. They are simply one manifestation of it and though they may be the most visible and, at first glance, the most political (and most clearly articulated) expression of it, they are far from necessarily being the most mature or even the most important, not only in the general social sense but even in terms of direct political influence. After all, 'dissent' has been artificially removed from its place of birth by having been given a special name. In fact, however, it is not possible to think of it separated from the whole background out of which it develops, of which it is an integral part, and from which it draws all its vital strength. In any case, it follows from what has already been said about the peculiarities of the post-totalitarian system that what *appears* to be the most political of forces in a given moment, and what thinks of itself in such terms, need not necessarily in fact *be* such a force. The extent to which it is a real political force is due exclusively to its pre-political context.

What follows from this description? Nothing more and nothing less than this: it is impossible to talk about what in fact 'dissidents' do and the effect of their work without first talking about the work of all those who, in one way or another, take part in the independent life of society and who are not necessarily 'dissidents' at all. They may be writers who write as they wish without regard for censorship or official demands and who issue their work—when official publishers refuse to print them—as *samizdat*. They may be philosophers, historians, sociologists and all those who practise independent scholarship and, if it is impossible through official or semi-official channels, who also circulate their work in *samizdat* or who organize private discussions, lectures and seminars. They may be teachers who privately teach young people things that are kept from them in the state schools; clergymen who either in office or, if they are deprived of their charges, outside it, try to carry on a free religious life; painters, musicians and singers who practise their work regardless of how it is looked upon by official institutions; everyone who shares this independent culture and helps to spread it; people who, using the means available to them, try to express and defend the actual social interests of workers, to put real meaning back into trade unions or to form independent ones; people who are not afraid to call the attention of officials to cases of injustice and who strive to see that the laws are observed; and the different groups of young people who try to extricate themselves from manipulation and live in their own way, in the spirit of their own hierarchy of values. The list could go on.

Very few would think of calling all these people 'dissidents'. And yet are not the well-known 'dissidents' simply people like them? Are not all these activities in fact what 'dissidents' do as well? Do they not produce scholarly work and publish it in *samizdat*? Do they not write plays and novels and poems? Do they not lecture to students in private 'universities'? Do they not struggle against various forms of injustice and attempt to ascertain and express the genuine social interests of various sectors of the population?

After having tried to indicate the sources, the inner structure and some aspects of the 'dissident' attitude as such, I have clearly shifted my viewpoint from outside, as it were, to an investigation of what these 'dissidents' *actually* do, how their initiatives are manifested and where they lead.

The first conclusion to be drawn, then, is that the original and most important sphere of activity, one that predetermines all the others, is simply an attempt to create and support the 'independent life of society' as an articulated expression of 'living within the truth'. In other words, serving truth consistently, purposefully and articulately, and organizing this service. This is only natural, after all: if living within the truth is an elementary starting point for every attempt made by people to oppose the alienating pressure of the system, if it is the only meaningful basis of any independent act of political import, and if, ultimately, it is also the most intrinsic existential source of the 'dissident' attitude, then it is difficult to imagine that even manifest 'dissent' could have any other basis than the service of truth, the truthful life and the attempt to make room for the genuine aims of life.

XVI

The post-totalitarian system is mounting a total assault on humans and humans stand against it alone, abandoned and isolated. It is therefore entirely natural that all the 'dissident movements' are explicitly defensive movements: they exist to defend human beings and the genuine aims of life against the aims of the system.

Today the Polish group *KOR* is called the Committee for Social Self-Defence. The word 'defence' appears in the names of other similar groups in Poland, but even the Soviet Helsinki monitoring group and our own Charter 77 are clearly defensive in nature.

In terms of traditional politics, this programme of defence is understandable, even though it may appear minimal, provisional and ultimately negative. It offers no new conception, model or ideology, and therefore it is not 'politics' in the proper sense of the word, since politics always assumes a 'positive' programme and can scarcely limit itself to defending someone against something.

Such a view, I think, reveals the limitations of the traditionally political way of looking at things. The post-totalitarian system, after all, is not the manifestation of a particular political line followed by a particular government. It is something radically different: it is a complex, profound and long-term violation of society, or rather the self-violation of society. To oppose it merely by establishing a different political line and then striving for a change in government would not only be unrealistic, it would be utterly inadequate, for it would never come near to touching the root of the matter. For some time now, the problem has no longer resided in a political line or programme: it is a problem of life itself.

Thus defending the aims of life, defending humanity is not only a more realistic approach, since it can begin right now and is potentially more popular because it concerns people's everyday lives; at the same time (and perhaps precisely because of this) it is also an incomparably more consistent approach because it aims at the very essence of things.

There are times when we must sink to the bottom of our misery to understand truth, just as we must descend to the bottom of a well to see the stars in broad daylight. It seems to me that today, this 'provisional', 'minimal' and 'negative' programme — the 'simple' defence of people — is in a particular sense (and not merely in the circumstances in which we live) an optimal and most positive programme because it forces politics to return to its only proper starting point, proper that is, if all the old mistakes are to be avoided: individual people. In democratic societies, where the violence done to human beings is not nearly so obvious and cruel, this fundamental revolution in politics has yet to happen, and some things will probably have to get worse there before the urgent need for that revolution is reflected in politics. In our world, precisely because of the misery in which we find ourselves, it would seem that politics has already undergone that transformation: the central concern of political thought is no longer abstract visions of a self-redeeming, 'positive' model (and of course the opportunistic political practices that are the reverse of the same coin), but rather the people who have so far merely been enslaved by those models and their practices.

Every society, of course, requires some degree of organization. Yet if that organization is to serve people and not the other way around, then people will have to be liberated and space created so that they may organize themselves in meaningful ways. The depravity of the opposite approach, in which people are first organized in one way or another (by someone who always knows best 'what the people need') so they may then allegedly be liberated, is something we have known on our own skins only too well.

To sum up: most people who are too bound to the traditional political way of thinking see the weaknesses of the 'dissident movements' in their purely defensive character. In contrast, I see that as their greatest strength. I believe that this is precisely where these movements supersede the kind of politics from whose point of view their programme can seem so inadequate.

XVII

In the 'dissident movements' of the Soviet bloc, the defence of human beings usually takes the form of a defence of human and civil rights as they are entrenched in various official documents such as the Universal Declaration of Human Rights, the International Covenants on Human Rights, the Final Act of the Helsinki Conference and the constitutions of individual states. These movements set out to defend anyone who is being prosecuted for acting in the spirit of those rights, and they in turn act in the same spirit in their work, by insisting over and over again that the regime recognize and respect human and civil rights, and by drawing attention to the areas of life where this is not the case.

Their work, therefore, is based on the principle of legality: they operate publicly and openly, insisting not only that their activity is in line with the law, but that achieving respect for the law is one of their main aims. This principle of legality, which provides both the point of departure and the framework for their activities, is common to all 'dissident' groups in the Soviet bloc, even though individual groups have never worked out any formal agreement on that point. This circumstance raises an important question: Why, in conditions where a widespread and arbitrary abuse of power is the rule, is there such a general and spontaneous acceptance of the principle of legality?

On the primary level, this stress on legality is a natural expression of specific conditions that exist in the post-totalitarian system, and the consequence of an elementary understanding of that specificity. If there are in essence only two ways to struggle for a free society — that is, through legal means and through (armed or unarmed) revolt — then it should be obvious at once how inappropriate the latter alternative is in the post-totalitarian system. Revolt is appropriate when conditions are clearly and openly in motion, during a war for example, or in situations where social or political conflicts are coming to a head. It is appropriate in a classical dictatorship that is either just setting itself up or is in a state of collapse. In other words, it is appropriate where social forces of comparable strength (for example, a government of occupation vs a nation fighting for its freedom) are confronting each other on the level of actual power, or where there is a clear distinction between the usurpers of power and the subjugated population, or when society finds itself in a state of open crisis. Conditions in the post-totalitarian system — except in extremely explosive situations like the one in Hungary in 1956 — are, of course, precisely the opposite. They are static and stable, and social crises, for the most part, exist only latently (though they run much deeper). Society is not sharply polarized on the level of actual political power, but, as we have seen, the fundamental lines of conflict run right through each person. In this situation, no attempt at revolt could ever hope to set up even a minimum of resonance in the rest of society, because that society is 'soporific', submerged in a consumer rat-race and wholly involved in the post-totalitarian system (that is, participating in it and acting as agents of its 'automatism'), and it would simply find anything like revolt unacceptable. It would interpret the revolt as an attack upon itself and, rather than supporting the revolt, it would very probably react by intensifying its bias towards the system, since, in its view, the system can at least guarantee a certain quasi-legality. Add to this the fact that the post-totalitarian system has at its disposal a complex mechanism of direct and indirect surveillance that has no equal in history and it is clear that not only would any attempt to revolt come to a dead end politically, but it would also be almost technically impossible to carry off. Most probably it would be liquidated before it had a chance to translate its intentions into action. Even if revolt were possible, however, it would remain the solitary gesture of a few isolated individuals and they would be opposed not only by a gigantic apparatus of national (and supranational) power, but also by the very society in whose name they were mounting their revolt in the first place. (This, by the way, is another reason why the regime and its propaganda have been ascribing terroristic aims to the 'dissident movements' and accusing them of illegal and conspiratorial methods.)

All of this, however, is not the main reason why the 'dissident movements' support the principle of legality. That reason lies deeper, in the innermost structure of the 'dissident' attitude. This attitude is and must be fundamentally hostile towards the notion of violent change as such to the system — and every revolt, essentially, aims at violent change — simply because it places its faith in violence. (Generally, the 'dissident' attitude can only accept violence as a necessary evil in extreme situations, when direct violence can only be met by violence and where remaining passive would in effect mean supporting violence: let us recall, for example, that the blindness of European pacifism was one of the factors that prepared the ground for the Second World War.) As I have already mentioned, 'dissidents' tend to be sceptical about political thought based on the faith that profound social changes can only be achieved by bringing about (regardless of the method) changes in the system or in the government, and the belief that such changes — because they are considered 'fundamental'—justify the sacrifice of 'less fundamental' things, in other words, human lives. Respect for a theoretical concept here outweighs respect for human life. Yet this is precisely what threatens to enslave humanity all over again.

'Dissident movements', as I have tried to indicate, share exactly the opposite view. They understand systemic change as something superficial, something secondary, something that in itself can guarantee nothing. Thus an attitude that turns away from abstract political visions of the future towards concrete human beings and ways of defending them effectively in the here and now is quite naturally accompanied by an intensified antipathy to all forms of violence carried out in the name of 'a better future', and by a profound belief that a future secured by violence might actually be worse than what exists now; in other words, the future would be fatally stigmatized by the very means used to secure it. At the same time, this attitude is not to be mistaken for political conservatism or political moderation. The 'dissident movements' do not shy away from the idea of violent political overthrow because the idea seems too radical, but on the contrary, because it does not seem radical enough. For them, the problem lies far too deep to be settled through mere systemic changes, either governmental or technological. Some people, faithful to the classical Marxist doctrines of the nineteenth century, understand our system as the hegemony of an exploiting class over an exploited class and, operating from the postulate that exploiters never surrender their power voluntarily, they see the only solution in a revolution to sweep away the exploiters. Naturally, they regard such things as the struggle for human rights as something hopelessly legalistic, illusory, opportunistic and ultimately misleading because it makes the doubtful assumption that you can negotiate in good faith with your exploiters on the basis of a false legality. The problem is that they are unable to find anyone determined enough to carry out this revolution, with the result that they become bitter, sceptical, passive and ultimately apathetic—in other words, they end up precisely where the system wants them to be. This is one example of how far one can be misled by mechanically applying, in post-totalitarian circumstances, ideological models from another world and another time.

Of course, one need not be an advocate of violent revolution to ask whether an appeal to legality makes any sense at all when the laws — and particularly the general laws concerning human rights — are no more than a façade, an aspect of the world of appearances, a mere game behind which lies total manipulation. 'They can ratify anything because they will still go ahead and do whatever they want anyway' — this is an opinion we often encounter. Is it not true that to constantly 'take them at their word', to appeal to laws every child knows are binding only as long as the government wishes, is in the end just a kind of hypocrisy, a Švejkian obstructionism and, finally, just another way of playing the game, another form of self-delusion? In other words, is the legalistic approach at all compatible with the principle of 'living within the truth'?

This question can only be answered by first looking at the wider implications of how the legal code functions in the post-totalitarian system.

In a classical dictatorship, to a far greater extent than in the post-totalitarian system, the will of the ruler is carried out directly, in an unregulated fashion. A dictatorship has no reason to hide its foundations, nor to conceal the real workings of power, and therefore it need not encumber itself to any great extent with a legal code. The post-totalitarian system, on the other hand, is utterly obsessed with the need to bind everything in a single order: life in such a state is thoroughly permeated by a dense network of regulations, proclamations, directives, norms, orders and rules. (It is not called a bureaucratic system without good reason.) A large proportion of those norms functions as direct instruments of the complex manipulation of life that is intrinsic to the post-totalitarian system. Individuals are reduced to little more than tiny cogs in an enormous mechanism and their significance is limited to their function in this mechanism. Their job, housing accommodation, movements, social and cultural expressions, everything, in short, must be cosseted together as firmly as possible, predetermined, regulated and controlled. Every aberration from the prescribed course of life is treated as error, licence and anarchy. From the cook in the restaurant who, without hard-to-get permission from the bureaucratic apparatus, cannot cook something special for his customers, to the singer who cannot perform his new song at a concert without bureaucratic approval, everyone, in all aspects of their life, is caught in this regulatory tangle of red tape, the inevitable product of the post-totalitarian system. With ever-increasing consistency, it binds all the expressions and aims of life to the spirit of its own aims: the vested interests of its own smooth, automatic operation.

In a narrower sense the legal code serves the post-totalitarian system in this direct way as well, that is, it too forms a part of the world of regulations and prohibitions. At the same time, however, it performs the same service in another indirect way, one that brings it remarkably closer — depending on which level of the law is involved — to ideology and in some cases making it a direct component of that ideology.

1. Like ideology, the legal code functions as an excuse. It wraps the base exercise of power in the noble apparel of the letter of the law; it creates the pleasing illusion that justice is done, society protected and the exercise of power objectively regulated. All this is done to conceal the real essence of post-totalitarian legal practice: the total manipulation of society. If an outside observer who knew nothing at all about life in Czechoslovakia were to study only its laws, he or she would be utterly incapable of understanding what we were complaining about. The hidden political manipulation of the courts and of public prosecutors, the limitations placed on lawyers' ability to defend their clients, the closed nature, *de facto*, of trials, the arbitrary actions of the security forces, their position of authority over the judiciary, the absurdly broad application of several deliberately vague sections of that code, and of course the state's utter disregard for the positive sections of that code (the rights of citizens): all of this would remain hidden from our outside observer. The only thing he or she would take away would be the impression that our legal

code is not much worse than the legal code of other civilized countries, and not much different either, except perhaps for certain curiosities, such as the entrenchment in the constitution of a single political party's eternal rule and the state's love for a neighbouring superpower. But that is not all: if our observer had the opportunity to study the formal side of policing and judicial procedures and practices, how they look 'on paper', he or she would discover that for the most part the common rules of criminal procedure are observed: charges are laid within the prescribed period following arrest, and it is the same with detention orders. Indictments are properly delivered, the accused has a lawyer, and so on. In other words, everyone has an excuse: *they have all observed the law.* In reality, however, they have cruelly and pointlessly ruined a young person's life, perhaps for no other reason than because he or she made *samizdat* copies of a novel written by a banned writer, or because the police deliberately falsified their testimony (as everyone knows, from the judge on down to the defendant). Yet all of this somehow remains in the background. The falsified testimony is not necessarily obvious from the trial documents and the section of the criminal code dealing with incitement does not formally exclude the application of that charge to the copying of a banned novel. In other words, the legal code — at least in several areas — is no more than a façade, an aspect of the world of appearances. Then why is it there at all? For exactly the same reason as ideology is there: it provides a bridge of excuses between the system and individuals, making it easier for them to enter the power structure and serve the arbitrary demands of power. The excuse lets individuals fool themselves into thinking they are merely upholding the law and protecting society from criminals. (Without this excuse, how much more difficult it would be to recruit new generations of judges, prosecutors and interrogators!) As an aspect of the world of appearances, however, the legal code deceives not only the conscience of prosecutors, it deceives the public, it deceives foreign observers, and it even deceives history itself.

2. Like ideology, the legal code is an essential instrument of ritual communication outside the power structure. It is the legal

code that gives the exercise of power a form, a framework, a set of rules. It is the legal code that enables all components of the system to communicate, to put themselves in a good light, to establish their own legitimacy. It provides their whole game with its 'rules' and engineers with their technology. Can the exercise of post-totalitarian power be imagined at all without this universal ritual making it all possible, serving as a common language to bind the relevant sectors of the power structure together? The more important the position occupied by the repressive apparatus in the power structure, the more important that it functions according to some kind of formal code. How, otherwise, could people be so easily and inconspicuously locked up for copying banned books if there were no judges, prosecutors, interrogators, defence lawyers, court stenographers and thick files, and if all this were not held together by some firm order? And above all, without that innocent-looking Section 100 on incitement? This could all be done, of course, without a legal code and its accessories, but only in some ephemeral dictatorship run by a Ugandan bandit, not in a system that embraces such a huge portion of civilized humankind and represents an integral, stable and respected part of the modern world. That would not only be unthinkable, it would quite simply be technically impossible. Without the legal code functioning as a ritually cohesive force, the post-totalitarian system could not exist.

The entire role of ritual, façades and excuses appears most eloquently, of course, not in the proscriptive section of the legal code, which sets out what a citizen may not do and what the grounds for prosecution are, but in the section declaring what he or she may do and what his or her rights are. Here there is truly nothing but 'words, words, words'. Yet even that part of the code is of immense importance to the system, for it is here that the system establishes its legitimacy as a whole, before its own citizens, before school children, before the international public and before history. The system cannot afford to disregard this because it cannot permit itself to cast doubt upon the fundamental postulates of its ideology, which are so essential to its very existence. (We have already seen how the power structure is enslaved by its own ideology and its ideological prestige.) To do this would be to deny everything it tries to present itself as and, thus, one of the main pillars on which the system rests would be undermined: the integrity of the world of appearances.

If the exercise of power circulates through the whole power structure as blood flows though veins, then the legal code can be understood as something that reinforces the walls of those veins. Without it, the blood of power could not circulate in an organized way and the body of society would haemorrhage at random. Order would collapse.

A persistent and never-ending appeal to the laws — not just to the laws concerning human rights, but to all laws — does not mean at all that those who do so have succumbed to the illusion that in our system the law is anything other than what it is. They are well aware of the role it plays. But precisely because they know how desperately the system depends on it — on the 'noble' version of the law, that is — they also know how enormously significant such appeals are. Because the system cannot do without the law, because it is hopelessly tied down by the necessity of pretending the laws are observed, it is compelled to react in some way to such appeals. Demanding that the laws be upheld is thus an act of living within the truth that threatens the whole mendacious structure at its point of maximum mendacity. Over and over again, such appeals make the purely ritualistic nature of the law clear to society and to those who inhabit its power structures. They draw attention to its real material substance and thus, indirectly, compel all those who take refuge behind the law to affirm and make credible this agency of excuses, this means of communication, this reinforcement of the social arteries outside of which their will could not be made to circulate through society. They are compelled to do so for the sake of their own consciences, for the impression they make on outsiders, to maintain themselves in power (as part of the system's own mechanism of self-preservation and its principles of cohesion), or simply out of fear that they will be reproached for being 'clumsy' in handling the ritual. They have no other choice:

because they cannot discard the rules of their own game, they can only attend more carefully to those rules. Not to react to challenges means to undermine their own excuse and lose control of their mutual communications system. To assume that the laws are a mere façade, that they have no validity and that therefore it is pointless to appeal to them would mean to go on reinforcing those aspects of the law that create the façade and the ritual. It would mean confirming the law as an aspect of the world of appearances and enabling those who exploit it to rest easy with the cheapest (and therefore the most mendacious) form of their excuse.

I have frequently witnessed policemen, prosecutors or judges — if they were dealing with an experienced Chartist or a courageous lawyer, and if they were exposed to public attention (as individuals with a name, no longer protected by the anonymity of the apparatus) — suddenly and anxiously begin to take particular care that no cracks appear in the ritual. This does not alter the fact that a despotic power is hiding behind that ritual, but the very existence of the officials' anxiety necessarily regulates, limits and slows down the operation of that despotism.

This, of course, is not enough. But an essential part of the 'dissident' attitude is that it comes out of the reality of the human 'here and now'. It places more importance on oft-repeated and consistent concrete action — even though it may be inadequate and though it may ease only insignificantly the suffering of a single insignificant citizen — than it does in some abstract 'fundamental solution' in an uncertain future. In any case, is not this in fact just another form of 'small-scale work' in the Masarykian sense, with which the 'dissident' attitude seemed at first to be in such sharp contradiction?

This section would be incomplete without stressing certain internal limitations to the policy of 'taking them at their own word'. The point is this: even in the most ideal of cases, the law is only one of several imperfect and more or less external ways of defending what is better in life against what is worse. By itself, the law can never create anything better. Its purpose is to render a service and its meaning does not lie in the law itself. Establishing respect for the law does not automatically ensure a better life for that, after all, is a job for people and not for laws and institutions. It is possible to imagine a society with good laws that are fully respected but in which it is impossible to live. Conversely, one can imagine life being quite bearable even where the laws are imperfect and imperfectly applied. The most important thing is always the quality of that life and whether or not the laws enhance life or repress it, not merely whether they are upheld or not. (Often strict observance of the law could have a disastrous impact on human dignity.) The key to a humane, dignified, rich and happy life does not lie either in the constitution or in the criminal code. These merely establish what may or may not be done and, thus, they can make life easier or more difficult. They limit or permit, they punish, tolerate or defend, but they can never give life substance or meaning. The struggle for what is called 'legality' must constantly keep this legality in perspective against the background of life as it really is. Without keeping one's eyes open to the real dimensions of life's beauty and misery, and without a moral relationship to life, this struggle will sooner or later come to grief on the rocks of some self-justifying system of scholastics. Without really wanting to, one would thus become more and more like the observer who comes to conclusions about our system only on the basis of trial documents and is satisfied if all the appropriate regulations have been observed.

XVIII

If the basic job of the 'dissident movements' is to serve truth, that is, to serve the real aims of life, and if that necessarily develops into a defence of the individual and his or her right to a free and truthful life (that is, a defence of human rights and a struggle to see the laws respected) then another stage of this approach, perhaps the most mature stage so far, is what Václav Benda has called the development of parallel structures.

When those who have decided to live within the truth have been denied any direct influence on the existing social structures, not to mention the opportunity to participate in them, and when these people begin to create what I have called the independent life of society, this independent life begins, of itself, to become structured in a certain way. Sometimes there are only very embryonic indications of this process of structuring; at other times, the structures are already quite well-developed. Their genesis and evolution are inseparable from the phenomenon of 'dissent', even though they reach far beyond the arbitrarily defined area of activity usually indicated by that term.

What are these structures? Ivan Jirous was the first in Czechoslovakia to formulate and apply in practice the concept of a 'second culture'. Although at first he was thinking chiefly of nonconformist rock music and only certain literary, artistic or performance events close to the sensibilities of those non-conformist musical groups, the term 'second culture' very rapidly came to be used for the whole area of independent and repressed culture, that is, not only for art and its various currents but also for the humanities, the social sciences and philosophical thought. This 'second culture', quite naturally, has created elementary organizational forms: *samizdat* editions of books and magazines, private performances and concerts, seminars, exhibitions and so on. (In Poland all of this is vastly more developed: there are independent publishing houses and many more periodicals, even political periodicals; they have means of proliferation other than carbon copies, and so on. In the Soviet Union, *samizdat* has a longer tradition and clearly its forms are quite different.) Culture, therefore, is a sphere in which the 'parallel structures' can be observed in their most highly developed form. Benda, of course, gives thought to potential or embryonic forms of such structures in other spheres as well: from a parallel information network to parallel forms of education (private universities), parallel trade unions, parallel foreign contacts, to a kind of hypothesis on a parallel economy. On the basis of these parallel structures, he then develops the notion of a 'parallel *polis*' or state or, rather, he sees the rudiments of such a *polis* in these structures.

At a certain stage in its development, the independent life of society and the 'dissident movements' cannot avoid a certain amount of organization and institutionalization. This is a natural development and unless this independent life of society is somehow radically suppressed and eliminated, the tendency will grow. Along with it, a parallel political life will also necessarily evolve, and to a certain extent it exists already in Czechoslovakia. Various groupings of a more or less political nature will continue to define themselves politically, to act and confront each other.

These parallel structures, it may be said, represent the most articulated expressions so far of 'living within the truth'. One of the most important tasks the 'dissident movements' have set themselves is to support and develop them. Once again, it confirms the fact that all attempts by society to resist the pressure of the system have their essential beginnings in the pre-political area. For what else are parallel structures than an area where a different life can be lived, a life that is in harmony with its own aims and which in turn structures itself in harmony with those aims? What else are those initial attempts at social self-organization than the efforts of a certain part of society to live — as a society — within the truth, to rid itself of the self-sustaining aspects of totalitarianism and, thus, to extricate itself radically from its involvement in the post-totalitarian system? What else is it but a non-violent attempt by people to negate the system within themselves and to establish their lives on a new basis, that of their own proper identity? And does this tendency not confirm once more the principle of returning the focus to actual individuals? After all, the parallel structures do not grow *a priori* out of a theoretical vision of systemic changes (there are no political sects involved), but from the aims of life and the authentic needs of real people. In fact, all eventual changes in the system, changes we may observe here in their rudimentary forms, have come about as it were *de facto*, from 'below', because life compelled them to, not because they came before life, somehow directing it or forcing some change on it.

Historical experience teaches us that any genuinely meaningful point of departure in an individual's life usually has an element of universality about it. In other words, it is not something partial, accessible only to a restricted community, and not transferable to any other. On the contrary, it must be potentially accessible to everyone; it must foreshadow a general solution and, thus, it is not just the expression of an introverted, self-contained responsibility that individuals have to and for themselves alone, but responsibility to and for the *world*. Thus it would be quite wrong to understand the parallel structures and the parallel *polis* as a retreat into a ghetto and as an act of isolation, addressing itself only to the welfare of those who had decided on such a course, and who are indifferent to the rest. It would be wrong, in short, to consider it an essentially group solution that has nothing to do with the general situation. Such a concept would, from the start, alienate the notion of living within the truth from its proper point of departure, which is concern for others, transforming it ultimately into just another more sophisticated version of 'living within a lie'. In doing so, of course, it would cease to be a genuine point of departure for individuals and groups and would recall the false notion of 'dissidents' as an exclusive group with exclusive interests, carrying on their own exclusive dialogue with the powers that be. In any case, even the most highly developed forms of life in the parallel structures, even that most mature form of the parallel *polis* can only exist — at least in post-totalitarian circumstances — when the individual is at the same time lodged in the 'first', official structure by a thousand different relationships, even though it may only be the fact that one buys what one needs in their stores, uses their money and obeys their laws. Certainly one can imagine life in its 'baser' aspects flourishing in the parallel *polis*, but would not such a life, lived deliberately that way, as a programme, be merely another version of the schizophrenic life 'within a lie' which everyone else must live in one way or another? Would it not just be further evidence that a point of departure that is not a 'model' solution, that is not applicable to others, cannot be meaningful for an individual either? Patočka used to say that the most interesting thing about responsibility is that we carry it with us everywhere. That means that responsibility is ours, that we must accept it and grasp it *here, now*, in this place in time and space where the Lord has set us down, and that we cannot lie our way out of it by moving somewhere else, whether it be to an Indian ashram or to a parallel *polis*. If western young people so often discover that retreat to an Indian monastery fails them as an individual or group solution, then this is obviously because, and only because, it lacks that element of universality, since not everyone can retire to an ashram. Christianity is an example of an opposite way out: it is a point of departure for me here and now — but only because anyone, anywhere, at any time, may avail themselves of it.

In other words, the parallel *polis* points beyond itself and only makes sense as an act of deepening one's responsibility to and for the whole, as a way of discovering the most appropriate locus for this responsibility, not as an escape from it.

XIX

I have already talked about the political potential of living within the truth and of the limitations upon predicting whether, how and when a given expression of that life within the truth can lead to actual changes. I have also mentioned how irrelevant trying to calculate the risks in this regard are, for an essential feature of independent initiatives is that they are always, initially at least, an all or nothing gamble.

Nevertheless this outline of some of the work done by 'dissident movements' would be incomplete without considering, if only very generally, some of the different ways this work might actually affect society; in other words, about the ways that responsibility to and for the whole *might* (without necessarily meaning that it must) be realized in practice.

In the first place, it has to be emphasized that the whole sphere comprising the independent life of society and even more so the 'dissident movement' as such, is naturally far from being the only potential factor that might influence the history of countries living under the post-totalitarian system. The latent social crisis in such societies can at any time, independently of these movements, provoke a wide variety of political changes. It may unsettle the power structure and induce or accelerate various hidden confrontations, resulting in personnel, conceptual or at least 'climatic' changes. It may significantly influence the general atmosphere of life, evoke unexpected and unforeseen social

unrest and explosions of discontent. Power shifts at the centre of
the bloc can influence conditions in the different countries in
various ways. Economic factors naturally have an important
influence, as do broader trends of global civilization. An
extremely important area, which could be a source of radical
changes and political upsets, is represented by international
politics, the policies adopted by the other superpower and all the
other countries, the changing structure of international interests
and the positions taken by our bloc. Even the people who end up
in the highest positions are not without significance, although as
I have already said, one ought not overestimate the importance of
leading personalities in the post-totalitarian system. There are
many such influences and combinations of influence, and the
eventual political impact of the 'dissident movement' is thinkable
only against this general background and in the context that
background provides. That impact is only one of the many
factors (and far from the most important one) that affect political
developments, and it differs from the other factors perhaps only
in that its essential focus is reflecting upon that political development from the point of view of a defence of people and seeking
an immediate application of that reflection.

The primary purpose of the outward direction of these movements is always, as we have seen, to have an impact on society, not
to affect the power structure, at least not directly and immediately. Independent initiatives address the hidden sphere; they
demonstrate that living within the truth is a human and social
alternative and they struggle to expand the space available for that
life; they help — even though it is, of course, indirect help — to
raise the confidence of citizens; they shatter the world of
'appearances' and unmask the real nature of power. They do not
assume a messianic role; they are not a social 'avant-garde' or
'élite' that alone knows best, and whose task it is to 'raise the
consciousness' of the 'unconscious' masses (that arrogant self-
projection is, once again, intrinsic to an essentially different way
of thinking, the kind that feels it has a patent on some 'ideal
project' and therefore that it has the right to impose it on society).
Nor do they want to lead anyone. They leave it up to each

individual to decide what he or she will or will not take from their experience and work. (If official Czechoslovak propaganda described the Chartists as 'self-appointees', it was not in order to emphasize any real 'avant-garde' ambitions on their part, but rather a natural expression of how the regime thinks, its tendency to judge others according to itself, since behind any expression of criticism it automatically sees the desire to cast the mighty from their seats and rule in their places 'in the name of the people', the same pretext the regime itself has used for years.)

These movements, therefore, always affect the power structure as such indirectly, as a part of society as a whole, for they are primarily addressing the hidden spheres of society, since it is not a matter of confronting the regime on the level of actual power.

I have already indicated one of the ways this can work: an awareness of the laws and the responsibility for seeing that they are upheld is indirectly strengthened. That, of course, is only a specific instance of a far broader influence, the indirect pressure felt from living within the truth: the pressure created by free thought, alternative values and 'alternative behaviour', and by independent social self-realization. The power structure, whether it wants to or not, must always react to this pressure to a certain extent. Its response, however, is always limited to two dimensions: repression and adaptation. Sometimes one dominates, sometimes the other. For example, the Polish 'Flying University' came under increased persecution and the 'flying teachers' were detained by the police. At the same time, however, professors in existing official universities tried to enrich their own curricula with several subjects hitherto considered taboo and this was a result of indirect pressure exerted by the 'Flying University'. The motives for this adaptation may vary from the 'ideal' (the hidden sphere has received the message and conscience and the will to truth are awakened) to the purely utilitarian: the regime's instinct for survival compels it to notice the changing ideas and the changing mental and social climate and react flexibly to them. Which of these motives happens to predominate in a given moment is not essential in terms of the final effect.

Adaptation is the positive dimension of the regime's response, and it can, and usually does, have a wide spectrum of forms and phases. Some circles may try to integrate values or people from the 'parallel world' into the official structures, to appropriate them, to become a little like them while trying to make them a little like themselves, and thus to adjust an obvious and untenable imbalance. In the 1960s, progressive communists began to 'discover' certain unacknowledged cultural values and phenomena. This was a positive step, although not without its dangers, since the 'integrated' or 'appropriated' values lost something of their independence and originality, and having been given a cloak of officiality and conformity, their credibility was somewhat weakened. In a further phase, this adaptation can lead to various attempts on the part of the official structures to reform, both in terms of their ultimate goals and structurally. Such reforms are usually half-way measures; they are attempts to combine and realistically co-ordinate serving life and serving the post-totalitarian 'automatism'. But they cannot be otherwise. They muddy what was originally a clear demarcation line between living within the truth and living with a lie. They cast a smoke-screen over the situation, mystify society and make it difficult for people to keep their bearings. This, of course, does not alter the fact that it is always essentially good when it happens because it opens out new spaces. But it does make it more difficult to distinguish between 'admissible' and 'inadmissible' compromises.

Another – and higher – phase of adaptation is a process of internal differentiation that takes place in the official structures. These structures open themselves to more or less institutionalized forms of plurality because the real aims of life demand it. (One example: without changing the centralized and institutional basis of cultural life, new publishing houses, group periodicals, artists' groups, parallel research institutes and work places and so on, may appear under pressure from 'below'. Or another example: the single, monolithic youth organization run by the state as a typical post-totalitarian 'transmission belt' disintegrates under the pressure of real needs into a number of more or less independent organizations such as the Union of University Students, the Union of Secondary School Students, the Organization of Working Youth, and so on.) There is a direct relationship between this kind of differentiation, which allows initiatives from below to be felt, and the appearance and constitution of new structures which are already parallel, or rather independent, but which at the same time are respected, or at least tolerated in varying degrees, by official institutions. These new institutions are more than just liberalized official structures adapted to the authentic needs of life; they are a direct expression of those needs, demanding a position in the context of what is already here. In other words, they are genuine expressions of the tendency of society to organize itself. (In Czechoslovakia in 1968 the best known organizations of this type were *KAN*, The Club of Committed Non-Communists, and *K231*, an organization of former political prisoners.)

The ultimate phase of this process is the situation in which the official structures – as agencies of the post-totalitarian system, existing only to serve its automatism and constructed in the spirit of that role – simply begin withering away and dying off, to be replaced by new structures that have evolved from 'below' and are put together in a fundamentally different way.

Certainly many other ways may be imagined in which the aims of life can bring about political transformations in the general organization of things and weaken on all levels the hold that techniques of manipulation have on society. Here I have mentioned only the way in which the general organization of things was in fact changed as we experienced it ourselves in Czechoslovakia around 1968. It must be added that all these concrete instances were part of a specific historical process which ought not be thought of as the only alternative, nor as necessarily repeatable (particularly not in our country), a fact which, of course, takes nothing away from the importance of the general lessons which are still sought and found in it to this day.

While on the subject of 1968 in Czechoslovakia, it may be appropriate to point to some of the characteristic aspects of developments at that time. All the transformations, first in the general 'mood', then conceptually and finally structurally, did not occur under pressure from the kind of parallel structures that are taking shape today. Such structures — which are sharply defined antitheses of the official structures — quite simply did not exist at the time, nor were there any 'dissidents' in the present sense of the word. The changes that took place were simply a consequence of pressures of the most varied sort, some thorough-going, some partial. There were spontaneous attempts at freer forms of thinking, independent creation and political articulation. There were long-term, spontaneous and inconspicuous efforts to bring about the interpenetration of the independent life of society with the existing structures, usually beginning with the quiet institutionalization of this life on and around the periphery of the official structures. In other words, it was a gradual process of social awakening, a kind of 'creeping' process in which the hidden spheres gradually opened out. (There is some truth in the official propaganda which talks about a 'creeping counter-revolution' in Czechoslovakia, referring to how the aims of life proceed.) The motive force behind this awakening did not have to come exclusively from the independent life of society, considered as a definable social milieu (although of course it did come from there, a fact that has yet to be fully appreciated). It could also have simply come from the fact that people in the official structures who more or less identified with the official ideology came up against reality as it really was and as it gradually became clear to them through latent social crises and their own bitter experiences with the true nature and operations of power. (I am thinking here mainly of the many 'anti-dogmatic' reform communists who grew to become, over the years, a force inside the official structures.) Neither the proper conditions nor the *raison d'être* existed for those limited, 'self-structuring' independent initiatives familiar from the present era of 'dissident movements' that stand so sharply outside the official structures and are unrecognized by them *en bloc*. At that time, the post-totalitarian system in Czechoslovakia had not yet petrified into the static, sterile and stable forms that exist today, forms that compel people to fall back on their own organizing capabilities.

For many historical and social reasons, the regime in 1968 was more open. The power structure, exhausted by Stalinist despotism and helplessly groping about for painless reform, was inevitably rotting from within, quite incapable of offering any intelligent opposition to changes in the mood, to the way its younger members regarded things and to the thousands of authentic expressions of life on the 'pre-political' level that sprang up in that vast political terrain between the official and the unofficial.

From the more general point of view, yet another typical circumstance appears to be important: the social ferment that came to a head in 1968 never — in terms of actual structural changes — went any further than the reform, the differentiation or the replacement of structures that were really only of secondary importance. It did not affect the very essence of the power structure in the post-totalitarian system, which is to say its political model, the fundamental principles of social organization, not even the economic model in which all economic power is subordinated to political power. Nor were any essential structural changes made in the direct instruments of power (the army, the police, the judiciary, etc.). On that level, the issue was never more than a change in the mood, the personnel, the political line and, above all, changes in how that power was exercised. Everything else remained at the stage of discussion and planning. The two officially accepted programmes that went furthest in this regard were the April, 1968 Action Programme of the Communist Party of Czechoslovakia and the proposal for economic reforms. The Action Programme — it could not have been otherwise — was full of contradictions and half-way measures that left the physical aspects of power untouched. And the economic proposals, while they went a long way to accommodate the aims of life in the economic sphere (they accepted such notions as a plurality of interests and initiatives, dynamic incentives, restrictions upon the economic command system), left untouched the basic pillar of economic power, that is, the principle of state, rather than genuine *social* ownership of the means of production. So there is a gap here which no social movement in the post-totalitarian system has ever been able to bridge, with the possible exception of those few days during the Hungarian uprising.

What other developmental alternative might emerge in the future? Replying to that question would mean entering the realm of pure speculation. For the time being, it can be said that the latent social crisis in the system has always (and there is no reason to believe it will not continue to do so) resulted in a variety of political and social disturbances (Germany in 1953, Hungary, the USSR and Poland in 1956, Czechoslovakia and Poland in 1968, and Poland in 1970 and 1976), all of them very different in their backgrounds, the course of their evolution and their final consequences. If we look at the enormous complex of different factors that led to such disturbances, and at the impossibility of predicting what accidental accumulation of events will cause that fermentation in the hidden sphere to break through to the light of day (the problem 'of the final straw'); and if we consider how impossible it is to guess what the future holds, given such opposing trends as, on the one hand, the increasingly profound integration of the 'bloc' and the expansion of power within it, and on the other hand the prospects of the USSR disintegrating under pressure from awakening national consciousness in the non-Russian areas (in this regard the Soviet Union cannot expect to remain forever free of the world-wide struggle for national liberation), then we must see the hopelessness of trying to make long-range predictions.

In any case, I do not believe that this type of speculation has any immediate significance for the 'dissident movements' since these movements, after all, do not develop from speculative thinking, and so to establish themselves on that basis would mean alienating themselves from the very source of their identity.

As far as prospects for the 'dissident movements' as such go, there seems to be very little likelihood that future developments will lead to a lasting coexistence of two isolated, mutually non-interacting and mutually indifferent bodies — the main *polis* and the parallel *polis*. As long as it remains what it is, the practice of living within the truth cannot fail to be a threat to the system. It is quite impossible to imagine it continuing to coexist with the practice of living within a lie without dramatic tension. The relationship of the post-totalitarian system — as long as it remains what it is — and the independent life of society — as long as it remains the locus of a renewed responsibility for the whole and to the whole — will always be one of either latent or open conflict.

In this situation there are only two possibilities: either the post-totalitarian system will go on developing (that is, will be *able* to go on developing), thus inevitably coming closer to some dreadful Orwellian vision of a world of absolute manipulation, while all the more articulate expressions of living within the truth are definitively snuffed out; or the independent life of society (the parallel *polis*), including the 'dissident movements', will slowly but surely become a social phenomenon of growing importance, taking a real part in the life of society with increasing clarity and influencing the general situation. Of course this will always be only one of many factors influencing the situation and it will operate rather in the background, in concert with the other factors and in a way appropriate to the background.

Whether it ought to focus on reforming the official structures or on encouraging differentiation, or on replacing them with new structures, whether the intent is to 'ameliorate' the system or, on the contrary, to tear it down: these and similar questions, in so far as they are not pseudo-problems, can be posed by the 'dissident movement' only within the context of a particular situation, when the movement is faced with a concrete task. In other words, it must pose questions, as it were, *ad hoc*, out of a concrete consideration of the authentic needs of life. To reply to such questions abstractly and to formulate a political programme in terms of some hypothetical future would mean, I believe, a return to the spirit and methods of traditional politics, and this would limit and alienate the work of 'dissent' where it is most intrinsically itself and has the most genuine prospects for the future. I have already emphasized several times that these 'dissi-dent movements' do not have their point of departure in the invention of systemic changes but in a real, everyday struggle for a better life 'here and now'. The political and structural systems that life discovers for itself will clearly always be — for some time to come, at least—limited, half-way, unsatisfying and polluted by debilitating tactics. It cannot be otherwise, and we must expect this and not be demoralized by it. It is of great importance that the main thing—the everyday, thankless and never-ending struggle of human beings to live more freely, truthfully and in quiet dignity—never imposes any limits on itself, never be halfhearted, inconsistent, never trap itself in political tactics, speculating on the outcome of its actions or entertaining fantasies about the future. The purity of this struggle is the best guarantee of optimum results when it comes to actual interaction with the post-totalitarian structures.

XX

The specific nature of post-totalitarian conditions—with their absence of a normal political life and the fact that any far-reaching political change is utterly unforeseeable—has one positive aspect: it compels us to examine our situation in terms of its deeper coherences and to consider our future in the context of global, long-range prospects of the world of which we are a part. The fact that the most intrinsic and fundamental confrontation between human beings and the system takes place at a level incomparably more profound than that of traditional politics would seem, at the same time, to determine as well the direction such considerations will take.

Our attention, therefore, inevitably turns to the most essential matter: the crisis of contemporary technological society as a whole, the crisis that Heidegger describes as the ineptitude of humanity face to face with the planetary power of technology. Technology—that child of modern science, which in turn is a child of modern metaphysics—is out of humanity's control, has ceased to serve us, has enslaved us and compelled us to participate in the preparation of our own destruction. And humanity can find no way out: we have no idea and no faith, and even less do we have a political conception to help us bring things back under human control. We look on helplessly as that coldly functioning machine we have created inevitably engulfs us, tearing us away from our natural affiliations (for instance from our habitat in the widest sense of that word, including our habitat in the biosphere) just as it removes us from the experience of 'being' and casts us into the world of 'existences'. This situation has already been described from many different angles and many individuals and social groups have sought, often painfully, to find ways out of it (for instance through oriental thought or by forming communes). The only social, or rather political, attempt to do something about it that contains the necessary element of universality (responsibility to and for the whole) is the desperate and, given the turmoil the world is in, fading voice of the ecological movement, and even there the attempt is limited to a particular notion of how to use technology to oppose the dictatorship of technology.

'Only a God can save us now', Heidegger says, and he emphasizes the necessity of 'a different way of thinking', that is, of a departure from what philosophy has been for centuries, and a radical change in the way in which humanity understands itself, the world and its position in it. He knows no way out and all he can recommend is 'preparing expectations'.

Various thinkers and movements feel that this as yet unknown way out might be most generally characterized as a broad 'existential revolution'. I share this view, and I also share the opinion that a solution cannot be sought in some technological sleight of hand, that is, in some external proposal for change, or in a revolution that is merely philosophical, merely social, merely technological or even merely political. These are all areas where the consequences of an 'existential revolution' can and must be felt; but their most intrinsic locus can only be human existence in the profoundest sense of the word. It is only from that basis that it can become a generally ethical — and, of course, ultimately a political — reconstitution of society.

What we call the consumer and industrial (or post-industrial) society, and Ortega y Gasset once understood as 'the revolt of the masses', as well as the intellectual, moral, political and social misery in the world today: all of this is perhaps merely an aspect of the deep crisis in which humanity, dragged helplessly along by the automatism of global technological civilization, finds itself.

The post-totalitarian system is only one aspect — a particularly drastic aspect and thus all the more revealing of its real origins — of this general inability of modern humanity to be the master of its own situation. The automatism of the post-totalitarian system is merely an extreme version of the global automatism of technological civilization. The human failure that it mirrors is only one variant of the general failure of modern humanity.

This planetary challenge to the position of human beings in the world is, of course, also taking place in the western world, the only difference being the social and political forms it takes. Heidegger refers expressly to a crisis of democracy. There is no real evidence that western democracy, that is, democracy of the traditional parliamentary type, can offer solutions that are any more profound. It may even be said that the more room there is in the western democracies (compared to our world) for the genuine aims of life, the better the crisis is hidden from people and the more deeply do they become immersed in it.

It would appear that the traditional parliamentary democracies can offer no fundamental opposition to the automatism of technological civilization and the industrial-consumer society, for they, too, are being dragged helplessly along by it. People are manipulated in ways that are infinitely more subtle and refined than the brutal methods used in the post-totalitarian societies. But this static complex of rigid, conceptually sloppy and politically pragmatic mass political parties run by professional apparatuses and releasing the citizen from all forms of concrete and personal responsibility; and those complex foci of capital accumulation engaged in secret manipulations and expansion; the omnipresent dictatorship of consumption, production, advertising, commerce, consumer culture, and all that flood of information: all of it, so often analysed and described, can only with great difficulty be imagined as the source of humanity's rediscovery of itself. In his June 1978 Harvard lecture,* Solzhenitsyn describes the illusory nature of freedoms not based on

---

*Editor's note [in Unwin Hyman edition]: This lecture is published as *Alexander Solzhenitsyn Speaks to the West* (London, 1978).

personal responsibility and the chronic inability of the traditional democracies, as a result, to oppose violence and totalitarianism. In a democracy, human beings may enjoy many personal freedoms and securities that are unknown to us, but in the end they do them no good, for they too are ultimately victims of the same automatism, and are incapable of defending their concerns about their own identity or preventing their superficialization or transcending concerns about their own personal survival to become proud and responsible members of the *polis*, making a genuine contribution to the creation of its destiny.

Because all our prospects for a significant change for the better are very long range indeed, we are obliged to take note of this deep crisis of traditional democracy. Certainly, if conditions were to be created for democracy in some countries in the Soviet bloc (although this is becoming increasingly improbable), it might be an appropriate transitional solution that would help to restore the devastated sense of civic awareness, to renew democratic discussion, to allow for the crystallization of an elementary political plurality, an essential expression of the aims of life. But to cling to the notion of traditional parliamentary democracy as one's political ideal and to succumb to the illusion that only this 'tried and true' form is capable of guaranteeing human beings enduring dignity and an independent role in society would, in my opinion, be at the very least shortsighted.

I see a renewed focus of politics on real people as something far more profound than merely returning to the everyday mechanisms of western (or if you like bourgeois) democracy. In 1968 I felt that our problem could be solved by forming an opposition party that would compete publicly for power with the Communist Party. I have long since come to realize, however, that it is just not that simple and that no opposition party in and of itself, just as no new electoral laws in and of themselves, could make society proof against some new form of violence. No 'dry' organizational measures in themselves can provide that guarantee, and we would be hard pressed to find in them that God who alone can save us.

XXI

And now I may properly be asked the question: What is to be done, then?

My scepticism towards alternative political models and the ability of systemic reforms or changes to redeem us does not, of course, mean that I am sceptical of political thought altogether. Nor does my emphasis on the importance of focusing concern on real human beings disqualify me from considering the possible structural consequences flowing from it. On the contrary, if A was said, then B should be said as well. Nevertheless, I will offer only a few very general remarks.

Above all, any existential revolution should provide hope of a moral reconstitution of society, which means a radical renewal of the relationship of human beings to what I have called the 'human order', which no political order can replace. A new experience of being, a renewed rootedness in the universe, a newly grasped sense of 'higher responsibility', a new-found inner relationship to other people and to the human community — these factors clearly indicate the direction in which we must go.

And the political consequences? Most probably they could be reflected in the constitution of structures that will derive from this 'new spirit', from human factors rather than from a particular formalization of political relationships and guarantees. In other words, the issue is the rehabilitation of values like trust, openness, responsibility, solidarity, love. I believe in structures that are not aimed at the 'technical' aspect of the execution of power, but at the significance of that execution in structures held together more by a commonly shared feeling of the importance of certain communities than by commonly shared expansionist ambitions directed 'outward'. There can and must be structures that are open, dynamic and small; beyond a certain point, human ties like personal trust and personal responsibility cannot work. There must be structures that in principle place no limits on the genesis of different structures. Any accumulation of power whatsoever (one of the characteristics of automatism) should be profoundly alien to it. They would be structures not in the sense of organizations or institutions, but like a community. Their authority certainly cannot be based on long-empty traditions, like the tradition of mass political parties, but rather on how, in concrete terms, they enter into a given situation. Rather than a strategic agglomeration of formalized organizations, it is better to have organizations springing up *ad hoc*, infused with enthusiasm for a particular purpose and disappearing when that purpose has been achieved. The leaders' authority ought to derive from their personalities and be personally tested in their particular surroundings, and not from their position in any *nomenklatura*. They should enjoy great personal confidence and even great lawmaking powers based on that confidence. This would appear to be the only way out of the classic impotence of traditional democratic organizations, which frequently seem founded more on mistrust than mutual confidence, and more on collective irresponsibility than on responsibility. It is only with the full existential backing of every member of the community that a permanent bulwark against 'creeping totalitarianism' can be established. These structures should naturally arise from *below* as a consequence of authentic social 'self-organization'; they should derive vital energy from a living dialogue with the genuine needs from which they arise, and when these needs are gone, the structures should also disappear. The principles of their internal organization should be very diverse, with a minimum of external regulation. The decisive criterion of this 'self-constitution' should be the structure's actual significance, and not just a mere abstract norm.

Both political and economic life ought to be founded on the varied and versatile co-operation of such dynamically appearing and disappearing organizations. As far as the economic life of society goes, I believe in the principle of self-management, which is probably the only way of achieving what all the theorists of socialism have dreamed about, that is, the genuine (i.e. informal) participation of workers in economic decision-making, leading to a feeling of genuine responsibility for their collective work. The principles of control and discipline ought to be abandoned in favour of self-control and self-discipline.

As is perhaps clear from even so general an outline, the systemic consequences of an 'existential revolution' of this type go significantly beyond the framework of classical parliamentary democracy. Having introduced the term 'post-totalitarian' for the purposes of this discussion, perhaps I should refer to the notion I have just outlined – purely for the moment – as the prospects for a 'post-democratic' system.

Undoubtedly this notion could be developed further, but I think it would be a foolish undertaking, to say the least, because slowly but surely the whole idea would become alienated, separated from itself. After all, the essence of such a 'post-democracy' is also that it can only develop *via facti*, as a process deriving directly *from life*, from a new atmosphere and a new 'spirit' (political thought, of course, would play a role here, though not as a director, merely as a guide). It would be presumptuous, however, to try to foresee the structural expressions of this 'new spirit' without that spirit actually being present and without knowing its concrete physiognomy.

XXII

I would probably have omitted the entire preceding section as a more suitable subject for private meditation were it not for a certain recurring sensation. It may seem rather presumptuous, and therefore I will present it as a question: Does not this vision of 'post-democratic' structures in some ways remind one of the 'dissident' groups or some of the independent citizens' initiatives as we already know them from our own surroundings? Do not these small communities, bound together by thousands of shared tribulations, give rise to some of those special 'humanly meaningful' political relationships and ties that we have been talking about? Are not these communities (and they *are* communities more than organizations) – motivated mainly by a common belief in the profound significance of what they are doing since they have no chance of direct, external success – joined together by precisely the kind of atmosphere in which the formalized and ritualized ties common in the official structures are supplanted by a living sense of solidarity and fraternity? Do not these 'post-democratic' relationships of immediate personal trust and the informal rights of individuals based on them come out of the background of all those commonly shared difficulties? Do not these groups emerge, live and disappear under pressure from concrete and authentic needs, unburdened by the ballast of hollow traditions? Is not their attempt to create an articulate form of 'living within the truth' and to renew the feeling of higher responsibility in an apathetic society really a sign of some kind of rudimentary moral reconstitution?

In other words, are not these informal, non-bureaucratic, dynamic and open communities that comprise the 'parallel *polis*' a kind of rudimentary prefiguration, a symbolic model of those more meaningful 'post-democratic' political structures that might become the foundation of a better society?

I know from thousands of personal experiences how the mere circumstance of having signed Charter 77 has immediately created a deeper and more open relationship and evoked sudden and powerful feelings of genuine community among people who were all but strangers before. This kind of thing happens only rarely, if at all, even among people who have worked together for long periods in some apathetic official structure. It is as though the mere awareness and acceptance of a common task and a shared experience were enough to transform people and the climate of their lives, as though it gave their public work a more human dimension that is seldom found elsewhere.

Perhaps all this is only the consequence of a common threat. Perhaps the moment the threat ends or eases, the mood it helped create will begin to dissipate as well. (The aim of those who threaten us, however, is precisely the opposite. Again and again, one is shocked by the energy they devote to contaminating, in various despicable ways, all the human relationships inside the threatened community.)

Yet even if that were so, it would change nothing in the question I have posed.

We do not know the way out of the marasmus of the world, and it would be an expression of unforgivable pride were we to see the little we do as a fundamental solution, or were we to present ourselves, our community and our solutions to vital problems as the only thing worth doing.

Even so, I think that given all these preceding thoughts on post-totalitarian conditions, and given the circumstances and the inner constitution of the developing efforts to defend human beings and their identity in such conditions, the questions I have posed are appropriate. If nothing else, they are an invitation to reflect concretely on our own experience and to give some thought to whether certain elements of that experience do not — without our really being aware of it — point somewhere further, beyond their apparent limits, and whether right here, in our everyday lives, certain challenges are not already encoded, quietly waiting for the moment when they will be read and grasped.

For the real question is whether the 'brighter future' is really always so distant. What if, on the contrary, it has been here for a long time already, and only our own blindness and weakness has prevented us from seeing it around us and within us, and kept us from developing it?

Translated by Paul Wilson

Alfred Herrhausen

New Horizons in Europe

Alfred Herrhausen was one of the most important industrialists and bankers in West Germany. Born in 1930, he
studied business administration at the University of
Cologne, graduating in 1952. For the next thirty-five years
he had a brilliant career in business, finance, and government, playing a pivotal role in the reorganization of the
German steel industry. In 1988 he became sole spokesman
of the Board of Managing Directors of Deutsche Bank.

Dr. Herrhausen understood that the success of *perestroika*
was in the best interests of the West and urged the international financial community to support the Eastern reform
process. "The investment will be worth it!" he said. The
following essay was originally given as the Arthur Burns
Memorial Lecture and represents Dr. Herrhausen's vision-
ary proposals for investment, trade, and other developmental support to aid this revolutionary movement.

I

I wish to focus on the topic of integration as a sort of
leitmotif, and by "integration" I mean the fundamental reshaping of Europe and the economic implications thereof. This
reshaping has two interconnected features: economic and political integration in the West and reform in Eastern Europe.

Let me begin with a short summary of developments in
Western Europe. Here, the process of integration which began
about 40 years ago has been given new impetus. After a long
period of stagnation, the European Community has finally

aroused itself and is now energetically addressing the many challenges facing it. The Single European Act of 1987 has provided an explicit framework for the completion of the single European market and for the establishment of an economic and currency union.

The program for the completion of the single market in 1992 is proceeding much faster than pessimists had expected although the pace is slower than that which optimists had hoped for. By and large, the envisaged time schedule will be adhered to. And, meanwhile, it has transpired that the growth and employment impulses of 1992 are going to be even stronger than originally predicted in the so-called Cecchini Report. In addition, they are materialising sooner. There are good prospects for strong growth in EC countries on into the early nineties. As a result, Europe is now in a much better position to cope with a recession in North America, should it occur, than was the case in the seventies or early eighties.

Next on the EC priority list is the gradual implementation of the European Monetary Union. Obviously, a single market calls for a single currency. Experience with the European Monetary System has, on the whole, been positive and the EMS will form the nucleus of the envisaged monetary union. There are, of course, a number of difficult problems still to be solved. Monetary Union means that participating countries will have to sacrifice much of their previous autonomy in the field of economic policy making. This concerns areas such as the exchange rate and monetary policy and, to a certain degree, will probably also extend to fiscal policy. I admit, the issues involved are thorny but, nevertheless, I am convinced that they can be resolved and that the year 2000 is a realistic goal for the implementation of monetary union.

EC integration is of manifest importance for third countries, too. They should perceive "Europe 1992" as part of a wider phenomenon, namely the world-wide interlocking of economies which is now called the globalization of business activities. European integration and that taking place between The United States and Canada under The Free Trade Agreement are not discrete phenomena. Rather, they are manifestations of a truly global process to which the ongoing efforts to make the Uruguay round of GATT negotiations a success are a further pointer. Against such a background, fears that the EC — fortress-like — will cordon itself off are obviously unfounded. Europe has to remain open and it will remain open for third countries in general and for its European neighbours in the East in particular.

The European Community of twelve different nations has gained new respect internationally. In addition, the progress achieved in implementing EC integration has proven that free nations can pool their energies on a voluntary basis without the emergence of a hegemonial power. This insight has been a source of inspiration for Eastern European countries and has prompted them to press courageously for self-determination — that is, for the right to develop their own models for political and economic reform.

II

Currently we are witnessing a series of developments in Eastern Europe which signify a genuine rupture with the past. Events are unfolding with breathtaking rapidity. "Glasnost" and "Perestroika", initiated by General Secretary Mikhail Gorbachev, have convulsed the Soviet Union. In other Eastern European countries, we are witnessing a peaceful revolution "from below" so to speak. Hungarians, Poles, Czechs and East Germans are all standing up and demanding freedom: freedom of opinion, freedom of speech, freedom to travel, self-determination including free elections. In short, they are demanding democracy, that is: "government of the people, by the people, for the people". At the same time, they are demanding a standard of living hitherto refused them. They are sick and tired of the disasters of socialist planning which has reduced potentially affluent societies to near-poverty.

Fundamental reform of the existing economic system, such as has already been initiated in Hungary, Poland and in the Soviet Union and which is in the offing for East Germany (and presumably for Czechoslovakia), with a view to putting greater emphasis on market mechanisms has its dangers. And whatever happens, reform is likely to be a long and arduous process. Major adjustment problems will be unavoidable and will have to be surmounted if transition to market mechanisms is to work, economic efficiency to increase and the standard of living to be raised. One is reminded of Alexis de Tocqueville's shrewd observation that authoritarian regimes run into difficulties precisely then when they begin to change for the better. My personal conviction is that political and economic reform will have to go hand in hand in order to achieve enduring success. The setback in China this summer, where reform had been restricted to the economy and where the old political structures had remained unchanged shows only too clearly that freedom is a comprehensive concept and cannot be confined to just one sector of national life.

The Soviet leadership has thus far declined a Western-style pluralistic democracy for the U.S.S.R. But with glasnost, a new election system and more autonomy for the individual republics, important steps have been taken in the direction of democracy. At any rate, political change has advanced much faster than economic reorganisation. If the government does not succeed in eliminating, or at least easing, bottlenecks in supply, the resulting disaffection could interact with inveterate, latent ethnic antagonisms and possibly erupt in increasingly bitter conflicts. To cope with the probable hardships of this winter may turn out to be particularly difficult.

Success with perestroika is, however, necessary and very much in the West's interest as well. It would also give other countries in Eastern Europe more scope to restructure society and the economy. Such success can even be seen as *the* precondition for further progress in reforming countries.

III

Let me expand a little on the specific case of Poland. In addition to the patent shortcomings in the way its domestic economy is organised, Poland is also grappling with an exceptionally large external debt of almost $40 billion. For domestic reforms to have at least a chance of success, the debt problem needs to be solved promptly. In the past, the banks have agreed to regular reschedulings, but now the onus is on government lenders assembled in the Paris Club to come up with a helpful contribution. They account for roughly two-thirds of the country's external debt. If there is to be a permanent solution, this will require enlarging the strategies hitherto adopted to include a reduction of debt or debt service. However, such support can only make a meaningful contribution to reform policy if it is used sensibly and efficiently, as was the case with the Marshall Plan funds in shattered postwar Western Europe.

But this — vital — precondition still has to be fulfilled, given the dominant role of the state sector whose bureaucratic structures have remained largely intact so far. What, then, is to be done? The indispensable aid from outside should, I feel, be supplemented by a temporary scheme whereby external donors also have a say in the application of funds provided. The task here is to ensure that new loans are channelled into promising projects. It is, therefore, to be commended that the export credit guarantees which the West German government is prepared to extend are largely project-oriented. In fact, it was a *Polish* idea that a committee of experts drawn from both countries evaluate likely projects in order to make sure that the costly mistakes of the seventies are avoided.

In this context, I proposed — on the occasion of this year's Annual Meeting of the World Bank and the IMF in Washington — the establishment of a development bank on the spot, that is in Warsaw. Its job would be to bundle incoming aid and deploy it in accordance with strict efficiency criteria. I could well imagine that such an institution might be set up along the lines of the German Kreditanstalt für Wiederaufbau, the Reconstruction Loan Corporation, whose origin goes back to the Marshall Plan.

Representatives of the creditor countries should hold the majority in the management board of this new institution. Such a Polish "Institute for Economic Renewal" (IER), as it could be called, would have two functions: it should help and monitor.

Since both these functions can only be exercised in close cooperation with the Polish authorities and with Polish trade and industry, genuine involvement on the part of the Institute in the Polish economy and the country's development process would be absolutely essential. It could be set up "until further notice" or come under Polish control after a transitional period. By channelling Western "help towards self-help" in the right directions, the Institute could play a constructive role in economic reform.

Similar institutions could of course be established for other countries. As an alternative to specific Institutes for each single country, France has proposed the creation of a European Development Bank in analogy to existing institutions for Africa, Asia and Latin America. The EDB would serve all Eastern European countries and operate in much the same way as the envisaged "Institute for Economic Renewal". The proposal which is very much in line with my ideas is presently under further consideration. I have, however, three specific pleas in this context: Firstly, funds provided for a European Development Bank should not be deducted from aid destined for the less developed countries in the Third World. Secondly, the bank should be established very rapidly. In today's situation, speed is of the essence. Thirdly, it should extend project loans to every East European country interested and which is prepared to accept some form of conditionality along the lines of that practised by the IMF. Membership in the IMF would be welcome, but must not be made a prerequisite for access to lending. Otherwise, of the reforming countries, only Hungary and Poland would be eligible, but not the GDR or Czechoslovakia. That would certainly be unfortunate.

IV

How should we appraise the current situation in the two German states? Germany is at the very center of recent European developments. As a consequence of the Cold War, our country has been — unnaturally — divided since 1948. For 28 years the Berlin Wall prevented East Germans from moving freely. In the course of the last two months, with a lot of courage, the East Germans have forced upon their government tremendous political changes which nobody, until today, would have thought possible. They culminated in the opening of the Wall — a development whose powerful symbolism captivated world opinion. Despite the general euphoria, one could not miss the irony: The Wall was built in an attempt to keep people in the country, and now it had to be opened for exactly the same reason. Of course, East Germany's position is different from that of Hungary or Poland and is much more difficult in certain respects. It is the "front-line state", if that expression is still admissible, of the Warsaw Pact. And it borders on the other German state with which it has always to compare.

The opening of the Wall has raised the question of German reunification. Preferably, we should speak about "unification". In my opinion, a single, united German state is clearly desirable, not because of the attraction of sheer size or any power that size might confer, but because — historically, culturally and in human terms — it is a natural aspiration. We in Germany are very grateful that the Bush Administration and the American people have considerable understanding for this view.

In some quarters in the West, there is concern that a unified Germany might withdraw from NATO and adopt neutrality in order to gain reunion. It is pointed out by some observers that this may now be all Mr. Gorbachev can hope to rescue from the present political upheaval in Eastern Europe. In my opinion, such a demand would nevertheless be ill-advised. Nobody, and not even the Soviets, can be interested in having a large country of nearly 80 million people isolated in the middle of Europe, uneasily veering between East and West. As far as my fellow countrymen are concerned, I am convinced that, confronted with that sort of choice, they would say: "No, thank you". It would certainly be illogical for us to loosen our ties with the Western community exactly at a juncture when our neighbours in Eastern Europe are becoming receptive to the Western ideas of democracy and market-oriented systems. Our government and our parliament have made it abundantly clear for anybody who cares to listen that the Federal Republic is not contemplating a "solo run".

It is not premature to analyse the possibilities and consequences of German unity. Two things, however, should be kept clearly in mind. Firstly, it is up to the people to decide where they belong, i.e. in the first place to the East Germans. That East Germans be given freedom and self-determination is more important than a united Germany. If, later, the attainment of liberty were to be followed by a decision on their part to have a closer relationship with the West or even unity that would certainly be welcomed in the Federal Republic. At this point, the question is still very much an open question.

Secondly, such an endeavour would be a difficult and certainly a long process in view of the large economic and social differences that exist today. Whereas East Germany has the highest standard of living in Eastern Europe, the gap to West Germany is considerable. Now that travel between the two parts of Germany in an East/West direction is unrestricted, the GDR will have to do its utmost to overcome economic stagnation, to increase efficiency, to improve the standard of living for its citizens and to take environmental issues much more seriously in order to remain attractive as a place of abode for its citizens.

How could this be tackled? It is clear that the present rigid and bureaucratic planning system has failed. The economy has certainly been badly mismanaged in the past but the system as such can probably be improved, at least to a limited extent. For example, prices could reflect production costs more closely; planning could be less rigid and allow more responsibility to the large concerns; foreign trade and foreign exchange rules could become more flexible. This is obviously what Mr. Modrow, the new prime minister, has in mind when he uses the formula: "No planning without market, but no market economy in place of a planning system". The precise meaning of this — somewhat equivocal — principle still has to be worked out, however.

While economic improvements within the system seem possible, I doubt that they will be sufficient to enable the large leap forward which is necessary. In my opinion this cannot be achieved without fundamental reform. A model which has been proposed by some people in both East and West Germany is the so-called "third way". This means a sort of "via media" which combines market prices with socialism, socialism being conceived of as public ownership of the means of production. In my view, that idea is pure illusion. You can have either method of coordination: central planning or free competition with moves in prices conveying signals to independent entrepreneurs. And for the price mechanism to work effectively, you need private ownership with a readiness to take risk and responsibility. Any unholy union such as a socialist market system based on the competition of enterprises under public ownership is doomed to failure. The examples of Yugoslavia or Israel have made this very clear. And of course, this line of reasoning applies not just to the GDR, but to other countries in the East as well.

I believe the performance gap cannot be closed without introducing a Western-style market-economy system, based on market prices *and* on private ownership. What the GDR needs is a combination of three reforms, price reform, currency reform and a reform of ownership, namely the reintroduction of private property rights in the most important parts of the economy. West Germany had it easier in 1948. Then, we only needed two measures, namely the currency reform, introduced by the Allies, and Ludwig Erhard's lifting of price controls, in order to pave the way to what became known as the German "economic miracle". A reform of ownership was not necessary. So it must be conceded that the task confronting Eastern Germany now is compounded by an additional, weighty factor.

Property reform will probably be the most difficult of the three fundamental changes. There are hardly any historical precedents for such an exercise. How should one approach such an issue? In my view there are two main strategies which could be combined. The first is to allow private enterprises to set up facilities without let or hindrance. Private companies could quickly expand in sectors hitherto neglected such as services and new technologies. They could also fill the gaps when state-owned concerns withdraw from some activities. This approach has the advantage that it could be put into practice immediately.

The second avenue would be the comprehensive privatization of government-owned companies. Technically, the easiest way would be to convert large concerns into public corporations and offer their shares to private investors. Employees could be given preferential treatment. Maybe management buy-outs could also be used. I am well aware that it is a very difficult attempt to transform a society which has lived under thorough-going socialism for forty years into a society of profit-minded shareholders. Of course, the process could and should be managed in stages and it should be closely coordinated with price and currency reform.

Price, currency and property reform would mean profound changes throughout society in Eastern Germany. Many people in the East, including some of the leaders of the present opposition groups, are already worried about the social costs of such adjustment. The rewards would certainly not accrue instantaneously. However, I am convinced that, given an adequate economic environment in the East and pertinent support by the West, the East German as well as the other Eastern economies could achieve impressive growth. I believe the GDR in particular could then catch up on the Western standard of living in about ten years or so.

V

As a consequence of change in the East, the Federal Republic itself is also facing a number of problems, in particular that of integrating the large inflow of people from East Germany and of ethnic Germans from Russia, Poland and other parts of Eastern Europe. It is estimated that in 1988 and 1989, 850,000 Germans from the East will have come to the Federal Republic. This is a large number corresponding to nearly 1.5% of total population. It must be recognised that such an influx has generated concern in some quarters. Especially those in search of work or housing are afraid that the newcomers will reduce their chances. Such attitudes are understandable to some extent, but nonetheless they are unjustifiably pessimistic. They have their origin in static thinking and fail to comprehend the stimulus that population growth and an enlarged labour force will have on the economy.

Fortunately, the inflow could not have occurred at a better point in time as economic growth is currently very strong. It is already difficult to fill existing job vacancies in a number of regions. The immigrants will step in as they are mobile and motivated. They are, on average, much younger than our population. Those from East Germany, in particular, have a good standard of education. They are ready to work hard in order to make a living. In addition, they usually arrive here with very few assets and are, virtually, in need of everything. In short, the inflow will bring a stimulus to both the supply and demand side of the West German economy. It has been estimated that immigration will boost growth by nearly 1% in 1990. So I think the influx of new citizens will — notwithstanding temporary friction in some parts of the economy, such as the housing market — be as much a boon as it is a challenge.

VI

Now, how should Western countries including Western Germany react to change in Eastern Europe? In my opinion, there should be consensus that the success of perestroika is also in the interest of the West. It will make the Earth a more peaceful planet. It will liberate tied resources from armaments to more useful and pacific purposes, such as environmental policies and aid for the less developed countries.

Therefore, the West should support the Eastern reform process. The investment will be worth it. I use the word "investment" because all help should be inspired by the guiding idea of the Marshall Plan which was to stimulate initiative on the part of recipient countries in order to put such countries in a position to achieve growth "under their own steam" in due course. And a second proposition is self-evident: we can give support only when the receiving countries actually request it.

I already mentioned some possible support measures such as export credits and the setting up of development banks. What else could be done by the EC and other Western countries? I would like to pinpoint three aspects:

1. The short-term priority should be to overcome food shortages. At the world economic summit, the EC was given the task of coordinating such help. Governments should also be prepared to provide short-term balance-of-payments loans in order to bridge the time between now and the point when reforms begin to make themselves felt.

2. The Community should open its markets to the East. The EC has already concluded trade agreements with Hungary and Poland. Other countries should follow. In the final analysis, trade is certainly to be preferred to aid.

3. Companies should be encouraged to seek cooperation with partners in the East. This would imply inter alia greater use of the joint-venture approach, something which is already possible in all Eastern countries with the exception of the GDR.

VII

As far as the entry of countries such as Hungary or Poland into the EC is concerned, I think the question is premature. EC-membership presumes a certain degree of homogeneity — particularly in terms of the economic system, but also in terms of infrastructure and — to some extent — of income levels.

We should also keep in mind that the EC is not just an economic, but very much a political endeavour. I am an avowed advocate of political union as a long-term EC target. Developments in the East should not beguile us into losing sight of this target. To grant access to every country which applies would certainly mean postponing or even abandoning political union as the ultimate goal of EC integration. Obviously, there are choices to be made. In my view, a thorough discussion of these issues over coming months is called for as a basic decision will have to be taken soon.

Emphasis on ultimate political union should not be misunderstood as a policy to close the EC to Eastern Europe. I have already stressed that markets have to be kept open. A realistic alternative to membership could be to negotiate some form of association similar to the agreements which the EC already has with a number of Mediterranean countries.

An interesting idea put forward by a German think-tank is that the Eastern European countries could join EFTA, the European Free Trade Agreement. This probably implies that EFTA would change in the direction of a more supranational structure. The EC is keen to improve relations with EFTA in order to create a large and dynamic European economic area.

Seen in this perspective, we could end up with three concentric circles in Europe. The EC would be the core, the second circle would consist of a possibly enlarged EFTA and the third would comprise other European countries which choose to stand on their own.

VIII

Ladies and Gentlemen, as we approached 1989 many of us may have thought that it was going to be just one of those ordinary years despite the fact that exactly 200 years ago we had the storming of the Bastille which ushered in the French Revolution, 75 years ago the outbreak of World War I and 50 years ago Hitler's reckless plunge into World War II. It is, already now, clear that 1989 will be perceived by history as the most important year since the outbreak of the Cold War between the East and the West. The ongoing – perhaps epochal – changes in Europe will have important consequences not only for Europeans, but also for the United States and its role in Europe. At the weekend, President Bush and Soviet leader Mikhail Gorbachev addressed this theme in Malta (which prompted the headline "from Yalta to Malta"). Let me just add here that it is, in my view, absolutely essential that close ties between the United States and the EC continue. To borrow a phrase from Richard Burt, Arthur Burns' successor in Germany, we have to develop a "mature partnership".

For the American political planner Fukujama, the nature of events in 1989 is so striking that he publicly declared that the "end of history" had been reached. He justifies this startling affirmation with his perception that communism has reached the end of the road and that the model of the open society and of market systems based on private property has fought and won a final victory. There are grounds to see things this way. There can be no doubt that socialism in its concrete historical form with its bureaucratic central planning and comprehensive government control of all segments of the economy and of society will have to abdicate.

Yet the struggle for open societies is not over. For one, we cannot be certain that there will be no orthodox "counter-revolution" in the East. Secondly, the intellectual fascination of a pseudo-market system based on public ownership is still great for many people and aversion to capitalism in many quarters remains intense, especially among intellectuals. Therefore, the contest between economic systems will probably continue, hopefully at a less "ideological" level. Thirdly, the market system in the West itself is by no means guaranteed forever. There is a perennial tendency to indulge in interventionist policies, to pursue levelling policies which penalise effort and initiative, for the state to encroach upon the domain of the private sector. In the eighties, supply side policies in the form of privatization, deregulation, and liberalisation combined with tax reduction and price stability have rejuvenated Western economies. But we should remain aware that this is a task which is never completed.

Freedom, and the openness that goes with it, does not simply happen. Mankind has to fight for it—time and again. The solidarity members in Gdansk, the citizens of Budapest and Prague and the peaceful demonstrators on the streets of Leipzig have achieved a victory against formidable odds thanks to the grit and determination which comes from an overriding desire for freedom and well-being—the same desire that drove generations of Europeans before them to the New World in the legitimate "pursuit of happiness", a fundamental human right explicitly cited in no less a document than the Declaration of Independence. Let us hope that their efforts towards establishing functioning democracies will eventually be crowned with success and let us contribute all we can to that success.

History, therefore, has not ended. On the contrary, I believe that precisely now we are on the threshold of a very significant phase in human history. Vast military pacts still confront each other and we continue to think in the categories of national egoisms, defending "spheres of interest", conducting espionage and investing untold billions in armaments.

But and notwithstanding this sombre scenario, is it really such an illusion to surmise that modern history, our history, probably needs a new vision, an entirely different program — one that is geared, not to conflict and menacement, but, instead, to combating the real problems of this world, be it at national level or within the context of international cooperation — real problems such as the North/South divide, the debt crisis, terrorism and crime, the scourge of drugs, AIDS, overpopulation and a potential ecological catastrophe! These are the issues we must address with a new sense of purpose and dedication.

In 1989, Alfred Herrhausen was assassinated, his car blown up by political terrorists.

Finis vitae ejus nobis luctuosus, amicis tristis, extraneis etiam ignotisque non sine cura fuit. (We grieved at his passing and his friends were saddened. People abroad and strangers, too, were affected.)

—Tacitus, *Agricola*, circa 43

PART II

The Two Germanys

Reiner Kunze

Tales from
The Wonderful Years

Reiner Kunze is perhaps the most widely known and respected East German writer to have escaped to the West. Born in 1933, he studied philosophy and journalism at the University of Leipzig, going on to win numerous prizes and awards for his many publications for both children and adults, which have been translated into three languages. He became the object of increasing official defamation and harassment and was expelled from the East German Writers Union as a result of the spectacularly successful publication of his book *The Wonderful Years* in West Germany.

About *The Wonderful Years*, Kunze has written: "My book is not a political pamphlet. It is not meant to attack anyone. I am not an enemy of the Republic. I am an enemy of lies." We include here several short vignettes from the "Café Slavia" section of *The Wonderful Years*, which Kunze wrote while living in East Germany in the 1960s.

1968

Come to the Slavia,
we'll hold our tongues.
—*Jiři Mahen*

Behind the Front

On the morning of August 22, 1968, my wife nearly tripped: A bouquet of gladiolus lay at our door. An elderly couple in the neighborhood had a garden and would sometimes bring us flowers. "They probably didn't want to disturb us last night," said my wife.

That afternoon, she came with three bouquets in her arms. "These are only some of them," she said. They had been left for her at the hospital where she works, and nobody but my wife was surprised. Everyone knows she's from Czechoslovakia.

The Coat

The cloakroom lady hung my coat in a dumbwaiter and let it descend into the basement, and I stepped into the café.

The geography was finally right for me: The huge windows, where I looked for a table, were in the direct firing line of one of the tanks that had come straight at me too.

I was in Prague.

I had translated Vladimír Holan's long verse narrative *Night with Hamlet* for a Hamburg publisher, and I couldn't let the book go to press without discussing the translation with the author. Since it would bring foreign currency to the National Bank, I had gotten a visa for Czechoslovakia, though travelers were not permitted to enter at that time.

Here, at the Café Slavia, I wanted to write postcards. The racks in the newsstands were adorned with huge art-postcards — old engravings showing medieval Prague under siege or a bird's-eye view of the Battle of the White Mountain in 1620, after which Bohemia was re-Catholicized and a large part of the Czech intelligentsia left the country.

Prague, December 9, 1968.

The waitress took her time, which I noted without impatience. I'm a tea-drinker, and the art of brewing tea is the only art that has yet to flourish in this land.

I wrote to Moravia and filled out two very carefully selected cards for Moscow, where friends had invited me to the Praga Restaurant in spring: we had toasted Czechoslovakia.

Forty minutes later, when I still hadn't ordered, I made a pleading gesture to the waitress — propriety, I felt, demanded it. But I had evidently underestimated the altitude of her line of vision. My next signal, which I was convinced *had* been noticed, was likewise to no avail.

I began to suspect that my table was not being served. However, the patron sitting down opposite me just a short time later hadn't even fully unfolded his newspaper when the waitress came and asked him what he'd like. She did not take my order. She turned her back and walked away.

All at once it dawned on me that troops from where I came from had invaded Czechoslovakia.

"Did you check this coat in the café?" My friends eyed one another sidelong. I had never noticed the label in the lining: *Inform*. And in Cyrillic letters: *Isgotovlyeno v GDR*. [Made in the German Democratic Republic.]

"Before you even sit down, the waiters already know," said the colleague as she poured the coffee.

Someone asked: "What were you doing?"

"Writing postcards."

"Don't tell me to the Soviet Union."

When I said yes, he choked. "It's obvious no young Donetz miner is strolling through Prague — and without a brigade at that."

"We ought to have a special I.D. card for friends," said the woman. And: "Drink up. We'll brew some more."

The news of my being refused coffee in the Slávka (as the Café Slavia is known in Prague slang) always preceded me. Wherever I was expected — I was received with coffee.

For three days and three nights, I drank coffee of such a potency that if translated into military terms, it would have put all the remaining invader tanks out of commission: the soldiers would have gone home wide awake.

My Friend, a Poet of Love

He is one of the most brazen men between the Morava and the Moldau, a breaker of taboos, a master of dogma-smashing irony: his writings helped to bring on the spring of '68.

"Around 3:00 A.M., a woman is standing at the door, calling my name, and tonight of all nights Alena is with me," he said. Alena is his wife. They didn't live in Prague. He only worked here and rented a room. "You know how jealous Alena is," he said. "Luckily, she sleeps like a child

"The woman outside is waiting, and I wonder who it might be: Jana? Evička? . . . Dáša? I had only met Dáša a couple of days ago. A wonderful girl! But if you've slept with someone only once, you don't recognize her voice right away. She calls again, knocks. Now Alena is stirring. I put my hand on her mouth and tell her not to move, it's probably someone who's been locked out of the bar but still wants to drink. Then outside, I hear her going away . . . At six-thirty, someone knocks again. The same voice. 'I'm going to open,' says Alena. 'You can't go to the door like that,' I say and try to talk her out of it.

"'I'm curious,' she says and gets her robe. When I see I can't avert the catastrophe, I withdraw to the bathroom. Alena comes back, pale. 'Prague is occupied,' she says, 'Soviet tanks are on Wenceslas Square.'

"Boy, if you knew how I felt: was I ever glad it was only the tanks!"

But Heroes (Motto of M., motorized artillery man)

First alert, late July. Three days, then over. All leaves canceled. Explanation: Black Lion NATO maneuver. . . . At the next alert, gun and ammo on the cot. Camouflage uniform. In the afternoon, Red Meeting. Every day, loading and unloading. . . . First scuttlebutt: Czech movie troop wanted to make film with help of West German army, which West German army used as pretext to march into Czechoslovakia. Disturbances in

Prague. . . . Officially confirmed at Red Meeting. Policy: Since
we have to reckon with West German army's refusal to stop at
our border, we may be forced to attack. . . . Our radio — big
superheterodyne — is jammed. All we can get is GDR stations.
Dial sealed with adhesive tape. Higher alert phase. 8/19: Early
alert. No more Red Meetings. 8/20, 0330: Fall in with battle gear.
Military gas masks passed out and Jumbo — nickname for anti-
nuclear tarpaulin. Some guys had had target practice only eight
times. Another advance — a quickie — except for officers and staff
sergeant. Then: Forward! Without being told the destination.
And without rest. In P., tank regiment on trailers. Morning of
21st: Reconnaissance on the car. Printed leaflets: Czechoslovakia
asks the Warsaw Pact for help. Fulfillment of obligations. First
test. Reminder of oath. Not a word on the reason for the call for
help. . . . Most men view the whole thing as a change of pace.
Only worry: getting back by October; concerned only the discharge candidates, whose hitch is up in October. . . . Through
North and Central Bohemia. 30 kilometers before B.: Halt.
Woods. The *Führer*'s bunker. Five tents. Every soldier has to dig
himself a hole. Pup tent over it, that's all. Gap between troops and
officers huge. Still. But mood: normal. Not much to do. Two to
four hours of political instruction daily. Same rationale: West
German army invasion, Black Lion NATO maneuver near the
border. Tape lectures, some with slides. Brilliant lecture on the
Beats with textual analysis of *I Set Fire*. I set fire, that's my fate.
Political aspect: Person doesn't think further. Lots of Beat poetry.
Also discussion on Beatles. Again with lots of music. Masses
calmed down. Politically too. The disturbances in Prague caused
by rowdies. Everything under control. The military action not
aimed at the Czech people. . . . Insulated from the outside
world. No newspapers. Just *Neues Deutschland* once. Mail: Just
open cards with army mail number. Model texts suggested:
"Don't worry, I'm fine." By chopper to Berlin. Postmarked
there. . . . Next to us, Poles, white stripe on helments. Next to
the Poles, Soviets. Each in a separate camp. . . . Suddenly, new
information about call for help: Disturbances in Prague were
against Dubček, and the police couldn't keep the situation under

control. Arms caches discovered. . . . Truck driver brought along a story: Buddy swapped army property for booze. Court-martialed and shot. . . . Panic. Red Meeting. Question: How is that possible in a Socialist army? . . . Printed handout: What Is My Fatherland? Commentary on oath of allegiance. Stress on seriousness of oath. Anyone taking it is under military jurisdiction. Severest punishment because of martial law. First indication that martial law was declared. Our cocks hit high noon! Terrified for our bare lives. Every step, every word could mean death. For instance when plastered. No morale. . . . Raw weather. Clothes clammy, dirty. The discharge candidates saw black: it was already mid-September! . . . Till then, normal movies: East German, Soviet. Nothing political. Entertainment. Now movies to juice up morale. French-Italian co-productions. *Tiger of the Seven Seas, The Three Musketeers.* When they didn't draw anymore — sex. Swedish flicks with English subtitles. Silent movies for us. But flesh. One was called *Black Gravel.* English, I think. Woman — mid-thirties, fairly well off, picks up guy on the street and exploits his manhood. Sucks him dry, wipes him out. Then throws him back into his asocial milieu. Only bed scenes. With fore- and afterplay. The warriors roared. . . . Gradually — through truckdrivers — things trickle in from outside: abortive attempts at contacting Czechs. Big awakening: "I thought *they* called *us?!*" Now it was clear why the Soviets were in Prague, and not us. We would have stirred up memories. . . . Squadron demoralized. Every other word is "home." For "Hi!" — "When are we going home?" Some officers almost chummy. Especially when a soldier on duty had a heated vehicle at night. . . . Finally it was announced that Dubček had been thrown out. He hadn't shown the necessary severity toward the class enemy. . . . From now on, every time something goes wrong, there is only one pet phrase: Dubček's final revenge! — If you cut yourself on a can-opener: Dubček's final revenge! — "Third Company — peel potatoes!": Dubček's final revenge! One question more pointed than the other. No one afraid anymore. The men would have shot only to protect their own lives. I grew up more in this time than in years! . . . Finally: alcohol. Official prohibition. Now a big bottle of beer every day. Hard stuff on the sly. If you had the bread. There was always someone. . . . We went back on October 28. Stopped in every large town. Young Pioneers. Banners. Tea. Mayor. Factory delegations. Pictures. Albums. School classes with flags. "Maneuver Ball" in the marketplace. The only women: Free German Youth girls. Finally something to hold on to. The whole thing—four days. The soldiers—pissed off. Looked like pigs. Underwear changed three times in two months. They stank. But they were heroes.

Handcuffs

After a final inspection . . . all of us, each escorted by one soldier, but without handcuffs, were taken to the courtroom for the first time, on November 19, 1945. . . .

—**Albert Speer, defendant in the Nuremberg War Crimes Trial**

"I was locked up for only four months; then came the amnesty," said S., an attendant in a Thuringian sanatorium. "I had made leaflets against the invasion of Czechoslovakia and tacked them up on trees and doorbells during the night of August 25. About eight or so. But I had more. I can't remember the text too well. It ended with: Citizens, Awake! . . .

"I wasn't treated so badly. Only at the remand prison: they pulled me out of the car by my hair. . . . And then I had to stand naked in front of the policemen and read the prison rules. . . . Once, the guards played catch with me—that is to say, I was the ball. You get shoved from one to another, and some of them stand in such a way that you don't see them; then you think you're falling. Afterwards, your knees are like jelly. . . . I was taken to the trial in handcuffs, with two guards escorting me across the prison yard. The sentence was a year and a half in juvenile prison. That's not reform school, it's tougher. But they said the court was taking my age into consideration and that was why the sentence was so lenient. I was fifteen."

Translated by Joachim Neugroschel

Reiner Kunze

Life and Consequences
Being a Writer in Divided Germany

Here is an essay by Mr. Kunze, written recently from his new home in West Germany, chronicling his difficulties as a writer in East Germany.

I

When the mail
passes by the window bloom
the ice-flowers yellow

This image would scarcely occur to someone who is not waiting in desperation for a certain letter, or for whom it is not a

matter of life and death that the letters journeying from or
toward himself reach their recipient.

> *Letter you*
> *two-millimeter-wide opening*
> *of the door to the world you*
> *opened opening you*
> *glowing*
> *light-filled, you*
> *are here*

No author who can move freely in the world will make these
associations at the sight of a newly arrived letter: "Letter you/
two-millimeter-wide opening/of the door to the world." One
has actually to live in a state where the courts impose a sentence
of six years imprisonment for "agitation against the State" and, as
proof of this agitation, accept an exchange of private letters that
had never been accessible to the public (as happened in the trial
of the engineer Burckhard Guenther on the 25th and 27th of
September, 1978, in Frankfurt/Oder) in order that when one
thinks about letters plays on words like "opened opening" and
"glowing, light-filled" present themselves. The poetic image that
rises up out of the unconscious has its own truth, and it dies at
the moment of falsification. . . .

Postal facts from our life in the DDR (the little archive on
which I am relying lay hidden for many years under the floor of a
public building in the DDR, and I owe it to a friend that I am in
possession of the documents again): a letter, mailed on December 22, 1969, in Frankfurt am Main, delivered in Greiz
(Thueringen) on February 2, 1970, time elapsed 43 days . . . a
registered letter, mailed on August 12, 1970, in Reinbek near
Hamburg, delivered in Greiz on October 6, 1970, time elapsed
56 days . . . a registered express letter, mailed on December 23,
1974, in Bad Vilbel, delivered in Greiz on January 19, 1975, time
elapsed 28 days.

A posting date, scratched out or covered with ink, a postmark
on the back whose halves do not meet at the edge of the flaps,
and broken seals were as much a part of the postal routine as

replies to tracers: "We regret that all inquiries were without result—one must presume that it was lost in the mails . . ." (Deutsche Post Office, Gera Regional Office, March 21, 1977 . . . "Since . . . the addressee denies having received it, clearly through an oversight it was never delivered . . ." (Greiz Postal and Long-Distance Communications Office, Telegram Tracers, January 19, 1977.

Letters containing statements about the time and place of an intended appointment were usually delivered a day after the date stated.

Unless I am mistaken, no author's copy of any book of mine that appeared in West Germany or elsewhere and was sent by post ever reached me. (Christmas, 1968, our daughter gave me some envelopes she had hand-painted, including one with a lion, and since the S. Fischer Publishing House was readying my children's book *Leopold the Lion* for the press, I enclosed my new year's greetings to the publisher in this envelope. As it happened, the envelope-lion became the book-jacket lion, and our daughter waited, now patiently, now impatiently, for the day when she would see *her* lion in print. But instead of the advance copy sent by express mail, she too received only the notice of confiscation. "Addressee: . . . Kunze, Marcela . . . Serial number: 1. Exact designation: *Leopold the Lion*. Intrinsic value in per cent: Book. Unit or quantity: Piece. Quantity: 1. Entry completed at Post Office 1. Erfurt, July 17, 1970.

Thanks to our friends' presence of mind and willingness to take risks I was still able to get sight of my books. When the reader of the Rowohlt Press was trying to bring me a copy of the volume of poetry *felt oaths [sensible wege]* and the DDR border police left the train compartment with his passport for a moment, he wrote a Leipzig address on a piece of paper, looked the one other traveller (whom he had not spoken a word to during the entire trip) in the eyes, put the scrap of paper and the book in a bag, and slid the bag under the seat. The reader was removed from the train and obliged to return to Hamburg—but the stranger took the book to the Leipzig address, where it was accepted on my behalf.

The first edition of the volume of poetry *at indoors volume [zimmerlautstaerke]* appeared in a paperbound series, and the first copy I held in my hands was bent in the middle—a girl from West Berlin had brought it over the border in her brassiere. (As symmetry would have it, I then came into possession of yet another bent copy.)

Entrusting a package containing a book manuscript to the mails would have meant running the risk of having the original seized and the copy found during a house search, which would have come to the same thing as the total obliteration of four or five years work. In addition, it would have meant the loss of the protection a book brings through the publicity it creates by its publication.

In paragraph 106 of the penal code of the DDR of January 12, 1968, relating to the severity of punishment for "agitation against the state," it is said that whoever produces "writings" that "defame the civil, political, economic, or other social relations of the German Democratic Republic" will be "punishable by imprisonment for from one to five years." And further on: "Whoever uses in the commission of this crime organs or facilities of publication that are conducting a campaign against the German Democratic Republic, will be punishable with imprisonment for from two to ten years . . . Preparations and attempts are punishable."

It would have been irresponsible to entrust the manuscript to a person who was allowed, on grounds of age or ill health, to travel in West Germany, for one would have brought this person too into danger. Accordingly, for one of my books I had a colleague in Westphalia provide me with extra-thin typing paper, and when the manuscript was ready, I divided it up into letters each weighing 20 grams. Then I travelled from one major city of the DDR to the next, in each city depositing one of the letters in the mailbox. All of them reached their destination and were forwarded by their various recipients to the press in Frankfurt, where the manuscript was reassembled.

Such was the reality, and the images that came to me one day would not have been able to do so without just *this* reality.

> *Letters you*
> *white lice in the*
> *fatherland's pelt, watch out,*
> *the mails are*
> *a comb!*

I remember the train journey when this idea came to me and image after image followed upon it. What had long been experienced suddenly revealed a poetic structure.

> *O from*
> *a foreign land, see*
> *the stamps . . . What*
> *is the land's name?*
>
> — — —
>
> *Germany, daughter*
>
> ★
>
> *O how*
> *beautiful the stamp is: the wolf and*
> *the seven kids and*
> *his paw is*
> *all white . . . Who*
> *wrote the letter?*
>
> *Perhaps*
> *the seven kids,*
> *perhaps*
> *the wolf*
>
> *. . . the wolf is dead!*
> *In the story, daughter, only*
> *in the story*

I wrote a cycle of 33 variations on the theme "The Mail" that I later shortened to 21 variations.

The DDR Ministry for Culture, however, refused the Educational Press of Berlin and Weimar its approval for printing the book that included this cycle. I never received any written communication concerning this prohibition, but one of the two readers who brought the manuscript back to Greiz drew a large snail creeping along through the night in our guest-book. On its back, it bore the emblem of the Educational Press (April 18, 1967).

When the Rowohlt Press published the volume of poetry in 1969, Max Walter Schulz said at the Sixth Congress of German Writers in Berlin, "When one reads the . . . poems, the fatal lyric region between introspection and anti-communism shows itself with brutal clarity . . . It is . . . a naked, irascible individualism, greedy despite its [display of] sensitivity for action, that peers out from its inner world, already collaborating with anti-communism, with willful distortion of the image of the DDR . . ." In her opening greeting , Anna Seghers, the then-president of the German Writers' League, had announced Schulz's speech as a "leading address," which meant that it represented the views of the leadership, and therefore, of the Party.

But a poem cannot turn back, and so the author has only the choice between turning back and the poem.

II

In May, 1970, the journal *Akzente* published four poems, among them this one:

Like Things of Clay

But I glue my halves together like a broken clay pot.
—Jan Skacel, letter of February, 1970

1
We wanted to be like things of clay
Existence for those,
who, mornings, around five, drink their coffee
in the kitchen

To belong to the simple tables

We wanted to be like things of clay, made
from earth from the fields

Also, that no one can kill with us

We wanted to be like things of clay

> *Amid*
> 　　*so much*
> 　　　　*rolling*
> 　　　　　　*steel*
>
> 2
> *We will be like the shards*
> *of things of clay: no more*
> *a whole, perhaps*
> *a flaring*
> *in the wind*

Both the presses in the DDR with whom I was still in contact responded with registered letters. New Life Press: " . . . we regret that we must inform you today that our Laszlo Nagy poetry album will appear without your versions. We were brought to this decision by the poems published by you in the journal *Akzente,* volume 5, 1970, that show us that you are no longer in accord with the cultural-political goals pursued by our press. The contract between the press and you as verse-translator is henceforth null and void."

And the People and World Press: "We hereby inform you that we will not publish your versions of the works of Gyula Illyes and Novomesky." The presses did not react spontaneously, but only nine months after the appearance of the number of *Akzente* in question — an infallible indication that a decision had been reached in the highest circles.

III

From now on, it was almost impossible for me to do readings anywhere except in churches. Since only events of a religious character did not require official approval, there were prayers before and after the reading, or the priest held a brief devotion and blessed the congregation at the end. Yet the need to gather under the roof of a church to hear an author read aroused emphatically political expectations and fostered the misconception that poetry is a political message in code.

Bicycling
Turning away, off
to the woods

The motorists smile
like grown-ups

And indeed, in the woods
on the branching path, the bike-rattles
clatter in the spokes

When we get down
as if from a shaken sieve, the mind is
fine sand

and tempts to play

When I read this poem aloud one evening—there were 300 men and women in the hall, spokespersons for the Catholic Student Associations of the DDR—it was only on the third attempt that I was able to go on to the end, since the audience burst into applause [each time] after the words "turning away."

These words touched upon one of their deepest yearnings—the longing to withdraw from the spirit-killing political and ideological indoctrination to which they saw themselves exposed even, in part, within the private realm. They felt themselves suddenly understood and validated. After a moment's irritation, I in fact did understand them, and it was legitimate that they applied the words "turning away" to their situation. But the poetic experience exhausted itself, for many of them, in their satisfaction from this sense of political agreement.

When we get down
as if from a shaken sieve, the mind is
fine sand

and tempts to play

"On the fact that works of art give people the possibility of passing beyond the reality which they inhabit and themselves are into the non-real sphere of the imagination rests one of the most precious gifts that art can confer, namely, its peace," wrote Romano Guardini. The dominance of the political kills this gift.

During my activity as a teacher at the University of Leipzig at the end of the '50s, a student came to me during a break in one of the seminars and warned me: the party had given him the assignment of reporting every politically suspect utterance of mine to the state security police. At the end of the seminar, another student, a woman, followed me into the room and delivered the same warning. Neither knew of the other's assignment.

At the Theodor Neubauer Secondary School in Greiz, a sixteen-year-old schoolboy was given the "signal honor," after several secret interviews, of helping the state security police to protect the teachers, the parents of his fellow students, and above all the security police themselves from mistakes — he had only to write down anything that people said that struck him as politically questionable and deliver the report every Thursday at 5 P.M. at one of the apartments rented by state security. One day, the youth forgot that it was Thursday and went to this apartment the following afternoon. At the door he met a classmate.

"You come here?" "You come here?!"

In the face of such [technical] perfection, one could be certain that there was no church-reading where state security was not present, and as the years went by, I acquired a certain knack for picking out these gentlemen — in my experience they were always men — from the audience. For instance, when the Catholic student representatives began to applaud after the words "turning away," a gentleman in the second row was at least as surprised as I was. Several times he glanced uncertainly from side to side, and when he seemed to sense that he would attract attention if he did not join in the clapping, he brought his hands together, hesitantly, three or four times. After the reading, he was the first to arrive at the restaurant where people wanted to sit down together in a more intimate circle, and nobody knew him.

After a reading at Greiz which, after a reminder about the respect due a church, had passed off without any expressions of feeling from the public, several audience-members were taken into custody the next day as they left the factory gate at the end of their shift and brought to the state security building. After an eight-hour-long interrogation, one woman was handed over in a state of nervous collapse to the Catholic priest, whom they rang up in the middle of the night and awakened from his sleep for the purpose, and he himself was sentenced to a fine. Much the same happened in Gera.

From the same period derives my knowledge that laser-beams can penetrate yard-thick concrete, so that with their help any conversation conducted in any house can be intercepted — except for conversations conducted in a wooden cubicle (for which reason a wooden enclosure was subsequently installed in the new building for the Standing Representation for West Germany in the DDR). One night, when I stepped out the door of our six-unit apartment house with a guest, a giant of a man was standing behind it with a sort of suitcase, and the guest, a diplomat from West Germany, said in an undertone, "Oh well, talking for the tape recorder again!"

What sort of apparatus there was in the cars, occupied by two or three men, which were often parked round the clock on the opposite side of the street, one can only guess.

IV

The consequences that can arise for its author after the publication of a poem are irrelevant during the creation of the text. I had to bear them in mind, however, when a book of mine was being printed in West Germany. When S. Fischer accepted the volume *at indoors volume [zimmerlautstaerke]* in 1971, with the poem "Like things of clay" among its contents, I often lay sleepless far into the night, turning this way and that in my mind how I would respond if the state prosecutor chose one poem or another as grounds for an indictment. I had offered this book to the Rowohlt Press, but a new reader had been taken on in Reinbek who brought back the manuscript that had luckily gotten through to the West and announced to me that with these poems he would not be able to win the revolutionary students in West Germany over for lyric poetry. I could not rule out the possibility that the West German critics would react similarly and in the DDR circumstances would be seen as especially favorable for my arrest. In order that I might be able to care for myself in prison, a doctor-friend who was familiar with my state of health instructed me in methods of pain-suppression and acupressure.

Except for imprisonment and destruction of our health, my wife and I were ourselves relatively invulnerable, so long as she could provide a living for us through her profession as a doctor. But the consequences touched our daughter too, and after our emigration to West Germany, my wife's parents in Czechoslovakia and my own parents in the DDR.

After repeated attempts to use the behavior of our daughter to show that she was spreading the ideology and morality of her father, the "class enemy" at school, one day she pleaded with us not to force her to go to school again. (At a parents' meeting, where the debate was over poems of mine and not the conduct of our daughter, one of the fathers said in my presence, "We will not permit our children to be contaminated by the daughter of such a man!") She joined a Christian home for the retarded in Berlin as part of the nursing staff, but state security kept the pressure on the director of the home to cancel the position and thereby make it impossible for her to stay in Berlin until, months later, the management took her into its confidence and begged her to give notice herself.

Then she worked in Jena, where she got to know a young man and moved in with him. An acquaintance who, unbeknownst to us, had been working for state security dropped his disguise — he was no longer able to reconcile certain methods with his conscience — and informed us that this young man had been sent to Jena with the express purpose of winning our daughter's trust. When we told her about this, she thought we had succumbed to paranoia, but the young man, who had really and truly fallen in love with her, obviously found himself with no way out and so committed suicide. Our acquaintance stated that the suicide note found on the young man was seized by state security officials.

My wife's father in Czechoslovakia suffered several heart attacks and was cared for by a young doctor who looked in on him without even being asked to. After he had not put in an appearance for some time, one day he came after dark and told my in-laws that he had been interrogated by the Czech secret police in a prejudicial manner en route to his first medical congress in West Germany. He had been forced to strip completely and was then asked what sort of contacts he had with the son-in-law. The doctor had been totally unaware of my existence. He asked my in-laws to forgive him for not being able to take care of them any longer — it was obvious that he was being watched.

Seriously ill, my mother had been unable to leave her house for years, and my father is too fragile to travel to us any more. An opportunity arose for them at least to see their son's face in an interview on the television program "Report," March 3, 1988. On the morning of the same day, I telegraphed them, "9 P.M. Warmest greetings. Reiner." The telegram was delivered the following day just after the end of the morning repeat of "Report."

Toward the end of 1988, efforts had been made by the West German Federal Chancellery to persuade the government of the DDR, after almost twelve years, to allow us to visit my 82-year-old parents — my mother was on her death-bed — for a few hours. The reaction of the DDR government was one of "harsh refusal." Three weeks later, my mother was dead, and her burial took place without us. Our daughter, who had joined us in emigrating to West Germany twelve years earlier, obtained the permission of the officials of the DDR to take part in the funeral, which was a relief to us, especially in consideration of my father. At the Gerstungen train station on the DDR border, however, she was taken from the train and sent back without any explanation.

V

After the change of head-of-state in the DDR at the beginning of the '70s, there were attempts at compromise. But as a writer I can enter into compromises only in an editorial role, not in literature, in the work itself. The poetic image is incapable of compromise, since it refers to truth. The originating idea excludes political calculation. Also, in the end it lies beyond the power of consciousness to determine what the reality is that poetic images or other artistic conceptions produce.

In the anthology *Letter with a Blue Seal* brought out by the Reklam Press, Leipzig, in 1973, eight of the "21 variations on the theme of 'the mail'" are missing. Since on the one hand I felt sympathy for those who were trying to insure that this anthology came into being and had to have an eye to politics, but on the other I was unwilling to contribute to deceiving the readers about the political conditions in the DDR, I left the same numbers over the surviving variations in the manuscript that they had borne in the complete cycle.

This clear indication of the omissions was refused as unacceptable, and there was insistence upon continuous numeration and alteration of the title, so it would not be visible how many variations the cycle includes. This would have meant disguising the act of censorship, and so I decided — trusting in the fact that readers of lyrics are close readers — on the heading, "From: variations on the theme 'the mail.'" And so it was possible, without spreading misinformation, for (among others) the variations "When the mail/passes by the window . . . " and "Letter you/two-millimeter-wide opening/of the door to the world . . . " to appear in the DDR, while texts like the following went unprinted:

> *Beautiful women*
> *went the rounds of the besiegers*
> *of Naples, the army*
> *sank under*
> *syphilis*
>
> *All news is*
> *women*

VI

Even if I had thought that I ought not to write it, or ought to write it differently, I would not have been able not to write, or to write differently, my book *The Wonderful Years*. For most of the people in the DDR, there had been no improvement during the period of attempts at compromise between a certain few artists and the regime, and for a writer reality is above all also the reality of others.

On the 21st of October, 1976, the director of the Children's Book Press of the DDR, where 15,000 copies of an edition of *Leopold the Lion* illustrated by Albrecht von Bodecker lay ready for delivery, wrote me a letter: "Distribution of the slanderous book, *The Wonderful Years*, in West Germany and distribution of a book by the same author on the part of the Children's Book Press are mutually exclusive." (It is probable that the printing of this DDR edition was destroyed, for later on it was disputed that the book had ever been printed. Someone unknown to me had brought a copy to Greiz, nonetheless, where my wife found it in a bag along with a sandwich she had put aside for herself.)

I was expelled from the Writers' League of the DDR, and the Director of the Section for Culture of the Central Committee of the Socialist Unity Party of Germany called me an "enemy of the State" in a speech delivered to editors of cultural publications. From that, and from what followed, we came to the choice that German authors have the privilege of making: leaving one's home and yet remaining in the same land and one's own language. After exile in theory—the writer and party official Erik Neutsch had already declared in 1975 at the University of Greifswald that Biermann, Heym, and Kunze were not part of DDR literature—came exile in fact. On the 14th of April, 1977, we emigrated to West Germany. We suffered as little from illusions as we knew what it means to be free. Born in 1933, up to this day I had lived exclusively under dictatorships.

VII

For many years we had received solidarity from West Germany, and without the certainty that there was a public ready to protest, the feeling of vulnerability might perhaps have begun to paralyze us. But it had not been solidarity *only* that we had received.

After the appearance of the volume of poetry *felt paths [sensible wege]* at the Rowohlt Press in 1969, another West German press invited me to the book-fair at Leipzig and explained to me that Rowohlt was not the right publisher for me. In case I was prepared to change publishers, they would consider offering me a lifetime contract. I would have felt it was shabby behavior on my part if I had accepted the offer, for I only felt my obligation to Rowohlt was ended when they later refused the book of poetry *at indoors volume.*

A year or two later, a reader for the publisher that had made me this offer struck up a conversation with me at a Leipzig streetcar stop, and I told him I had finished a new book. "Yes," he said, "but unfortunately, a lot has changed since." After the hostile statements by Max Walter Schulz at the Writers' Congress they could no longer risk taking me on as one of their authors, since they could not risk jeopardizing their ties to DDR publishers. For example, they were working on a common project of an encyclopedia in many volumes, and a large part of their books were printed in the DDR—and of course much more cheaply than anywhere else in the world . . . Any contract with a press in West Germany had to be approved before it was signed by the DDR Copyright Bureau, and the press had to pay over the author's fee to the DDR State Bank, which gave the author .98 DDR marks for each German mark. If the contract was not approved, and one signed it nonetheless, the result was usually that suit would be brought for the maximum penalty, at that time a fine. In this case too, the author's fee had to be remitted to the DDR State Bank—the penalty for diversion of foreign monies was imprisonment.

While the S. Fischer Press was preparing the book *Leopold the Lion* in the spring of 1970, while we were at the Leipzig book-fair, I informed the reader who was accountable at that time that the fine for signing the contract had been duly paid. The reader was astounded: a fine? Then he would not bring the book out either. He didn't want DDR officialdom to start "shutting doors" in his face, and he wouldn't consider risking his good relations with Batt, the director of the Hinstorff Press . . .

During a conversation in Berlin, a member of the ministerial council of the DDR remarked, more by way of a well-meant, timely warning than out of cynicism, that I took too simple a view of the world. No matter how unobtrusively I had my manuscripts taken into the West, as soon as they arrived there, the DDR had a copy on its desk too. I was unable to confirm the veracity of this claim, but when at one of the last book-fairs that I visited as a citizen of the DDR a man who was a colleague of my West German publisher at the time absolutely insisted on trying to persuade us to take part in currency illegalities — he missed no opportunity to press his case — my wife and I began to feel we had grounds for reflection.

VIII

In the first years after our emigration, I once said that many people in West Germany did not realize what they had, and some people cannot forgive me for it even today. Unfortunately, I still see no reason to change my opinion. In fact, many are unaware what limitations of their personal freedom they do *not* suffer from, what ideological indoctrination they are *not* exposed to, what means for claiming their rights are *not* withheld from them, or what possibilities for pursuing an intellectually stimulating life they do *not* lack. They are unware of how they are *not* treated as wards, how they are *not* compelled to collude in the lie, and how much fear has so far been spared them. To their benefit and to their misfortune, they are so very unaware that they are incapable of changing places in imagination with someone who lives a life founded on other experiences. And the inability to make such connections is one of the causes of the sometimes ruthless ideologizing of intellectual life in West Germany.

In her book on Maria Svetayeva, Maria Rasumovsky quotes Majakovsky, who said at the enlarged plenary of the Russian Writers' League on the 26th of September, 1929, "Someone has claimed the poet Svetayeva writes good poems, they just don't hit the mark . . . She's one of those people who 'go their own way,' who have gone around campaigning for Gumilyov's poems to be published again, since they are 'good in themselves!' My opinion is that something that is aimed against the Soviet Union, against us, has no right to exist, and it is our business to paint it as black as we can . . . ! " A person exposed to this way of thinking — exposed in the awareness that he will never be able to escape from it — sometimes feels afraid in West Germany (just as he would, sooner or later, feel afraid in every other country of the West — only, I wonder whether it would happen so often, or with such a chill in his heart). . .

During an autograph party in Koblenz, a girl asked me just why I had come to the West.

I said because it was very likely I would otherwise have spent a number of years in prison.

"Really?" she said. "And is that so bad?"

Part of the yard of our house is a little slope that we have made into a forest. One day, we noticed that at different spots the undergrowth and the foliage on the lower branches were dying. They had been sprayed with an herbicide. In our mail box a copy of the weekly *Die Zeit* lay open. The heading said "No Crisis," and the article referred to my resignation from the League of German Writers (VS).

Later on, in the summer the leaves of individual trees began to wither, and I decided to dig one of them up. Someone had cut the trees down and, carefully camouflaging what they were doing, pushed them back into the ground. In the mailbox lay a mass-magazine with a political attack.

After the volume of poetry *everyone's only life* appeared, I received a newspaper clipping of the S. Fischer Press ad on which the restrained use of lower-case in the quoted text was

marked in red. Footnote: "It's a disgrace to our culture!!!
. . . Wherever German is spoken, the Duden [dictionary]'s is the
only script that's valid! . . . Only our twisted birds of the left
. . . make use of the writing of the terrorists."★

Another response to this volume of poetry that came through
the mails consisted of the ripped-out page containing the poem,
"Meditation on a Torso" and a typewritten postscript.

> ### Meditation on a Torso
> > . . a (late antique) marble
> > statue of Venus . . . , which
> > through the obligatory casting
> > of stones by centuries of
> > pilgrims to St Matthew's
> > who were supposed to show
> > that they were abjuring
> > paganism by this act, has
> > been reduced to unrecognizability (catalogue)
>
> The darkness in the fist
> is a piece of the darkness in us
>
> Whoever raises their fist raises
> The dark as badge
>
> And in the moment that we stone,
> darkness in us is
> thick as in the stone

Below the poem are the typewritten words, "The bourgeoisie is
much in your debt! The fist of the revolution will reach
you! . . ." Such are the formulations of intellectuals.

To be a writer means also accepting one's own life as a
consequence of the esthetic.

Translated by Patrick Diehl

★ In German, the normal spelling would be *Terroristenschrift*; here, the word had
been spelled *terroristenschrift*, with the lower-case first letter underlined.

Edith Anderson

Town Mice and Country Mice
The East German Revolution

Edith Anderson is an American writer and journalist who from 1960 to 1967 was Berlin correspondent of *The National Guardian*. The German exile she had met in New York in 1943 went home after the war, became editor-in-chief of a large literary publishing house, and sent for her. Consequently, for half her life she has lived in a divided Germany, first West, then East.

After her husband's death, Ms. Anderson stayed on in East Berlin, where she has a family. She is currently writing a memoir entitled *Cold War Marriage*. The following essay is an eyewitness account of recent private and public events amid the cataclysmic changes she has seen during the crucial days of the 1989 revolution in East Germany.

Coming back from Marienbad last April I got a ride with my sanatorium roommate and her husband as far as Dresden, where my grandson picked me up to help with the baggage, and we took a train bound for East Berlin. It was a day like midsummer and getting hotter.

We found two seats at the door end of a stuffy compartment for six in a nonsmoker. Opposite us was a sober, trustworthy looking chap of twenty-eight to thirty improving each shining hour by doing paperwork connected with his job. At the window on his side sat a young, almost attractive lady about his age, smartly dressed by East German standards, and desultorily reading a paperback.

They were obviously not together. There was an unoccupied seat between them, and they used the formal *Sie* to one another when speech was absolutely unavoidable, such as, "Do you think you could get the window open?" (Nobody could.) Across from her, next to me, was a bright-eyed little man in his fifties who turned out to be a Russian.

We went straight to the dining car, the young man having kindly agreed to mind our things, and when we came back we saw shed sweaters on the empty seat. The window was slightly open. The two young people were conversing quietly. My grandson asked me to help him with his English homework, and we were deep into it when I noticed that our neighbors opposite were calling each other *Du,* the familiar form, and talking politics.

But strangers did not talk politics on East German trains unless they were drunk, in which case everyone else studiously ignored them. People who for decades lived side by side in the same apartment house, even a small one like mine where you greet every inhabitant by name, didn't talk about politics, although one tenant might drop a significant word to an especially trusted person and the other might raise a meaning eyebrow — nothing you could quote. You never knew who might be a spy from the State Security (called *Stasi* for short, though always in a lowered voice after a cautious glance around). But here the quiet, well-behaved young man, not drunk at all, was literally getting hot under the collar, ripping off his tie, saying that the people of this country had just about had it.

"I give it one more year before something busts," he said.

"Six months," she replied with a hard look. She wasn't drunk either.

His head steaming, the young man went out into the corridor to smoke, pulled down the window for air, then turned around and, overcome by bravado, shouted through the open compartment door, "All right, call the police! I'm waiting!" He half laughed, felt a bit foolish, because who was going to turn him in — an obviously American grandmother and a schoolboy? Or the Russian bursting with *perestroika* and *glasnost*? He had been trying eagerly to get into the conversation, except his German wasn't good enough.

My grandson was alarmed. He whispered, "He's exaggerating, isn't he?"

I answered gingerly, not being sure of his mother's truth policies, "Well, a lot of people here are very angry." But I felt my own scalp creep, as if some law of nature had broken, a sheep instead of baaaing shouted in a human voice, "Enough!"

The young woman had hit it right on the nose: six months. The unthinkable happened here.

In May there were local elections in which the count was rigged to look as if nearly 100 percent of the voters were content with the slate foisted on them. This was not new in itself. Manipulation had long been suspected, but hitherto it had not been quite so brazen. And it used to be easier to push people intimidated by successive regimes to the polls to approve candidates of whom they knew nothing. All they knew was that everything would remain as it was, or deteriorate. East Germany's legislatures were pathetic ciphers yessing decisions made by a nonelected caucus. The fact that quite a few responsible and conscientious individuals sat there in silent resignation only emphasized the helplessness of the whole people. Not a single channel for democratic action existed.

A man known to be from the State Security, the *Stasi*, always the same coldly handsome and unbending man, rang doorbells in my house before elections and pressed on every tenant a numbered pink voting card intended to make us fear the consequences if we failed to turn it in for a ballot.

East Germany was run by a party known as the SED, usually called the Communist Party by foreign journalists because it was too much trouble to explain the initials. It consisted of approximately 1⅓ parties that had merged a year after World War II ended: the old, decimated KPD—Communists—and a leftist breakaway from the revived SPD—Social Democrats. The name

SED simply meant Socialist Unity Party of Germany. The unity proved to be that of a crocodile with its meal.

Three years later, in response to the founding of the Federal Republic of Germany in the Western occupation zones, the Soviet Union launched in its own zone a German *Democratic* Republic, on whose surface lightweight "bloc" parties bounced about like corks. There were a Peasants' Party, a Liberal Party, a National Party, and a Christian Democratic Union, none of which had anything to say but created the illusion that various interests were represented. They all occupied actual headquarters, had a few names included on slates, and published shadowy little captive newspapers that lay about at the hairdresser's or in dentists' waiting rooms.

By May 1989, however, watchers fed up with not being represented managed to witness the count in enough polling stations to be sure the official figures were the most outrageous fraud perpetrated to date. Naturally, they could not publish their findings anywhere, but in such cases West German radio helped. Since no candidate represented genuine opposition, the voters could only cross out names. Many had crossed out the entire slate. A popular young lawyer, Gregor Gysi, asked by a client to check the ballots in her polling station, was denied access. A low rumble like the beginning of an earthquake was heard in the GDR. After a while it seemed to die away.

It had not died away. Too many other things were wrong, worst of all the soothing syrup of the media. Too much was missing from the shops. A taken-for-granted item would disappear, come back, disappear again. Meat in the window of the butcher shop nearest my house consisted at one point of unidentifiable remnants; the sausage smelled and tasted as if meant for uncritical dogs. Women's clothes were frumpy. They hung unbought on the same racks for as long as three years. Or they were ridiculously ostentatious, besides being out of style (if they ever had been in style) and costing a fortune.

There were no spare parts to fix home appliances or cars. Assembly lines were halted for want of supplies from auxiliary plants. It was the same on building sites, and the workers stood idle and furious. What good was this kind of socialism? Why did everything work so smoothly in the Germany next door? Who in the GDR was responsible for this balls-up?

The rulers and the people hadn't been introduced. The rulers lived in Wandlitz on a lake north of Berlin in houses surrounded by forest, which in turn was enclosed by barbed wire. It was taboo to the media. The private lives of the occupants were so perfectly shielded from scrutiny that it was easy to believe such unattractive people had none. News photos showed the Politburo, or it might be the Council of Ministers, facing the camera as a line of boring old men in dark suits and conservative ties standing neatly side by side at some official function. In one shot I recall they had all placed the tips of their shoes at the exact edge of a rug, as if touching the floor would incur a heavy penalty.

A closer look at the photos revealed a token woman in the Politburo lineup, dressed as nearly like a man as possible. In the Council of Ministers, the wife of the head of state could be found in another rectangular costume with lapels. She was the Minister of People's Education.

They were not actually hated, because no one knew what they were up to. They were resented though. They obstructed the view. Of reality. Primarily they obstructed it for themselves. They did not perceive that the intelligence of an unhappy people was being criminally wasted.

A couple of years ago the West German magazine *Stern* interviewed Politburo member Kurt Hager, one of whose functions was the tyrannical fondling of "culture." He preens himself on his theoretical acumen. He has a professor title. In reply to *Stern's* query, "Will there be *perestroika* in the GDR too?" Hager said snottily, "Would you, when your neighbor puts up new wallpaper, also feel obliged to repaper your home?"

West German publications could not be had in the GDR, but the interview was reprinted there as if it were something to be proud of. The wallpaper sideswipe at Gorbachev and at the people's own hopes infuriated everybody and became one of the banana peels on which the Party slipped.

In August, hearing that Hungary had taken down the barbed wire separating it from Austria, some East Germans on vacation in Hungary tried to cross over and proceed to West Germany. The Hungarian frontier guards were uncertain how to deal with this, but a fermenting government in Budapest soon jettisoned its scruples about offending, perhaps mortally wounding, a Warsaw Pact partner and ordered the guards to let East Germans go where they pleased. Other GDR vacationers holed up in the West German embassy in Budapest, causing intense discomfort to the staff and themselves, and waited for an agreement with the GDR that would enable them to go to West Germany legally.

A handful who had taken their holidays in Czechoslovakia, which was still loyal to the GDR, swam the treacherous currents of the Danube to reach Hungary and either made it with nothing left but the clothes they had on or drowned.

Few people over thirty-five were among the growing band of infatuated East German adventurers so confident that they could make out in West Germany. Many of them carried infants, pushed strollers, dragged tired and protesting little children by the hand. Some had had the hardihood (or were good enough mechanics) to drive all the way to Hungary in a Trabant, the cheaper make of East German car, which breaks down at a dirty look.

At last an East German representative arrived at the groaning West German embassy and issued departure permits to the recreant citizens who had put their government in such an embarrassing position. He promised a train that would carry them straight through to the West, but he could not state just when, so nobody was prepared for the announcement one day that a bus was parked outside to take them to the station.

Unimpeded ones grabbed their few belongings and ran for seats. One bus would never hold them all. In their wake staggered girls trying to clutch babies and baggage without dropping anything. Men managed better. Clumsier people fell in the headlong rush and were accidentally kicked before they could roll out of the way. Terrified like everyone else that this bus might be the last chance to reach capitalism, a few Trabant owners left their cars at the roadside to join the stampede.

They had paid from eight thousand to nineteen thousand marks (the latest price) for those cramped little plastic cars. They had waited years to get them. Even for the better class and far more expensive Wartburgs the waiting list was interminable. (To the standard question of reporters, "Why are you leaving the GDR?" a lout whose only encumbrance was a premature beer belly complained that he was "sick and tired of having to choose between a Trabant and a Wartburg.")

As it happened, that bus for which cars were sacrificed was only the first, nor would the train be the last or the only chance to reach the Federal Republic of Germany.

But once on board and heading west, with disheveled clothes straightened and faces washed, the travelers seemed to recover poise and take pride in their achievement. Despite unexplained delays that made the train twelve hours late in Passau, they still looked bright and attractive as they stood at open compartment windows beaming, holding up tots and shouting "Freedom!" to the crowd of well-nourished Bavarians on the station platform. Many of these had waited all night to greet the train. They called out emotionally as they handed up bouquets, "We're all Germans!" "We're one people!" "Good luck to you!"

It was impossible not to be moved and at the same time sick at heart. Very few of these victims of the tug-of-war between Western and Eastern propaganda would find a job. There were already four million unemployed in West Germany, including those who had long since given up trying and been dropped from the rolls. And where would they live? West Berlin alone had 12,000 unfortunates sleeping in the streets. In the FRG 819,000 people are now (as of November) waiting for a place of their own, but no moderately priced housing has been built in years under the Christian Democratic administration.

If any subsequent trainload was met at the border with flowers, TV cameramen did not trouble to record it. The news next day was people having second thoughts in Frankfurt, where many changed trains. A few girls turned away to hide tears when asked about their destination. A young husband was shown on the station platform sobbing helplessly in his wife's arms, both of them blind to the camera, which then shifted to their untended suitcases lying nearby on the floor as if waiting to be stolen. Without comment the sequence ended with a panorama of empty freight containers in an asphalt wasteland, street after street of them close together, as yet untenanted. Was this just a movie-lot nightmare? Did it really exist?

These pictures deterred no one who was determined to go. The initial trickle of escapees turned into a gold rush. Literally. By mid-September the hundreds became thousands a day heading out of the socialist world for the big rock-candy mountain. They had been watching it longingly on West German television all their young lives. They knew from the commercials exactly how they would furnish their homes and make them shine.

The GDR having surrendered its principles in Budapest, the West German embassy in Prague also filled up with refugees. These were not necessarily on vacation. Prague is so near that it could be used as a convenient back door for unwilling GDR citizens, provided they were allowed to cross the West German frontier. As yet they were not; the Czechs were adamant. The refugees slept on double-decker cots crammed into the staff lounge, breathed each other's carbon dioxide, ate charity meals, and used up the embassy's water. Those unable to squeeze inside camped with their children in the muddy garden, shivering in autumnal cold, the unluckier ones sloshing through puddles in their summer sandals.

The reason embassy staffs endured this bedlam (in Warsaw also, to a lesser extent) was a part cynical, part political one. The FRG claims GDR citizens as its own, hence it "owes" them unconditional hospitality when this happens to suit the aims of the administration. West and East Germans alike, so Chancellor Helmut Kohl insists, are part of a greater Germany, which extends from the river Maas in Holland to the Memel in Latvia and from the Adige in Italy to the Straits of Belt in Denmark—according to a stanza of the anthem "Deutschland, Deutschland über alles." The stanza had been deleted for the sake of appearances, but it is now being taught again in West German schools.

When the Prague embassy's plumbing got hopelessly clogged and sanitary conditions indoors and out so noisome that a city-wide epidemic looked likely, the mortified GDR government had no choice but to relieve the Czechs. It instructed them to let its pestiferous subjects enter West Germany without papers, no matter how many might still arrive. As arrive they did.

Yet if they had not done so, more and more each day, the East Germans clinging to home would not have risen in horror at this hemorrhage of manpower and the total ruin they saw coming. It was the runaways, the blithest, least responsible, most uninformed and egotistical sector of the people who polarized still indistinct feelings in all the rest and started an avalanche of dramatic changes that culminated, faster than anyone could have imagined, in irreversible mutiny. It was a historical irony unique among revolutions.

"We're staying here!" roared the first irate hundreds of marchers in Leipzig. By October a hundred thousand skilled workers and professionals had left. Name any calling—whatever anyone needed, the people qualified to deliver it were gone. Education was "free," in other words the nation paid for it, and now the government did nothing but wring its hands while an incalculable investment bled away.

"We're staying here!" cried more and more Leipzigers with riot police at their heels, clubbing, kicking, tripping, and sending them flying, arresting whomever they could grab, but the demonstrations were repeated and sparked to Dresden, Halle, Plauen, Gera, Rostock. Not yet East Berlin. As the capital of the GDR it was the only halfway privileged city.

Leipzig led them all. There the Party apparatus had been most rigid and the people most bitter over decades of intellectual bullying, inferior diet, housing permitted to crumble on its foundations. Every Monday night, after work and a church service, thousands and then tens of thousands set out to demonstrate. They were not necessarily religious. Churches were the only places where people could meet and talk.

It seemed strange that the dogged thousandfold chant of we're-staying-here in no way reassured government leaders, nor were they (as one might imagine) the least bit grateful or proud that workers in a workers' state were marching only after the day's work was done. On the contrary, this terrified them, especially when the shouts changed to *"We are the people!"* No matter how often police smashed up signs calling for democracy, plurality, free media, and free elections, there would be another demonstration and more insubordinate slogans the next night.

The government lost its head. Dithering, it placed severe restrictions on travel to Czechoslovakia, then lifted them a few days later, letting more hundreds of people out. With the fortieth anniversary of the GDR at hand, the seventy-seven-year-old Erich Honecker frantically cast about for a way to save face before Gorbachev.

He had invited his great ally to be guest of honor at the October 7 festivities. He hoped that the sight of a vigorous people's idol beside him on the reviewing stand would make him look more plausible and at the same time help stave off counter-revolution. He seemed to have forgotten the effect of a Gorbachev visit in China. He also forgot that there had never been any revolution to counter.

To make sure nothing spoiled his celebrations, Honecker had Unter den Linden blocked off to everything but a display of military bluff, followed after dark by a torchlight parade of thousands upon thousands of baby-faced adolescents from the provinces in the blue shirts of the youth organization. They were evidently quite excited to be on famous Unter den Linden and gazed about in wonder at the palatial edifices whose windows flashed red from the torches they were carrying so carefully. As they passed the reviewing stand, the nearest of these children looked up with shy smiles at long-suffering Gorbachev. His face was a study. What he said to Honecker in private had availed nothing.

At this hour a young man I know who lives near the Gethsemane Church, a sanctuary for protest in a rundown district, was trying to take his two small girls home from a children's party, but he was stopped by a police cordon and ordered back to safety; they would not be able to reach home.

The small girls with their cut-out paper lanterns and miniature flags probably saved their father from a drubbing or worse. Anyone caught in the vicinity of the Gethsemane Church that night was bestially mishandled, not just the few hundred demonstrators carrying lit candles in token of their peaceful intentions. Nearly fifteen hundred were seized, mostly onlookers or passersby. Some were old, a few were pregnant. While fireworks thundered and showered pretty pink and green stars over East Berlin, these people were hustled in paddy wagons to three different security prisons, where they were forced to strip naked. They were viciously beaten. Many had to stand facing a wall with arms raised and legs wide apart for twelve hours and more.

Apparently this was nothing to what was planned for Leipzig two days later. It was a demonstration Monday. First warnings of a bloodbath came from hospital employees alarmed by the delivery of unusual amounts of blood for transfusions and medication for tear gas injuries. Other persons noticed police officers carrying gas masks. Reverend Peter Zimmermann of the Nikolai Church was alerted, and he contacted Kurt Masur, the Gewandhaus Orchestra's civic-minded conductor. Masur got hold of a few sober Party functionaries and with the minister they constituted themselves as a committee and telephoned Egon Krenz in Berlin. He was the Politburo member in charge of security.

Krenz had made himself unpopular by following orders from Honecker to visit Peking after the Tienanmen massacre, and praising Chinese Party leaders for their wise statesmanship.

Now, however, he agreed that political disputes should be settled by political means and promised the committee that no violence would occur. There was in fact a lowering police presence that evening in Leipzig, and the 70,000 marchers held onto each other tightly for the first time. But Krenz kept his word, contravening a direct order from Honecker.

On October 18, in an attempt to save their own necks, the Politburo persuaded Honecker to step down. The leader's mantle was passed to his one-time protégé Egon Krenz, at fifty-three the youngest among them by a generation. A tall, burly man, he had most often been seen smiling approval just behind little Honecker and was widely considered a yea-sayer with nothing much in his head. Overnight he became General Secretary of the SED and simultaneously Chairman of the State Council. In other words, he was head of government. It was not exactly a democratic procedure that endowed him with these two posts, but to be fair there were no democratic procedures in the GDR.

After Honecker's resignation "for reasons of health," another Politburo member, the media muzzler Joachim Herrmann, was sacrificed to public disaffection. Immediately *Sputnik*, the GDR-banned Soviet feature magazine (in German), was reordered by the post office, and the newspapers grew so frank and fascinating that people combed them from front to back and had no more time to read books.

Except one — if you could get hold of a copy. That month the sensational revelations of a nearly forgotten man appeared in West Germany, entitled *Difficulties with the Truth*. It described how, under the reign of SED chief Ulbricht (deceased in 1973) and his sadistic secret-service whip Erich Mielke (still on the Politburo up to December 1989), the outstanding publisher Walter Janka had been sentenced to five years "intensified" solitary confinement, allegedly for counterrevolutionary activities. The real reason was an old grudge of Mielke's that dated back to the International Brigades in Spain. Janka doesn't go into the details in the fragment published — only three chapters of a full autobiography to appear in the fall of 1990. He doesn't even identify his tormentor by name, but knowing Janka I can easily imagine how a cur like Mielke would have resented him, a real man, one with a mind of his own who spoke it and never bowed or scraped in his life.

As we now know, it was Mielke who on October 7 ordered the police brutality that began at the Gethsemane Church. "Beat them to a pulp, the swine!" he bellowed, according to a policeman's testimony before an investigating committee.

Making people strip naked the better to humiliate them was a specialty of Mielke's. But in 1957 before new arrivals in his state security prison dropped their clothes on the floor of the entrance area, they first had to stand at attention and stare steadily at a gigantic portrait of Stalin lest they failed to grasp in whose spirit the prison was run. It was the only portrait of Stalin that had not been removed from the GDR after the twentieth Party Congress, but Stalin's spirit was everywhere. Hence the title *Difficulties with the Truth,* signifying the anguish of a committed Communist who could not come to terms with Party cruelty.

No one was permitted to know where the innocent man was held, nor did we dream under what conditions: in an unheated cell that he was never allowed to leave; denied an additional blanket on icy nights, denied yard exercise, a bath, medical treatment, never seeing another human face except the jailer's, forbidden all reading matter. Four years of this. The full term was commuted only because of anxious, persistent protests from authors outside the socialist world who had had personal dealings with Janka ("I would put my hand in fire for him," wrote Erika Mann). And in the twenty-nine years of semiobscurity that have passed since his discharge, he was never rehabilitated because, as a no-longer-sung SED song went, "The Party, the Party, it is always right."

As the book was not yet available in the GDR, the most telling and shattering parts were read aloud by an actor in the Deutsches Theater, East Berlin, on Saturday night, October 28. Many people wept. The reading was repeated a week later, broadcast and televised.

The timing of the revelations, no coincidence, certainly contributed to the fall of the Politburo and what passed for a government.

It was writers and artists, first prudently enlisting the cooperation of Mayor Krack and the chief of police, who organized the demonstration of November 4 in Berlin that turned the tide; but the multitude of half a million who poured into the great central square was a cross-section of the whole population. They overflowed Alexander Platz, spread out in all directions as far as the eye could see, and changed the image of Germany.

Volunteers wearing armbands that said "No violence" wandered among the people as troubleshooters, but there was no trouble. Girls pinned flowers to the uniforms of astonished policemen, a sixties gesture hitherto unknown in the GDR.

All at once the listless, passively grumbling citizens of East Berlin were articulate, free and open, serious, thrilled. Platform speakers and demonstrators reciprocally uplifted and transformed one another in a tremendous explosion of unity and self-discovery.

But woe to him who mounted the platform and uttered a word of cant. There was a mass allergy to Party jargon so potent that it gave Berlin's Party Secretary Günter Schabowsky the shock of his life. The very words "my Party" spoken in a proprietary way called forth shouts of contempt. Smiling, Schabowsky looked quite amiable, but when the crowd drowned him out his forehead distorted into two ugly bulges. The reddening face clenched to a fist as he leaned forward threateningly, yelling unheard against a tornado of boos and shrill whistles that finally blew him from the platform.

A speech especially moving for its sincerity and sense was made by the minister Friedrich Schorlemmer of Wittenberg (Martin Luther's town), a gaunt, genial, sandy-haired man descended from a friend of Marx and Engels. He told the demonstrators that a coalition of reason was needed, not just emotion overflowing its banks.

"We have lived in a stooping position, dulled and patronized," he said. "Today we are coming to ourselves. We can be proud. We will not be kept in reins any longer. But fear is not yet overcome. Today the police hold out a velvet paw, but many fear the claw beneath." He entreated justice "to an SED that is changing. Our country is on the rocks," he said. "We cannot rebuild it without the SED, but the SED *need not be in charge.* Democracy now or never! More kindness and warmth! As Luther said, 'Let minds grapple, but fists be still!'"

The lawyer Gregor Gysi also asked for justice — for Egon Krenz, whose name elicited hostile noises the moment it was mentioned. "I happen to know," Gysi said, "that on October 9 in Leipzig it was Egon Krenz who made the decision between a Chinese and a democratic solution to the crisis in the GDR. He decided for democracy." No one had heard this before. Liking Gysi they wanted to believe him, but there were skeptical boos. "Egon Krenz deserves a chance," persisted the lawyer, who for his part made no bones about being a Party member. Which nobody minded. At this time Gysi was defending the right of a reformist citizens' organization, New Forum, to legal existence. "But," he said, to cheers, "this has to be the last time anyone becomes head of state in the GDR without being elected."

It was a day of rejuvenation. Christa Wolf, sixty, whose novels have long been heavy with gloom, looked at least fifteen years younger. Within two weeks she had written four brilliant polemical pieces. She spoke of revolutionary renewal. "We must not sleep away the chance this crisis offers," she warned. "We must not, through mistrust, endanger the dialogue we have begun." Before her allotted five minutes were up she exclaimed, "Police: Change your duds and come with us!" — "Dream wide awake!" — "A suggestion for May First: The leaders march past the people!" — "Picture this: Socialism, and no one's leaving!"

As the crowd laughed and applauded, she added, "Those are not my words, I'm reading them from your posters. They come from the literary treasury of the people."

More barbed slogans and cartoons had been painted on wallpaper in derision of Kurt Hager and plastered to the sidewalk in front of the Ministry of Culture.

The last of twenty-five speakers to mount the platform and the one lightest on her feet was the eighty-one-year-old, extremely corpulent actress Steffie Spira. She threw up her head, stood erect like the soldier she is, and said in a strong voice, "I left this country in 1933 with nothing in my hands, but in my mind Brecht's poem in praise of dialectics. It ends like this:

> *When the rulers have spoken*
> *The ruled will speak.*
> *You who are lost, fight!*
> *Those who have grasped their situation — how can they be*
> *   stopped?*
> *For the victim of today is the victor of tomorrow,*
> *And out of Never grows Now!*

"I wish my great-grandchildren a time without schoolyard calls to the colors. Without compulsory patriotism classes. Without blue-shirted youth carrying torches and being forced to parade past higher-ups."

Here she raised her hand above her, conjuring up Erich Honecker in his gray fedora playing father of his country, while Politburo members bored out of their minds flanked him on either side. This was the price they had to pay on every national holiday for their considerable privileges. More considerable, as it turned out, than we ever suspected.

On the street just behind the platform scaffolding stood Berlin's arrogant Party Secretary Schabowsky alone, ignored, still trying to take in what had happened to him. The Party leadership had fatally underestimated a demonstration called by mere artists and writers, and he had been left holding the bag. As the crowd thinned out, Pastor Schorlemmer noticed him, came over, and laid a brotherly arm around his shoulders.

"I see," said Schabowsky with an effort. "As a soulsaver you're trying to console me, is that it?"

Schorlemmer smiled without replying and Schabowsky managed to recover the use of his limbs and go home to Wandlitz to digest the lesson he had received.

"This was the greatest historical event since the French Revolution," said an unexpected personality next day, West Berlin's relatively new Social Democratic mayor. A quiet and collected, modest man who can fight, Mayor Walter Momper became an insistent partisan of the GDR. "Where democracy is concerned the West can learn a few things from the GDR," Momper said, "social responsibility, for example, and disgust with an elbow society." He appealed to the West not to endanger the "magnificent" happenings in East Germany and denounced Chancellor Kohl's "flagrant inability" to recognize their significance.

Egon Krenz, however, had missed the boat again. Now he hastily called a demonstration of his own. It was well attended, partly because so many workers wanted to give him a piece of their mind. He tried to mollify them, promised that more reforms would be instituted and wrongs righted. He never forgot to smile except when the furious whistling, chanting, and booing so dismayed him that the starch went out of his mask. He still did not know what time it was.

Having moved house helter-skelter from Wandlitz to Berlin, he found a girl from East German TV at his door with a camera crew first thing next morning. They were allowed to photograph the family at breakfast, sitting on too-shiny copies of antique chairs. Then Krenz took the visitors into a small reception room, where the girl fired questions from the hip in rapid succession without once looking friendly. "Why are you shielding Erich Honecker?" she demanded.

Krenz replied, "There is such a thing as political *Kultur*."

At an impromptu meeting around the front steps of the Central Committee building after the committee had resigned in a body, Krenz desperately promised waiting workers to keep the same promises he was always promising to keep.

"Too late!" they shouted. They wanted any mention of the SED's "leading role" deleted from Article I of the GDR's constitution. A couple of days afterward Krenz announced that he agreed with this. Too late. It had deleted itself.

The whole Politburo was forced to resign and with it willy-nilly Egon Krenz as General Secretary. A figure without substance, he then gave up his second post as Chairman of the State Council. Neither post was needed. There will be no new Politburo and no State Security Ministry to terrorize and spy on citizens. A new constitution providing new structures of government is being worked out by representatives of the formerly impotent "bloc" parties, the Evangelical Church, the reformed SED, and a dozen new citizens' organizations with various special interests.

Only the People's Chamber, now democratic in its composition, functions as a real parliament. It elected as Prime Minister Hans Modrow, sixty-two, a lifelong Communist banished to the provinces by the Politburo for his embarrassing honesty and integrity.

But now a welter of corruption among the GDR's former leaders began to come to light. It was flabbergasting in its dimensions. No private lives? Embezzlement was their private life. They took foreign exchange from government coffers. They appropriated public lands as private hunting grounds, with wanton ignorance slaughtering animals to no purpose and ravaging their habitat. The tearful-looking head of the so-called trade union federation, Harry Tisch, stocked up 20 percent of an entire province for his absurd butchery and camouflaged the territory with road signs identifying it as army property. Wiping his streaming eyes, he also used a large cruise ship meant for trade unionists' holidays as his own yacht, entertained his cronies on it, and paid the bills out of the federation's treasury. Others at no expense to themselves had luxury homes built for their middle-aged children and adult grandchildren, ordering only the finest materials from capitalist countries.

The full extent of the mafia run by those homely men in the dark suits and conservative ties is not yet known. A river of filth flows from Wandlitz and has many tributaries.

The result was that half a million SED members, as many people as overflowed Alexander Platz on November 4, handed back their Party books. Some quit out of revulsion, rage, heartbreak; others because as disappointed opportunists they expected no more favors.

The question of how old, committed Communists who had suffered for their beliefs could now have sunk so low was raised by Gregor Gysi in his report to an emergency Party Congress. Briefly his explanation was Stalinism, the cold war, an ill-considered decision in 1956 to create a Wandlitz for the protection of top leaders, and in consequence their gradual, at last total, isolation from the people and reality.

"It has to do with a whole system that is wrong," he said. "Domination by one party leads to domination by its leadership, and domination by the leadership necessarily leads to domination by the top leader and his advisers. If these are the wrong kind, that's what happens."

Toward morning Gysi was elected Party Chairman, with the mayor of Dresden as his deputy. The title General Secretary was dropped. After seventeen hours of exhausting discussion no one had come up with a satisfying name for the reformed party, so they decided on SED-PDS (Party of Democratic Socialism), which not only looked like alphabet soup but still contained three fatal letters: S-E-D.

Not even Gysi realized that other people no longer cared to distinguish between criminal leaders and an honest rank and file, between Stalinism and socialism. Quite suddenly, overnight it seemed, everyone but themselves hated the SED. Not until a sign began to appear in demonstrations saying "Gysi — Stasi — Nazi" did it strike them in the pit of the stomach.

Gregor Gysi is a pale, prematurely bald man with a lightning intelligence and the tenacity of a first-rate lawyer. He has no leadership ambitions, was virtuously coopted into his thankless new post, but was too idealistic to turn it down. He gave up his law practice. He was certainly the only candidate who, all other things being equal, had any conception of how to handle this deepest crisis his country had ever faced, and to do it within the limits of democratic legality. Unfortunately, all other things were not equal. From moment to moment the situation changed like the design in a kaleidoscope that is rolling downhill. He has suffered some stunning shocks. One was the resignation from the SED-PDS of his own deputy, Mayor Wolfgang Berghofer, who only ten days earlier had referred to Gysi in a talk show as "my comrade in arms." Berghofer took with him thirty-nine other members of the Dresden city government. The ground under the Party's feet had grown too hot for smart politicians.

For the outside world it was the opening of the wall on November 9 that constituted the great event. Of course the wall had to be opened, and would have been, but why that very minute and all at once? The move was ordered in blind haste by Egon Krenz to appease the people and save his position. By panicking he threw away a hand full of aces, a primary bargaining point in negotiations with West Germany. The result of this idiocy was the uncontrollable mess his successors inherited.

Freedom to travel, if only from East to West Berlin, is a blessing mixed with gall when your only money is nonconvertible. It is the old story of the town mouse and the country mouse.

West Germany has long donated a hundred west marks once a year to any visiting country mouse who cared to collect it. After the wall opened the country mice had to stand in long lines like beggars at a soup kitchen to get this money. Most admitted it made them feel ashamed. A hundred marks don't go far. What would these people do next time? None of the alternatives was conducive to GDR independence.

They could exchange their nonconvertible east marks in the west at a horrendous loss; by the second week of freedom the rate was twenty to one. The east marks, literally thrown out the window, then return in Western hands to East Germany and buy up — for example — subsidized products. In this way town mice eat country mice out of house and home.

East Berliners can lay off sick and work a few hours a day or full time in West Berlin, using part of their earnings to pay bills cheaply in the East and the rest for luxuries. During this time they have produced nothing in their own country.

Or they can leave outright, and they do. The exodus has not diminished. This is precisely what happened before the wall was built in 1961; hence the wall.

There are differences between then and now. For one, some influential people in the West, not only West Germany, have developed an admiration for the GDR since its revolution, in much the same way as anti-Semites changed their feelings about Jews after Israel won the Six-Day War. There was a growing interest among politicians and businessmen in helping the GDR's economy get on its feet instead of sucking out its entrails and gobbling the rest when it could no longer help itself. A January poll in West Germany found 53 percent of its entrepreneurs seeking some form of cooperation with the GDR. Volkswagen pioneered in planning an improved Trabant to be built in Karl Marx Stadt. But all these friendly hands held out hopes, not consummation. Real help was dilatory, awaiting the results of a free election. Scheduled for May 6, it was moved up to March 18 to stem the exodus.

Would it? The two thousand still leaving each day had fewer illusions about quick success. It was a stable society that they longed for.

Meanwhile the East German government had a new adjunct, the Round Table, actually rectangular and very long. Here sat — or stood in furiously wrangling clusters — representatives of all the old parties, the churches, and the aggressive, politically raw little parties and organizations — twelve? eighteen? — that had rapidly mushroomed in the name of democracy. Their function was primarily advisory. Impossible to remember their various names, New Forum, Democratic Awakening, Democracy Now, United Left, etc., or what they had said they stood for last week. Their televised sessions sometimes looked like a mass cockfight.

This calmed down abruptly after the New Forum made a serious mistake, calling what they thought would be a civilized demonstration (their spokesman was a professor of philosophy) at Stasi headquarters. It quickly got out of hand. Convinced that the Stasi had not really shut up shop, some demonstrators stormed the place, smashed in the gates, doors, desks, files, threw furniture out of windows, sent reams of paper flying down stairwells. Many were in a rage because fired Stasi employees were awarded a year's severance pay. Others joined in the riot out of a frightening unleashed hatred that was only looking for an outlet, any outlet. But no one was left in the building.

Many thoughtful East Germans have realized for a long time that some kind of confederation with West Germany was desirable, but they did not want the exorbitant *Anschluss* demanded last year by Chancellor Kohl—quite rudely demanded—in a hasty ten-point takeover ultimatum that would have ripped from the GDR its last shreds of pride. The European Community has condemned Kohl's plan. Nobody in Europe wants another united and overbearing Germany.

Nobody except neo- and other Nazis, who have been crawling out of the woodwork all over Germany. In West Germany they have been allowed to run for office and have won more seats in every local election by demanding the restoration of prewar borders. When their leader in the "Republican" Party, former SS man Franz Schönhuber, claimed in November to have underground cells in the GDR, nobody here believed it, but they do now. Anti-Semitism, hushed up by the Honecker government, never reported, rose to stark visibility when the Republicans scored their first election success. Two years ago a young woman I know found a star of David and the words "Jews get out" scratched into her door. Gravestones in Jewish cemeteries were and are regularly knocked over or defaced. And now the neos have invaded Leipzig.

The Monday demonstrations there never stopped, they became a kind of ugly sport. Their composition changed as they grew in numbers and belligerence. The new crowd no longer shouted "We are the people," but "We are *one* people," "Germany *one* Fatherland," "Red Army clear out!" and of course "Gysi—Stasi—Nazi" although the difference between themselves and Nazis is hard to discern. Older and cruder demonstrators began to predominate in mid-December, waving West

German flags (i.e., East German ones from which the insignia was removed) and threatening opponents of instant *Anschluss* in a Greater Germany. Two such opponents—and this took guts—held up a streamer quoting the last line of Brecht's *Arturo Ui*, a grim satire on Hitler: "The bitch who bore him is still in heat."

But such people are afraid to appear anymore. Assorted rabble come over the border every Monday night and hand out eagerly grabbed literature and posters sent by the "Reps." No one stops them. No one confiscates the material.

Berlin's police chief, the latest one (there has been considerable turnover), stammeringly explained on television why policemen are suddenly so backward about stepping in. "Our police are confused," he said. "They were trained to protect a class, the SED, and were reprimanded when they did. Now they're told they have to *protect* the people, but that might also turn out to be wrong."

Has it really been a revolution? Or is it only what Bishop Werner Leich of East Germany calls it, "a period of agitated transition"? Perhaps a revolution is just that.

Eric Gabriel

November in Berlin

Eric Gabriel is an American who has lived in West Berlin since 1985, after originally growing up in New York in the Bronx and the section of Manhattan called Hell's Kitchen. Author of the novel *Waterboys* (published by Mercury House in 1989), he has written numerous short stories published in the United States and Germany. Winner of the National Arts Club Award in 1983, he is also an accomplished musician, playing the piano in West Berlin nightclubs.

Mr. Gabriel's essay offers a unique perspective on what it was like to be in Berlin both before and after the heady days in November 1989 when the infamous Berlin Wall came down and its "evil spell" on history was finally broken.

A Friday afternoon in the Tiergarten, the large park in the middle of West Berlin. The weather is mild for the first weekend of November, but fumes from hundreds of coal stoves leave a grayish haze in the sky and a slight needling in the nose, which reminds you that it's winter. A pale moon shadows the silvery ball atop the television tower in East Berlin. The tower is a fixture of the eastern skyline, a response to the Funkturm in the West. The ball is mirrored with numerous metal panels resembling something in a disco. A last bit of sunlight leaves a cross-shaped reflection on it, which accounts for its nickname: St. Ulbricht, the cathedral of socialism, recalling the East German head of state Walter Ulbricht under whose leadership the tower was erected. Walter Ulbricht was also responsible for another fixture of the Berlin cityscape: the wall. At the edge of the Tiergarten, at

193

Potsdamer Platz, a piece of that wall has been taken away, allowing East Berliners to pass through and see what they haven't been able to see for the past twenty-eight years: the other side of it.

That Friday, about twelve hours after East Berlin opened its border to the West, I biked to Checkpoint Charlie. This border crossing point is normally reserved for the Allies and is crowded mostly in summer, when Americans flock to East Berlin to see how ugly and gray life is under Communism. Once it marked the beginning of Berlin's great white way on the Friedrichstrasse and later it marked where tanks faced each other during the darkest days of the cold war. That Friday, the streets were packed with people streaming past the East German border guards, their ID cards freshly stamped with an exit visa. Cars from East Berlin slowed to a crawl alongside the crowds of West Berliners waiting just over the white stripe painted on the asphalt, cheering every car with an East German license plate, handing cans of beer to the drivers. (Cars with East German diplomatic plates got no cheers. They'd always been able to cross the border freely.) The West Berliners were euphoric, the way the French must have been, meeting Lindberg after his flight across the ocean. Considering what had separated East from West before, the comparison is no exaggeration.

Berlin at the turn of the century was an imperial capital with wide streets and millions of people. After World War II and the building of the wall, West Berlin shrank not only in size and population but in scale. The Kudamm—Kurfuerstendamm, West Berlin's shopping and entertainment district is always crowded, but otherwise West Berlin always seemed to be the calmest big city in Europe. With the border open it regained some of its turn-of-the century chaos as its population doubled in a matter of hours. Streets once easy to navigate from one end to the other swelled with people. Whole stretches of subway lines could no longer operate. The smallest streets bustled.

In a city where traffic lights are ordinarily more important than pedestrians, motorists tolerated masses of people crossing streets in the Italian fashion—every which way. The Kudamm became a pedestrian zone altogether. West Berliners, normally blasé toward the wall, suddenly rediscovered it, turning the area between that opening at the Potsdamer Platz and the Brandenburg Gate into a promenade. People smiled for no reason, and total strangers struck up conversations with each other; commonplace behavior in New York, uncommon — even suspicious — here. East German border guards, the last of the unyielding, unsmiling Prussians, seemed friendly. I saw three wearing roses in their lapels, given them by East Berliners returning home.

It was strange to see so many people standing on every corner, noses buried in street maps. There are always enough tourists in West Berlin, yet the city is no tourist mecca on the order of Paris or Rome; people in search of *Mitteleuropa* go to Vienna. The East Berliners weren't put off by any lack of points of interest. When I asked people what they planned to do while in West Berlin, most replied, "I want to see what the place looks like."

And then the Trabbies. Next to bad coffee and the low speed limit on East German highways, the Trabbies (from *Trabant*, German for "satellite," no irony intended) are what come to mind when West Germans think of The First Worker and Farmer State on German Soil (the GDR's official subtitle). A rather homely looking car reminiscent of a 1960 Rambler with a two-cylinder engine, Trabbies reach a top speed of sixty-five and come in colors that used to be termed easy on the eyes, i.e., dull. Emission control standards prohibit Trabbies from being driven in West Germany but an exception was made for the East Germans. And suddenly West Berlin was full of them. "Trabbies on the Kudamm," read one headline, as though the sight of them side by side with the Mercedes cruising past the expensive stores showed that things had truly come full circle. The air took on that unmistakable East European heaviness, noticeable even in a city like Berlin, long reputed to have the worst air on the continent. The Trabbies were a phenomenon all to themselves. The first Trabbie stolen. The first Trabbie smash-up. Trabbies have also been reported with slashed tires and smashed windows: backlash against the "other" Germans.

West Berliners could enjoy being tourists without ever leaving home; the sheer number of people from the East—and their Trabbies—made it feel as though they'd actually brought East Berlin along with them. I found myself looking at people I passed on the street, wondering, East or West? It wasn't that hard to tell: who else would be taking a stroll on my street—no tourist attraction—at ten o'clock on a weekday morning, family in tow? I walked into my corner drugstore to find it full of people "just looking." In a drugstore. I saw people riding the elevated subway line with their noses pressed against the window, scrutinizing the scene passing below. Beside them sat the locals—Turkish women doing their knitting or rows of bored-looking punks. When I asked an East Berlin couple their impressions, "It looks like Berlin," they said.

Not everybody in the East came to West Berlin, though. Ex-GDR-Chief Erich Honecker is rumored to be in Switzerland.

The breaks in the wall, necessary because the regular border crossing points couldn't handle the flow of people waiting to enter West Berlin, seemed to signal that the evil spell of history was broken as well. People stared unbelieving, as East German cranes lifted away the slabs of concrete along the Bernauerstrasse, setting them down nearby like the monoliths of a new Stonehenge. It was along this stretch of the wall that people once flung themselves out of the windows of the adjacent buildings to escape into the West. The break at Potsdamer Platz was fraught with equally dramatic overtones. Once the heart of Berlin, with more traffic than any other spot in Europe, Potsdamer Platz is now a dusty no-man's land, severed by the wall, the grimness relieved only by the bright orange car of the nearby magnetic railway shuttling back and forth overhead. It is a place where history seems especially cruel, even if you don't know that Hermann Goering lived nearby in the Leipziger Strasse, or that Hitler's Reichschancellory stood right around the corner. Nearby, before the Brandenburg Gate, another historical pulse point and Berlin's symbol, people climbed up onto the rim of the wall during the night of November 9. West German police had to stop them from taking pickaxes to it, and still many did.

Television crews set up shop nearby, waiting for the moment when the wall before the Brandenburg Gate will fall. Meanwhile, East German border guards are now stationed along the rim, lit by the lights of the television crew, looking like actors frozen in a *tableau vivant* against the neoclassical backdrop of the Brandenburg Gate, as though in a production of a Greek tragedy.

West Berlin has taken on the character of Germany during its economic miracle phase of the 1950s. Lines of East Germans can be seen standing in front of the banks and post offices to pick up their hundred marks "welcome money," given out by Bonn to overcome the discrepancy of value between the West and East German mark, a difference of ten to one. The media report the impact of the wall being opened in terms of sales volume, as a Christmas season sale might be. (West German stores are preparing for what promises to be the most lucrative Christmas shopping season in years.) Newspapers print photographs of happy East Germans celebrating their purchases of goods unavailable in the East. The bitter strife over the store closing hours has been temporarily forgotten so that merchants eager for their share of those hundred marks may keep their stores open late. Produce stands have been set up on every other corner to exploit the East's chronic shortage of — and the East Germans' hunger for — fresh fruit. If the wall was a symbol for East Germany's isolation from the West European mainstream, the banana has become synonymous with its reentry.

To see the masses of people trudging back to the border crossing points loaded down with full plastic shopping bags, it seemed the most important way in which the West differed from the East was not by virtue of personal freedom but rather purchasing power. People coming over at Checkpoint Charlie were met with large signs put up by a food store chain offering a free pound of coffee. Those leaving were given free packs of cigarettes. A small demo was held on the Kudamm, presumably for the benefit of the East Germans, protesting the "capitalistic reunification." It received little sympathy. "You don't know how good capitalism is," someone shouted. "Go over there if you like it so much." Still, it was hard to see Wittemburg Platz knee-deep

in plastic cups and empty Coke cans and not think that opening
the border did nothing more than channel money into West
Berlin cash registers. On the other hand, how could one expect
the East Germans to be any different from their cousins in the
West? It would be like Americans expecting Europeans to be old-
fashioned and charming.

I fell into conversation with a woman drinking champagne
with her husband on the street — "bars" became another sidewalk
industry — minutes after crossing into West Berlin. She spoke of
the thrill of looking at what was in the window of a computer
store. She didn't say she wanted to buy a computer, or would
have if she'd been given more than that hundred marks. Mate-
rialism? More praise of capitalism? No, simply wanting to feel
that one is in touch with the rest of the world. East Germans
have long complained of being second-class citizens. For years,
the East German government has dealt with the problem in a
manner any Western businessman would approve of. Exquisit
and Delikatess stores in every East German city offer western
goods — at phenomenal prices — which gave something for East
Germans to spend their money on.

"Imagine being kept in a room and then the door opening,"
the woman drinking champagne said. I remember first hearing
about the wall as a kid, seeing a man on the cover of *Life*
magazine lowering himself down a rope in what looked like a
mine shaft. It was like something out of the movie *The Great
Escape.* The wall conjured up images of barbed wire and concrete, the trademarks of the dreary, repressed Eastern bloc. (The
museum near Checkpoint Charlie is a veritable archive of wall
propaganda developed by the West, something like Radio Free
Europe in 3-D.)

I knew about Germany being divided, of course — it had to be,
I was told, so they wouldn't start World War III. But, like all good
Americans, I was poor enough at geography so that I didn't know
exactly how. I'd envisioned the country being split in half, with
Berlin in the middle. Even after I knew about the true arrangement I would have to go to Berlin to realize how, for example,
they separated the subway systems. (That became clear enough

when I rode through those dimly lit stations in East Berlin where East German police watched through little windows in the bricked-up walls.) Even having seen pictures of the wall hadn't prepared me for it live; at first glance I'd thought that the concrete barrier I was walking past separated and encircled an industrial area.

Those subway stations were only part of it. I discovered new incongruities daily: streets divided down the middle. Railway tracks breaking off in midair over a trestle and, perhaps most poignantly, the Brandenburg Gate, the old entrance to the city, sealed shut. The wall left the city with two different official names. East Berlin is referred to in Berlin (West) as Berlin (Ost). "WB" is all that labels the blank space on the left side of the East Berlin subway maps. Road signs in the German Democratic Republic lead West German motorists to a place called "Westberlin" but the East Germans exit at "Berlin, Capital of the GDR," which, as the joke goes, is the capital with the longest name in the world.

If the wall must have seemed inconceivable to Berliners at the time of its construction — imagine one running down Broadway, for instance — for those living there or coming to the city afterward, a wall-less Berlin was equally inconceivable. At an exhibition of public transit in Berlin, I overheard two elderly women arguing about the number of the streetcar line that once ran from Schoeneberg to Pankow, a journey impossible without a visa (and a mandatory exchange of twenty-five German marks) today, although you can still see the tracks where they slip under the wall at Potsdamer Platz. For all my initial shock, I was surprised at how soon I got used to the *Mauer*, calmly including it in travel directions (He lives on Adelbertstrasse, right near the wall . . .) and routing my bicycle around it, as though East Berlin were an industrial area. But I could never see the wall without experiencing a little shiver, and the wall itself never seemed quite as sinister as the concrete watchtowers looming up behind it.

West Germany's single national holiday is June 17, commemorating a strike and protest march of East German workers through the Brandenburg Gate into the Western sector of the city in 1953. Soviet tanks crushed the action. The West Germans seized upon the event to trumpet the freedom of the West, designating it, with some irony, The Day of German Unity, as well as renaming the street leading up to the Brandenburg Gate the Street of June 17. There has been talk of declaring November 9 a national holiday, substituting it for June 17. (I saw a new street sign "renaming" the Street of June 17 appropriately.)

The idea of a new national holiday shouldn't be taken lightly; it would be only the second such holiday. National pride is a touchy subject in West Germany since World War II. (Official jargon prefers the word *federal* to *national*.) One finds relatively few statues of historical figures in West Germany, compared with the rest of Europe. It is clear that West Germans see the opening of the wall as the beginning of a new era. Stripping June 17 of its special status would mean abandoning what the Greens consider to be West Germany's insistence upon reunification as well as an arrogant exploitation of history for the use of Western propaganda. Unfortunately, November 9 already has something to commemorate: the anniversary of the *Reichskristallnacht*, the "national pogrom" of 1938, when virtually every synagogue in Germany was burned, thousands of Jewish businesses were plundered, and countless Jews were murdered and imprisoned. Last year, vigils and exhibits — and the Jenninger address — marked the fiftieth anniversary of the event. This year it has gone by almost unnoticed. Declaring November 9 a national holiday marking the events of 1989 would banish the events of 1938 to obscurity.

Dealing with the past — what the West Germans refer to as *Vergangenheitsbewaeltigung* — seems especially critical now, when the issue of reunification has the potential for stirring up a new wave of nationalism and increased hostility against those seeking political asylum and foreigners, East Germans included. These days, *Die Deutschland Frage* — the German Question — concerns itself primarily with bridging the gap between West and East German marks, rather than between the way each Germany has dealt with the past; West Germany, with money, mostly, and East Germany, by throwing the responsibility onto the West. I didn't

see any flag waving at the border crossing points. But at a city hall
rally just after the border was opened, Chancellor Kohl and Lord
Mayor Walter Momper – and even Willy Brandt – tried to lead
the crowds in the singing of the national anthem. The question
of a national identity, never far below the surface of (West)
German life, seemed to hang in the air of West Berlin along with
the fumes of the Trabbies.

I share the euphoria of the Berliners. I am neither a native
Berliner nor a German, nor did I have family on the other side of
the wall coming to meet me, but my joy was absolute when I
heard the news of the wall being opened. And it baffled me: how
could I, a Jew, share such happiness with . . . Germans? A mere
fifty years before, the masses of people moving down these same
streets were not East Germans on their way to the Kudamm but
Jews on their way to the death camps. I had to put aside my
euphoria long enough to wonder, What about all these East
Germans and West Germans, falling into each other's arms, tears
of joy in their eyes? Did such thoughts dim their euphoria? Or is
the question unfair ?

Perhaps. A fairer question, if no less painful, perhaps, might
be: in the middle of all this hoopla, is it clear to the Germans of
both sides that the wall, viewed in the West as a symbol of
Eastern-bloc repression, is inextricably linked to the Second
World War, a war the Germans unleashed upon Europe? Will the
opening of the wall be seen as an attempt to dispel the fears and
mistrust lingering after that war, or simply as a politically – and
financially – expedient way of eliminating a thorn in the side of
the West and a source of tension for the East? The recent
congress of the conservative Christian Democratic Party, to
which Chancellor Helmut Kohl belongs, gave the subject of
reunification top priority. It seemed irrelevant that East German
groups such as the Neues Forum and the new Liberal Democratic Party have committed themselves to building a new East
German society rather than simply dissolving into the West. At
that city hall rally Lord Mayor Walter Momper spoke against
calling November 9 a Day of Reunification but for calling it a
Day of Reunion instead. Willy Brandt urged people to accept the

existence of two German states. When Kohl tried to speak, crowds booed him away. But for many West Germans, the logical outcome of the borders being opened is reunification.

Not far from Checkpoint Charlie are the remains of the Gestapo headquarters, where the cells once used for torture have been unearthed. Across the street — on the other side of the wall — stands a building that once housed the Luftwaffe. I wondered what would have been the mood at the border if Checkpoint Charlie had been nearer to the Gestapo area, if people coming from East Berlin had had to pass by the narrow underground passages before seeing the glitter of the Kudamm? What if the reunion between East and West Germans had had to take place there? I wondered if perhaps it should have been arranged that way anyway.

And yet I was euphoric when they opened the wall. I enjoyed the luxury of being able to feel truly good about a development in world politics. I could hardly remember the last time I had. When American troops pulled out of Vietnam? When the Shah was ousted from Iran or Somoza from Nicaragua? It certainly has been a while. It's hard to know what will happen in the weeks ahead. But to think that, barely weeks before, thousands of East Germans were packing into West German embassies in Prague and Warsaw to get their exit visas for West Germany. And before that, others were sneaking out in the trunks of cars or tunneling under the wall to escape. Now they're organizing independent political parties. They're coming for the day and then going home. The East Berliners I spoke with said that moving to West Berlin was out of the question, since they had jobs and, above all, apartments in East Berlin. "I ordered a couch that's coming next week," someone said, "and I also have to feed my dog."

Günter Grass

Don't Reunify Germany

Günter Grass is Germany's most celebrated contemporary
writer, a creative artist of remarkable versatility: novelist,
poet, playwright, essayist, graphic artist. Among his many
famous works are *The Tin Drum, Dog Years, From the Diary
of a Snail, The Flounder,* and *The Meeting at Telgte.*

Born in Danzig in 1927, Mr. Grass is also a committed
political activist who has remained a leading voice for
reason, gradualism, and moderation. In this essay he offers
an unpopular view of reunification, expressing serious reservations about a confederation of the two Germanys,
which he worries could become an excessive, swollen, and
dangerous colossus.

Twenty years ago, [President] Gustav Heinemann spoke of
"difficult fatherlands," calling one by name: Germany. That
astute appraisal is now being confirmed. Once again, it looks as if
a reasonable sense of nationhood is being inundated by diffuse
nationalist emotion. Our neighbors watch with anxiety, even
with alarm, as Germans recklessly talk themselves into the will
to unity.

Day by day, the people of the German Democratic Republic
are struggling for greater freedom and razing the bastions of a
hated system by nonviolent means. This is an event unique in
German history — a successful revolutionary movement. What is
actually happening, however, is in danger of receding into the
background.

Other, secondary concerns are thrust to the fore. Numerous
West German politicians demand the stage, and with it, of

course, the spotlight. The West German Government, its Minister of Finance in the vanguard, drapes its cornucopia in glittering
promises, then dangles it ever higher, demanding that the revolutionaries take ever riskier leaps to get it.

Meanwhile, the Chancellor attempts to direct the world's
attention to himself and his 10 point program. And that patch-
work program, wrapped in statesmanlike oratory, met with
applause! A few reasonable rudimentary suggestions obscured its
contradictions and the omissions made with an eye to re-elec-
tion, including once again the refusal to recognize Poland's
western borders with no qualifications.

Disenchantment came the very next day. The hoax lost its
appeal. Reality — in the form of our neighbors' justifiable fears
rooted in their own experience — caught up with the Bundestag.
The "reunification" bubble burst because no one of sound mind
and memory can ever again permit such a concentration of
power in the heart of Europe. Certainly the great powers, with
the accent now on victorious powers, cannot; nor can the Poles,
the French, the Dutch, the Danes.

But neither can we Germans. Because there can be no
demand for a new version of a unified nation that in the course of
barely 75 years, though under several managements, filled the
history books, ours and theirs, with suffering, rubble, defeat,
millions of refugees, millions of dead, and the burden of crimes
that can never be undone.

Such a nation — no matter how much good will we think
we've come to show in the meantime — should never again ignite
political resolve. Instead, we should learn from our compatriots
in the G.D.R., for they were not given freedom as a gift, as were
the citizens of the Federal Republic, but had to wrest their
freedom from an all-embracing system. They have had to struggle to achieve it on their own, while here we stand amid our
riches, poor by comparison.

So what is this arrogance, with its boasts of a favorable balance
of trade and great glass houses? What is this "we know better"
about democracy, when our grade on the first exam is "satisfac-

tory" at best? What is this exultation at their scandals over there, when stench clings to our own?

And measured against the modest wishes of those we presume to call the have-nots on the other side, what is this imperiousness incarnate in the person of Helmut Kohl?

Have we forgotten? Do we want to repress now, too (being masters at repressing), how the smaller German state was weighed down, far more than is just, with the burden of a lost war?

Consider the possibilities open to the G.D.R. after 1945 — and their present day effects. No sooner had greater Germany's systematic coercion lost its power than the Stalinist system took hold with new, though familiar forms of coercion.

Economically exploited by the Soviet Union (itself exploited and ravaged by the greater German Reich), confronted by Soviet tanks during the workers' uprising of June 1953 and then finally trapped inside walls — the citizens of the G.D.R. have had to pay, and as proxies for the citizens of the Federal Republic, to pay and pay again. It was not we who bore the chief burden for a world war that all Germans lost. No, they bore it, in unfair measure.

And so we owe them quite a lot. What is needed is not a patronizing "quick boost" or a brisk buyout of the "bankrupt G.D.R.," but rather a far-reaching equalization of burdens, payable at once and with no conditions. We can finance the debt we owe by cutting our military budget and imposing on every West German citizen a surtax commensurate with his or her income.

Only then, when our compatriots in the G.D.R. — exhausted, up to their necks in water and still fighting for freedom piece by piece — receive justice from our side, only then can we speak and negotiate as equals, they with us and we with them, about Germany and Germany, about two states with one history and one culture, about two confederated states in a European house. The precondition for self-determination is all-encompassing independence, and that includes economic independence.

The hocus-pocus of reunification rhetoric is seductive but gets us nowhere. Once it is set aside, it becomes clear that the suggestion of Hans Modrow, the Prime Minister of the G.D.R., for a contractual community is well suited to the present situation and its eventual possibilities.

This would allow for a commission, with equal representation from both countries, to coordinate obvious matters such as transportation, energy and postal service — and to oversee the equalization payment that the Federal Republic owes the G.D.R. An additional task in the service of peace would be a step by step reduction of defense budgets, as well as coordination of joint German responsibility for development aid to the third world.

The commission could likewise enrich with new meaning Johann Gottfried Herder's concept of national culture. And, not the least of its tasks, it could put a halt to environmental pollution, which disregards all national boundaries.

All such efforts and more like them, if they are successful, will make room for further German-German advances, and so smooth the way for a confederation of the two states, if that is what is wished. But with one precondition: the renunciation of a single state on the basis of reunification.

Union with the G.D.R. in the form of annexation would involve losses that could never be made good. For the citizens of a subsumed state, there would be nothing left of their hard-earned identity — achieved at last at the cost of exemplary struggles. Their own history would sink beneath the dull weight of a standardized history. Nothing would be gained except an alarming excess of power, swollen with the lust for more and more power.

Despite all our protestations, even well-intentioned ones, we Germans would once again be feared. For our neighbors would gaze at us with justifiable mistrust and from ever-increasing distance, which would very quickly give rise to a renewed sense of isolation and with it the dangerous self-pitying mentality that sees itself as "surrounded by enemies." A reunited Germany would be a colossus, bedeviled by complexes and blocking its own path and the path to European unity.

On the other hand, a confederation of the two German states, and their declared renunciation of a unified state, would benefit European union, especially because, like the new German self-conception, it too will be a confederation.

Translated by John E. Woods

PART III

Poland

Ewa Kuryluk

Poland – the World's Guinea Pig

Ewa Kuryluk is a writer, artist, and art historian of Polish descent who has lived in New York since 1981 but has made several trips home during recent years. Having published many books in both Poland and the United States, she is also cofounder and coeditor of the Paris-based Polish magazine *Zeszyty Literackie* and contributes regularly to the *New York Times Book Review*, *The New York Review of Books*, *Arts Magazine,* and *The Drama Review.*

In the following anecdotal account, Ms. Kuryluk offers a very personal view of particular events she has experienced in Poland as Solidarity struggled toward its ultimate victory.

At times history hibernates, at times it runs like a gazelle. On December 13, 1981, the world learned about the imposition of martial law in Poland. In the previous night thousands of Solidarity activists (and many of my friends) were removed from their beds and transferred to camps, and all phone connections with my country were cut. At that moment I was installing my first one-person art show in the United States in a state of shock. I was perplexed by the terrible speed of events. But even more paralyzing was the prospect of hibernation, the fear that our struggle against totalitarianism had been stopped for God knows how long; that once again Poles would have to put up with the "tropical heat of Siberian nights" and excell in jokes in order to survive a futile epilogue of repression; and the fear that for decades I wouldn't be able to return home. Although I reminded myself that a dying horse kicks and that terror, instead of slowing things down, often speeds them up, I dreamt the best minds of my generation going down the drain and saw myself arriving in Warsaw one day at the beginning of the twenty-first century — a gray-haired woman and a stranger.

But history chose not to behave like a marmot. And seven and a half years after the cold winter of the military coup I found myself on a Pan Am jumbo jet flying to Warsaw — the capital of a country that had again acted as the world's guinea pig. Poland took up the interrupted experiment of returning from communism to capitalism and from the "progressive" dictatorship of the proletariat to the "reactionary" parliamentary democracy. The experiment, if successful, had shattering philosophical and political implications. It would question Marxism's main dogma: that the course of history is predetermined and leads from the hell of capitalism to the paradise of communism. And it would disprove the system's basic claim: that the Party has been chosen by the working class to conduct the historical mission of marching everyone to the gates of heaven — a supreme goal only imbeciles and criminals could fail to recognize. While the fall of the dogma remains to be seen, the arrogant claim has recently been refuted. When, in June 1989, Poland held the first mostly free elections of the Communist block, the Party was voted out and almost everyone, and in particular the proletariat, wanted to march backward, not forward. Since Big Brother was suffering from his own *perestroika* headache and couldn't lend his strong arm, the Polish United Workers Party decided to let the unspeakable happen — rather than risk an explosion. Thus political pluralism was reintroduced, and the Sejm, for almost half a century a dead duck of a parliament, was reactivated. A white, quiet building in the back of which our family had lived since 1946, it was now populated by the democratic opposition.

The opposition included a few of my old friends, "Rabbit's Friends and Relations," as they are referred to in *Winnie the Pooh*. A brilliant translation of the English book was published shortly after October 1956 (the end of Stalinism), became the bible of our childhood, and led us to cultivate the Pooh-Piglet type of talk — an unconscious reaction to the false pathos of newspeak. When my plane took off from JFK in the hot and humid midsummer night of late July 1989, I heard some of the official names of the Rabbit's Relations ("crawling revisionists," "agents of imperialism," "banana youth," "antisocialist elements," "Zionists") buzzing in the air; I smiled, covered myself with a blue blanket, and went to sleep enveloped in the comforting sense of victory, which had come sooner that anyone would have expected.

I was awakened by the pilot's voice announcing that we had crossed the Atlantic, reached Europe, and in about two hours would be landing in Warsaw. Passengers lined up in front of the bathroom and nervousness began to creep from the back of my mind, reminding me that "our" majority had won, but "their" minority still ruled. Finally, as the plane touched the ground of the shabby Okecie airport, the voice of a particularly cautious Rabbit's Relation, today a resident of the Upper West Side and my neighbor, reached me from across the ocean: watch out, they may pretend that from now on they'll play chess; but, really, they'll only play their old asshole game.

Indeed. My passport had been extended by the New York Consulate of the Polish People's Republic and carried the stamp "valid." But the security officer opened it and said: invalid. But it's written valid, I insisted looking into his eyes. He avoided my gaze, and I realized that, while he had been informed about chess being in, his knowledge of its rules was vague and he felt compelled — a nostalgic slip of the tongue — to bring back the taste of the old game he had always been so good at. Poor man! He waved his hand with resignation, returned my passport, and mumbled: if you plan to leave, you need a green exit card.

And so I passed, catching the sight of my mother's face glued to the dirty glass wall separating us from the crowd on the other side. Exhausted old women predominated (our flight was delayed, and there were no chairs in the waiting hall). Many of them were overweight, some terribly skinny, and most looked like working-class women. And yet, as I examined their worn-out faces (I had time, the luggage belts were broken), I recog-

nized the familiar features of the Polish intelligentsia and realized that many of them belonged, like my mother, to the country's elite. How, then, was I to imagine the real proletarians, the
underpaid females retiring from the textile factories at Lodz or
the workers of Silesia, one of Europe's most polluted areas? They
too, I thought, were now coming to airports, seaports, and
railroad stations to greet their children arriving from all over the
world. Since 1981 half a million people, the majority of them my
age, had left.

The dubious welcome and the mess made me immediately
grasp what had changed and what hadn't. Clearly, the authorities
were subdued, but their cat-and-mouse mentality had remained
the same. Of course, the Polish pussy, compared to its cousins
east, west, and south, had always had a relatively human face and
not too sharp claws. Still, its scratches did hurt. Absent for eight
years, I had forgotten the pain. Now the memory returned
almost too quickly.

Before coming to Poland I favored a gradual transition of
power: let the defeated Communists form their own government; triumphant opposition, satisfy yourself with the role of a
shadow cabinet, don't rush. Upon my arrival in Warsaw I felt my
moderation melt. Yes, I could watch heated parliamentary
debates and delight in the fact that the familiar faces of the
former state enemies were transmitted daily by the state TV; and
yes, once a week I could enjoy "Studio Solidarnosc," an exclusive
Solidarity program, for an entire hour — at least in theory, since
in practice it was often severed in half by censorship. But, on the
other hand, my days were cut short by having to stand in lines —
for bread or stamps or aspirin — and by hunting for a washing
machine that would replace our long broken one. The hunt,
discouraged by everyone including my mother, who had started
to wash her bedsheets in the kitchen sink, made me discover the
lack or shortage of everything — and the simultaneous persistence
of the system's love for trompe l'oeil. Each friend whom I asked
where to look for washing machines advised me to go to Hala
Mirowska, a Warsaw department store, which recently had been
shown on television: during her last visit to Poland

Mrs. Thatcher had obtained splendid mushrooms there in a shopping mall setting. So I went to Hala Mirowska but found the same old, run-down place, and my question: where is the washing machine department? was answered with: what?

Returning from my futile expedition, I couldn't help recalling the excellent impression Stalinist jails had made on Mrs. Roosevelt. The following night I dreamt about green cardboard, which, for some obscure reason, I wished to use instead of canvas. It had been locked in a sinister sort of building around which I kept circulating. In New York I would have interpreted my dream as purely erotic, but in Warsaw it smelled of something less attractive than sex. Had Freud experienced totalitarianism in his youth, would he have written a different *Traumdeutung*?

In the morning I directed my steps to the passport office, a filthy labyrinth of subdivided corridors and halls, and selected a medium-long line in front of what seemed to be the entrance to the right room. There was a piece of paper taped to the door and covered with childlike script: Exit and Related Matters. Two hours later, my passport in my sweaty hand, I entered the room and asked: could I get a green exit card? A female security officer took my passport, glanced at it and replied: not valid for exit. I felt as if I had been caught in flagrante delicto — in bed with my dream. Speechless, I stared at the flakes of dandruff that had accumulated on the collar of the woman's uniform. A fat fly took off from the ceiling and began to circulate above her head. She moved her hand, as if to repel the insect, opened a drawer, took a piece of cheap greenish paper and placed it in front of me. I grabbed it, walked out of the room, and hurried onto Crow Street — not a dove anymore. Perhaps the dandruff did it. Or the fly. Anyhow, I was convinced that Solidarity had to come out of the shadow.

As I continued on Crow Street, I remembered Adam Michnik's article "Your President, Our Prime Minister" published in the July 2, 1989, issue of *Gazeta Wyborcza,* the daily he had founded before the elections. Opposing the party line of the opposition, he postulated a model in which a Communist president would coexist with a Solidarity prime minister and government. I'd heard about Michnik's view when I was still in another world — a Fellow at the National Humanities Center in North Carolina — and disagreed with him. I found that he was asking for too much, and I welcomed the critical article "Hurry Slowly," written by Tadeusz Mazowiecki, the chief editor of *Tygodnik Solidarnosc*, and published in the July 14 issue of his weekly. Upon my arrival in Warsaw I discovered that many people feared the speed suggested by Michnik. However, my own position began to shift and, as I was about to turn from Crow Street into Jerusalem Avenue, the shift was concluded: Adam is right! We have to hurry quickly!

In the evening I was invited to a party where the Michnik-Mazowiecki controversy was discussed and wanted to present my new position. But instead of stating it in a few words, I was overcome by excitement and delivered a speech full of common-places: we need "our" prime minister and "our" government today and not tomorrow! I shouted. Soviet-sponsored Commu-nism has ruined Poland. Years, if not decades, are needed to rebuild the economy, restore agriculture, overcome the gigantic foreign debt. People who have voted for Solidarity cannot wait any longer. They have to see a tiny bit of improvement, otherwise they'll explode. Everyone knows that there are no carrots to be distributed. But sticks are plentiful, and you, Solidarity guys, have to start diminishing their number. Do what you can do. Replace totalitarian injustice with a comprehensive legal system. Teach the *apparatchiks* the art of complying with the letter of law — and *Kinderstube*. And if they cannot learn these simple skills, let them plant carrots. We have too many passport officers, too few gardeners.

Silence followed, then an old friend asked: any problems with your passport? No, I answered. Then why are you into cultural revolution? He laughed and added: this I call American extrem-ism; it must come from too much jogging. But here we need to hurry slowly, otherwise our history will die from a heart attack. Be good, Ewa, let it take a break.

Maybe history wanted to take a break, but it couldn't. On August 1 the government's new "market policy" (no ration cards, no control of food prices anymore) went into effect. It was to stimulate the private sector, in particular peasants who, for the first time since the Communist takeover, were allowed to sell their pigs and potatoes for as much as they wanted; and, one hoped, it would increase the amount of food, relate prices to salaries, and shorten lines. But in a country where food production and distribution were still state monopolies and private enterprise was largely limited to country folks (the majority of them poor, old, and totally mistrustful of any government reform) the sudden introduction of a laissez-faire policy created, as Solidarity had predicted, chaos and panic.

August 1 was also the day my mother and I took a break. A quarter of a century ago our family had spent a summer vacation in a baroque chateau transformed into a recreation home for artists and scholars. I had promised my mother that we would return one day. Now, we both believed, the day had come, and we embarked on our small sentimental trip. The bus we wanted to take to the village south of Warsaw did not arrive, so I caught a taxi. The astronomical fare upset my mother, and to calm her I explained that the thousands of zlotys I had just paid amounted to two subway tokens when converted to dollars on the black market. You forget, my mother responded, that there is no black market anymore. Now people carry their money to *kantors* (private exchange offices), change them to dollars or rather, you're right, to tokens, and put them under their mattresses. Does this strengthen the Polish economy? Or the American? It might, I replied. How? Citibank could open a branch or two and transfer the hard currency under Polish bedding into American CDs.

Once in the countryside, we tried to keep our upper lips stiff and avoid heavy topics, We chatted about a swan family swimming across our pond, strolled in the park, and largely ignored the lack of milk at breakfast, so far the only sign of the new market policy. But our sense of vacationing on top of a volcano grew stronger every day. As August progressed, bad news kept getting worse. Inflation soared to 300 percent or 500 percent or 1000 percent, depending on the region. In some foodstores everything was sold out by 9 A.M. From other shops goods disappeared for a while and, when they reappeared, their prices doubled and tripled even as people stood in line. Thus migrations in search of supplies started. And while most women hoarded, most men calculated. Those whose monthly salaries now sufficed for five days went on strike.

Meanwhile Poland had no government but only a fresh power trio: the old emperor in new clothes. It consisted of General Jaruzelski, "their" president, General Kiszczak, "their" prime minister, who looked extremely genteel in his checked English-style suits, and a civilian, Mieczyslaw Rakowski who had just proved a complete failure as prime minister yet was now leading the Party. There was a pathetic touch to the group, since each man had to pretend to be the opposite of what he had been known for, but the case of Rakowski was particularly ironic. Normally, the post of first secretary represents the epitome of power in a Communist country. But Rakowski obtained it too late. When he finally succeeded, he found himself presiding over an association of veterans whose cause had lost.

General strike was in the air. And "their" prime minister invited everyone to participate in his government. But everyone refused. The explicit "never" of Solidarity was followed by the more subdued "nos" of the Peasant Party and the Democratic Alliance. In the past, these two small parties had been the puppets of the Communists. But at the beginning of August 1989, they began to remember their injured pride, redefine their long erased identities, and show signs of independence. It became clear that no figure of public standing would join Kiszczak's cabinet.

In the second week of August, the radio in our room fell sick with hiccups and the local newspaper stand had been burglarized and closed, so we relied on television and gossip. Both media were upset about a Lech Walesa proposal to form a government that would include Solidarity, the Peasant Party, and the Democratic Alliance. And exclude the Communists? Tension increased, and people started to speak in apocalyptic terms. The metaphor of the ship enjoyed the greatest popularity. The man, from whom I bought a pound of very green apples for the substantial sum of 2,000 zlotys, remarked with a sigh: ah, if I had 2,000 greens (dollars), I would jump off this ship, before it goes down. In the evening TV treated us to a blond beauty wailing about "our red and white boat seeking a safe haven" and to *Ship of Fools*. At midnight a melancholy middle-aged commentator compared Poland to the *Titanic*.

The comparison made me notice the extremely loud orchestra playing on board. No evening passed without an international piano or rock festival, a jazz or dance event inaugurated in a spa or in the middle of nowhere; and in Warsaw, 60,000 Jehovah's Witnesses gathered for their first world congress on Communist ground. They prayed, sang, performed mass baptism, and exchanged addresses in the Stadium of the Decade, a huge sports arena they had rented from the state, renovated and furnished with pools of water. *Polityka,* the official weekly, which once had been headed by Rakowski, praised the Witnesses for replacing fifty miles of broken boards, repainting all the benches, and installing modern toilets. Further the paper reported that the congress was attended by 15,000 brothers and sisters from the Soviet Union, many of whom had been punished for their faith with up to twenty-five years of jail or camp; this was their first trip abroad, and they considered it the beginning of a new era.

In addition to modern hits, the orchestra played war melodies. Especially popular were songs of the Warsaw Uprising that had broken out on August 1, 1944, had been carried by the enthusiasm of twenty-year-olds and had ended in death and destruction. The decision to rise against the Nazis was taken by the London-based Polish government. According to postwar Soviet and Polish propaganda, the government had been "a bunch of reactionaries and idiots" who kept Stalin in the dark. But in fact Stalin was informed, and he even encouraged the Uprising. The insurrection started when the Red Army was already on its way to Warsaw and thus could assist the Poles. But Stalin stopped the front at the outskirts of the city on the east bank of the Vistula, and for forty-six days had his soldiers watch the city struggle — and go under. When the order to cross the river was finally given, the capital was in ruins and a cemetery.

Warsaw was rebuilt, but the Uprising remained a taboo topic. Only in August 1989 could the Soviet role finally be mentioned in public; and a monument to the revolt was erected on one of Warsaw's main squares. The story of the Warsaw Uprising touched upon two other taboos: the Ribbentrop–Molotov Pact, a secret partition of Poland (on September 1, 1939, Hitler invaded the country from the west, and on September 17, Stalin annexed its eastern territories); and the Katyn massacre of Polish officers (they had fled to Russia after the outbreak of the war and were killed by the Soviets who, however, accused the Nazis). Jacek Kuron, the founding father of Polish dissent, addressed a tearful crowd gathered at the Warsaw Powazki Cemetery for the restoration of the Katyn Memorial, a piece of sculpture that had stood there once before. One night it had disappeared and was found only now — in a police storage room. The Hitler–Stalin Pact also had been found recently in Soviet archives and was passionately debated this summer. Two questions were repeatedly asked: did the Pact encourage Hitler to invade Poland? And, if so, was Stalin coresponsible for starting World War II?

On August 15 we returned to Warsaw by taxi (buses were on strike), just in time for the political gallopade. When, on the afternoon of August 17, I walked into the editorial offices of *Gazeta Wyborcza* (which, I noticed with delight, were located in a former kindergarten), electricity was in the air and Helena Luczywo, one of the editors whom I remembered from childhood but now hardly recognized, greeted me with: we're about to become a government paper. And a man whose familiar face I couldn't identify added: by next week we'll have "our" prime minister; and you're going to write for us on what's new in New York.

And so it was. On August 24 the parliament elected the Solidarity candidate Tadeusz Mazowiecki, the man who six weeks earlier wanted to "hurry slowly," in an almost unanimous vote (378 for, 4 against). The next day *Gazeta* published Michnik's article "My Best Wishes to Our Prime Minister," a tour de force of charm and wit. He wrote: "none of my opponents has publicly admitted his mistake in an equally short time and in an equally gallant manner." I read his piece in a bus carrying me to a PEWEX (dollar store) on Rose Street, where my month-long hunt was crowned with success. I returned home with a fancy Italian San Giorgio washing machine and — a Diana of dawning democracy — I embraced my mother and exclaimed: we shall overcome. However, the urgent question of who would remove the old and install our new *machina* soon cooled me down.

In the evening, watching our prime minister, whose exhausted face was beamed at us from around the corner, I couldn't help remarking how *he* would have to find the right people to remove the old junk and put up the new stuff. And he needs a friend or relation in America to pay for it, my mother completed my thought. In greens.

Later that night I went for a stroll in the back of the Sejm, quiet by then, and along the upper border of the Park of Culture. A monster of garden architecture, the park descended all the way to the Vistula and consisted of cement-made terraces, gigantic staircases, statues of male and female proletarians, vases, columns, fountains, and other Stalinist-style paraphernalia. By now everything was half-broken and enclosed with wooden fences hiding the vistas I had longed to see. On my way home I stopped in front of a bust showing a good-looking young gentleman with an impressive moustache. His name was Francesco Nullo, and he was a native of Bergamo and a Garibaldian. When the 1863 insurrection against the Russians had broken out, he rushed to Poland, heading Italian volunteers, and was killed in battle. To commemorate their local hero, the citizens of his town presented Warsaw with his pretty likeness. The monument was put up at the end of our short, narrow street and the beginning of the park. As a child I passed here every day, and I regarded Nullo — what a name! — as part of my life.

Illuminated by the faint light of a single lamp, Francesco's profile looked a little sad. A romantic idealist, he died, like Lord Byron, for the freedom of a foreign country. Such a sacrifice is not necessary today, I whispered, touching my fingertips to the fine features of his bronze face. It's a pity you can't be our emissary and tell the world that Poland needs help to shake off totalitarianism without violence and bloodshed—and that the world needs Poland. At this time of transition, a period slightly reminiscent of your own revolutionary day, armed struggles can easily erupt in Riga or Peking. Our experiment, if successful, can convince humanity that a peaceful path is possible. The survival of the Polish guinea pig is in the interest of all Rabbit's Friends and Relations. We count on their common sense, as our ancestors counted on your courage.

A man stopped and stared at me—a lunatic talking to a monument. The moon emerged from below our house. A plane flew above Nullo's head and reminded me that in three days I would be back in New York. There, idiot, you can address a live audience, I admonished myself, and walked home: to Frascati Street No. 1.

Leszek Balcerowicz

The Price of Polish Economic Reform

Leszek Balcerowicz is a member of Solidarity and Minister of Finance in the Central Council that governs Poland. What follows in this address to the Sejm, the lower house of the Polish National Assembly, is his proposal for the fundamental restructuring of his nation's economy, including quick stabilization measures and extensive systemic changes to control inflation, balance the budget, change the balance of payments, provide credit, incentive, and developmental funds, improve financial management of state enterprises, revise taxation, reduce subsidies, make new investments, and carry out extensive privatization of state property—all goals that he acknowledges to be difficult and formidable but absolutely necessary.

I

Mr. Speaker, may it please the house. The government entrusted me with the honorable task of presenting to the house proposals of great significance. Sejm decisions on matters that the documents being submitted concern will, in fact, determine the implementation of breakthrough changes in the Polish economy. They will open for every citizen and for all of Poland new prospects for a dignified life, free development, and fruitful work which brings satisfaction.

Council of ministers chairman Tadeusz Mazowjecki, while presenting the new government's program in September, spoke about the need to halt the destructive inflation and about the need to restructure the economy and base it on models that have been tested.

This need was reiterated by the further development of the economic and social situation. The system we have inherited from our predecessors can no longer exist. It has become the source of disintegration of the economy, disorganization and degradation of life, and dehumanization of interpersonal relations.

Polish society understands this. Society's support for the government and for the social forces backing it, despite the difficult living conditions, is indebted to this understanding. Our proposal is an economy based on market mechanisms, with an ownership structure that occurs in highly developed countries and that is open to the world: an economy whose rules are clear to everyone, in which it is the abilities, knowledge, talent, skilled hands, and willingness to work that count. One must end the fake game in which people pretend that they are working and the state pretends that it pays them. The alternative we are proposing is a real life instead of a pretend one.

For the first time for many years the aims set for society are clear and pragmatic. They were not invented in nineteenth century doctrines but they are concrete aims, and are perceived as such beyond the Baltic Sea and the Elbe River. Societies whose institutions and solutions we want to implement are not ideal and free from difficulties, but they do have the conditions in which to develop and to solve their problems on their own.

We are aware of the fact that the fundamental restructuring of the economic system will be implemented in extremely difficult conditions. Lasting systemic faults that are the result of the extremely irrational system of managing the economy for many years form especially part of these conditions. The accumulation of the effects of these faults and the errors of the economic policy of the previous government have contributed to the exceptionally sad results of this year. A dramatic acceleration of inflation has taken place. The economic imbalance has deepened. There has been a fall in production and supply of goods. The budget deficit has been disastrous. The dramatic economic situation at the end of this year is also marked by such phenomena as a decline in the national income, a reduction — the greatest for eighteen years — in the number of apartments handed over for use, a decrease in the coal extraction output, and a reduction in animal production output. The living conditions of people, including the poorest groups, are more difficult. The emigration of the young continues. The ecological conditions are deteriorating.

The efforts of the government since mid-September have made it possible to halt or to limit some of the unfavorable processes. The increasing trend of the budget deficit has been halted. The increase in the population's incomes stopped preceding the increase in prices. The financial situation of many enterprises has improved. Nevertheless, the conditions in which the program of changes is starting are still very unfavorable, even dramatic. However, it must be clearly said: waiting will not improve conditions but will make them even more difficult. The Polish economy is seriously ill. An operation is needed: a deep surgical cut to remove inflation, which is devastating the economy.

May it please the house, when talking about undertaking such an operation we must be aware of the fact that society will agree to it and — what is a fundamental condition — will undertake the process of transformations itself when both the long-term aims and the anticipated effects of the restructuring of the economic system are clear to it. Thus, what are we expecting? What will this process give to the people?

We would like this process to lead us to a situation that is regarded as normal in developed countries of the world and in our country has hitherto been regarded as an inaccessible ideal.

Such a situation occurs when people are rewarded for their hard work, enterprising spirit, and abilities to put their talents to good use, when their work is used in such a way that it brings profit and satisfaction, when the results of this work are not wasted but allocated, according to the will of the country's citizens, for the development of the country's civilization, for its cultural achievements, and for the protection of life and the natural environment.

II

Ladies and gentlemen, the extremely difficult starting situation forces us to undertake measures simultaneously on two platforms: the platform of extensive systemic changes and the platform of rapid stabilization measures. We know well that all citizens of our country are awaiting, above all, the effects of the announced change in the economic system; however, for the time being we must apply the tough logic of the process of transformation initiated in Poland the moment Tadeusz Mazow-jecki's government was set up. It is not possible to construct a lasting structure of the national economy without ensuring stable foundations for it in the form of a strong currency. For this reason stabilization measures should be given precedence. Priority should be given to the rapid elimination of inflation and restoration of economic balance. Already, galloping inflation makes many economic measures pointless, makes citizens adopt wrong approaches and attitudes, and makes effective switching to a new system of managing the economy impossible. Allowing this situation to remain unchanged would mean permitting a hyperinflation in which prices would rise from day to day. This would mean a total breakdown of the economy.

Counteracting inflation takes place in accordance with certain rules. It must take place quickly and resolutely, in a concentrated and universal manner, and it must embrace the entire national economy and entire society.

It should take place quickly because postponing the struggle against inflation leads to failure. In the world economy we know of no slow process of overcoming such enormous inflation with a positive result. Apart from that, there are justified fears that the reserves of society's patience, which is in fact limited, could soon be exhausted if this tedious process is protracted.

It should be done in a concentrated manner because the policy of strict curbing of income increases is inadequate. The entire economic policy must contribute to the struggle against inflation in this decisive period. This means balancing the budget, balancing the demand and supply of credit, stabilizing rates of exchange of foreign currencies, and so forth.

Relaxing one link results in endangering the remaining links by excessive tension and, as a consequence, their failure as a whole. Such a program of fighting inflation is difficult for society. Reducing the amount of money in circulation and reducing demand will therefore lead to insolvency of some enterprises and to their bankruptcy, to emergence of local unemployment, and to emergence of a temporary decline in manufacturing output. Such phenomena, together with an inevitable increase in prices at the beginning of the new year, will result in a temporary reduction in the living standard of the population. I know about it, we know about it, and we do not intend to conceal it from anyone. However, there is no other solution, particularly because even larger scale difficulties would appear if any other means were applied. So, you must answer the question: what is better — to live constantly with high inflation in a situation of a growing chaos, or to agree to hardships at this time in order to live later in a country with a stable and normal economy?

We must also explain here that the so-called pay in real terms is a notion transferred from countries having market economies. In our present conditions, real pay is not fully real. The living standard is determined by the exent of real consumption of market goods and services and not by what we could theoretically buy for our wages.

We have experienced this several times in recent years when the government made decisions on increasing wages that were not followed by an appropriate increase in the supply of market goods. Lines grew longer. Profiteering and the black market flourished. For, the fact that you have money does not mean that you can make a purchase that you intended to make. The pay in real terms is the part of our pay for which goods and services can be purchased.

III

May it please the house, the line of action I have presented here is expressed in government documents being submitted for discussion today. These documents can be divided into two groups. The first group is draft acts submitted to the parliament annually. They are: the budget bill, the balance of payments of the state, the balance of the population's money incomes and expenditures, the credit plan, guidelines for the credit policy, and the bills on the culture development, the professional incentive, and the science and technology development funds. The second group contains draft laws introducing changes in the economic system. That is, they are changes in the financial management of state enterprises, in the principles according to which economic activity is conducted in Poland in small-scale industry by foreign legal and physical entities and in economic activity with the participation of foreign subjects, in the taxation principles, in the law on the National Polish Bank, in the currency and customs law, in the law on employment and on special conditions on terminating contracts of employment with employees for reasons concerning work enterprises, in the principles of organizing credit conditions, and in laws on taxation of legal entities for increasing wages, and also in laws on counteracting monopolist practices.

Changes in the budget system mean the elimination of the deficit, above all, by reducing the present enormous amount of subsidies. The share of subsidies in budget expenditure should be reduced by more than half, from 31 percent in 1969 to 14 percent in 1990. The number of subsidized groups of goods and services will be reduced. Subsidies for the municipal and housing economy, municipal and intercity transportation, coal, bread, low-fat milk, and curd cheese will be maintained, although on a reduced scale.

Expenditure on central investment projects, particularly long-term and capital-intensive projects, and expenditure on public security and national defense will be reduced. Financing from the budget for the statutory activity of sociopolitical organizations will cease, with the exception of cases in which the organizations implement tasks delegated by the state. The source for financing these organizations should be income from member contributions, funds, and economic activity. The number of the so-called special aim funds, which ensure the financing of certain expenses from state funds outside the budget, will be curbed.

The budget will be balanced not only through reducing expenditure but also through efficient recovery of money owed. This means, above all, the need to introduce changes in the taxation system. The idea is both to make real the amounts that are indispensable in conditions of high inflation and to reduce the extent and scope of tax relief, which in effect constitutes hidden subsidies.

The application of a highly developed system of tax concessions would, in essence, lead to the creation of costly fiscal privileges. Economic units that maintain such concessions achieved them, after all, at the cost of the rest, reducing their development possibilities. At the same time, we ought to stress that these concessions influenced only to a small degree the desired behavior of economic subjects. It is enough here to point, say, to the example of concessions resulting from improvements in quality, whose application was not, after all, marked by positive results. A move away from extended tax concessions [is necessary], in a direction in which the rational economies of developed countries are going. Tax concessions, however, will be applied to a certain extent in such important social spheres as protection of the environment, the production of materials and products for housing construction, and the introduction of scientific and technological progress.

The great emphasis on restriction of budget expenditure does not mean that we are totally moving away from the application of subsidies, constituting one of the elements of state intervention in the economic sphere. Taking into account the importance of agriculture, the government intends to maintain subsidies aiding biological progress, technology, agricultural production, scientific research in this field, and the development of the economic and social infrastructure in rural areas. A discussion of the most important intentions of the government in this sphere is to be found in the assumptions for agricultural policy in 1990, which were submitted for examination by the esteemed house by the council of ministers.

The scope of goods covered by turnover tax will be expanded, including products sold in Poland for hard currency and for private import. Tax changes in 1990 will constitute the introduction to a fundamental reform of the tax system in coming years. The basis for fiscal and credit policy must be adapting the volume of money to the possibilities of the economy and thus a break with the illusion that problems can be solved by amassing money. This also concerns credits. The interest rate must, therefore, balance the demand for credit with the supply, resulting from the size of bank deposits. A positive interest rate must also compensate for the effects of inflation. In this situation, what is imperative is to move away from the hitherto widely applied preferential setting of interest on credit. This is because it erases the difference between subsidizing and giving credit. In justified cases the backing of economic projects will occur straight from the budget and not through the banks.

To restore health to fiscal policy, what is extremely important is the immediate separation of the central bank from the budget. It is precisely this change that we are proposing in the draft law, submitted to the esteemed house. Its acceptance will put an end to the possibilities of financing the budget deficit through the issue of money without backing.

We are ascribing new functions to pricing policy. Marked inconsistency has hitherto prevailed in this area. On the one hand, we had to cope with the wide range of free-market prices; on the other, many prices of the basic means of production were administratively blocked, motivated by the needs of the struggle against inflation. In reality, this was a struggle against the symptoms of this disease and not with the disease itself. The continuation of this policy would lead to results that everyone knows very well: lines in the market; shortages of goods and chaos; a bad price structure in the system of the functioning of the economy;

and an incorrect economic calculation. Currently, the basic element of pricing policy will be liberalization. The freeing of prices with the simultaneous intensification of financial policy ought to allow us to eliminate universal shortages. The government, however, does not intend to resign from the control of prices, with the aid of antimonopoly legislation.

For the process of inflation, the overcoming of inflation, not to be too prolonged, we ought from the very beginning to make realistic the hitherto substantially reduced prices of coal and power and other basic economic commodities. They must be raised to a level whereby they could for a certain period be stable and so not stimulate the further increase of other prices. The most difficult period for income policy occurs within the first, decisive stage of the anti-inflation operation.

It is necessary to ensure that pay rises and other income be clearly lower than price rises. The freezing of pay rises is necessary for the money and market equilibrium. The issue is that people's financial resources do not exceed the value of the goods and services available on the market. The stopping of pay rises is also necessary for social reasons, although it may seem paradoxical. Experiences of the past years indicate that enterprises trying to keep their staff give them pay rises, even if later they do not have the resources for development or settling their obligations. In the conditions of the strict financial policy that we must carry out, such actions would lead to a large number of bankruptcies, and following that unemployment and a fall in material production. So if we did not stop pay rises it would contribute to the fall in supply with all its social consequences. The income policy proposed today is made even more difficult by the fact that so far incomes have always been rescued at the last minute, and now neither managements nor crews are prepared for the new situation. Intensive stopping of pay rises however is only temporary. The period of its duration depends, most of all, on the extent of inflation.

IV

May it please the house, the stabilizing of the economy will allow for efficient implementation of systemic changes. If the esteemed house passes and the senate confirms the proposed package of laws, then in 1990 detailed solutions will be made specific and their implementation will begin. Above all, one must list here intentions aiming at the transformation of the ownership structure of the economy. Changes of this scope obviously cannot take place immediately. It is necessary, however, to take advantage of huge resources of motivation for efficient work, resources that are connected with the feeling of ownership. Gradual but decisive restructuring of the ownership structure will bring about the situation in which state enterprises will, for a long time, play a significant role in the Polish economy. Therefore, they will have an indispensable legal and economic independence. Work on legal and organizational forms of these enterprises will be carried out. Changes will also be made in their economic and financial systems, changes that are similar to changes in other economic spheres.

At the same time solutions are being prepared that will make it possible to carry out an extensive privatization of state property, which will be carried out by public sale of shares in enterprises. We envisage at the same time giving preference in buying shares to employees of these enterprises. Preference would also be given to other persons acquiring a small number of shares.

The emergence of communal property as a separate entity will be an important element in the property transformation. This will be connected with the emergence of true territorial self-government and thus will create conditions to give full independence to the communities of towns and parishes. Also, there will be significant changes in the cooperative movement, which will create conditions for the authentically independent activity by various cooperatives.

The changes in property ownership and, following this, organizational changes in the economy will be conducted with energetic combating of monopolistic structures and practices.

The proposals for relevant solutions have been included in the draft law submitted to the Sejm. Here, the point is in particular to prevent the collusion of economic units, which would eliminate competition, and to counteract production and trade aimed at increasing prices. The effectiveness of these actions should increase owing to the creation of the independent antimonopoly office.

The introduction of the new economic order depends to a large extent on the function of money in the economy. That is why it will be so important to continue the reconstruction of the banking system. It will involve, above all, supporting the creation of commercial banks, including a network of local banks. We hope that the newly created banks, including those with foreign capital participation, will become a factor encouraging the development of the Polish banking system.

The unified exchange rate of currency will be an important element of the system changes. It will make it possible to achieve internal convertibility of the zloty. The administrative rationing of foreign currency will therefore be abolished. The rates of exchange, in connection with the whole economic policy, will be shaped in such a way as to contribute to the rapid control of inflation. An additional safeguard will be a stabilization fund, amounting to approximately $1 billion, whose award we are expecting in the next few days. I trust that this fund will be made available soon enough and with conditions that will correspond to the pace and significance of measures being undertaken by Poland and the declarations that have been made several times by countries of the West.

The new policy of exchange rates will allow us to carry out an evaluation of the true effectiveness of foreign trade. In this situation the need for export concessions will disappear. The system of subsidies will be maintained only in relation to the turnover with CEMA countries because the zloty's exchange rate against the transferable ruble will not be shaped at the level of its balance. [Sentence as heard.] Together with the internal convertibility of the zloty there will be a liberalization in foreign trade, by limiting the list of goods that require concessions, alleviating the rules on issue of permits for export and import, and unifying the customs tariff.

Negotiations are coming to a close with IMF representatives. In the near future a so-called letter of intent should be signed, containing the decisions associated with the adjustment program for the year 1990. I wish to stress that its basis is the economic program of the government, presented in October 1989. The acceptance of the adjustment program by the IMF authorities is the condition for gaining access to the international credits of financial organizations, that means the IMF itself, the World Bank, and also foreign aid organized on a wide scale. This help should make possible the partial amelioration of the effects of the restoration of internal equilibrium and also contribute considerably to the reduction of the burden of debt servicing.

We will seek, in accord with our creditors, the full postponement of repayments falling due in the year 1990. We will also undertake negotiations with the aim of reducing indebtedness. The condition for the effective change of the structure of Polish industry and also the growth of its production is foreign credit support and also the facilitation of access to modern technologies. The governments of many countries have declared they will grant us credit guarantees to finance import of supplies and also investments. Access to credits on preferential conditions has also been declared. The exploitation of all these credit facilitations will demand significantly greater responsibility from the takers of credit than has been the case in the past.

The creation of a favorable climate of aid for Poland on the part of highly industrialized states has been favored by the acceptance by the U.S. Congress of a program on this matter. It contains decisions on the amelioration of the burden of our debt servicing, the shaping of a favorable stance toward Poland by the IMF and the World Bank, support for the stabilization program, and also the development of private initiative in Poland.

The EEC and the Council of Europe have also come forward with initiatives for economic aid. An important form of aid is the facilitation of access to the markets of Western countries for Polish goods, participation in the training of Polish specialists, the preparation of economic experts' reports, and also cooperation in environmental protection. We have already gained help in food supplies and in access to certain credits. More significant sums will strengthen our economy gradually, in the coming years, conditional on the successful implementation of the economic program.

These sums must be exploited to make our economy competitive on the world market. Such a possibility should also be created by the [transfer] to Poland of funds in the framework of various kinds of aid and the influx of foreign capital on sovereign conditions specified by us. An indispensable condition is, however, that galloping inflation be overcome and that normal economic conditions be created. No serious foreign entrepreneur will do business in a country that is disorganized by inflation.

V

May it please the house, the new conditions that will be created by the change of economic system that is being proposed show the need for the formulation of a new social policy to protect society against the burdens of the stabilization program and to achieve a better quality of life. It will be based upon a significant growth in the importance and breadth of initiatives and local resources, smaller than hitherto interference by the state, and limited involvement by the central budget.

The basic priority in the social policy of the state in 1990 will be the defense of social security. This means the strengthening of the system of welfare protection serving to shield the families that are economically weakest, pensioners, annuity holders, and persons temporarily unemployed. It is obvious that the coming times will demand from everyone appropriate participation not only in the benefits flowing from economic and market values. They will also demand a surrender to the obligations and even rigors resulting from their principles. It can also not be denied that they will demand from those working an effort corresponding to their material aspirations.

Yet no one should feel threatened about the material bases for his existence. The system of social security payments has been left untouched, and the resources for the welfare items in the budget are growing faster than other incomes. The main areas of welfare protection will be: first, the reform of the system of welfare aid to link more closely its organizations with local government, the direct and specific advance of payments, and the starting up of authentic civic activity for the sake of those most in need; second, the maintenance of quarterly revaluation of pensions and annuities, relative to the envisaged growth of remunerations in the socialized economy in successive quarters, and more beneficial principles than hitherto for establishing minimum pensions and annuities; finally, third, a system for effective help for persons temporarily without work. Eventual group redundancies will undoubtedly create a new, materially and above all psychologically difficult situation for persons who will experience these redundancies. The Ministry of Labor and Social Policy is preparing a package of measures for this difficult circumstance that takes advantage of the experiences of highly developed countries in counteracting unemployment and also assuring effective and fast material and training assistance.

Moreover, it is worthwhile to point out social aspects of ownership transformations, which in 1990 will gain a legal basis and will begin to take force. The possibility of purchase of stakes and shares by significant social groups, work crews included, will serve toward fulfilling their life ambitions and in the future also toward increasing income.

May it please the house, the change we are making is a breakthrough. It has a unique character. We have a pioneering role. The world watches Poland with attention. Deciding on this step, we realize its unique character and dangers, but at the same time we are fully convinced about the reality of this task, about its social righteousness. The opportunity ahead of us must not be wasted. We realize that social trust is connected with the expectation of concrete, wise, and fast action. People will not forgive our sluggishness. The situation in the world is also changing. When the government was installed, it worked in conditions different from today's. The development of events in Europe carries hope but also challenges. We are glad of democratic changes in other countries in Central and Eastern Europe, because they also strengthen the movement of international solidarity. But we will have to keep pace with the increase of economic and political power of our partners, especially that of our Western neighbors. We want to be a strong partner for the whole of Europe, East and West, whose interests are not only perceived but also observed. Therefore, any delay in economic changes can constitute an unforgivable mistake.

The laws presented to the esteemed house contain solutions that create a basis for healing the economy and propose to cut to the minimum the period of suffering due to the tempo of changes. This work has been done in a very short time, the more so when one takes into consideration the wide international contacts and agreements required to ensure the efficiency of the government's economic program. I ask the esteemed house that extraordinary circumstances be taken into consideration and that the house assess the proposed laws before the end of this month. These dozen or so days may decide our future years.

I am aware that this will mean concentrated and speedy work, which may have a negative effect on the formal quality of the documents. It appears, however, that in this situation not fully perfected solutions that have been applied at the right time are better than documents that are faultlessly prepared but overdue.

May it please the house, I wish to thank the deputies and senators most sincerely for their assistance to and understanding of the government to date in the period of working on the economic program. This program is certainly a difficult one: difficulties alongside the catastrophic economic situation; behavioral habits and the attitudes of people that were shaped during the period of the state's economic monopoly and the lack of democracy in public life; shortages of simple economic reserves; the training of a section of staff that does not meet the qualifications of the program; uncertainty as to the quantity and time of arrival of foreign assistance, indispensable in the initial period.

There are, however, also positive aspects, which, in my opinion, predominate. These include, above all: courage, solidarity, and the selflessness of the public; its will to achieve changes in Poland; its political wisdom, manifested particularly in recent years; the high qualifications and skills of the young generations; and advantageous external conditions. This is the capital with which we are starting.

Conditions for the favorable restructuring of the economy also exist. These include: the further progress of democracy, the ability of various political groups to cooperate to acheive a superior goal. We are also counting on that which is most important: understanding and an active stance by the public, particularly in the difficult transitional period. The government has up to now experienced such understanding. Society, despite the growing problems of daily life, the danger and uncertainty of tomorrow, has given its confidence to the government, confirming its highly commendable solidarity. This is proof of the enormous possibilities of our society, which in conditions of freedom and sovereignty is capable of achieving even the most difficult goals.

The strength of Polish society and the conviction that we have a well-aimed program are the source of the confidence and belief of the government. People want and need the Poland that we are proposing. We need therefore consistency and joint effort to create such a Poland.

Thank you for your attention.

Adam Michnik

The Moral and Spiritual
Origins of Solidarity

Adam Michnik, forty-three, is one of the founding members of Solidarity, the editor of Poland's first independent
daily, *Gazeta Wyborcza,* and a member of the Polish parliament. Named "European of 1989" by the French magazine,
La Vie, he is a brilliant essayist, political writer, and historian whose underground writings caused him to be
imprisoned for over five years by the totalitarian regime he
eventually helped to overthrow.

Reviewing his book *Letters from Prison* in its August 15,
1986, issue, *Publishers Weekly* noted, "His program of open
resistance stresses the importance of ordinary citizens' protest in their daily lives . . . . Michnik is an original, strong
voice, and the fierce eloquence of his prose comes across in
this translation . . . ."

What follows is Mr. Michnik's personal reflections on the
moral, spiritual, and political significance of recent revolutionary events, and the implication for the future.

An intimate bond exists between force and deception. This
concept, expressed by Alexander Solzhenitsyn,[1] is exceptionally
valid in describing the state of affairs in the totalitarian world in
which it has been our fate to live. What does it mean to live a lie?
It means above all to establish all one's relations with other
people as relations based on pretence. It means I look a person in
the eye while actually watching his hands. It means that I assume
he is capable of cheating. It also means that I have the same

opinion of humanity in general and of myself. To live a lie means to establish my relations with the world as relations of constant threat. The world wants to do me wrong, and I must defend myself by creating a make-believe world. Deception becomes a method of self-defense.

Living in a totalitarian system, we have all practiced deception. But if we say that our deceit — our deceit in self-defense — served as our dissent against totalitarianism, then we are lying, since to answer deceit with deceit is to answer evil with evil. It is to answer force with fear. This is why we participated in the mock elections, wrote fallacious articles, raised our hands at absurd meetings, and cheered at organized mass demonstrations in support of the totalitarian system. We did this out of fear, we were deceitful out of fear, and in this sense fear of imprisonment made us deceitful. Fear of repression made us obedient. Our obedience was a form of deception based on fear.

Then, at a certain moment, extremely difficult to pinpoint, each of us living with a gag in his mouth and with his body in a totalitarian plaster corset began to break open this corset and to spit out the gag. Our first steps were, and continued to be, like those of a child, stumbling every once in a while. If our first words have so much in common with the babbling of a mute, we must remember, after all, that these steps and these words are not this time the product of deceit or of fear but are really a rejection of deceit, a rejection of fear.

It is immeasurably difficult to trace the path on which a person, first in captivity, later gaining his freedom, rebellious, consequently encounters other people just like himself, and at a certain point, as in Bulat Okudzhava's well-known song, extends a hand to the other person, and they walk on together. "Let us join hands, friends, so that they will not pick us off one by one," sang Bulat Okudzhava, calling us to join the dance, and that, I daresay, was the moment when Okudzhava's gift of poetic clairvoyance gave him a glimpse of the Russian intelligentsia joining hands.

My personal experience is the experience of a man who attempted several times to join such a chain of friendly hands, who was imprisoned for the first time twenty-five years ago in March 1965, who participated in the 1968 student uprising in protest against the anti-intellectual and anti-Semitic hue-and-cry organized by the Communist bureaucracy in Poland, who stubbornly wanted to be part of the independent community, and who saw that this community was being systematically disrupted by the force of police crackdowns.

The first time I succeeded in becoming a link in such a chain of friendly hands was when the Workers' Defense Committee (WDC) was organized in 1976. This was something quite new. Previously the workers would rebel and the intelligentsia would remain calm, either out of conformity, out of fear, or out of a failure to understand, looking with eyes open and mouths shut at antilabor repression. If the intelligentsia, writers, artists, and students rebelled, then the workers remained deaf and dumb, in degrading humility and fear. Sometimes it happened that, to keep the intellectuals quiescent, anti-intellectual sentiments were fomented among the workers, and these incited antilabor and antiplebeian sentiments, guaranteeing the humility and submission of the intellectuals.

The WDC was an attempt to break through this accursed barrier of isolation. The WDC was formed on the initiative of a dozen or so people of different ideological leanings, different traditions, different backgrounds, and different generations, who shared the desire to defend the persecuted workers, to defend the people who, in June 1976, went out into the streets of Radom and Ursus to demonstrate their disapproval of the social policy of the Communist bureaucracy — the drastic price hikes meant to substitute for much-needed economic and political reforms in Poland. To all people in their right minds, to all realists of that time, the people who formed the WDC appeared mad. Ordinary people asked, "Are they hitching their wagon to a star? Are they trying to part the Vistula with a rod? Does this group of thirty people want to challenge the Communist bureaucracy? We all know that is simply impossible. These people have gone mad or worse. Who cares if these people exist, if they suggest to the world that the impossible is in fact possible? Aren't these people provocateurs and cryptocommunists?"

In this mood of suspicion, the hidden bond between force and deception once again coalesced. The cementing element in this bond is fear. Out of fear of force we are deceitful. We deceive ourselves about the members of WDC, saying in Warsaw parlors that they are, at bottom, even worse than those in power because they are Communists with blinders on. We say this to justify to ourselves our own lack of courage, our own conformity, which allowed us to turn our backs on those who were wronged and degraded, those who most needed help, the workers of Radom and Ursus.

The WDC used the strategy of Columbus's egg. They declared publicly that they were organizing as a workers' aid institution, they called on public opinion for assistance and solidarity, and, finally, they signed the declaration with their own first and last names, giving their addresses and telephone numbers. They issued a challenge to the Communist bureaucracy saying, "You signed the Helsinki Declaration on Human Rights, and we want to and will make practical political use of your signature. Here it is: here is our Workers' Defense Committee."

We ourselves did not know at the time that in founding the WDC we were somehow laying the cornerstone of the first independent civic institution to exist on this scale. The WDC campaign as a whole had a model in Polish civic life: the Catholic Church. Not all WDC members were Catholics, although the overwhelming majority of Poles are Catholics. Not all of them would admit at the time that the Catholic Church was actually the first to provide definite proof that it was possible to be an independent institution in a totalitarian political environment, and that the Church itself demonstrated the first type of antitotalitarian action.

Ignacy Tokarczuk, the industrious bishop, by building churches without the approval of the administration (which did not issue permits for building places of worship) showed how it was possible to organize people to build these churches and at the same time, in the process of building, to fulfill the spiritual needs of the oppressed community. On the one hand, they built a church, a building to which people could come to meet God, and, on the other hand, they built the real community that develops around the task of building a church. In this sense, the WDC was the first institution to attempt to build on the model par excellence created by the Catholic Church in Poland in the sphere of the civic community and in the political sphere.

The ethos of the WDC (one must speak of its ethos rather than its program) was the rejection of violence. The WDC program was simple: to reconstruct the civic community, to build its institutions, to revive all of the spheres that had died under the Communist regime. Under the Communist regime, where a person is the property of the state and the state is the property of the bureaucracy, interpersonal bonds die. One does not look a person in the eye, one looks up to receive instructions or down to pass instructions on. The WDC wanted to be a gathering of people who looked each other in the eye. The WDC wanted to prove that it is possible to challenge force and deception, to reject force, consciously choosing conflict without force, and to reject deceit by speaking the truth. In its ethos the WDC was aware as never before that there are causes for which it is worth suffering and giving one's life, but there are no causes for which it is permissible to cause suffering and kill. The WDC rejected revenge. The WDC wanted to wage a war for human dignity without hatred.

Obviously, I am speaking (writing) here about ethos. In the WDC, there were different people, and certainly none of us had achieved that moral elevation; but not only how we live but also how we would like to live is important, after all.

Let me venture the opinion that the ethos of the WDC had a substantial influence on the ethos of Solidarity. During the period after the famous August strike when the workers of the Gdansk shipyard, rejecting force, managed to gain autonomous, independent, free trade unions for themselves in Solidarity, and later when this whole field of freedom began to be revived, the idea of a civic community formulated by the WDC was most fully expressed here. Even later, after December 13, when the police came to our homes and broke the doors open, when we were dragged to police stations and carted off to prisons, the other face of the WDC ethos was revealed — the rejection of force.

Solidarity did not respond with force to the force of the Communist bureaucracy. It responded with something that could be called a strategy of the silence of the sea, a strategy of turning one's back on the authorities. The authorities were severe but no longer persuasive. The community had its back turned, but it was no longer silent. People were speaking to each other. People simply did not want to talk to the authorities. They responded to force by boycotting Party–state institutions.

The refusal to use force remained a lasting component of the strategy of Solidarity. Because of this, in later years, except in times of crisis, the Round Table strategy was possible. The Communist bureaucracy probably intended the Round Table as a kind of trap for Solidarity. Perhaps it was an attempt to gain legitimacy for its own authority, or perhaps it was an attempt to coopt some segments of the democratic opposition into the camp of the authorities in order to gain credibility in this community. But the Round Table became something else: a way for the authorities to legalize Solidarity, and not for Solidarity to legalize the Communist authorities.

The Round Table paved the way for a reevaluation of the previous eight years; it paved the way for rehabilitation of the people who opposed the military state; it paved the way for the first democratic parliamentary election of 35 percent of the Diet and 100 percent of the Senate. The Round Table made it possible for Poland to use elements of the Spanish route to democracy, a scenario in which the reform wing of the ruling camp could find a common language with the democratic opposition, which does not desire a confrontation and understands that political compromises are a necessary condition for democratic order. Finally, the Round Table, with its tradition of thinking in terms of compromise, but consistent and future-directed compromise, was able to bring about a state of affairs in which it became possible for the Communist Party to yield the administration to Solidarity.

The type of reasoning initiated in the WDC epoch, reasoning in which there was equal room for inflexible opposition and for flexible compromise, in the end apparently gave rise to a political system in which cohabitation was possible, in which President Jaruzelski, author of the military state, and Premier Mazowiecki, victim and prisoner of the military state, could coexist, in which this same Mazowiecki and Deputy Premier General Kiszczak could coexist, and, finally, in which all of the above could coexist with Solidarity, the vigorous movement of national and civic emancipation directed by Lech Walesa.

No one can predict how far-reaching these changes will be. Let us hypothesize two logics. One is the logic of epuration, a purification of what was called in post-Nazi Germany de-Nazification. It is the logic of settling accounts. But another logic is possible, the logic of the Spanish road to democracy. In this logic there is room for adaptation to democratic order and to democratic habits on the part of all those connected with the *ancien régime,* with the old administration, who want to and can manage to adapt.

This is a logic that allows us to declare the war has ended, a logic in which there are victorious and defeated ideas and victorious and defeated political movements, but there are no people who are victorious for all time because they were right or people who are forever damned because they were wrong. This is a logic of adaptation, a logic of compromise, a logic of reconciliation. It is in Poland's favor that hatred is not a part of the Polish moral ethos, and it is in Poland's favor that each of us truly understands what a priceless virtue it is to be able to forgive the guilty in public and private life.

The great contemporary Polish poet Zbigniew Herbert wrote in his famous poem "The Unmasking of Mister Cogito" what seems at first glance to be contradictory: "And do not forgive, for it is not within your power to forgive in the name of those who were betrayed at daybreak." Does this mean that Herbert is opposed to forgiving the guilty? No. Herbert is simply opposed to deceit. Herbert says that the truth must be spoken aloud, the guilty must be named, to be forgiven. This is a reference to the Gospel. Christ said: "Love your enemies." . . . One can only forgive only the wrong done to one, not the wrong one does. It is not in my power to forgive in the name of someone else, but I have the right to explain that the ability to forgive is a virtue and that the effort to gain revenge, although understandable, is not a virtue.

It is almost impossible to love one's enemies as Christ commanded. Nevertheless, it seems that, if all of us in the antitotalitarian opposition have managed to accomplish anything in life, then it is only because there were some among us who knew how to forgive. And when I think today of those great people who created the ethos of the democratic opposition, of people like John Paul II and Cardinal Wyszynski, of people of the Catholic Church in Poland and the Protestant Church in Germany, of Andrei Sakharov and Jack Kuron, when I think of all these many people, people who are so different, then I ask myself whether there was some kind of religious background to this antitotalitarian struggle in which I had the good fortune to be a participant. And I answer yes, there was such a background.

We are all witnesses to something that I would call a religious renaissance. This is not simply an increase in the power of the Church and a mass return to religious practice. It is not a collective conversion. It is simply a collective return to issues of transcendence, to issues of whether there is any order that is absolutely hard and fast. I personally think that each of these people, regardless of their declarations and convictions concerning the rationality of the world order, of there being no higher value than human life, people like Andrei Sakharov (who was not at all a believer) lived and acted exactly as if they were bathed in the light of religious reflection and the struggle for fidelity to natural law. It was as if God were watching over them continuously from on high, as if they were aware of the presence of God. We might say that the experience of these people involved in the antitotalitarian opposition was of an ineluctably transcendent nature.

It is no accident that writers such as Kolakowski, Solzhenitsyn, Milosz, and Konwicki, the Romanians Dinescu and Plesu, the Hungarians Janos Kis[2] and Sandor Csoori,[3] the Bulgarian Blaga Dimitrova, the Yugoslavs Danilo Kis[4] and Dobrica Cosic, the Czechs Havel, Kundera,[5] Vaculik,[6] and Simecka,[7] all of these people, associating with people of high moral value, realized at a certain point that they must choose between material comfort — the comfort of money or lucrative positions — and moral comfort that might be accompanied by suffering and poverty, and they chose moral comfort.

Why did they do so? We leave this question unanswered. Perhaps because we cannot answer this question, we tend to rate our behavior as worthy of merit or damnation. To this ignorance we owe our ability to think well or ill of our actions, to consider certain of our deeds as morally right or wrong, and we also have the dignity and the privilege of judging that a moral sin is our fault, but moral merit is our own merit.

Finally we wonder what has now changed? What sort of world is this, that it is not already a world of real communism? While the old order no longer exists, the new order does not yet exist. In other words, our lot now is freedom, but democracy is not yet our lot. We still do not have sufficiently developed institutions of a democratic infrastructure. Talking to people from the West, we feel impatient when we are unable to explain this to them.

Why can't we explain it? Perhaps because, being aware of the inadequacy of their language relative to ours, we are nevertheless unable to suggest using our language and its precise categories. Before our very eyes, the language of the left was destroyed. Before our very eyes, the following words died: communism, the left, social justice. We have neglected onomastics. We know, of course, that the concept of social justice is the most vague of all the concepts of real politics. What does equality of all people mean? Such equality is possible only in captivity.

Let us speak more carefully. Justice means that one person would not look idly at the misfortune and poverty of another. The fact of the matter is, however, that this postulate cannot be directly translated into the language of a political program. Whoever tries to do this opens new gates to new concentration camps.

My country is confronted by entirely new challenges. The Polish political scene will be unlike anything else. It will not continue the factions from the pre-Communist epoch, nor will it continue the divisions of right and left, as in Western Europe. Those divisions appear to be a modern European masquerade.

What will the real divisions then be? Let us take two examples. First, let's look at the argument about the form of the market. We agree that a market is necessary, but what kind of a market? A ruthless market according to Milton Friedman and Chicago Boyce, or perhaps a "market with a human face," a market that will not, in its ideological consequences, be an apology for egotism, brutality, and the Roman maxim *Homo homini lupus*. A market in which mercy rather than ruthlessness will pay, because only this kind of a market will allow the redistribution of goods needed to save our country from violent upheavals of social discontent.

Second, let's look at the division between a European and a nation-centered orientation. The first option rejects Communism in the name of human rights, in the name of a pluralist democracy and human dignity, in the name of the Christian principle of one shepherd and one flock. The second option, the nation-centered orientation, rejects Communism only because it is not ingrained, because it is foreign to the national tradition, because it is Soviet.

It is true that Communism is foreign, not ingrained, and Soviet. But the evil present in Communism cannot be reduced to this. Communism is above all antihumanitarian, aimed at the destruction of the human personality, and for this reason antinational, and not the reverse (it is not that Communism is antinational and therefore aimed at destruction of the human personality). Whoever claims otherwise is expressing implicit approval of a future anti-Communist dictatorship in place of the Communist dictatorship and is at the same time approving all that nationalism leads to — intolerance, xenophobia, and hatred.

Each great change occurs in stages. The first stage of this antitotalitarian revolution, this "velvet revolution," according to Václav Havel, was the battle for freedom. We succeeded in winning this battle. We are free. We have emerged from the underground into the sun of freedom. But we still cannot say what we emerged as. Did we emerge truly free, or did we emerge with a face deformed by hatred? Did we emerge infected with the totalitarian bacillus of political intolerance? These are questions of fundamental importance.

Today this velvet revolution is entering a new stage. The essence of this new stage is a struggle not for freedom but for power, a struggle for revenge. It is the struggle between two spirits present in our culture, the spirit of tolerance, the Christian spirit, which, it is true, sometimes speaks in lay language, and the spirit of hatred, of vengeance, a pagan spirit, which, it is true, sometimes speaks in the language of Christian faith. This actually has determined the course of history in this part of the world, where our countries form a mosaic of nationalities, languages, religions, and cultures. This richness and pluralism of culture gave birth to unique values that came to make up the culture of this part of Europe, but at the same time the mosaic can become a real threat because it contains the seeds of nationalist conflicts.

Stalin was indeed a genius of a tyrant. He constructed the post-Yalta boundaries of Europe in such a way as to make them the source of all subsequent national conflicts. These boundaries are neither logical nor just, but an attempt to change the boundaries today would be a greater triumph of illogic and would engender even greater injustice. Here once again we rise to battle with Stalin. The temptation to national wars must be his greatest posthumous triumph. It was Stalin who programmed the shape of our "native Europe" (to quote Milosz) in such a way that this shape became a point of departure for subsequent national hatreds. Our native Europe is threatened with balkanization, it is threatened with becoming a place of tribal wars and hatreds.

This may happen. Many sociological theories suggest it as a likely scenario. But we must not capitulate before the laws of sociology. I must find in myself the courage to spit in the face of these laws and to say that I will not listen to these sociological predictions whose object is hatred and harm. I will go forth alone, if need be, against these predictions, armed with the basic values of my culture, armed with the conviction that the most important thing in my life is not to be on the side of a cause that is victorious through force but to be on the side of a cause whose splendor is its rightness.

Otherwise, in the words of Simone Weil, justice will be an eternal fugitive from the camp of the victors.

Translated by American Translators International, Inc.

Editors' Notes

1. Alexander Solzhenitsyn wrote *The Gulag Archipelago, Cancer Ward,* and *One Day in the Life of Ivan Denisovich,* inter alia.

2. Janos Kis wrote *Politics in Hungary: For a Democratic Alternative* in 1989.

3. Sandor Csoori wrote *Memory of Snow* in 1983.

4. Danilo Kis, a Yugoslav, wrote *Encyclopedia of the Dead* in 1989 and the Foreword to Karlo Stajner's *Seven Thousand Days in Siberia,* published by Farrar Straus Giroux in 1988. *Library Journal,* reviewing this book in January 1988, commented, "Though Stalinist terror has been graphically described before, few accounts are as horrifying as Stajner's . . . ."

5. Milan Kundera, a Czech, wrote *The Unbearable Lightness of Being* in 1984.

6. Ludvik Vaculik, a Czech, wrote *A Cup of Coffee with My Interrogator* in 1987. He was banned from publishing after the Soviet invasion of Czechoslovakia in 1968. Accordingly, he used the classic Czech genre known as *feuilletons.* These were short literary essays that many Czech writers used and circulated to a wider readership.

7. In 1985, Milan Simecka wrote *The Restoration of Order: The Normalization of Czechoslovakia 1969.*

PART IV

Czechoslovakia

Josef Škvorecký

Czech Writers: Politicians in Spite of Themselves

Josef Škvorecký has lived in Toronto, Canada, since leaving Czechoslovakia in 1969. The author of numerous stories and novels (including the recently published *End of Lieutenant Boruvka*), he is now retired as professor of literature at the University of Toronto, but he continues with his wife to run the Sixty-Eight Publishers Corporation, which specialized in unofficial Czechoslovak literature. Among the authors he has published is Václav Havel.

In the following essay, Mr. Škvorecký celebrates the past and current role of novelists, poets, playwrights, essayists, and scholars in Czechoslovakian history — as spokesmen, politicians, and public tribunes; as saviors of the language and of the national soul — and applauds the fact that in the end it has been the writers who have prevailed, to topple the forces of oppression and lead the revolutionary renewal.

Sitting in a dirty bar in Prague, Nathan Zuckerman contemplates an incredible scene conjured up in his mind: "Styron washing glasses in a Penn Station barroom, Susan Sontag wrapping buns in a Broadway bakery, Gore Vidal bicycling salamis to school lunchrooms in Queens." Then he looks at the filthy floor and sees himself sweeping it. The scene may appear incredible, but Zuckerman's inspiration, in Philip Roth's "Prague Orgy," comes from stark Prague reality. Many eminent Czechoslovak writers have been working at such jobs ever since the tanks rolled

253

into Czechoslovakia in 1968 to put an end to what now appears to have been a sort of off-Broadway preview for Mikhail S. Gorbachev. But given the political role of writers in Czechoslovakia, it is no more surreal that the dissident playwright Václav Havel, during the recent events, should have quickly assumed the leadership of the opposition.

When in 1982 our Czechoslovak émigré publishing house in Toronto, the Sixty-Eight Publishers Corporation, brought out the *Dictionary of Czech Writers* (of the 20th century), it contained entries for almost 500 people whose work had been banned in toto or censored to such a degree that its character was drastically changed. The dictionary listed novelists, poets, playwrights, essayists and scholarly writers and, except for a small handful, the censored writers included everybody who really counts in present-day Czech letters: people such as Milan Kundera, Ludvik Vaculik, Václav Havel, Bohumil Hrabal, Ivan Klima and the Nobel Prize laureate Jaroslav Seifert. In view of this sorry state of affairs, Louis Aragon's remark calling Czechoslovakia a "Biafra of the mind" and Heinrich Böll's description of the country as a "cultural cemetery" were hardly exaggerations.

If, in the 1970s, an American tourist found himself in a Prague hospital, his bedpan might indeed have been emptied by Ivan Klima; the floor of his room might really have been swept by Lenka Prochazkova, a good novelist of the postinvasion generation, and his beer might have come from a barrel rolled onto the brewery truck by Václav Havel.

In societies that curbed liberal freedoms or grossly violated justice, poets, fiction writers, playwrights have traditionally been more than purely literary figures. Milton wrote not only *Paradise Lost* but also a tract on free speech; Swift was not just the author of *Gulliver's Travels* but of a pamphlet on Irish famine; Zola's fame does not rest solely on his contribution to literary naturalism, but also on his involvement in the Dreyfus affair.

In cruel autocracies, such as Russia under the reactionary czars or modern totalitarian dictatorships, the writer's political alter ego has often overshadowed his life as a man of letters. He (or she) didn't even have to produce outspokenly political stuff: the very fact that he put on paper images of life much closer to truth than those offered by censored journalism – not to mention bootlicking ideologists – turned him, in the minds of his readers, into something considerably more important than just a raconteur. A writer, in such societies, became a public figure – in contrast to free societies, where he is essentially an entertainer, even if performing at a level where entertainment appears deadly serious and immensely meaningful.

For close to four centuries – except for the brief interlude of the First Republic between 1918 and 1938 – Czechs and Slovaks have not known the freedoms enjoyed by the British throughout most of their modern history, and by the Americans since they emerged on the world stage as a nation. The battle on the White Hill near Prague, fought in the same year the Pilgrim Fathers reached the shores of America, not only put an end to the political independence of the Kingdom of Bohemia; it also marked the beginning of both political and religious suppression conducted by the Hapsburgs and by their efficient clerical henchmen, the Jesuits. The Society of Jesus first of all put an end to the highly diversified Czech literature by burning every Czech book they could lay their hands on, primarily the Protestant Bible, a text comparable in beauty and linguistic importance to the King James version. The Czech nation was, so to speak, beheaded, for most of the Protestant intelligentsia, the leading intellectual force of the time, were either executed or forced into exile.

Representative of this first great drain in Czech history was the departure for the Netherlands of Jan Amos Komensky, the bishop of the Moravian Brethren and the founder of modern pedagogy, known internationally under his Latinized name of Comenius. According to Cotton Mather's *Magnalia Christi Americana*, Gov. John Winthrop offered him the presidency of the then-new Harvard College, and Comenius might thus have become the predecessor of the numerous Czechoslovak scholars turned American professors after the Nazis and later the Marxist-Leninists outdid the Society of Jesus in thwarting Czech humanities. But Comenius was too old, the trans-Atlantic journey too strenuous; he stayed in the Netherlands and never came to America. His followers did: the Moravian Brethren, largely Germanized when they finally reached the virginal continent from their German exile, but professing the religious and humanist views of their Czech spiritual father.

The beheaded nation lost its literature and, within less than half a century, the Jesuits managed to transform a people who a century before Luther, as followers of the martyred Jan Hus, had been pioneers of religious reform and individualism, into one of the most devout Roman Catholic peoples of Europe. Not only that. Since all higher education was now in German, and German became the prerequisite for all who sought any kind of intellectual or bureaucratic career, the Czech language, by the mid-eighteenth century, was little more than part of folklore. The world of books — except for prayer books for the common folks — became entirely German.

Then *ex occidente* came *lux*. Ironically, it was one of the most German of German philosophers, Johann Gottfried Herder, whose work gave the most decisive push in the direction of national rebirth. To Herder's romantic mind, language was more important than constitution and politics: language should determine all patterns of human life, including forms of government. And languages, like individual people, were marvelously diversified. Therefore, a nation's soul was its language.

It's not hard to imagine the eagerness with which such ideas were absorbed by men and women who found themselves in the schizophrenic situation of rediscovering their often remarkable history as a nation distinguished by its own language, yet speaking that language poorly, if at all. But the German philosopher inspired them even further: in his major work, *Outlines of the Philosophy of Man,* he predicted a great future for the Slavic nations "once they are liberated from the shackles of slavery."

So about 200 years ago these mostly German-speaking Czech intellectuals set to work reconstituting the nearly extinct tongue so that it might become the soul of the reawakened nation. They did it through the printed word.

It wasn't an easy task. In the West, the intervening century and-a-half since the genocide of the Czech intelligentsia and of their language had witnessed the emergence and development of modern fiction and the beginnings of modern science and technology, with the corresponding broadening of vocabulary and poetic usage. Countrified Czech could hardly have coped with such realities if it hadn't been for the efforts of the enthusiastic German-educated linguists. It verges on a miracle that, in the span of less than a century, they were able to develop the poetic but primitive dialect of the farmers into a linguistic tool fully capable of meeting the needs of sophisticated literature and of the scientific age.

The work started with translations rather than with original works: the reconstructors were linguists rather than littérateurs. By 1872 there was no longer a shortage of original poetry or prose either.

Given the extraliterary impetus for this development, it should not be hard to understand that all this ferment was not viewed solely as artistic activity, and not even as something that, in the first place, belonged to literature. To translate, to write was a patriotic duty for those who were capable of doing so. Those who were not considered it *their* patriotic duty to read and discuss what others had written. Thus the writer became everything he had always been in unfree societies: spokesman, politician, public tribune. But on top of that he turned — in the Herderian sense — into the savior of the language, that is of the national soul. When Jaroslav Seifert in 1956 proclaimed that Czechoslovak writers were the "conscience of the nation," he was only reiterating a very old notion.

To carry such a heavy burden in addition to the regular burden of writing well caused various side effects — some benign, some malign. On the bright side, it shaped the Czechs into a people of the book in the secular sense of avid, or at least habitual, readers of belles-lettres. In our own century this tendency was enhanced by the radical censorship imposed on printed matter by the Nazis and by the Leninists. Both made good books into forbidden fruit—but mostly Czechoslovak books only. What, under the totalitarians, was not permitted to the living domestic writer was often tolerated in a dead one, and certainly in a foreigner. The dead and the foreign were unenlightened as yet by the various but always the only true *Weltanschauungs*, and therefore under no obligations to write strictly along the lines of the reigning ideological dictates. And so in spite of the close watch over the publishing business, the liberating message of good books got through.

On the dark side, the "patriotic duty" syndrome caused various troubles even before our times, for the best writers in particular. A Byronic poem, "May," written in 1836 by Karel Hynek Macha—a germinal work of modern Czech poetry—was ravaged by almost all contemporary critics because the rhymed tale about patricide and the spectacular execution of a romantic "rebel without a cause" contained all kinds of gore except the patriotic variety. In verse of exquisite brilliance the poem also evoked the beauty of the countryside; but that, without the patriotic peppering, was also a sin of pure lyricism, much later labeled "formalism."

The Czech writer, from the beginning of the renaissance of Czech literature in the early nineteenth century, had been constantly admonished to mix politics with poetics; indeed, occasionally he was even exhorted to describe Czech life not merely as it is but also—perhaps predominantly—as it should be: an ominous foreshadowing of the demands of the much later Socialist Realism. When Milan Kundera angrily objected to the characterization of his novel *The Joke* by some American reviewers as "a major indictment of Stalinism" by insisting that "*The Joke* is a love story," he was not being absurd—although without the book's particular "joke" and its Stalinist repercussions, its particular "love story" would never have happened. He spoke with 150 years of similar simplified readings of works of art in his bones.

However, the Czech writer was not merely asked to produce engaged literature; more often than not he was also expected to take a direct part in Czech political life. The homes of patriotic families, in the years leading up to the stormy years of 1848, had been adorned with portraits of the scholarly writer-cum-politician Frantisek Palacky, in whom the near-deification of the pen-pusher reached its apogee: he earned for himself the unofficial title of Father of the Nation both for his extensive political and cultural activities (in 1848 he was acknowledged leader of the liberal camp) and for his authorship of the magisterial *History of the Czech Nation*. Begun in German, finished in Czech, this classical work rehabilitated the anti-Catholic Hussites and discredited the Jesuits. A similarly split personality was the founder of independent Czechoslovakia, Tomas Garrigue Masaryk, a philosophy professor and the author of many important books, including literary criticism and one of the first systematic critiques of Marxism. In midlife he turned predominantly political, and eventually ended his long career as the first President of Czechoslovakia, a kind of philosopher-king who, in the sea of fascist and semifascist lands in the Europe of the 1920s and '30s, created an island of liberal democracy, unprecedented in those regions.

Among Masaryk's greatest admirers was a gentle fiction writer by the name of Karel Capek. Although he spent most of his life in a state that was the very opposite of oppression—the original cause of the problematic symbiosis of politics and poetics in the same mind and body—he divided his diligent working hours regularly between intensely politicized cultural journalism and the writing of fiction, plays and translations of French poetry. He paid tribute to the President—with whom for many years he met weekly—in the charming "Conversations with Masaryk" a truly pioneering work of political journalism that, in fact, became the main channel through which the thoughts of the philosopher-statesman reached less sophisticated audiences. At the same time, Capek was a marvelous writer of short stories that were mostly devoid of political engagement, and a pioneering author of brilliant essays on what today is called popular literature.

However, the threat of deadly oppression reached this sensitive man from neighboring Germany, and so he too slipped into this traditional mode of the duty-laden Czech littérateur and produced a series of increasingly political dramas. Having begun as a fairly good playwright with pieces like *R.U.R* (for Rossum's Universal Robots — and yes he did coin the word *robot* from the Czech *robota* meaning compulsory work such as rendered by feudal serfs) and *The Makropoulos Affair,* which was made into the much more familiar opera by Leoš Janáček, he ended with tear-jerking antifascist melodramas such as *The White Illness* and *Mother.*

To put it bluntly, the traditional duty — even though its fulfillment did make a lot of sense in the shadow of Nazism — marred Capek as an artist, and today he is sometimes remembered in the West for the definitely weaker part of his oeuvre, while his truly great storyteller's art is virtually unknown on these shores.

On the other hand, his very practical devotion to the cause of democracy gained him — in a way — the distinction of becoming the archetype of the Czechoslovak writer victimized by totalitarian barbarians. The Munich tradegy killed him: he died barely three months later of a broken heart. In just three months, and a few hours after the Nazi Army had entered Prague on March 15, 1939, the Gestapo knocked on Capek's door. But only his wife was at home; her gentle husband was dead — I'm tempted to say safely dead, for I cannot bear the thought of this man who was the embodiment of human decency in the world of the Nazi gulag.

During the fifty years following that fruitless knock on the door, many Czechoslovak writers went through the ordeal of the camps, and even of the gallows and the firing squad. Capek's brother, Josef, a writer and artist, died in Bergen-Belsen. Karel Polacek, the Jewish virtuoso of the Czech language, died in Auschwitz. Vladislav Vancura, the author of fictions made known in the West thanks to new wave movies such as *Marketa Lazarova* and *Capricious Summer,* was shot in the aftermath of the assassination of Reinhard Heydrich, the Nazi Governor of Bohemia. A few years later, the scholarly writer Zavis Kalandra swung on Stalinist gallows, and the fragile, sick and unique lyricist Jan Zahradnicek survived his release from long years in jail for only a couple of months. To enumerate those who served various terms in the jails of the two dictatorships, from Arnost Lustig to Václav Havel, would take up far too much space.

If the summons to patriotic duty of nineteenth-century authors was questionable and sometimes tragic, the Communist estheticians turned it into a tragic farce. Formalism and cosmopolitanism became high literary crimes. Inspiration by the eternal joys of sexual love led to accusations of "apolitical writing," of which Jaroslav Seifert was guilty most of his literary career. The first generations of German-speaking Bohemians' spontaneous and largely genuine love of their nation became mandatory and metamorphosed into the hypocritical servility of "socialist patriotism"; this bred such strange literary forms as the "builders novel" of Socialist Realism, at one time quite seriously regarded as the highest art form in history. In the end — after the Soviet invasion of 1968 — "socrealism" became mandatory and was written into the statutes of the Writer's Union. Whoever was not a "social patriot" did not need to apply.

The well-known paradox emerged: writers in this new and strange post-1968 colonial society were either rich or lived as paupers on the semilegal outskirts of society, periodically in and out of jail. There was almost no middle ground. The social status of an author depended on his willingness to conform to poor old J. K. Tyl's well-meaning early nineteenth-century demand that the writer describe life not only as it is, but also as it should be. The socrealist theoretician's contribution to the ancient patriot's innocent formula was the leaving out of "only" and "also." The monetary rewards of socialist patriotism were ample and numerous, and after the invasion of 1968, among the general corruption and governmental blackmail, they grew out of proportion. In the '70s, a poet producing one volume of rhymed political trash per year, of which fewer copies were sold than given free to the author, was not unusual, and the most obnoxious party-sponsored "cultural" magazines paid special bonuses for mere willingness to write for them.

It is, however, a well-known lesson of history that ideological purity is deadening and the products of the puritanic muse are, in the end, read only by those who, for professional reasons, have to read them: critics currying favor with the Government. The purity of patriotic artifacts soon become mixed with unpatriotic dirt, both in the Stalinist 1950s and in the neo-Stalinist post-1968 era. In the '60s, "liberal" to some degree thanks to the presence of reform-minded comrades in the apparatus of decision and supervision, the first remarkable post–World War II Czech novelists and playwrights emerged: Hrabal, Havel, Kundera, Jiri Grusa, Vera Linhartova, Josef Topol and others.

In the '80s, after literature had been almost smothered by demands more rigid than ever before—and made even more absurd by the memory of the years in between—the Communist Party dropped many of the most obnoxious literary orders (such as obligatory optimism), and a grotesque form of neonaturalism appeared—a kind of muckraking whose targets were various societal evils, such as prostitution, bribery and the black market. The trouble with this sort of artistic "courage" was that authors were cautiously circling along the periphery, carefully avoiding any criticism of the root of the evil—that is, of the system. That is why no really first-class writers have emerged from this period so far. Of course, we have not yet seen what lies hidden in the desk drawers of the circumspect muckrakers.

But if literature became corrupted, crippled, distorted, suppressed and to a great extent silenced, politics as a profession and as a meaningful field of human activity was, during the Communist era, eradicated. The politician either metamorphosed into the Leninist yes man or disappeared into jail or into exile. To a much greater degree than in the benevolent autocracy of old Austria, in Zola's bourgeois France or in the Russia of the more enlightened czars, the Czechoslovak writer began to assume the role of, first, a conveyer of semilegal thought—that's when the art of writing and reading between the lines developed—and later, the public tribune. He was soon followed by his modern derivation, the auteur film maker, and eventually by the humanist intellectual. Meetings of artists' unions became surrogates for political rallies and party conventions; problems of esthetics, if discussed at all, took a very distant back seat to the questions of the *res publica*. Out of these tumultuous gatherings, the contemporary type of Czechoslovak politician was born: the writer, substituting for the banned, extinct, nonexistent political professional. Foremost among this new breed of politicians were Václav Havel and Ludvik Vaculik.

However, the era of noisy union meetings ended with the intervention of the tanks. Havel, Vaculik et al. lost the microphone. But due to some unclear — and probably, from the party's point of view, pathological — process in the organism of the Communist power structure, which may perhaps be diagnosed as senescence, these scribbling "criminals" were neither physically liquidated nor totally silenced: that is, they were not silenced abroad. New voices within Czechoslovakia joined them to form a hard core of literary dissent, the most visible and influential pressure group of the post-invasion era: Karel Pecka, Eda Kriscova, Alexander Kliment, Lenka Prochazkova, Ivan Klima, Iva Kotria, Zdenek Urbanek, Eva Kanturkova, Egon Bondy, Jan Treulka, Milan Uhde, Zdenek Rotreki — to name only some, and only authors of belles lettres — were among them. There were also scholars, philosophers and theologians. Although vilified, jailed, harassed and perpetually interrogated, they were treated so on the overt suspicion of "criminal" activities, and not because they dared send out their manuscripts for publication by émigré publishing houses operated mostly by writers who had left the country. That traffic in books was a police mystery, thanks to which a strange circulation was established, depending in both directions on illegal means of delivery: manuscripts flowing from Prague to the West, their printed versions returning back to Prague and also sent to various Western countries of the modern Czechoslovak diaspora. In spite of all the efforts of socialist realists, Czechoslovak literature refused to die.

For twenty years the courageous men and women of the Czechoslovak underground seemed to be little more than a voice of one crying in the wilderness. And courageous they were, principled beyond belief. When Václav Havel, in jail and facing charges of subversion, was given a chance to emigrate to the United States, where Joseph Papp offered him a job as a dramaturgist at the Public Theater, he was willing to accept, but only on the condition that charges against all his co-defendants be dropped. The Government naturally could not afford such a loss of face, and so instead of New York, the playwright was taken to a prison job in the foundries. He almost died there when he developed pneumonia that was—perhaps deliberately—neglected by the prison doctor.

In 1977 these men and women of letters founded Charter 77, a group of the courageous ones who challenged the Government to respect its own Constitution. That, too, for many years appeared to be only a tiny voice calling in the desert. But some heard, and—together with many others all over Eastern Europe—the tiny voice grew stronger. In November 1989 the voice became a roar, eventually enveloping even the cautious, the timid and the hesitant. The writers, in the end, toppled the leadership of the party.

Václav Havel

Four Essays

Here are four more short essays by Václav Havel: the first on seeing Gorbachev from the crowd outside the Prague National Theatre in April 1987 as Havel was taking his dog for a walk; the second on the political climate in Czechoslovakia during 1988 as events began to accelerate toward revolution; the third his concluding statements to the appeal tribunal of the Prague Municipal Court in 1989, when he was once again convicted and sentenced to prison; and the final, less than a year later, his New Year's Day 1990 address as president of Czechoslovakia.

Meeting Gorbachev

The proposed visit by the Glasnost Tsar to the very country that is governed by those opposed to glasnost has evidently aroused many expectations. It has brought an unprecedented number of journalists to Prague. They arrive in good time; it is the Glasnost Tsar himself who keeps postponing the trip. And so the waiting newsmen occupy themselves as best they can. Dozens of them call on me; they all want to know what I think of the new Tsar. But it is embarrassing to have to keep repeating the same thoughts over and again, especially as none of them seems at all original to me: whatever I say, I am struck by the feeling that I have heard it or read it before somewhere.

Finally he arrives, and I can relax. The journalists now have something more interesting to do than listen to me telling them things they have already written.

I live near the Prague National Theatre; it's half-past nine in the evening, not a reporter in sight, so I take my dog for a walk. And what do we see? Endless rows of parked limousines and a vast number of policemen. Of course: Gorbachev is in the National Theatre watching a gala performance. Unable to resist, I make for the theatre, and thanks to my dog, who clears a path through the crowd, I manage to struggle through to the front. I stand and wait; the show must be over any minute. I look around at the people on the pavement and listen. They're just passers-by, not an organized 'rent-a-crowd', nor even people who came to catch a glimpse of Gorbachev—just nosy individuals, on their way to or from the pub or out for an evening stroll and who, like me, noticed something unusual and stopped out of curiosity. Their talk is full of sarcasm, aimed in particular at the long ranks of secret policemen, who remain impassive, obviously under orders not to do anything that might cast a shadow on Gorbachev's visit.

At long last the police suddenly came to life, the limousines' lights are switched on and their engines started, the dignitaries begin to trickle out of the theatre. And, lo and behold, there he is, Raisa at his side, plain-clothes cops swarming all around them.

Just then I have my first surprise: all these cynics, all these sarcastic wits, who just a few seconds before were making merciless fun of their rulers and their bodyguards, were suddenly transformed, as if by magic, into an enthusiastic, frenetically cheering crowd, fighting to get as near as possible to the leader-in-chief.

No: this is not about 'eternal friendship with the Soviet Union'—this is something more dangerous: these people are cheering a man who, they hope, is bringing them freedom.

I feel sad; this nation of ours never learns. How many times has it put all its faith in some external force which, it believed, would solve its problems? How many times had it ended up bitterly disillusioned, forced to admit that it could not expect help from anyone unless it was prepared, first and foremost, to help itself? And yet here we are again, making exactly the same mistake. They seem to think that Gorbachev has come to liberate them from Husák!

By now the Glasnost Tsar has reached the spot where I am standing. He is rather short and stocky, a cuddly ball-like figure hemmed in by his gigantic bodyguards, giving the impression of someone shy and helpless. On his face is what I take to be a sincere smile, and he waves to us in an almost conspiratorial way, as if greeting each and every one of us individually.

And then comes my second surprise: all of a sudden I find myself feeling sorry for him.

I try to imagine the life he must lead, all day long in the company of his hard-faced guardians, no doubt with a full agenda, endless meetings, negotiation-sessions and speeches: having to talk to a great many people; remember who is who; say witty things but at the same time make sure they are the *correct* things to say, things that the sensation-seeking outside world can't get hold of and use against him; needing always to be seen smiling and attending functions such as tonight's, when he would surely have preferred a quiet evening and a rest.

But I quickly suppress this twinge of compassion. After all, I say to myself, he has what he wants. He obviously enjoys this sort of life, or he wouldn't have chosen it in the first place. I refuse to feel sorry for him, rebuking myself for acting like all those idiots in the West who melt like snowmen in the sun as soon as some East European potentate smiles charmingly in their direction. Be realistic, I admonish myself; stick to what you've been handing out to all those foreign journalists for the last three days.

Gorbachev, the same man who here in Prague praised one of the worst governments our country has had in modern times, is walking just a few yards away from me, waving and smiling his friendly smile — and suddenly he seems to be waving and smiling at *me*.

And so to my third surprise: I realize that my sense of courtesy, compelling me to respond to a friendly greeting, works more quickly than my sense of politics, for here I am, shyly raising my arm and waving back to him.

Suddenly the small, ball-like figure disappears inside his official limousine and is driven off at a hundred kilometres an hour.

The crowd disperses slowly; people continue their journey home or to the pub, wherever it is they were going before coming across this unexpected excitement.

I walk my dog home and try to analyse my reactions.

And so to my fourth and last surprise: I don't feel the slightest regret at having given Gorbachev that shy little wave. I really don't have any reason not to return the Glasnost Tsar's greeting. It is, after all, one thing to respond to his smile, but something else again to try and excuse my own reaction by blaming him for smiling in the first place.

Translated by George Theiner

Cards on the Table

For Czechoslovakia, 1988 was not just a year of several notable round anniversaries. It was also a year of great political importance for our country — as we have come to expect of years ending in an eight. Admittedly there has been no dramatic turn of events, either for the better or for the worse, but something did happen, nevertheless: the cards were put on the table, so to speak.

At long last, people started to assert openly that they no longer intend to put up apathetically with the imposed status quo and that they have the capacity to do something more for freedom than just sympathising tacitly with Charter 77 when listening to foreign broadcasts at home, swapping *samizdat* literature secretly with their workmates, or occasionally applauding some less inhibited theatrical production within the darkness of an auditorium. This was proved by the many thousands of citizens who had the courage to take part in independent demonstrations. But there are other signs as well: everywhere people are talking far more openly than before, even within highly official structures. More and more "licensed" artists, academics and journalists are beginning to call a spade a spade regardless of possible consequences. It looks as if the barrier that has been laboriously constructed between society and those citizens ready to speak their minds is beginning to crumble and fall away. People seem to have had their fill of the government's inability to solve the problems it has heaped upon itself, and they are growing tired of their own cautiousness.

But the regime has put its cards on the table too. Not only has it restructured itself in such a way that absolutely nothing is now left to chance — whereby it has destroyed any remaining illusion that society might have — it has even gone so far as to demonstrate quite unambiguously — either through the use of water-cannon, further arrests, bans of every kind, or hopelessly halfhearted reforms — that what really lies behind all its talk of "restructuring" and "democratisation" is the preservation of the existing totalitarian structures at all costs. "There will be no dialogue," declared Mr. Štěpán breezily from the platform on Wenceslas Square, and he went on to show what he meant in eloquent fashion the following day when he took personal charge of the (happily erratic) water-cannon. There is only one possible interpretation of his words: abandon all hopes you may have of any real shift or change of direction.

The cards are on the table. How the game will proceed from here on is anyone's guess. While it is true that the water-cannon are not particularly functional, it is equally true that civic awareness will not suddenly start to function trouble-free after twenty years of neglect. So the game is not going to be an easy one — for any of the players. What is most important is that the "game" has started at all: or more precisely, that it has entered a new phase — one in which it is impossible to pretend that there is nothing to play for.

And as happens at such moments of truth, something has surfaced, as it always does when a totalitarian system of a Communist type gets itself into a crisis (or alternatively, when it tries to reform itself). Its cornerstone and formal self-justification, the notorious dogma of the leading role of the Communist Party — a dogma that is incompatible with the democratic functioning of any constitution — has been called into question. In other words, the idea of *pluralism* has emerged, the idea that no ideology, doctrine or political force should a priori and for all time (i.e., through constitutional legislation) dominate all others, but that everyone has an equal right to seek political power.

There is nothing new about this, of course. As a result of the political ferment that we are witnessing almost everywhere in the Soviet bloc, the idea of pluralism is emerging all around us. The way the Communist leadership reacts to it varies from country to country. Gorbachev speaks of "socialist pluralism," by which he most likely means a plurality of views both within the Communist Party as the leading force, and outside it. When Rakowski talks about political pluralism, he probably has in mind giving opposition forces a few seats in the government and parliament as a safety valve for social discontent and a way of diverting attention away from his worst nightmare: trade-union pluralism. So far, it is the Hungarian Party leader Imre Poszgay who has gone furthest in this direction, particularly in his unambiguous declaration that there would be no place at all in the new Hungarian constitution for a clause stipulating the leading role of the Party.

In Czechoslovakia, this idea was proclaimed openly in October in the manifesto of the recently created Movement for Civil Liberties (HOS), significantly entitled *Democracy for All*. It is no coincidence that it happened this year in particular: if the time has come for putting cards on the table, then this card — the last, but in its way the most important of all — had to be played too.

The value of the *Democracy for All* manifesto does not reside in the originality of its thinking. Most of what it says has long been taken more or less for granted by all sensible people here (which does not mean to say that certain details of the manifesto might not prove controversial).

Its value lies in the fact that it sets out all these different self-evident truths in a single document, and does so publicly, as a basis for political activity, and not as someone's private viewpoint.

What HOS will develop into only time will tell. Maybe it will quickly become an integral feature of our country's life, albeit one not particularly beloved of the regime (rather like Charter

77). Perhaps it will remain for the time being merely the seed of something that will bear fruit in the dim and distant future. It is equally possible that the entire "matter" will be stamped on hard (although criminal investigation has so far been initiated solely into "the matter", and no one has yet been charged or arrested in connection with it). But whatever happens, one thing is already clear: the logic behind the constitutional enshrining of the leading role of one particular party has been openly called into question and these misgivings have been voiced and disseminated along with other fundamental concerns. This is of enormous significance. What has been done in this way can no longer be undone. This public declaration of the emperor's nakedness will go on sounding in the ears of all onlookers as long as he remains without clothes, or at least until fear has stopped up the last receptive ears (which is by now a most unlikely alternative).

Of course, many other hopeful things happened in 1988 apart from that manifesto. But even if nothing else had happened it would have been a great deal. Whatever turn the game takes now, one thing is certain: it will be impossible to ignore this new card. Besides there is no telling whether this particular card could ever have been played without the others.

The fact that 1988 saw an end to the taboo about the leading role of the Party (among other things) as well as a call for the rehabilitation of politics may well be important in the long term. However, there is an issue that seems to me even more important for us in the here and now. I refer to a "leading role" of rather a different kind, namely, what is to gain the upper hand in the immediate future: the awakening spirit of freedom, common sense and civic awareness, or the water-cannon?

It could well be the water-cannon, of course. But its domination will certainly not last forever. Soaking people to the skin and scaring them is one thing, eliminating civil discontent is another. Water-cannon are more likely to intensify the latter, rather than eliminate it. Above all, there is no way now they will avert the logical consequences of the present political and economic events.

So we should enter the new year without any illusions, but also with the assurance that the prison warden who talked to me in my cell on October 28 was not wrong when he said: You've got truth on your side!

Translated by A. G. Brain

Address to the Court

Václav Havel's concluding statement at the appeal tribunal of the Prague Municipal Court on March 21, 1989

Members of the court, members of the public,

The events just prior to my arrest, the manner of my interrogation and the conduct of my trial have all given me a fairly reliable notion of the actual reasons why I am in prison. However, since I lack any concrete evidence to prove my assumption, it must remain a hypothesis. Nonetheless, it all hangs together so well that I feel I am entitled to talk about it here.

After 3 P.M. on January 16, the State Security (StB) received the news that representatives of independent citizens' initiatives had tried to lay wreaths in memory of Jan Palach near the St. Wenceslas statue. StB officers immediately arrived at Wenceslas Square, where, at 3:25 P.M. they also noticed me among the group of people gathered there, and started to keep me under surveillance.

I did not lay any flowers by the statue. I did not behave at all conspicuously and did not come into any contact with the police. It would therefore seem that somewhere lengthy consultations were taking place about whether I should be arrested or not. Apart from that, they were most likely waiting for the right group to arrive, i.e., the officers who have me "in their care," in other words, who know something about me and could put pertinent questions to me at an interrogation. That phase lasted about an hour and culminated in my arrest at 4:30 P.M. in front of the Pragoimpo building, just as I was leaving Wenceslas Square. The haste with which the StB officers pushed their way through the crowd toward me is evidence that they feared I would leave Wenceslas Square and deprive them of at least formal grounds for my arrest. I was not arrested as someone obstructing a public servant in the performance of his duty, but quite simply because I was who I was.

I then waited some eight hours at the police station in Skolská Street to learn what they intended to do with me. The interrogation I underwent was a fairly general affair, which touched on various different matters and did not point toward any specific suspicions that might be confirmed or disproved. On the contrary, it was clear that they did not yet know whether I was actually to be charged with anything, and if so, with what.

The decision was eventually reached. Accordingly, I was detained and later charged and remanded for an alleged breach of the peace. However, since my mere presence on Wenceslas Square did not provide sufficient concrete grounds for charges to be preferred against me, let alone for me to be held on remand or convicted, they also took certain other actions into account, namely, statements of mine that had been broadcast by foreign radio stations concerning the events of January 15, for which I would seemingly not have been prosecuted otherwise. This second count was therefore included in my indictment for purely functional reasons, so they would have at least some sort of grounds for the indictment and verdict.

The fact that my indictment was re-formulated several times, that my case was first discussed at a ministerial council even before Major Zák had written his report on my arrest, not to mention the desperate and largely unsuccessful attempts to obtain witnesses who might say something specific against me, as well as many other factors, all create in me the strongest of impressions that it was first decided that I should go to prison and only afterwards was an effort made to contrive some legal grounds.

The trial was properly and objectively conducted. All the more astonishing therefore was the verdict, which was totally at variance with the evidence produced. It struck me that the decision had been taken before the trial, and somewhere other than in the courtroom. And this only confirmed my impression that I had been arrested because I was who I was, and was convicted only because I had been arrested.

Consequently, the verdict appears to me as no more nor less than an act of vengeance for the fact that I hold the views I hold and do nothing to conceal them. The actual terms of the judgment seem to me to be a substitute for something else, and a very poor one at that. In the circumstances, it strikes me that the verdict would have been far more honest had it merely stated: "Václav Havel, you are getting on our nerves, and so you will go to prison for nine months."

In the recent period, and in fact in connection with my own case, there have been several occasions on which the independence of our judiciary has been asserted. I sincerely trust that this appeal tribunal will demonstrate that independence by ordering my release.

Translated by A. G. Brain

Václav Havel's final statement at the court hearing on February 21, 1989

Madam Judge,

Since I have already commented sufficiently on the individual arguments of the indictment, both during the pre-trial proceedings and in this court, I do not intend to repeat myself but will merely sum up my position. I believe that no evidence has been produced to prove either incitement or obstruction of a public servant in the performance of his duties. I therefore consider myself innocent of these charges and demand my release. Nonetheless, I would like, in conclusion, to say something about one aspect of the whole case that has not been touched on so far.

The indictment states that I "attempted to disguise the anti-state and anti-socialist character of the planned rally." That statement, of which, incidentally, no concrete proof is given — nor can it be — imputes political motives to my actions. I am therefore within my rights to dwell for a while on the political aspects of the entire case.

First of all, I must point out that the words "anti-state" and "anti-socialist" have long since lost all semantic meaning, having become, in the course of their many years' entirely arbitrary use, no more than a derogatory label for all citizens who inconvenience the regime for whatever reason, and it has absolutely nothing to do with their actual political opinions. At various periods of their lives, three General Secretaries of the Communist Party of Czechoslovakia — Slánský, Husák and Dubček — were described in these words. Now the same label is applied to Charter 77 and other independent citizens' initiatives, simply because the government disapproves of their activity and feels the need to discredit them in some way. As can be seen, the indictment in my case also indulged in the same kind of political abuse.

What is the real political purpose of our activity? Charter 77 was created and continues to function as an informal community endeavouring to monitor respect for human rights in our country, including compliance with the relevant international covenants or with the state constitution, as the case may be. For twelve years now, Charter 77 has been drawing the attention of the state authorities to serious discrepancies between their legal commitments and what is the actual practice in our society. For twelve years it has warned about various disturbing phenomena and signs of crisis, and exposed violations of constitutional rights, as well as arbitrary behavior, bungling and incompetence on the part of the authorities. In pursuing these activities, Charter 77 is expressing the views of a broad section of our society, as I am able to gauge for myself every day. For twelve years we have been inviting the state authorities to take part in a dialogue about these matters. For twelve years, the authorities have ignored our campaign and merely imprisoned or prosecuted us for our part in it. Notwithstanding, the regime now acknowledges many of the problems that the Charter exposed years ago and that could have long been solved, had the authorities heeded its voice.

Charter 77 has always stressed the nonviolent and legal character of its activities. It has never been its objective to organise street disturbances. I myself have stressed publicly on repeated occasions that the degree of respect accorded to dissenting and critical-minded citizens is a measure of respect for public opinion in general. On repeated occasions I have stressed that continued disdain for peaceful expressions of public opinion can lead only to increasingly open and forcible social protest. I have repeatedly stated that it will be to no one's advantage if the government waits until people start demonstrating and taking strike action, and that it could all be easily avoided if the authorities were to start engaging in dialogue and displaying a readiness to listen to critical voices. No heed has ever been paid to such warnings, and the present regime is now reaping the fruits of its own contemptuous attitudes.

One thing I will admit: on January 16 it was my intention to leave Wenceslas Square as soon as I had laid my wreath in memory of Jan Palach. In the event, I stayed there for over an hour, chiefly because I was unable to believe my eyes. Something had happened that I would have never have dreamed possible. The police's entirely futile interference with those who wished, quietly and without publicity, to lay wreaths near the statue, succeeded instantly in transforming a random group of passers-by into a crowd of protesters. I realised just how profound civic discontent must be if something like that could happen. The indictment quotes me as telling our country's leaders that the situation was serious. In point of fact I told them that the situation was more serious than they thought. Then on January 16, I suddenly realised that the situation was more serious than even I had previously thought.

As a citizen who wants to see things take a calm and peaceful course in our country, I sincerely trust that the state authorities will at last heed the lesson and initiate an earnest dialogue with all sections of society, and that no one will be excluded from that dialogue for being labeled "anti-socialist." I sincerely trust that the state authorities will at last stop playing the ugly damsel who breaks the mirror in the belief that her reflection is to blame. That is also why I trust I shall not be convicted groundlessly yet again.

Václav Havel's statement after the verdict

Since I do not feel guilty, I have nothing to feel remorse for, and if I am to be punished, I shall regard my punishment as a sacrifice in a good cause, a sacrifice that is negligible compared to Jan Palach's absolute sacrifice, the anniversary of which we were intending to commemorate.

Translated by A. G. Brain

Excerpts from New Year's Day Address by the President of Czechoslovakia, Václav Havel

For 40 years you have heard on this day from the mouths of my predecessors, in a number of variations, the same thing: how our country is flourishing, how many more millions of tons of steel we have produced, how we are all happy, how we believe in our Government and what beautiful prospects are opening ahead of us. I assume you have not named me to this office so that I, too, should lie to you.

Our country is not flourishing. The great creative and spiritual potential of our nations is not being applied meaningfully. Entire branches of industry are producing things for which there is no demand while we are short of things we need.

The state, which calls itself a state of workers, is humiliating and exploiting them instead. Our outmoded economy wastes energy, which we have in short supply. The country, which could once be proud of the education of its people, is spending so little on education that today, in that respect, we rank 72d in the world. We have spoiled our land, rivers and forests, inherited from our ancestors, and we have, today, the worst environment in the whole of Europe. Adults die here earlier than in the majority of European countries. . . .

The worst of it is that we live in a spoiled moral environment. We have become morally ill because we are used to saying one thing and thinking another. We have learned not to believe in anything, not to care about each other, to worry only about ourselves. The concepts of love, friendship, mercy, humility or forgiveness have lost their depths and dimension, and for many of us they represent only some sort of psychological curiosity or they appear as long-lost wanderers from faraway times, somewhat ludicrous in the era of computers and space ships. . . .

The previous regime, armed with a proud and intolerant ideology, reduced people into the means of production, and nature into its tools. So it attacked their very essence, and their mutual relations. . . . Out of talented and responsible people, ingeniously husbanding their land, it made cogs of some sort of great, monstrous, thudding, smelly machine, with an unclear purpose. All it can do is, slowly but irresistibly, wear itself out, with all its cogs.

If I speak about a spoiled moral atmosphere I don't refer only to our masters. . . . I'm speaking about all of us. For all of us have grown used to the totalitarian system and accepted it as an immutable fact, and thereby actually helped keep it going. None of us are only its victims; we are all also responsible for it.

It would be very unwise to think of the sad heritage of the last 40 years only as something foreign, something inherited from a distant relative. On the contrary, we must accept this heritage as something we have inflicted on ourselves. If we accept it in such a way, we shall come to understand it is up to all of us to do something about it.

Let us make no mistake: even the best Government, the best Parliament and the best President cannot do much by themselves. Freedom and democracy, after all, mean joint participation and shared responsibility. If we realize this, then all the horrors that the new Czechoslovak democracy inherited cease to be so horrific. If we realize this, then hope will return to our hearts.

Everywhere in the world, people were surprised how these malleable, humiliated, cynical citizens of Czechoslovakia, who seemingly believed in nothing, found the tremendous strength within a few weeks to cast off the totalitarian system, in an entirely peaceful and dignified manner. We ourselves are surprised at it.

And we ask: Where did young people who had never known another system get their longing for truth, their love of freedom, their political imagination, their civic courage and civic responsibility? How did their parents, precisely the generation thought to have been lost, join them? How is it possible that so many people immediately understood what to do and that none of them needed any advice or instructions? . . .

Naturally we too had to pay for our present-day freedom. Many of our citizens died in prison in the 1950's. Many were executed. Thousands of human lives were destroyed. Hundreds of thousands of talented people were driven abroad. . . . Those who fought against totalitarianism during the war were also persecuted. . . . Nobody who paid in one way or another for our freedom could be forgotten.

Independent courts should justly evaluate the possible guilt of those responsible, so that the full truth about our recent past should be exposed.

But we should also not forget that other nations paid an even harsher price for their present freedom, and paid indirectly for ours as well. All human suffering concerns each human being. . . . Without changes in the Soviet Union, Poland, Hungary and the German Democratic Republic, what happened here could hardly have taken place, and certainly not in such a calm and peaceful way.

Now it depends only on us whether this hope will be fulfilled, whether our civic, national and political self-respect will be revived. Only a man or nation with self-respect, in the best sense of the word, is capable of listening to the voices of others, while accepting them as equals, of forgiving enemies and of expiating sins. . . .

Perhaps you are asking what kind of republic I am dreaming about. I will answer you: a republic that is independent, free, democratic, a republic with economic prosperity and also social justice, a humane republic that serves man and that for that reason also has the hope that man will serve it. . . .

My most important predecessor started his first speech by

quoting from Comenius. Permit me to end my own first speech by my own paraphrase. Your Government, my people, has returned to you.

Translated by the New York Times

PART V

Hungary

Tamas Aczel

Hungary Hearts

Tamas Aczel was born in Budapest and received both his B.A. and his M.A. at the University of Budapest. He published four novels and four books of poetry in Hungary, winning the Kossuth and Stalin Prizes for literature, before he fled his native land in 1956.

Mr. Aczel is now a professor of English at the University of Massachusetts. In English he has written one nonfiction work, *The Revolt of the Mind,* and the novels *The Ice Age, Illuminations,* and (forthcoming) *The Hunt.* The following article represents his firsthand account of the initial euphoria and subsequent problems of the revolution in Hungary.

Budapest

"How is it," a friend asked, with a wink of gleeful sarcasm, "that whenever you happen to be in town, the Party dissolves itself and turns into another one?" In the mild October sunshine, we were sitting on the terrace of a famous pâtisserie in the middle of Belváros, the Inner City, now only a shadow of its old elegant hauteur, yet bearing its historical catastrophes and private misfortunes with dignity. It was true. I had not "happened to be in town" (my native city) for thirty-three years. The last time I'd seen those streets and houses around us, the ruling Communist Party had dissolved itself and become a new "socialist" Party, founded by Prime Minister Imre Nagy and some of his reform-minded friends. They were joined by János Kádár, who within a couple of days walked over to the advancing Russians and offered himself as their satrap in Hungary for as long as they wanted him. They wanted him for thirty-three years. When I left the country in November 1956, it was at a historical turning point. Now I came back, for the first time, at another one. Clio had been good to me, I told my friend, jokingly. He seemed to agree.

Later that week, as I watched the nationally televised Congress of the Old Party turning itself again into a New Party — the agonies of death and rebirth under the indifferent glare of arc lamps — I realized how serious my joke must have sounded. On the podium, before an astonished nation, speaker after speaker denounced the mistakes and horrors of the past and rhapsodized about the miracles of democracy. It was a time of confessing guilt, accepting responsibility, pledging purification. In an explosion of remorse, the leaders of the past were asking the people of the future for the remission of their sins. It was a spectacular performance, something historically unique, unparalleled — even during the past few tumultuous weeks in East-Central Europe. One by one, with gritted teeth, the Communists of Poland, East Germany, and Czechoslovakia had given up Party rule. But they were careful to preserve the Party itself; they kept its organizational network intact, its financial sources hidden, its gunpowder dry, even if they were forced, as in Poland and East Germany, to dismantle their private armies, the militias. In Hungary the Communist Party collapsed under the weight of popular pressure, and all that remained was a grumbling group of apparatchiki threatening to establish a Communist Party. They were welcome to do so, according to the press, though it didn't appear to be a promising venture.

When my plane banked and glided smoothly out of the soft gray cumuli, suddenly I saw the old familiar postcard panorama of the city: the Danube, the bridges, the Gothic turrets of the Parliament, the walls of the Citadel, the graceful contours of the Royal Palace. I knew that beneath the old landscape I was going to find an array of new landscapes, new panoramas. But first I couldn't resist immersing myself in the warm waves of onrushing nostalgia. Having been an Orwellian "un-person" for so many years, I found it natural simply to venture into the city and seek out the places where I was born and grew up. The river was the same, lazy and gray; the Royal Palace had been rebuilt; my old alma mater was sootier, the house where I was born more desolate, but the Sunday morning High Mass in one of the most beautiful baroque churches of the city was elevating and moving, as if the old medieval hymn to the Virgin — "Do not forget us, poor, poor Magyars!" — had been suddenly endowed with a new meaning.

It didn't take long to realize that the country too was on a nostalgia binge, floating in an inflated memory-boat on the sweet seas of yesteryear. From the TV and the radio, from taverns and music halls, the sentimental melodies of my childhood and youth assailed me relentlessly. The audience loved it. If for me it was slightly intrusive and insistent, for those who had endured the sharp-edged ideological puritanism of the past four decades it was an opportunity of forgetting and remembering simultaneously.

There was, of course, a much more important form of remembering, though not forgetting. Wherever I went in the city I saw — on street corners, in the underground passages of the Metro, on public squares — book vendors setting up their primitive bazaars for selling the memories of the past forty years in astonishing numbers. Anthologies reprinting the speeches or writings of the executed Imre Nagy and his friends and associates, memoirs (even of former Party functionaries), analyses of the Stalinist and post-Stalinist eras, sold by the hundreds of thousands. One anthology was said to have sold 100,000 copies within a week. These books, hastily printed and brought to that insatiable market as soon as it was technically possible, filled the gap between the once-unmentionable past and the free present, and created a bridge to understanding the future. According to the latest statistics, I was told, by mid-October 400 independent publishers had been operating countrywide. The number is staggering, especially if one knows that this is a country about four times the size of Massachusetts, with 12 million inhabitants. Partly, of course, all this was clever business by clever businessmen who smelled profit in the sudden possibilities of freedom, an early manifestation of competitive capitalism. But mainly it was the reflection of a burst of desire to know, an insatiable hunger for what was once forbidden fruit but now became, as a kilo of apples, accessible on street corners. Reliable information on cheap paper at a reasonable price: no wonder the books sold like candy.

This was all part of the glorious euphoria that had swept over the country, at first gradually, but later with increasing rapidity, ever since the beginning of 1989. It had reached its peak on June 16, at the public burial of Nagy, his friends, and other victims of the terror that followed the suppression of the 1956 revolt. In the presence of hundreds of thousands, the symbolic significance of the burial became more than obvious; it become overwhelming, an emotional and historical milestone in the development of a new tradition: Hungarian democracy. Much to my surprise, at the opening of the radio's running commentary on the funeral, a famous actor had read a poem of mine, one I had published in a Paris-based Hungarian-language magazine twenty years ago. I knew I was now on my way back to being a "person" in my native land.

Literature, of course, had for 400 years played an immensely important part in Magyar society. About the time Sir Francis Drake set out to sail around the world, the great poet Bálint Balassi set out from Hungary to Krakow. Sir Francis was lured by the glitter of the unknown, its famed treasures and treasured fame; Balassi, perhaps, by some beauties in certain houses of ill-repute on Drodzka Street, or, conceivably, by the masterly Renaissance chapel of Bartolomeo Berecci. Behind Drake's flapping sails were a strong queen and a vigorous country; behind Balassi's tired steed, a lovelorn mistress and a Hungary about to be buried under the tidal wave of the Sultan's armies. "Farewell," Balassi opened his famous valedictory poem, "farewell my sweet homeland, good Hungary, shield of Christianity." But he couldn't stay away for long; he knew what his moral and soldierly commitments demanded of him. He returned to take up the sword, and died, five years later, shielding Christianity and his country on the walls of Esztergom.

Since his death, poets in Hungary saw their patriotic duty as a moral commitment to their nation, and the people looked upon them as their prophets and visionaries. In every major turning point in the country's history, poets and intellectuals were in the forefront of the battle. They were there, in impressive numbers and courage, in the years of oppression before and after 1956, and led the charge against the system to a triumphant end. When, one evening, around nine o'clock, I turned on the TV, I wasn't surprised to find one of the country's finest writers sitting in front of the camera, answering questions about the nation's problems from a lone interviewer. And instantly his transformation began. This famous author of many books and movie scripts, whether intentionally or not, was assuming the traditional mantle of the seer. He offered his vision of the nation's fate in a conversation, one on one, with history, but his rhetoric sounded hollow, his wisdom marred by banalities. I wondered if there was a channel in the West that would give ninety minutes of prime time for such a performance. It was, no doubt, a classic Magyar phenomenon, which on one hand reflected an enormous respect for the nation's intellectuals, but on the other showed the problems of a tradition that, under increasingly different circumstances, was turning into an empty shell.

I mentioned this to some of the leading young intellectuals, and they seemed to agree. It was clear to them that if a new road was to be carved from the rocky hillside of history (as one of them put it), the nation must face new images of itself. With the establishment of the rule of law over the rule of man, a reinterpretation of tradition was clearly on the agenda. Now that an effective political and economic democracy was emerging, the opposition was becoming an active and institutionalized power, and the conflict between the government and the opposition was a battleground of ideas and not a field for executions. The fires of 200 years of romantic populism were slowly turning into an ash heap.

Here, I felt, I was approaching the wellspring of the new Hungarian democracy. For with the euphoria of this year of triumph fading into the grayness of every day, the problems of politics and economics must now be dealt with on a practical level with practical solutions. And those problems were enormous and unique: nobody had ever attempted the transformation of state economies into the private, market-oriented economics of the West. Elections were fine, but soon the question would be *how* the ideas can be translated into practice. Who owns the state-owned factories? What is the mechanism of finance and commerce? What happens to collectivized agriculture? It was clear to me that for Hungary the days of passion were now over, and the days of reason were beginning.

After the fight for a unifying purpose reached its climax and triumphed in the Nagy funeral and the abdication from power of the Communist Party, one could already detect fragmentations within the new democratic parties and organizations. Other signs of conflict and contradictions were also becoming visible: the realization of democracy under ordinary circumstances. It is a very healthy development — no more emotional demonstrations against a hostile power, no more rhapsodies or flowery speeches, no more bitter lamentation over the cruelty of Magyar fate.

When the plane banked and rose, and the familiar postcard panorama suddenly disappeared under the soft, gray cumuli, I knew that I was leaving a country that, perhaps for the first time in its thousand-year history, held the promise of letting its people determine their own fate. Hard work based on hard ideas was now the order of the day. *For* a fledgling democracy.

George Paul Csicsery

The Siege of Nógrádi Street, Budapest, 1989

George Paul Csicsery was born to Hungarian parents in Germany in 1948 and has lived in the United States since 1951. Mr. Csicsery is an award-winning independent film-maker who now makes his home in Oakland, California. He is also a journalist and writer whose articles, reviews, and interviews have appeared in numerous books and magazines, including *Savvy, Parenting, Film Quarterly,* and *West Magazine.*

Active in the distribution of Hungarian documentary films in the United States, Mr. Csicsery was last in Hungary during August 1989 to direct a "Nova" documentary about mathematician Paul Erdos. The report below from that trip documents his observations of East Germans camping near the West German embassy in a fashionable neighborhood of Budapest, hoping to cross freely over the Hungarian border into Austria. The pressure from these refugees put the Hungarian government into an awkward dilemma, caught between the two Germanies. It also signaled the beginning of the end for the Honecker Communist regime in East Germany. And it heralded important revolutionary changes in Hungary itself: the subsequent destruction of the Communist Party and the birth of a new Republic of Hungary.

During August of 1989 there was a joke making the rounds in Budapest about getting directions to Austria. "Follow the trail of abandoned Wartburgs in the woods. When there are no more, you're there." The woods and fields near Hungary's border with Austria were indeed littered with vehicles left behind by East Germans who had driven up to the border, then crossed on foot. An enterprising repo man could have made a killing by hauling abandoned cars back to East Germany and reselling them.

For many of the 12,000 East Germans who poured across the Hungarian border into Austria with the blessings of the Hungarian government on Sunday, September 10, the happy outcome was by no means inevitable. Some had waited in Budapest since July, hoping for a chance to leave for West Germany, but living with uncertainty. The Hungarian government might have at any moment succumbed to the formidable pressure exerted by its Warsaw Pact ally, East Germany, and sent them home to certain severe punishment.

Budapest's West German consulate—an extension of the embassy across the Danube in downtown Pest—is located on Nógrádi Street, a steep winding road in the fashionable hills of Buda. There are attractive new condos and two-story family houses sprouting up alongside the old world-mansions, many of which are embassies and consulates. But for nearly a month the serenity of the neighborhood was disrupted by increasing numbers of East Germans camped out on sidewalks, in bushes, in driveways, and in cars. The consulate and neighborhood were literally under siege.

By August 14, Telo, a student in his early twenties, had been living on Nógrádi Street for ten days. Julia, an eighteen-year-old temporarily staying with friends, had been showing up daily for a month. She had left Dresden four weeks earlier and had yet to call her parents. She wanted to call them only after she was safe in West Germany. All she knew now was that she was never going back to East Germany.

Most of the sixty to seventy East Germans who made the street their home during Budapest's hot summer days and balmy nights were young people, but there were also families, their Trabants and Wartburgs parked along the sidewalk, blankets stretched over open doors to provide shade for the children in the ninety-five-degree heat.

The bizarre encampment, which at night looked more like a beer party, would never have existed had not the Hungarian government decided in May to dismantle the Iron Curtain along Hungary's 215-mile border with Austria. Television footage of Hungarian soldiers rolling up barbed wire had broadcast Hungary's desire to cultivate ties with the West. For Hungarians, the dramatic gesture was largely symbolic, since they had already gained the right of unrestricted travel in January. But for Romanians, East Germans, and Czechs, all still ruled by hard-line Stalinist governments, an open Hungarian border to the West presented an unprecedented opportunity. In East Germany and Romania especially, most people could only dream of traveling West. Getting permission to visit Hungary — a fellow Warsaw Pact nation — was relatively easy. But with the Hungarian border to Austria suddenly open . . .

During July 1989, some 200,000 East Germans took their summer vacations in Hungary. When 100 of them occupied the West German embassy in downtown Budapest and demanded exit visas to West Germany, they were given safe passage. Word of this easy exodus spread among their compatriots, most of whom were camped in the dozens of resort towns surrounding the warm waters of Lake Balaton, seventy miles to the south.

During the summer, the beaches of Lake Balaton are regularly inundated with German-speaking tourists. There are more vacancy signs in German, advertising *zimmer frei,* than in Hungarian. For West Germans and Austrians, Lake Balaton has long been an economical alternative to more exotic Mediterranean vacations. To East Germans in 1989, it was the warmest water they could get near legally. But in 1989 Lake Balaton saw an added influx of thousands of Western tourists who habitually vacationed in Italy. Algae pollution in the Adriatic Sea had produced a major ecological disaster, rendering the beaches along 170 miles of Italian coastline unapproachable for months.

To the East Germans, just being around so many of their more affluent Western kin, with their high-tech campers and shiny

Mercedeses, sharpened the contrast. Getting to know them close up merely rubbed salt in the wounds. If the Hungarians and Poles could dump forty years of Stalinism without being bullied back into the fold by the Soviets, what's wrong with the German Democratic Republic, they asked.

The answer was another occupation of the West German embassy in Budapest early in August, this time by 170 East Germans. Within days other smaller groups, like the one on Nógrádi Street, were waiting for Hungarian exit visas to Austria.

During the day the crowd on Nógrádi Street swelled to several dozen more people; new arrivals appeared daily, some straight from East Germany, but most from the vacation camps around Lake Balaton. People converged on the gates of the West German consulate to learn about diplomatic developments and to carry on day-long discussions with West German consular officers — several had been flown in by the Bonn government to look after the physical needs of the East Germans in the street. The growing knot of campers encouraged the newcomers. It was easier to make a decision about whether to stay or go home when you saw people around you take the fateful step of overstaying their visas. The group provided a sense of security, even to people who did not need to sleep in the street.

Katryn, a trim twenty-nine-year-old auto mechanic from Dresden, was lucky enough to be staying in a house with Hungarian friends. But she routinely came to Nógrádi Street during the day with her two-year-old son Bill to wait. Katryn and her twenty-eight-year-old house painter husband, Stefan, had talked about leaving East Germany for three years but had never found an opportunity. Then, during their vacation to Hungary, Stefan bolted across the border to Austria illegally. That had been five weeks ago.

"I would like to take my son and go be with my husband," Katryn said. Stefan was waiting for them to join him in Rheinheim, West Germany. Katryn had spoken to him on the phone but had no idea when she and Bill would see Stefan again. On August 18, Katryn and Bill were still sitting on the sidewalk across the street from the West German consulate in Budapest.

As the hot days dragged on and the protracted negotiations between the two Germanys and the Hungarian government remained deadlocked, the toll on the now-fugitive East Germans began to show. Blistering heat and humidity, lack of sanitary facilities, and stories of East German agents kidnapping their own citizens from the streets of Budapest added to the tension.

At midnight, Heinz, a twenty-three-year-old electrician from Leipzig with long blond hair and an earring, sat on the same narrow strip of lawn across the street from the locked West German consulate where he had been sitting for a week — waiting and drinking beer. He wore the only clothes he had brought for his vacation, a cutoff denim vest and shorts. He had no shoes.

Like many of the young East Germans who had decided not to return home, Heinz had been on vacation at Lake Balaton when several of his friends had decided to make a break for West Germany through Austria. Heinz had often thought of going to West Germany; in the past year, political conditions in East Germany had deteriorated.

"A year ago we were still forced to sing the praises of the Soviet Union," Heinz said. "Today anybody in East Germany who dares to say anything positive about the Soviets or Gorbachev ends up in prison." Heinz went along with his friends to camp out on Nógrádi Street and wait.

By August 14, despite the discomfort, boredom, and uncertainty about how things would turn out, Heinz had little to lose; his visa to visit Hungary had expired. If he went back to East Germany, Heinz believed that he faced a seven-year sentence just for overstaying his visa. He was also sure that West German media pictures had shown his face and that East German agents who drove by Nógrádi Street had photographed him. In the eyes of East German authorities, hanging around Nógrádi Street was enough to make Heinz a marked man. Besides, West German relief organizations and consular officials had started distributing food and money to the fugitive East Germans.

There were other risks. It appeared that the East German government was actively harassing its disobedient citizens. On August 16 the newest occupants of Nógrádi Street adopted a policy of leaving their encampment for supplies and meals only in groups. The night before, Klaus, a twenty-one-year-old from Dresden, saw two people from the camp hustled into a car and driven away by some men who had been hanging around a café down the street. Klaus assumed that the two had been kidnapped by East German agents, and he warned the others not to go anywhere without at least three companions.

"It's enough for an East German car just to drive by the encampment," Klaus said. "If their plate numbers are recorded, they might as well not bother going back home. They'll be jailed for just being curious about us and stopping to talk."

The Hungarian residents of Nógrádi Street, while generally sympathetic, eyed the East German refugees with suspicion. It was a suspicion bred of having tasted the bitter fruit of German political upheavals twice already during the twentieth century. Hungarians like to see themselves as the victims of German political disasters during both world wars.

Following World War I, Hungary ceded over 60 percent of its territory to neighboring countries and lost a third of its population—largely because France, Britain, and the United States wanted to punish imperial Germany. An estimated two million Hungarians now live in Romania as the result of the Treaty of Trianon in 1920. During World War II, the Hungarian government entered a military alliance with Germany in order to regain some of its lost territories and to keep the Germans from occupying Hungary directly. The tactic worked for a while. Hitler did stay out of Hungary's internal affairs until 1944, when he caught the Hungarians trying to negotiate an early surrender to the Western Allies. Offended by such duplicity from an ally, Hitler deposed the monarchists in a dramatic coup and imposed a government led by Hungarian Nazis, who called themselves the Arrow Cross Party. With their S.S. masters lending an enthusiastic hand, the Arrow Cross—who had been out of favor and occasionally in jail under the monarchists—began to settle scores. In the short time allotted to them, the Nazis managed to murder thousands of people, including several hundred thousand Jews and other Eastern Europeans who had taken refuge from Hitler in monarchist Hungary. They had to work fast, because in March 1945, after a two-month battle that devastated Budapest, the Red Army wrested control of Hungary from the Germans, and the Nazis became the hunted. It was during this darkest moment of Hungary's history that Swedish envoy Raoul Wallenberg saved 100,000 Hungarian Jews from deportation to German death camps only to be captured by Russian troops entering Budapest.

To most Hungarians, being a sideshow in a mostly German circus was the direct cause of their country's forty years of bondage to the Soviet Union. After Hitler they experienced Stalin at his prime. During the late 1940s and early 1950s, a Western bourgeois society was reduced to a Stalinist dictatorship. During the early '50s an estimated 10 percent of the male population of Hungary spent time in prison for political reasons. The Hungarian revolution of 1956 was a first attempt to break out of the Soviet orbit. It was crushed and 10,000 Hungarians lost their lives as Soviet tanks reimposed Moscow's will. Another 200,000 fled to Austria during the two weeks it took the Russians to establish a new, loyal, Hungarian government. This is why the 1989 gesture of rolling up the barbed wire between Austria and Hungary carried such a powerful symbolic message for Hungarians. Creating an open border somehow balanced the tragedy of 1956. They could now come and go as they pleased; no longer would they be shot by their own border guards. Even more important, this time the Soviet Union did not interfere. For the first time since 1938, a Hungarian government acted independently of its powerful neighbors. It had been a long road from 1956 to 1989, and to some Hungarians the noisy young East Germans were now endangering the delicate Hungarian process of slipping quietly out of the Soviet bloc. Why did they have to choose Hungary as the place to confront their own repressive government?

"Why here?" asked Julia Hentes, who tended her petunias a few feet from a row of sleeping bags full of East Germans pressed against her fence. "It's a problem of the two Germanys. Why do they have to involve us again?"

During the war, Hentes, a retired accountant, had been bombed out of her family home in Buda in an air raid. She spent the next eight years in the countryside, first with relatives, then — when the Communists took over in 1948 — in officially assigned quarters with a family of strangers. It wasn't until 1960 that her husband landed a job as an engineer in Budapest, enabling them to move into a room of a cousin's apartment in the city. The Henteses saved their money and bought a plot on Nógrádi Street. They spent nine years building a house, which they finally occupied in 1979. Now, the petunias along the fence and the geraniums in the window are Julia's pride and joy. It had been years since she thought that international politics would ever intrude on her doorstep again.

Noise, congestion, and hygienic problems caused by seventy people living on a narrow strip of grass and sidewalk for weeks irritated other neighbors as well. An architect was sure there had been some burglaries since the East Germans had arrived. But despite complaints from the neighbors, not a single Hungarian police car came up the hill to Nógrádi Street during the weeks that it was occupied by the East Germans. Hungarian authorities pretended that there was no crisis.

The first official act of recognition that something unusual was taking place came on August 18 with the appearance of a truck carrying two portable toilets. They had been rented from the city for the East Germans by the West German consulate.

On August 14, the day after 170 East Germans occupied the West German embassy in Pest, the Nógrádi Street consulate was padlocked to prevent a similar occupation. An Alsatian shepherd dog patrolled the low wrought-iron fence, dissuading anyone from climbing in. Representatives of the West German foreign office spent the day in closed sessions with Hungarian government officials discussing what to do with the growing number of East Germans who wanted to leave Hungary for West Germany instead of going home. At the end of the day no decision was announced. For the people waiting in the withering heat and humidity there was no sign of a resolution. That night, several of the East Germans on Nógrádi Street packed into their cars and headed for the Austrian border to cross on their own.

The East Germans knew that Hungary had ordered its border guards not to fire on people who tried to cross the border illegally. The escapees abandoned their cars in the woods and simply walked over to Austria. Close to 7,000 successfully took this route as August dragged on without a breakthrough in the government negotiations.

To keep up appearances, the border guards occasionally caught a few of the East Germans and sent them back to Budapest. Only one incident marred the generally cordial relations that had developed between fleeing East Germans and the Hungarian border guards responsible for returning those they could capture without violence. On August 22 a frightened East German youth attacked a young Hungarian soldier at the border and was killed in the ensuing scuffle.

The incident highlighted the growing dilemma of the Hungarian government, which for weeks had been looking for ways to let the East Germans go without incurring the wrath of their government. Hungary was bound by treaties signed with East Germany to keep its citizens from going West without East Germany's permission. But Hungary had also recently signed the United Nations agreement on refugees, and, according to its provisions, if an East German suddenly called himself a refugee, the Hungarians were obliged to treat him as such. The issue was complicated by West Germany's long-term policy of automatically conferring West German citizenship upon every East German who asked for it. No matter what it decided, the Hungarian government could not please both Germanys.

There was also the far from trivial issue of solidarity with Warsaw Pact countries. East Germany, like Czechoslovakia and Romania, was among the hard-line states that had rejected Hungary's reforms. Throughout most of 1989 it appeared that the Soviet Union's European satellites were dividing into two camps, with Poland and Hungary moving toward a neutral position that would be friendlier to the West.

The tension between Romania and Hungary was already at a point where Hungarians were saying that it might be a good idea to keep Soviet forces in Hungary to help defend against a surprise attack by Romania. Ceauşescu and members of the Romanian General Staff had made threats ever since the Hungarian government had openly accused the Ceauşescu regime of pursuing a genocidal policy aimed at the two million ethnic Hungarians who live in western Romania. During 1989, over 16,000 Romanians sought refuge in Hungary. The Hungarian government welcomed them, set up refugee camps, and frequently denounced Ceauşescu's violations of human rights at international forums. When Barbara Bush visited Budapest during the summer of 1989, the Hungarians made a point of taking her to one of the refugee camps for Romanians.

Hungary's relations with Czechoslovakia were also strained. In March, Hungarian Greens had forced the parliament to back out of a giant hydroelectric project that Hungary had embarked upon in partnership with Austria and Czechoslovakia years earlier. The project involved a diversion of water from the Danube at the cost of severe ecological damage to the entire region. When Hungary backed out of the deal, the Czech government was furious. Another humiliating insult to the hard-line Prague government was a Hungarian television interview with Alexander Dubček. The Czech foreign ministry protested the March broadcast, accusing Hungary of meddling in the internal affairs of Czechoslovakia.

In deciding what to do about the East Germans, the Hungarian government also had to consider the country's growing economic relationship with West Germany. At a time when Hungary's foreign debt stood at $17 billion (a higher per capita rate than that of any other Eastern European country), could Hungary afford to alienate West Germany — the country with the strongest potential and inclination for capital investment in Hungary?

On the morning of August 18, Nógrádi Street was strangely quiet. There was not an East German in sight. The only remaining traces of the occupation were the cars abandoned by owners who had left for the border. A sign on the gate of the still-padlocked consulate advised East Germans that the Hungarian Maltese Caritas charity organization was setting up a camp for them at a Catholic church in Zugliget, another suburb of Buda nearby. Food, shelter, and sanitary facilities were available free of charge. The siege of Nógrádi Street was over, but the opening of refugee camps in Budapest and around Lake Balaton meant only that the crisis was moving to a new, more organized phase. The Hungarian government's headaches were just beginning.

The weekend of August 19–20 is Hungary's most important national holiday. August 20 is traditionally celebrated as St. Stephen's Day, in honor of Hungary's first king and his conversion of the Hungarians to Christianity in the year 1000. Since 1948, Hungarian Communists have also observed the holiday, calling it Constitution Day. In 1989, Budapest celebrated August 20 with a vengeance – a dozen different events featured something for every political and cultural palate.

The annual Communist pageant was held on Margaret Island in the middle of the Danube. The river was also the site of speedboat races, an event that has replaced the aquatic military display that had been a highlight of the festivities during Stalinist years. Anchored on the Pest side of the Danube was a riverboat with an orchestra that played Strauss waltzes and operettas, a reverberation from Budapest's fin de siècle splendor.

But the crowning event was the annual religious procession at the Basilica, where for the first time since 1945 the remains of St. Stephen's right hand, set in an ornately bejeweled reliquary, were carried through the streets of Pest. The procession turned into a nostalgic celebration of national reconciliation, replete with the ironies of Hungary's twisted history.

Thousands of elderly peasant women in colorful folk costumes flocked to the city from the country's most remote villages. They marched, carrying statues of the Madonna and hand-woven banners proclaiming the names of their municipalities. With them marched priests from a dozen formerly outlawed Catholic orders, including Benedictines, Franciscans, Paulists, and Piarists. The relic was preceded by the Knights of the Order of Malta and by the nation's leading bishops. The entire route and the relic itself were flanked by Hungary's traditional scouts — boys in short pants and girls — all in khaki, with bright green neckerchiefs and a distinctive white sprig called angel's hair in their caps.

A year earlier, the only youth organization allowed in Hungary had been the Communist Young Pioneers. The traditional scouts had survived since World War II only in Western countries, and were legally allowed back into Hungary only after Károly Grósz — the hard-line Communist prime minister ousted just months earlier — had admitted during a 1988 visit to New York that he had been a member of the scouts himself before becoming a Communist, and that it had been a mistake for the Communists to outlaw the youth organization in 1948.

The procession's most astounding sight was the People's Army Band, led by a Catholic priest dressed in church vestments, playing an ancient hymn to the Virgin Mary. Next to this, the presence of Mátyás Szürös, president of parliament, walking a few steps ahead of the visiting daughter of Otto von Hapsburg — son of Hungary's last king — seemed anticlimactic. The solemn procession, with its uniquely Hungarian blend of anachronistic elements, was televised throughout the land.

The holiday also featured a Pan-European Picnic held at the Austrian border near the city of Sopron. The plan for Austrians and Hungarians to celebrate good neighborly relations included a "border walk" from Hungary to Austria on August 19 and 20. During the preceding days, the Hungarian and Austrian media gave the event extra publicity, making sure that every East German in Hungary would know about it. Not surprisingly, when the border opened, some 900 East Germans swept across to Austria in a charging mass. They could care less about neighborly relations between Austria and Hungary; within hours they would be in West Germany.

Everyone involved understood that the Hungarian government was exploiting the Pan-European Picnic and had overlooked other illegal border crossings to avoid an open confrontation with East Germany.

Instead of defusing the crisis, the maneuver merely whetted the appetites of new potential escapees. There were still thousands of East Germans vacationing in Hungary at the end of August. Many of them suspected that their chances of getting to West Germany would never again be as good. Their suspicions were reinforced when East Germany announced that it would no longer issue visas for its citizens to visit Hungary.

Before the dam finally burst on September 10, there was one more attempt by Hungary to diplomatically circumvent the twenty-year-old convention with East Germany. During the last week of August several hundred East Germans left Hungary for the West with documents issued by the Red Cross.

During the first week of September, the number of illegal crossings reached 200 a day. Hungary's foreign minister, Gyula Horn, had failed to get the two Germanys to resolve the problem without pushing Hungary into choosing between them. On Sunday, September 10, Hungarian authorities finally decided to let the East Germans go without documents. Erich Honecker was furious. East Germany accused Hungary of violating its obligations and damaging its long-term interests. But the damage was to East Germany's unbending regime. If it wanted to restrict the movements of its own citizens, East Germany could now do so only within the confines of its own territory.

With the gauntlet down, over 12,000 East Germans left Hungary that first night. This time they were taking their smelly Trabants and Wartburgs with them, crossing out the first and last letters of their country stickers as soon as they drove into Austria, turning "DDR" into a single "D" for Deutschland. Few of them could imagine that less than six months later their country, the DDR, would itself be on the verge of disintegrating into a single Deutschland.

The young people who had spent the hottest part of August camped out on Nógrádi Street in Budapest were just settling in to new lives as West Germans when a second wave of East Germans took refuge at the West German embassies in Prague and Warsaw late in September. These people too wanted to go to West Germany, whatever the cost. Then, as the fortieth anniversary of the founding of East Germany approached, discontented East Germans took to the streets of their own cities. On October 9, up to 70,000 demonstrators in Leipzig were shouting "Gorby, Gorby." Within days, East German newspapers were criticizing their own government and long-quiescent minor parties had roused themselves to challenge the Communists. Honecker's days were numbered.

During the same week, the Hungarian Communist Party self-destructed and reemerged as a new Socialist Party, but only 50,000 of the 750,000 members of the old party bothered to rejoin. A week later the party lost the authority to organize at factories and institutions, and its 65,000-member armed Worker's Militia was disbanded by order of parliament. On October 23, the anniversary of the 1956 Hungarian revolution, Parliamentary President Mátyás Szürös — the man who had marched a few steps ahead of a Hapsburg on August 20 — announced that the Hungarian People's Republic was no more. He proclaimed the birth of a new Republic of Hungary.

In November, the Berlin Wall — that most enduring symbol of the separation of East and West — was breached from the Eastern side by crowds of young people with champagne bottles. East Germans had found the most direct way to reach West Germany. The West German consulate on Nógrádi Street in Budapest was open for business as usual. None of the neighbors even stopped to think that the reunification of Germany had been set in motion on their own quiet street in Budapest. As far as they are concerned, the Germans have gone back to Germany — until next summer.

PART VI

Romania

Norman Manea

Romania: Three Lines
with Commentary

> *". . . the Demon of sadism and
> stubborn stupidity."*
> *"If only our administration and
> politics were on the same level
> as the arts."*
> *"A country inhabited by people
> and books."*

Norman Manea was born in 1936 at Suceava in Bukovina,
Romania. In 1941 he was deported to the concentration
camp of Transnistria in the Ukraine, where he remained
with surviving members of his family until April 1945.
Returning after the war to Romania, he was educated at
Suceava and in Bucharest at the Institute of Civil Engineering and worked from 1959 to 1974 as an engineer.

His extensive writing began to appear in 1966: essays,
articles, stories, and novels that earned him international
critical acclaim as well as a uniquely uncomfortable position in the Romanian Communist state. For many years
censors and other forces of oppression in the Ceauşescu
regime attempted to silence his powerful voice of social and
political criticism.

In 1989–90 Mr. Manea was an International Fellow at
Bard College, where he wrote the following essay. It presents an extensive account of his own experience of Romanian literary history, emphasizing the important role of

artists and intellectuals in the current violent revolutionary process of his native country.

I

"In legionnaire,[1] bourgeois, nationalist Romania I saw the demon of sadism and stubborn stupidity incarnate before me." Although these words by Eugene Ionesco first appeared in Romania in 1946, he did not elaborate on them until many years later, in the volume *Présent passé — Passé présent* (Paris, 1969).

That sentence has haunted me in recent years. Especially the question of how many words — and which words — would have to be changed in order for the statement to apply to our current situation.

As a child I lived through the ordeal of hatred and war in legionnaire, bourgeois, nationalist Romania. Later I looked at many books, documents, literary and artistic representations, all sorts of studies, to try to comprehend the Nazi phenomenon not only in its German but also in its other European varieties, and to find an explanation for these terrible derailments of history, of society, of the psyche (which is to say, of humanity itself); an explanation for the bewilderment and despair of constantly growing strata of the population; an explanation for the gradual extinction — through terror — of civil society and the transformation of everyday life into a state of siege in which the external "enemy" becomes a pretext for the extermination of "suspects" inside the citadel.

But only in the last years did I begin to understand the mechanism that sets off such inexorable disasters. Romania, under the most cruel and dark dictatorship, pressed by a deepening economic, political, and moral erosion, presented me with the very model of a collapse in which, this time, I did not play the part of a guinea pig — as I did in my childhood — but of an observer, and even of a not yet completely disarmed "suspect."

More than once I was reminded of Bergman's film *The Serpent's Egg*, of the stultifying atmosphere of the last years of the Weimar Republic, of the mixture of paranoia and disorientation, of the ways in which discouragement turns into resignation, then submission, and how general dissatisfaction hurries to find marginal targets; of how, given conditions of unalleviated material want and systematic terror, stupidity and violence will erupt wherever they can.

Still, let me hasten to say that—despite quite a few similarities—the Romania of the eighties was not the legionnaire, bourgeois, nationalist Romania of the prewar and wartime period.

The recent controversies in the West over the similarities between Nazism and Communism overlook, perhaps not entirely innocently, the much more important differences between the two systems.

The acceptance of clichés that meet the very common need for comforting simplifications appears to be associated with the naive conviction that to demonstrate the equally catastrophic effect of all dictatorships is to hold them all equally culpable; but this would lead to a relativization of guilt, and therefore, ultimately, to exoneration.

Not even the way that the two systems sometimes "borrow" methods from one another makes them equivalent. Those who want to understand something essential about "real socialism" (but also those interested in the character and consequences of "national socialism") should begin by studying the important differences between Nazism and Communism. Communism espouses a generous and widely accepted humanitarian ideal and utilizes subtler, more duplicitous strategies, which may at least partly explain its respectable age and incomparable expansionist force. Nazism was, in all its deeds and misdeeds, consistent with its own program, and those who followed it, at least in the initial stages, embraced that program knowingly and "legally." Communism, on the other hand is, in the balance sheet of relations between utopian vision and reality, in sharp contradiction with itself, and imposes its system on the masses by force. A contradic-

tion between ideology and the concrete necessities of government, between the posited ideal and the reality that challenges
it — but paradoxically, this contradiction also offers the Communists their relative capacity for recovery, for regeneration, and of
course also for mystification. And it is in this ample field of
inconsistencies and incongruities that demagogy operates and
society manifests its elasticity; it is here that vital processes — the
movements of ordinary daily existence — act.

Comparisons between the two systems, however, are not unin-
teresting, nor are their similarities insignificant. The unlit streets
of Bucharest, the unheated apartments, the interminable lines
for basic foodstuffs, the ubiquity of the police and its collaborators, the diversionary attacks on national minorities, the increasing brutality in human relationships, the monstrous pressure
exerted by the bureaucracy on every sphere of material and
spiritual life — all this reminded me again and again of Bergman's
film about the years before Hitler's seizure of power; of that
stifled atmosphere, that confused immobility perpetually poised
between implosion and explosion. Life as a series of postpone-
ments, a tumorlike growth of mistrust and fear, an all-encompassing schizophrenia. A step-by-step reduction of private life,
and finally its abolition, as time itself becomes subject to ever-
increasing taxation and eventually total *expropriation* by the state:
the hours sacrificed to standing in lines, to ritual political meetings and to rallies, on top of the hours at work, and the hours of
helpless exposure to the inferno of public transportation on the
way to and from work, meetings, and shopping; and when you
were finally home in your birdcage, you found yourself lost,
mute, staring into an emptiness that could be defined as infinite
despair.

The vacant stare, the mind in a void, tortured by the question
of whether the evil embodied in its one face (one computer
portrait of evil in hundreds of printouts) was due to an unfortunate accident, a derangement of history itself, and therefore not
to an individual psychological disturbance; or whether it was
something latent in all people at all times that had now erupted
as this monstrous collective face?

Everywhere there was the insidious, dilated presence of the monster called the Power.[2] In one's home, in one's thoughts, in the conjugal bed. The power of darkness. The black hole haunted by the demon of sadism and sly, stubborn stupidity. Tirelessly active impersonality, self-affirmed by a huge cult of the dictator's personality, proving itself and confirming its power by suppression. The void that knows no barrier. The polarization of malignant energy. *He, She*: "the others." Nepotism as an instrument of tyranny. The festivities of power, stupidity, and perversion. Macabre collective pathologies. Fear. Apathy. Depersonalization. Rhinocerization (in Ionesco's terms). The demon of sadism and stubborn stupidity.

Where are the limits of self-preservation, how much can the human being endure, and to what transformations is he prepared to succumb — willingly or under terror? Fear, exhaustion, disgust — at work, standing in lines, reading the same stupid newspaper all over again, watching the two hours of daily nausea on TV. The registration of your typewriter with the police, the underequipped and overused clinics, the feeling that you could die at any moment, and that every hour of survival merely retarded, prolonged, dismembered this slow dying, day after day, week after week. You would gradually stop seeing your friends because the buses ran very infrequently and were overcrowded, and it had become impossible to get from one end of the city to the other, and because you had nothing — food, drink, or even cigarettes — to offer them when they came to visit. Because you were sick of repeating the same lament for the billionth time, and because you didn't want to face the other's defeat — marked each time by new wrinkles — and recognize it as your own.

And the lie became more insolent by the day. Despair confined by neurosis. Resignation poisoned by cynicism. These were only the most obvious manifestations of a multifaceted social condition whose paradoxically destructive coherence mocked all attempts at logical explanation. A general picture borne out by any random sequence of personal events, the raw materials of biography.

The first half of 1986 involved me in an exhausting struggle with the censors, who had put a halt to the printing of my novel *Plicul negru* (*The Black Envelope*). A fight with a stubborn, demonic adversary who kept inventing fresh and absurd demands. Half a year of daily wrangling over particular pages, sentences, words. (Of the taboo words at least these should be mentioned: cold, dictator, sex, coffee, darkness, fascism, God, queues, whore, demolition, nationalism, breasts, Stalinism, meat, suicide, police informer, abortion, legionnaires, neurosis, rape, tyranny, homosexual.)

In May, I took part in a colloquium "On the Contemporary Romanian Novel" in the Transylvanian town of Tîrgu-Mureş. Since an explosive Writers' Conference in 1981, the official procedure for all writers' meetings was as follows: Suppress all contacts with the public (even the brief press reports about these events had to be cryptic and disinformative), tape-record all comments, frustrate all demands, send all proposals to be "checked" by the security organs whose job it is to update the dossier of each of the participants. My friendly relations with colleagues at the literary journal sponsoring the colloquium persuaded me to accept the invitation.

Present at the conference, in addition to the fifteen or twenty writers who had been invited, was a delegation of the Bucharest Council for Socialist Culture and Education, some local cultural activists and party functionaries, as well as several unknown figures whose appearance and bearing betrayed the particular higher "institution" to which they belonged. On the conference table, naturally, stood a tape recorder.

I was determined not to speak. And yet, listening to the all-too-clever and sly arguments of a talented colleague about the primacy of the aesthetic as the only legitimate literary criterion, I couldn't restrain myself. I contradicted his statements about the irrelevance of politically tendentious "ballast" and tried to show that, on the contrary, the "aesthetic" retreat from everyday life with its urgent issues explained why contemporary Romanian literature had not yet produced a very large number of major novels. Perhaps because "aesthetics" had not become "East-ethics"?[3]

My use of this pun was, of course, not unconsidered; nor was my concluding reference to Borges and Sabato. I was careful not to make explicit reference to the similarities between Argentina and Romania, which were very much on my mind in those days. I am referring not just to similarities of structure and temperament but also to the chasm between tremendous artistic potential and the most sinister political reality. (While writing the novel *The Black Envelope,* during Romania's current disaster, I was engaged in a steady internal dialogue not only with the obscure and strange organization of the blind in Ernesto Sabato's novel *On Heroes and Tombs* but also with the Argentine dictatorship.)

The next day, just before my flight back to Bucharest, an editor of the local literary review warned me in confidence that a State Security officer had visited him and some of his colleagues that morning to ask them for their opinion about my comment at the colloquium and, in general, about my character.

There were four of us on the way to the airport. At the control booth, we had to show our tickets and our I.D. papers. A routine check — the three with whom I was traveling were already on their way to the gate — but lo and behold, I was singled out for special treatment. The officer on duty took my I.D. "Just checking," he said. My three colleagues turned around and waited in solidarity with me for my case to be resolved. The explanations given us by the soldiers at the gate revealed nothing more than the sadistic indolence displayed by hostile and stubborn stupidity in any contact with civil society.

"Routine procedure," a friend and connoisseur of this kind of provocation would later explain to me. "Nothing important, really. They just wanted to let you know they've got their eye on you. Which you should have suspected anyway."

Sometime in the next few weeks I applied for a trip to the West as a tourist. I had unofficially heard that I had been awarded the fellowship of the DAAD Kunstlerprogramm in West Berlin for 1987. The Romanian "Postal Service" had (of course) made sure that the official letter of invitation did not reach me — which, paradoxically, turned out to be to my advantage. Had I received the letter, I would never have been granted permission to live and work in West Berlin for a year, since these types of permission are given — or rather, as a rule, refused — at the highest level of the country's hierarchy.[4]

There were many people at the local police precinct in charge of foreign travel that day in June. I had time to read the bulletin boards in the waiting room. One displayed the mug shots of delinquents and described the infractions they had perpetrated — three young men who had been accomplices in an incident of assault and theft. The captions under their pictures were virtually identical: so-and-so, born in such-and-such a place, without occupation, no previous criminal record, has committed, in complicity with so-and-so, assault and theft against such-and-such a citizen, and has been taken into custody for the purpose of due punishment. This text, full of grammatical errors, was repeated under each of the frowning and shaven-headed young faces, with one exception: the last and youngest, aged sixteen, was described as not just "without occupation," but as a "Gypsy without occupation." This in a police district station in the year 1986! Hanging next to numerous posters full of citations from the Constitution of the "multilaterally developed" society,[5] which, everyone knew, made ethnic discrimination or incitement to such discrimination a punishable offense.

In the middle of October I found in my mailbox the miraculous notification, stamped as "special" by the Ministry of the Interior — my permission to travel! It was hard to fend off the hysteria that follows in the wake of euphoria, the sensation that you are being shadowed at every step, an uncertainty that makes you a plaything for the sadistic entertainment of the authorities, who are fully capable of annulling the validity of their own permits.

If misfortunes never come alone, happy events sometimes come in bunches also. In the next few days I learned that my book, *Pe contur* (*Delineations*), had been awarded a prize by the Writers' Union, which had just convened to choose the best books published in 1984.[6] Just a few years earlier, I had been exposed to vicious attacks in retaliation for my public critique of a neo-fascist editorial that had been published in the goonishly nationalistic "cultural" weekly of the Bucharest Communist Party Council.[7] So my pleasure at receiving the prize was tempered by a certain degree of mistrust.

In November, I took the train to my native town of Suceava in the north, to say good-bye to my parents before traveling abroad. Sharing my compartment, opposite my reserved seat, was a passenger in a suit and tie, with no baggage other than an attaché case, very deeply absorbed in reading a newspaper — the "shadow" that had to accompany me to my destination, and perhaps further ("just to let you know they've got their eye on you").

There were giant posters all over the city: "Days of Culture in Suceava." First a day of music, then a day of sculpture, then of literature, film, theater, etc. The names of those who were to engage in dialogue with the stars from Bucharest had been chosen according to the recently established sandwich system: for the sake of calculated confusion, pair a genuine writer with a talentless blowhard, an opportunistic scoundrel with an honorable artist — and you have a legitimate combination, fully approved.

On that cold and dreary autumn day, as I headed for the grocery store to see which food line I might join, I couldn't have cared less for this "cultural" event. This was the city of my childhood and my youth, and my only purpose in being here was to soak up as much as I could of the heavy hours of parting.

But I was stopped by a neighbor, a local journalist. He was going to the literary event and insisted that I go with him. I was embarrassed. There was a humbly reproachful hint that I was keeping myself aloof, not just from the literary and political scene but also from former associates and colleagues, evidently because I considered them "provincial." He seemed positively hurt, and I, unfortunately, gave in.

When I found myself in the office of the director of the local House of Culture, where the party activists and local journalists were already assembled, I felt even more awkward and strange. Unshaven, tired, preoccupied, wearing a crumpled sweater, I stood as a real intruder among men and women who had dressed up for the festive occasion. But the director seemed delighted that my unexpected presence would add a "well-known novelist" to the panel discussion of "Tradition and Innovation in Contemporary Romanian Literature." I objected that my name had not been announced on the posters, that I had nothing to say on this topic, that I wasn't even dressed for the occasion. He would not accept a refusal. It was too late.

Soon, the "Bucharest writers" made their appearance, coming from their hotel. Instead of the seven who had been announced, there were three. Actually only two, as one was introduced as a journalist for the Communist Youth newspaper *Scinteia Tineretului.*

A poet, a critic, a novelist — an ideal trio for the panel. We went up on the stage and sat down. The audience consisted of fifty people, most of them children between ten and fifteen, and about ten teachers from the local schools. It was agreed that we would take questions from the audience to simplify the discussion. Many minutes passed before anyone plucked up the courage to break the silence. This gave me time to observe the children squirming in their seats, wearing winter coats and fur hats, and their teachers, also in coats and hats; for the auditorium was, needless to say, unheated — a fact that would have been a far more appropriate subject of discussion than the state of contemporary Romanian literature.

An elderly lady, looking like an Austrian housemaid, in a thick gray overcoat cut in military style and a hunting cap tilted at a coquettish angle, launched the first question: "What's going on with the Nobel Prize? Why haven't we got a Nobel Prize? Why has no Romanian writer ever received the Nobel Prize?"

The brilliant poet, aroused by the childishness of the question, displayed his ironic verve but then passed the essentially unanswered question to his friend. Without excess of modesty, the professor confessed that he had been for many years Romania's consultant to the Nobel Foundation (a fact he had never divulged in public before), went on to mention his frequent trips to the West and his friendly relations with various literary figures of world stature, decried the commercialization of culture in the West and the unfair way in which the world treated non-Western and particularly Romanian culture. And then came the surprise ending that was the goal of all his meandering: "A few years ago, Saul Bellow visited us here. When I met him I asked him: 'Tell me, sir, who is behind you? Who is backing you? Who actually gave you your Nobel Prize?'" The pubescent audience and the apathetic educators suddenly showed visible signs of life inside their heavy coats and beneath the fur hats they had pulled tightly over their ears .

The speaker prolonged the strategic pause a bit, then resumed his aria: "These are the facts. Someone is pulling strings, let's face it. Why not place a finger on the open wound? Nelly Sachs is an absolutely mediocre poet. And these Jews . . . all these Jews write in old languages that no one understands." He turned to the poet, asking him for help: "What's his name, the one who got the Nobel Prize a few years ago?"

The poet leapt to his assistance: "Bashevis Singer."

Enlightened, the professor found his stride again. "Exactly, Singer, that's the one. I found a few books by this Singer in translation. I read them very closely, and I can assure you: absolutely worthless. He's certainly not a writer."

I was not, under the circumstances, in the mood to defend the merits of such an eloquent witness as Nelly Sachs or a writer as interesting as Isaac Bashevis Singer. Nevertheless, I felt obliged to qualify the professor's all too categorical statements. I pointed out the difference between athletic achievements, which are established by the precise measurement of inches and seconds, and works of art, which are difficult to evaluate with perfect objectivity. Literary awards, I said, are rarely perfect calls, and this holds as true for the Romanian Writers' Union as it does for the Nobel Foundation. The judgment need only be plausible — that is, it must fall within a certain zone of artistic merit. Hankering for prizes, in any case, is a sign of frustration; and frustration in no way stimulates artistic creativity, which requires solitude and originality, not honors and publicity.

I reminded the professor of our having sat, several years before, at a literary conference in Belgrade where our hosts over-whelmed us not only with volumes by Yugoslav writers that had been translated abroad but also with lengthy bio-bibliographical tomes, in major languages of international communication, about Yugoslav literature. This, I said, Romania was still unable to offer. The professor nodded agreement, but I was not at all sure he remembered those days in Belgrade, for I had seen him there often dead drunk, bereft of the good-natured mask he assumed for his hypocritical speeches about freedom of speech and the end of censorship in Romania.[8]

After a few more questions and answers, the professor informed the audience about the projects of the publishing house he directed. He complained at some length of the problems confronting a Romanian editor, but stressed the paternal care and support for culture shown by the country's president, the secretary general of the Party, whom he had had the honor of meeting on several occasions, and of whose generous and far-sighted views on culture and art he had personally apprised himself. And then, once again, an astonishing finale.

"Nevertheless," he said, "new obstacles keep arising. Let's face the truth squarely. Why pretend? A few years ago I was visited by two professors from Israel. I knew them. They were formerly from Romania. They asked me: 'What are you doing with the Eminescu[9] edition? Is it out yet?' 'Well, no,' I replied, 'and it's your fault. Your chief rabbi's behind the delay, if you really want to know.' And that is the truth. Let's not mince words!"

Leaving the auditorium, I expressed to the poet my indignation at the cynical behavior of the professor. To speak that way in front of a roomful of children, in secret agreement with the local cultural officials, and spread such shameless lies! Anti-Western and anti-Semitic Party propaganda!! When he knows perfectly well that cultural institutions in the West aren't all dominated by political interests, that all Western culture isn't perverted and commercial, and that the complete edition of Eminescu is not being delayed just because of his anti-Semitic texts but also because of his anti-Russian texts and for other, more complex reasons. How vile! To exploit the trust of children like that! Instead of explaining to them why it is they don't have enough to eat and why it's so cold in their homes and in that auditorium!

The young poet, already not so young, did not allow himself to be contaminated by my naive indignation. He made a calming-down gesture with his hand and reminded me that the professor had earned his stripes in the service of a certain higher cause. I knew the "institution" he was referring to, but still I did not understand why what had just happened was therefore negligible.

"It's silliness, small potatoes," he said. "It's not worth talking about, it's really not worth talking about."

When I told my friends in Bucharest about my experience, they were no less outraged than I was. But at the Council for Socialist Culture and Education, the Suceava incident was being considered from a very different point of view: an investigatory commission was set up to determine who had given me the illegitimate authority to present my views at the conference, in defiance of the council's exclusive jurisdiction in such matters.

I had known for many years the idiotic fear and hypocritical sadism of Party functionaries appointed to "cultural" work. I had felt it more than once, like so many others. Nevertheless, I was shocked to learn, two months after that literary colloquium in Suceava, that "for ideological reasons" the Council for Socialist Culture and Education had revoked the prize recently awarded by the Writers' Union to my book *Pe contur* (the one published two years earlier). Then it all came back to me: the debilitating war with the censors, the vicious press campaign against me, the incident at the airport in Tîrgu-Mureş, the House of Culture in Suceava, and along with these personal memories, Eugene Ionesco's small text: "In legionnaire, bourgeois, nationalist Romania I saw the demon of sadism and stubborn stupidity incarnate before me."

It was still as true as ever. Only the first two locative terms would have to be changed. It was no longer legionnaire but "socialist" Romania. And the demon was no longer incarnate in the bourgeoisie but in the State Security apparatus.

II

For some time there has been much talk about Central Europe. To the extent that the discussion of this still vaguely defined notion is not dominated by an exclusive club mentality but rather by a search for an inclusive, cooperative solution, the long-term prospects for this part of Europe could be truly spectacular. But even in the absence of a clear definition of its key term, the debate is of burning interest.

In his excellent article, "Does Central Europe Exist?" (*The New York Review of Books,* October 9, 1986), Timothy Garton Ash analyzes the opinions of Havel, Michnik, and Konrad on the subject, showing their defining criteria to be based on cultural tradition and stages of development instead of geography. (Thomas Masaryk, for instance, included in his definition the Scandinavians and Baltic peoples, along with Poles, Czechs, Slovaks, Magyars, Serbocroats, Romanians, Bulgarians, Albanians, Greeks, and Turks, but excluded Germans and Austrians since they chose to place Europe's center in Berlin and Vienna respectively.)

If "membership" in Central Europe is essentially a spiritual matter, then our point of departure should be the "distinctive skepticism" — "a bit mysterious, a bit nostalgic, often tragic, and even at times heroic" — that Havel refers to in "The Anatomy of Reticence," but also the *"kulturpolitische Antihypothese"* proposed by Konrad, for whom the Central European Spirit belongs to the "rational, humanist, democratic, skeptical, and tolerant" West. And in the last analysis, both Havel's and Konrad's views converge in that "civil society" for which Michnik pleads.

Given these premises, Romania could present convincing arguments for belonging to Central Europe. Unfortunately, "real socialism" in Romania abused the European norm in important ways. Especially during the seventies and eighties, this country reminded one not only of China's and North Korea's "proletarian dictatorships," or of Latin America's right-wing dictatorships, but also of long past periods of despotic barbarism that bequeathed to our times what we typically think of as Balkan "underdevelopment."

Painfully I recall the words of the musician George Enesco: "If only our administration and politics were on the same level as the arts, we would be one of the happiest countries on earth."

Skepticism has always been a Romanian trait, especially in people's attitudes toward politics and politicians, and usually toward the very idea of political engagement.

The mediocrity of so many contemporary political leaders in both large and small countries, the moral duplicity that reveals itself in their rhetoric, can only reinforce that skepticism. Eventually it degenerates into indifference and contempt.

A national history consisting of a series of catastrophes, a geographic position at the crossroads of East and West, directly in the path — and at the mercy — of interests more powerful than one's own: all this probably teaches caution. What can you do? You have to survive. Do you become a fatalist? Do you develop an acutely suspicious ear? Do you gamble and play? Your volatile temper is spiced by humor and muted by that quality of *bun simt*,[10] for which you are famous, which owes much more to an archaic, pagan, instinctual wisdom than it does to the constructs of ideology, be it religious or atheistic. Romanians like to repeat, often with an undertone of regret and even of guilt, "We haven't produced any saints" — or, in ironic self-exculpation, "The Romanian is born a poet."

Caution toward ideologies and suspicion toward politics do not, however, necessarily lead to moral stability. The noncommittal stance doesn't have just positive effects. Among its frequent consequences are, unfortunately, compromise and complicity. The deformation of high principle to the point of caricature can discredit faith in principles as such. The social mechanism begins imperceptibly to function in the good old "natural" ways, by mutual favors and force of circumstance, proliferating corruption, Byzantinism, demagogy, abuse of power, and nepotism on a truly fantastic scale. Under these conditions, what is normally called life is pushed into the background and locked in a system of ciphers and codes.

There were press reports in 1986 that in a park in Zagreb, Yugoslavia, a young intellectual made a mimed protest speech before a crowd that had gathered spontaneously, a speech without words (to avoid being accused of breaking the law). It seems, however, that the audience understood his message perfectly. In Romania, this coded type of communication — in response to the brutal machinery of repression — permeated the whole of society, not just private relationships. Precise knowledge of a system of signs — perceptible only to initiates, and often implied rather than expressed — was indispensable in any exchange between individuals and groups. A whole society, under surveillance around the clock, split between feigned submission and masked refusal.

While working on my novel *The Black Envelope,* especially in the description of the association of deaf-mutes, which I had, conceived as a pseudosocialist equivalent of the evil organization of the blind in Ernesto Sabato's *On Heroes and Tombs,* I was forced to meditate at length on this theme of coded communication.

The censorship's brutal and repeated intervention reduced my book to a system of coded innuendoes inaccessible to all but the most sophisticated readers, except for the details that refer obviously (though still in code) to the banalities of daily life. The mysterious mark that begins to appear on the faces of one's fellow citizens, a scar right next to the eyebrow, refers to a certain overused wink that serves as a signal of mutual accord at all levels of the hierarchy; and of course, in the book, it serves as a reference to every sort of hidden and compulsive signal — a sort of nationwide tic.

I visited the Bucharest association of deaf-mutes. I was shocked by the miserable condition of the handicapped in a handicapped country: here was the extreme limit of the social and moral crisis in which the whole population had been plunged. I was also horrified by the cynicism of the authorities, who saw fit to oppress even this suffering minority to the point of complete mental and moral degradation. The deaf-mutes' newspaper in Bucharest was in no way different in language and layout from *Scînteia*[11] or, from any provincial party publication. Perhaps it was no accident that it was called *Our Life*.

The traditional mistrust in those who govern, the gulf between leaders and led, had grown to grotesque proportions in the last decade. Politics and politicians were seen as embodiments of stupidity or baseness (usually in combination), always surrounded by the aura of the ridiculous.

Everything political seemed tainted — not only those in authority, but sometimes even their opposition. Those who committed themselves politically on one side or the other were automatically suspected of some petty personal motive masquerading as high principle. It is no wonder that under such conditions sensible people stayed away from politics and even from the serious discussion of politics.

The nonpolitical stance thus became a refuge, a safe retreat, since one's abstention was not declared openly, and became active only in exceptional instances.

There was, however, a spirit of revolt. The reproach of passivity frequently leveled at Romania was only partially justified. Of course one cannot speak of a revolutionary tradition in Romania, but one shouldn't forget that in no other European socialist country has surveillance been as total and repression as severe.

The lack of revolutionary tradition is evident even in the few noteworthy uprisings and rebellions of recent Romanian history. The peasant revolt of 1907 and some of the workers' strikes in the twenties and thirties were simple explosions resulting from intolerable conditions.

Nevertheless, there were revolts. The miners' strike in 1977 and the protest demonstration in Brasov in 1987 — an officially organized election-day march that shifted abruptly into unrestrained popular fury against the officials — were not the only events of this kind. Smaller eruptions evaporated in the absence of any support or response from abroad. They had little chance of success in any case.

The spontaneous character of collective revolts was replicated in the outbursts of individuals as well. It is worth noting that, among the relatively few Romanian dissidents, many were Party members — which means that at least part of the time, and with reservations, they were willing to support the establishment.

More often than not, the decision to break with the system took place in a fit of rage. Immediately one was confronted with the fact that one stood alone and could not count on support from anyone. Recovery of one's courage and dignity often set in when despair over one's own unhappiness and indignation at the general misery combined and intensified to a degree that could no longer be endured. But the expression of social outrage usually remained limited to private explosions. For years there was a lack of any public discussion, for years the whole nation was exposed to the repressive monotony of a primitive, demagogic, cynical party jargon and to the quick repression of the Securitate. Could that be why even the most virulent protests had an improvisatory, rhetorical character?

Caragiale, the great Romanian playwright, wrote about this flaw: "We are all irritable, but only a few of us are expressive." The comment is witty but does not explain anything. The real reason why most attempts at opposing the Romanian regime were dissipated in improvised, transient, isolated explosions was the virtual impossibility of reestablishing the very foundations of genuine social dialogue. Even with the recovery of a more democratic way of life, Romania will probably suffer profoundly in the future from this dark and too long period of terror.

Of all the countries that might claim membership in a non-Communist Central Europe, Romania is probably the least talented for Communism. Paradoxical as it may seem, it is precisely the absence of a revolutionary tradition that explains the catastrophic, "un-European" situation in the Romania of the last two decades.

In 1945 the Romanian Communist Party had no more than 1,000 members.[12] It is easy to see why now, at the moment of the dictator's sudden and brutal collapse — after four decades of Communist politics and administration — it would have been hard to find 1,000 authentic Communists in Romania. Unfortunately, it has also become relatively easy to see why, under these conditions, Romania under Ceauşescu had over 3.5 million Communist Party members.[13] It may have been per capita the largest Communist Party in the world!

The Party card represented nothing more than a certificate of adaptation, a proof of one's social normalcy, which was added to all the other documents in one's personal record. To inflate a party to such proportions is tantamount to annulling it. This might have been interpreted as the outcome of a sane and intelligent strategy if the power once held by the Party had not long passed into the hands of the State Security force. The advantages of Party membership were of a purely potential kind; they depended on the individual's opportunistic energy and on the cynicism that comes to the aid of the self-preservation instinct.

The situation could take on grotesque, tragicomic forms. It would be hard, for example, to forget the commotion surrounding the Romanian publication of Mircea Eliade's *History of Religious Beliefs and Ideas* in 1981. The oddness of this event was exacerbated by the book's title in an officially atheistic country at a time when the censors were frenzied by strict orders with regard to anything resembling religion. What gave the contradiction a near-scandalous aura was the well-known fact that Eliade had belonged to the extreme right before the war, and that after the war he had deserted to "American imperialism."

The book's relatively small edition added to the general excitement: interested readers had to hustle for a "connection" in a bookstore, and naturally many were unable to secure a copy of the book. Actually the edition wasn't all that small — there was even a second printing — but most copies were sold through the hierarchy's "special channels." Obtaining *The History of Religious Beliefs and Ideas* was the privilege of those who called themselves atheists and revolutionaries, sworn enemies of all renegades and imperialists, etc., etc.

"If only our administration and politics were on the same level as the arts" — there would presumably have been far fewer Party members per capita in Romania. Even in recent years, when applying for membership in the Party had become a routine gesture — or perhaps especially then — the percentage of Party members among writers fell far below the national average, even though the Party never tired of asserting and proving its leading role in the Writers' Union, as in all other institutions. And the proportion was even lower among writers of real value — by which I mean those who were faithful to their vocation, who preserved their identity, and whose works, though written in a coded language, were unequivocally opposed to Romania's administration and policies under Ceauşescu. Therefore the population looked to the honest and gifted writers and artists with high esteem and trust even when they were silenced.

"Our cultural level is shockingly disproportionate to the rest of our social life. If only our administration and politics were on the same level as the arts, we would be one of the happiest countries in the world."

The last Writers' Union Conference, which took place in 1981,[14] was a genuine form of revolt. Had the speeches made then become known to the public (they were never published or taped, since no one was allowed to enter the room with a tape recorder), people would have been surprised, to say the least, at the vigor and frankness with which writers spoke out about Romania's crippled cultural life.

"Misplaced Europeans" is how one contemporary Romanian novelist defines his compatriots (reminiscent of Borges's "The Argentinian is an exiled European"). But Romanians have always had an astounding capacity for regeneration, for finding the strength to recuperate rapidly in the uncertain intervals between disasters. And forms of life, of creation, of resistance often sustained themselves in Romania, as far as was possible under this cruel, savage dictatorship, through culture.

III

On receiving the literary prize of the city of Bremen, Paul Celan emphasized that he came from a little-known landscape, "a country inhabited by people and books." Celan was referring to the Bukovina of his adolescence, but these words could apply to Romania as a whole.

Paul Celan came from cosmopolitan Bukovina, where Romanians, Jews, Germans, Poles, and Ukrainians lived together in a space that vibrated with a spiritual atmosphere of its own. Constantin Brancusi comes from poor Oltenia, the "land of quick thoughts and words," George Enescu from that lyrical and charming part of Moldavia that is considered "the placenta of Romanian culture." The iconoclast philosopher Emil Cioran was born in Rasinari, a typical Romanian village in southern Transylvania, not far from the German-founded "burg" of Sibiu, a city with a distinctly central European air, and Eugene Ionesco is a child of Bucharest, that metropolis glittering with irony and elegance, where misery is disguised as paradox and sarcasm as bantering cordiality. Panait Istrati is the child of a port on the Danube over which float the shining mirages of freedom and infinite space. Romania — a disconcerting mixture of contrasts: the Turk and the Tartar from the moonscape of torrid Dubrudgea, the competent yeoman from Banat, where so many Swabians found themselves a new fatherland, or the Saxonians of Transylvania in their centuries-old dialogue with Hungarians and Romanians.

But the nostalgia that writes these lines remembers not only the fishing village[15] where summer vacations among friends and the closeness of the sea seemed almost to cancel the sadness of the whole year, or the Carpathian forests that awakened such grandiose reveries in me when I was an adolescent; it turns back also to the young peasant woman who braved both war and the freezing wind of the Ukrainian steppes to save us, and to friends to whom literature has remained the Archimedian point and the North Star; to the vanished years when first love and the city library were my best schools; to my mother's fresh grave. This longing is for everything—people and books, suffering, hope, rebellion—that animates that irreplaceable realm we call a human life.

Anyone visiting Romania in the last decade could hardly imagine the once hospitable beauty of the country and the vital, spirited charm its everyday life once possessed; and I don't mean only the brief, relatively peaceful period between the two wars when Romania was striving for democracy, or only the few all too transient thaws of the postwar period.

During the relatively liberal decade of 1965–75, Romania was by no means prosperous, nor can one say that people's everyday life was permitted to unfold spontaneously and naturally. Yet the memory of that time has a tonic vibrancy: that allegro humming of sprightly Latinity, of wit and melodious decorum; you could move more freely, speak more freely about people and books. It was as if, overnight, people and books had risen from the dead—congenial talk, glittering parties, melancholy strolls, the excitement of venturing on some project—all this had come back to life. The new climate was not, as in other socialist countries, a reactivation of political involvement in response to a policy shift on the part of the leadership; it was a brief opportunity to set aside the government's political agenda and return to the simple enjoyment of life, in a country where people have always preferred songs to prayers and solemn oaths. That period stimulated economic initiative only to a negligible degree, but its benefit to art and literature extended into the next decade. We took advantage of any small chance to be in touch with the arts and the movements of thought in the West, and it was possible to take an independent position on social and political issues, and to express it in one's own personal style.

Glasnost was, in Romania, the implicit program of art and literature, before the terror of a frightened, hysterical censorship stifled it in recent years. The cultural landscape remained fragmented and discordant. Many Romanian books exhibited real expressive power and critical consciousness. Of course, as in every totalitarian state, you could also find many demonstrations of the most abject cynicism and opportunism, especially among the "official" (established) writers and those still striving for the laurels of state approval. But for a convincing and reliable diagnosis of the country's spiritual condition, one needed only to compare the official writers' demagogic declarations of fealty to their rulers with the disgust that is expressed between the lines in their books.

The Janus-head mentality creates some bizarre situations. For many years, one could watch on the press and on television the spectacular performances of a cynical and well-paid poet, a sort of state-sponsored disc jockey who liked to serve up all the favorite tunes of power — the folk song, the patriotic march, the ode to the Führer — until one day he fell into disgrace and vanished. Harder to understand — especially in times of misery and despair — were the services performed for the system by an old and celebrated philosopher who, after years of monastic seclusion, allowed his own extremely right-wing ideas, for which he had been imprisoned for years, to receive official sanction because they offered the leaders a new legitimacy.

For some writers, fashioning slogans and inane propagandistic metaphors was "merely" a routine; in other cases, this practice entailed a much more serious form of degradation.

Well-known writers even agreed to lend their pens or the journals they edited to the service of the State Security. They poisoned the cultural atmosphere and persecuted their colleagues on the "blacklist" with tireless, diabolical energy. The future chronicles of our present history will list the names of a number of "Romanian artists" and "Romanian writers" among those who left an indelible stain on the country.

And the others, the ones who maintained a proud silence, or exploded with suicidal rage? The resistance of so many honest and talented artists, writers, and intellectuals? Their contempt for politics, their aloofness from power, their improvised elitist self-isolation, their disdainful withdrawal from the struggles of the *vulgus*?

The fundamental condition of those who were honest, those who resisted, was a protracted state of latent explosion. In a culture obsessed with aesthetics and favoring an ironic aloofness from ethical imperatives, in a Romania devastated by compromise and complicity, where neither books nor people had a voice, a genuine writer could not in the long run endure the aggression that philistinism and cowardice fostered all around him. What sort of commitment could one ask of him? An unwavering faith in the primacy of the aesthetic as the prerequisite for ethical engagement? Aesthetics as East-ethics, then? The vocative pun found more than one echo. A recent novel by an author of the younger generation ends with the exclamation: "I need this East-ethics!" The unhappiness, the frustration, and the humiliation became more and more explosive, not just for the intellectuals but for the entire country.

Adaptability, skeptical pragmatism, and jovial resignation dominated Romanian reality for a very long time, to the detriment of political engagement, of coherent resistance, of constructive energy. Romanian — and naturally not just Romanian — beauty is more easily found in the individual than in the collective, behind the scenes rather than on center stage, in the dubious and roundabout solution (often preservative of some amply human resource) than in the firmness and clarity of a fixed position. After all, goodness is quiet and modest, it has trouble shielding itself against the noise and aggression of evil; and truth, too, survives in fractured, equivocal forms, finds refuge in obscurity and ingenious codes.

People and books . . . It seemed that an indestructible hedonism had always animated the people and the books of the Romanian landscape. A paradoxical priority was given to the immediacy of human relations, and also to relationships with landscapes and all the other existential pleasures that are the gift of a friendly climate. Paradoxical not because of the ineluctable contradictions of human interaction but because of an occasional suspension of essential moral criteria.

Recently I talked to an American intellectual who knows Romania well. I asked him what he found most surprising about the country. "Human relationships," he said. "The relationship between the 'good' and the 'bad,' if I may use these conventional terms. The abyss between good and evil people seems nowhere to be greater; or more precisely between those who feel drawn to humane principles and those in the voluntary service of evil. And yet they cooperate. I can't imagine a stranger, more puzzling collaboration."

Many Romanians considered this paradox — perhaps quite rightly — the result of a humanizing process rooted in that famous *bun simt* that is often cited as the foremost feature of the national character, a mode of communication that limits itself to the domestic and earthy zone of daily existence. But the authorities banked on this self-limitation; they manipulated it. In a society that permitted differences of opinion only in the private sphere, all the impulses that elsewhere would lead to frank argument or expressions of tolerance generated discord instead, and dishonesty, indifference, apathy. An apathy that irritated the rulers whenever one of their "grandiose projects" miscarried, but that suited them very nicely when it got in the way of a united and collective movement of revolt.

It is true that, even during the hardest times, Romanians have known how to build enclaves in which reason and normalcy could be preserved. Culture was maybe the most important of these enclaves. Unfortunately, after the war, the gulf between word and deed, between professed and genuine conviction, between political theater and social reality, widened.

During the last decade, this "sad country blessed with humor," as one of her great poets called her, was presenting herself, as so often in times of crisis and collapse, with a host of oppressive questions.

The disaster was absolute: the "evil" had to all appearances silenced the "good." A whole nation subjugated, hungry, humiliated, and forced to celebrate the crime ceaselessly. People and books alike thrown into the abyss. A country that destroyed its own monuments, its own memories; that was undergoing its own "racial purification" with the emigration of its last Jews, the massive departure of its German minority, and the escalating conflict with the Magyar minority; a country that was making the megalomaniacal claim — like some other great nations with a rich cultural heritage at similar junctures of imminent collapse — of a glorious lineage reaching back some 2,000 years and whose plans for more "multilateral development" extended into the next millennium, in blind disregard of our unstable nuclear era; a country that was governed by the dictator and his police like a penal colony, and that promised to transform all its citizens gradually into hard-working, infantile, submissive wage slaves for the sake of future penal colonies, 2,000 more years of stumbling through the dark, of multilateral degeneration.

At the end of an age that brought so many peoples the end of colonialism — and with it their entry into their own history — Romania seemed about to depart from history altogether.

And then, suddenly, the latest and most astonishing paradox of all: this defeated nation explodes in a singular display of courage and fighting spirit to take its place at the very forefront of contemporary history. In the second half of December 1989, Romania reclaims her dignity, rediscovers her heroes, the last but the biggest (because the most difficult) step in the restructuring of Eastern Europe. Overturned at last, the cruelest and darkest dictatorship!

The world now has to look to Romania with admiration. And to her writers as well. The recent upheavals, across Eastern Europe, have proved the importance of culture, its role and mission in the fight for freedom. We must hope that this resource will also prove itself in the coming very difficult period of moral recovery on the way to democracy and prosperity.

It is not by chance that today's Polish prime minister is a journalist and the president of Czechoslovakia a playwright. The great news of change and liberation was announced in Romania by a gifted and courageous poet. Let us hope that this beginning promises a happier future for the books and the people of this unforgettable landscape.

Translated by Joel Agee

Notes

1. Romania's native fascist movement was called the Legion of the Archangel Michael and later the Iron Guard. Its members were called "legionnaires."

2. In his recent article "The End of Communism in Poland and Hungary," *The New York Review of Books,* July 15, 1989, Timothy Garton Ash used "the power" in this same sense in his reflections on Poland: "Almost no one imagined that the great gulf between 'the power' and 'the society,' between Jaruzelsky and Walesa, could be so swiftly bridged."

3. The Romanian language allows the punning reference to *est* — east — in the word *estetica*.

4. Scientific exchanges and research trips in Romania fell under the auspices of the National Council for Science and Technology, headed by Elena Ceauşescu, President Ceauşescu's wife and number two in command of the country.

5. Nicolae Ceauşescu originated the concept of Romania as a "multi-laterally developed" society in the 1970s. The notion seemed to announce the advent, in a liberalized Romania, of a socialist society presumably superior in character to the Stalinist model of socialism with its emphasis on heavy industry. But the notion also signaled Romania's growing autarkic tendencies. The concept was consistently used in the official press throughout the disastrous period of backwardness and impoverishment of the 1980s, when Romania became a nationalistic, Stalinist, "non-European" dictatorship.

6. Awarding prizes in 1986 for books published in 1984 was one of the less bizarre aspects of the activities of the Romanian Writers' Union — strangled in the last few years, when even the most ordinary actions had to first be approved by "higher organs."

7. In response to my critical article published in the magazine *Familia,* several issues of *Saptamina* and other official newspapers in 1982 carried articles with anti-Semitic overtones denouncing me as a foreign, cosmopolitan, liberal, anti-Communist element.

8. In the late 1970s the Romanian censorship organ, *Directia Presei,* was dissolved. Censorship, however, did not end but was diffused, passing into the hands of individual editors of books, periodicals, etc. In the mid-1980s a central censorship organ was reinstituted, a *lectorat* within the Council for Socialist Culture and Education, i.e., a group to oversee and advise the individual editors. This amounted to a stricter form of publication control than the institution liquidated in the 1970s. Now there was double censorship — self-censorship by the writers, who can expect to be held accountable for their decisions, and by the control forum appointed to check up on them.

9. Mihai Eminescu, Romanian national poet, a great artist with a conservative, at times nationalistically accented, political vision.

10. Literally, "good sense." The word connotes a kind of instinctual delicacy in human relations, an unaffected, spontaneous sense of tact and decency. The German word *Menschlichkeit* is perhaps a close cognate.

11. *Scînteia* is the Communist Party daily and the largest newspaper in Romania.

12. Michael Shafir, *Romania* (Boulder: Lynne Rienner Publications, 1985), p. 27.

13. Over 3.5 million was the official figure quoted often in the Romanian press in recent years.

14. Although the Romanian Writers' Union was supposed to meet in conference every four years according to the statutes approved by the Party itself, no such meeting of writers had been allowed since 1981.

15. I am referring to 2 Mai, a fishing village on the Bulgarian border that became a chic but unpretentious resort for the Bucharest intelligentsia. People either camped in tents by the sea or boarded with the families of local fishermen. Since 1982, the construction of a military port nearby, restrictions on camping, and the arrest and unexplained death of one of the 2 Mai regulars (whose personal journal was used against him) have made this a much less inviting spot for many.

Author's Note: While the author did not participate directly in the Romanian revolt of 1989, and his essay deals only with the period immediately prior to the revolt, it conveys a sense of the moral decay, cynicism, ugly humiliation, and not-so-subtle brutality of that time and place.

PART VII

The Baltic States

Thomas A. Oleszczuk

The Peaceful Revolution in Lithuania

> *Once again there will arise self-governing people's states. And then they can decide for themselves what mutual agreements and unions they will sign and enter into as nations and states.*
> —*Vytautus Landsbergis, President of* Sajudis, *speaking to the Congress of People's Deputies in Moscow*[1]

Thomas A. Oleszczuk was born in 1948, a fourth-generation American of Polish descent. Currently a professor of political science at Merchant Marine Academy in New York, he has written numerous articles for the *American Political Science Review, Comparative Politics, Soviet Studies,* and *Review of Politics.* He is the author of *Political Justice in the U.S.S.R.: Dissent and Repression in Lithuania 1968–1987.*

Mr. Oleszczuk has specialized in writing about dissent and political change in and about Eastern Europe for twenty years, and is currently working on a book of comparative Baltic nationalism called *Baltics to the Balkans.* Here is his view of the dynamic political pluralism and acceleration of reform in Lithuania today, which has had such a powerful effect upon Gorbachev and the Soviet Union.

February 1990 was a time of drama. The session of the Central Committee of the Communist Party of the Soviet Union was to have done something about the stubborn Lithuanian Communist Party, which had declared its political independence only a few weeks before. Yet, no sanctions were imposed. Instead, Mikhail Gorbachev used the opportunity to push the Central Committee to accept political pluralism, even as nationalists in Lithuania were preparing to dislodge Communists in republic-wide elections. Once again, as in the previous year and more, the "unthinkable" was happening east of the Elbe River.

The recent developments in the small non-Slavic republic on the Baltic cast a bright light on the dynamics of change throughout what has been called "the Soviet Empire." The sources and dimensions of those developments, which predate Gorbachev's leadership, illuminate the prospects for the future facing him, other Communist officials, and the peoples of the entire political system. The lessons of Lithuania for the Soviet Union are the counterproductiveness of state coercion, the intersection of pressures for reform "from below" and "from above," and the limited maneuvering room for middle roads of reform.

State and Society in Lithuania

The current Western media analysis of the drama of the Soviet Union has been seriously flawed. The focus is on confrontation at the top — which leaders are talking to whom, what choice of words or policy proposals are made at public forums to undermine opponents. This ignores the acts of the masses, which form the social context for those confrontations.

What has to be understood is the underlying, pre-Gorbachev pressure for independence in Lithuania.[2] A small country with about 3.6 million citizens, mostly non-Slavic Lithuanians, Lithuania has always faced Westward culturally. Since the forced incorporation of Lithuania into the USSR in 1940, official policy has dictated suppression of the distinctive features of the political culture: its anti-Russian nationalism, anti-atheistic Catholicism, and anti-Communism. These features had firm roots in the interwar Lithuanian state, and even drew upon nineteenth-century developments. Thus, it is not surprising that this suppression was not complete, or that Stalinism in Lithuania would be its own "gravedigger," ironically mirroring the way the bourgeoisie was supposed to destroy capitalism, according to Marx.

Several strands of dissent developed. One was nationalist. Despite the Soviet regime's putative "internationalism" (under which the many nationalities could flourish), the language and secular culture endured, under close state control. Preservation of these differences from the dominant Russian majority always formed a backdrop to discontent, which fed upon anti-Russian sentiment. By the 1960s, underground literary and historical works in Lithuania were reaffirming the worth of Lithuanian life and decrying Russian domination. The prewar national flag and anthem, shrines of nationalist poets and leaders, and the old holiday of independence (from the disintegrating Russian Empire at the end of World War I) were more and more often used by Lithuanians expressing their national identity, despite the penalty of arrest.

Closely allied to nationalist dissent was religious dissent. Lithuania's Catholicism was officially supervised by the republic government's Committee on Religious Affairs, chaired by an atheist, but religious resistance to anticlerical propaganda never entirely disappeared. By the early 1970s, a religious underground of increasing strength, with a pervasive information network and covert seminary, had developed. More and more often, religious ceremonies with nationalist connotations were attended openly by hundreds, then thousands of worshippers. The activities of those who dissented grew in number and sophistication, with the late 1970s seeing several extensive petition drives, occasionally garnering nearly 200,000 signatures (for the return of the cathedral in Klaipeda, which had been confiscated by civil authorities). Moreover, the religious dissidents established an ongoing system of publication, centered primarily in the periodical *Chronicle of the Catholic Church in Lithuania* (which survived numerous waves of repression and emerged ever stronger).

A more general anti-Communism expressed itself in the rise of a third kind of dissent: human rights activists, who founded such organizations as the Lithuanian Helsinki Group and the Catholic Committee to Defend the Rights of Believers. The perceived sacrifices of the interests and dignity of individuals were challenged by those Lithuanians (like others elsewhere in the Soviet Union) who insisted upon protection from the arbitrariness of the state coercive apparatus.

This last strand of dissent suggests a paradox. The regime's lack of success in dealing with citizen resistance was *reinforced* by the state's attempt to repress. The government defined many actions as illegitimate and punished individuals for them. But both definition and punishment led to more dissatisfaction, as those not directly repressed objected, which led to further attempts by the courts and psychiatric hospitals to intimidate dissidents. This process, called "the dialectic of dissent and repression" by Robert Sharlet, brought in new people and united them in opposition to Communist leaders at all levels.[3] What arose in the 1970s was a real social movement, in which people acted collectively to achieve unofficial goals using their own resources against the established order.

Solidarity in Poland is the best known East European social movement. Its experience during martial law was similar in many ways to that of the Lithuanian movement of the decade before. Both used the infrastructure of the Roman Catholic Church as an organizational resource across the country, although in Lithuania the personnel of the church (priests and other local religious leaders) were much more active. Both states targeted dissidents differentially, generally avoiding church figures for fear of popular outrage. This fear was justified, as evidenced in Lithuania in 1970–71 after the arrests of several priests and in Poland after the killing of Father Jerzy Popieluszko, both followed by dramatic increases in protest. In both cases, the power of repression was ultimately ineffective, with the violation of human rights itself fueling development of the social movement.

The rise of a social movement under such circumstances means the emergence of a "civil society" in competition with the state.[4] This term means that individuals worked together for the good of the community outside of and often against the state's directives. Such collective action brought trust and personal efficacy. Although the costs of "being caught" by the police could be high for individuals, the movement provided succor. It also indirectly reduced the climate of fear enveloping people, by encouraging small group cooperation in discussions and other ways, and by constraining the regime from more massive use of force and intolerance. Ironically, as the movement gained in strength, the de facto "tolerance" for dissent increased dramatically. Arrests and trials for political reasons continued, but the movement grew much faster than such measures could deal with.[5]

The Gorbachev Era: Acceleration of Change

When Gorbachev became general secretary of the CPSU, he initially rejected the possibility of dissent, but gradually he moved to change the system in ways that actually promoted the fortunes of those who opposed existing policies and institutions. For the first six months, in official statements and policy, his leadership was indistinguishable from that of the Brezhnev generation. Indeed, Gorbachev's first speech to the Central Committee as general secretary used the Stalinist phrase "the cleansing of alien phenomena."[6] However, from October 1985 to January 1987, he made concessions under internal and international pressure: he proclaimed a need for legal reform as part of *perestroika*, accepted human rights as an issue for international diplomacy, and allowed more lenience in individual cases of repression. Nonetheless, this was a period of a "dual track" approach, during which he generally maintained repressive policies. *Glasnost* was to be a privilege extended only to those supporting *his* positions against the bureaucracy.

From early 1987 through the end of 1988, Gorbachev moved quite far in reform on human rights. With the release of Andrei Sakharov, followed by hundreds of other political and religious prisoners, the openness of the system was implicitly widened to include the formerly outcast. Legal reforms began, and the local authorities in many areas increasingly accepted the activities of "informal groups" (which *Pravda* at one point estimated to number 60,000). Repression of human rights declined markedly, except for certain nonestablishment religious groups (like the Evangelical Baptists) and non-Russian nationalists along the southern periphery (like Kazakhs, Armenians, and Georgians).

This "liberalization" was characterized by a withdrawal of close central control over various aspects of life. It proceeded "from the top," at Gorbachev's Politburo's directive, and it went only as far as republic and local authorities allowed. Thus, for Lithuania, the social movement until late in 1988 coexisted uneasily with the government. The latter continued harassment and even juridical repression, while the former pressed further and further in public activities. The Independence Day celebrations in February led to police violence in the face of thousands of demonstrators in many cities.

This would be the last time the republic government would respond to dissent in the old hard-line way without immediate consequence. Since late 1988, the Soviet Union and the Lithuanian Republic have moved into a new phase: "pluralization," the acceptance of increasingly independent power centers outside the Communist Party hierarchy. The pressures for policy innovation and structural renovation have in this phase pushed "from below" as often as, or more than "from above."

At the all-union level, pluralization was initiated from above, with elections for the newly created Congress of People's Deputies. The last-minute arrangement for Sakharov's selection and the prominent place of honor accorded him by Gorbachev were signs that not only could people criticize but they could also "participate" in decision making even if outside the Party.

In Lithuania, on the other hand, the pressures came first from below. A large informal group in support of Gorbachev's reform, called the Lithuanian Movement for Perestroika (*Sajudis*), arose in June 1988 to find the republic leaders recalcitrant. Only the replacement of the republic Party leader in October shifted the course of events. Then the organizations outside the Party began having an upward-spiraling impact on Lithuanian and Soviet affairs.

This displacement of leadership occurred for both republic and all-union reasons. At the republic level, it was primarily because popular discontent focused on the leaders' refusal to change old ways.[7] Within weeks of its founding, Sajudis was able to mobilize 50,000–60,000 in late June to protest the Party leaders' abuse of power within the Party, namely the undemocratic and manipulated elections to the nineteenth CPSU Conference. Within days, there were again demonstrations against the leadership's traditional use of the media to distort reports of the meeting to its own advantage. Then Sajudis sponsored numerous gatherings as it roused support for reformist, nationalist positions, while the Party establishment pressured it by cutting it off from the media and hindering its activities bureaucratically (delaying or canceling permission for meetings, forcing a choice between Party and Sajudis membership, etc.).

The conflict came to a head in late September 1988 after the Party leadership violently broke up a meeting of tens of thousands sponsored by the Lithuanian Freedom League, an affiliate of Sajudis, and simultaneously arrested several hunger strikers protesting the continued detention of political prisoners, despite the widely publicized release of hundreds of others across the USSR. Further intense protest led to the release of those prisoners and the ouster of the rigid Ringaudus Songaila from the top Party post, replaced by Algirdas Brazauskas, a pro-reform secretary of the Lithuanian Central Committee who had even spoken at the June protest of Sajudis.[8]

Moscow's commitment to change also played a role in this transfer of power within the Lithuanian Party. Gorbachev has slowly worked to rid himself of nonreformists in positions of responsibility. He has taken a masterful approach to power, seizing the personnel levers without too much heavy-handedness. Opportunities to push out old-line Communists have frequently presented themselves as these officials deal ineffectively with more demands from informal groups for change. For instance, Gorbachev had sent Alexander Yakovlev to the Baltic republics in August 1988 to press the local leaders to avoid violence and to promote reform, including concessions to the nationalist demands then being expressed at various meetings (for the legalization of the old national flag and anthem, for example). In October, Moscow did not support the hardliner Songaila in the intra-Party dispute following the September violence, paving the way for Brazauskas.

Gorbachev's role in this process is clear. His program of reform has, from the beginning, been sabotaged (through inaction, at least) by the Party–state bureaucracy. He has needed to develop outside allies like Sajudis who could squeeze the bureaucrats from below while he tried to move the society to reform from above. He thus has made attempts to bring intellectuals, the young, workers, even the religious to his side, and has promoted the rise of informal groups through which these outside allies could act.

The Current Situation

The dynamics of politics today in Lithuania can be summarized easily: political pluralism. The acceleration of reform has led to the diffusion of power away from the old Party–state.

The Communist Party of Lithuania is admittedly still the dominant institution of the republic, given the interpenetration of economic and governmental institutions based on the Soviet *nomenklatura* system (Party approval of managerial appointments). However, the Party is steadily losing influence, even as it reforms, to Sajudis, which has developed into the major voice of the population. Sajudis has support in all the cities and towns and throughout much of the countryside, with the exception of some non-Lithuanian areas. It swept last year's Congress of People's Deputies elections (winning thirty-six of forty-two seats, and it could have done even better) and is preparing for a strong performance in imminent republic elections.[9] Such widespread support has bent the Communist Party to adopt much of Sajudis's program and to continuing cooperation with it. Indeed, this cooperation has now reached the stage of cooptation: the December 1989 Lithuanian Party Congress that declared its independence from the CPSU in Moscow also elected several Sajudis leaders to its Central Committee and Politburo.

Although Sajudis was radicalized by the stubbornness of the Party through much of 1988, it has lost much of the political initiative to the Lithuanian Freedom League, one of its constituent organizations, dominated by former dissident leaders.[10] This group has always been more openly nationalistic, more daring, and more willing to confront authority. Its first rally (preceding the birth of Sajudis by nearly a year) protested the forty-eighth anniversary of the Nazi–Soviet Pact. Black armbands commemorated the Baltic dead resulting from that pact; chants of "Freedom!" accompanied the singing of the old Lithuanian anthem. Later, at the "constituent assembly" of Sajudis, one of the League's leaders, Antanas Terleckas, publicly proclaimed the goal of complete independence. This cast down the gauntlet after greetings from General Secretary Gorbachev to the assembly were conveyed by Brazauskas. It was the kind of radicalism that caused Sajudis concern, but to which it succumbed.[11]

Although its platform was very similar to Sajudis's, the League radicalized Sajudis in more than style and timing. On military policy, the League called for a national army separate from the Red Army and began mass protests on this in January 1989. Although these were joined by Sajudis representatives the following month, it was not until the League had agitated at numerous meetings and was gaining popular support for the issue in October that the Kaunas branch of Sajudis committed itself. It promised to defend the increasing number of young men who were refusing conscription, an issue that still is unresolved.[12]

Both organizations often aided other, smaller groups, such as the Lithuanian Helsinki Group and the Lithuanian Association for Human Rights, that had been part of the dissident movement and whose leaders had been dissident activists. Similar, newer groups evolved rapidly after mid-1988: the Committee for the Rescue of Lithuanian Political Prisoners, the Group for the

Support of Former Political Prisoners, the Committee for the Defense of the Rights of Criminal Prisoners, the International Society for Human Rights, and the Union of Exiles.[13]

This pluralization of the political system goes beyond the confines of the underground social movement, of course. Active organizations now represent specific causes that did not find special voice earlier. There are groups of workers, industrialists, farmers, ecologists, pacifists, reserve military officers, women, writers, and the young, some of which are breakaways from the old Party–state structure. Also, since the accession of reformers to the Party leadership, several political parties have been created or reestablished. These include the Lithuanian Democratic Party, the Social Democrats, the Christian Democrats, the Greens, the Party of Lithuanian Youth, the Party for Humanism and Progress in Lithuania, and the National Union of Lithuania.[14]

Thus, the contemporary scene has the older dissident figures in many organizations trying with some success to influence the major decisions of the times, via the League–Sajudis–Party connection. Supplementing them, the social movement has itself emerged from the underground and produced numerous nongovernmental organizations, with the values of national identity and human rights predominant. The Party no longer represses but listens to voices from outside the establishment.[15]

Options for Gorbachev

Under Stalin, Communists were frequently confronted with only one possible choice: follow his directives even if they were wrong. Gorbachev and his Party supporters face a "reformist dilemma of the single alternative." Times have changed, and Gorbachev is not able to command, much less limit, his followers with the threat that anything else is counterrevolution and deserving of the punishment given to traitors. Instead, it is he who has few options. In Lithuania, he has no real choice: either he accepts the acts of the reformers there, or he ends the reform in toto.

The Baltic republics show no sign of accepting a limited role in a new Soviet Union. They do not buy Gorbachev's offer of new "forms of federative relationships." Instead, all three republics are moving toward independence, with the Lithuanians now in the lead.

Until the end of last year, Gorbachev had evolved a tripartite strategy on the national question. He had used force in the Caucasus and Central Asia, mainly in response to interethnic violence, and had not pressed hard for reform in the absence of strong reformist groups in those areas. In the Baltics, he had encouraged change and tolerated nationalism, which did not erupt into violence and which gave him allies for reform. In the remaining, mostly Slavic, areas he tried to encourage reform completely outside a nationalist context.

This tripartite strategy now lies in ruins. Although Gorbachev can temporarily coerce unruly nationalism in the south (with long-term negative consequences even there), he cannot proceed with tolerance of the Balts while moving more cautiously among the Slavs. The three-way policy is not maintaining Soviet unity among the various nationalities.

It must be admitted that coercion in the southern republics has not automatically threatened *perestroika*. To stop violence among the peoples of the Caucasus and Central Asia does not entail a rejection of reform: those repressed were not, after all, reformers. That would not be the case in the western republics, where economic reform and nationalist movements are closely linked.

Gorbachev cannot use tanks against his own allies even when they oppose him, for that would imply the bankruptcy of his reform, admitting that the people cannot do without strong central control in *all* their affairs. He can try wooing his Baltic allies. The moves to a multiparty system and to private property represent acquiescing after the fact to the experiments of the Balts, as well as a great deal more, of course.

However, it is not clear how he can keep them in the Union more than temporarily by such concessions. The underlying centrifugal factors predate his leadership and can rapidly escalate, as they have through the social movement of Lithuania and through pluralism itself later. Only a few years after Gorbachev came to power, the previously unthinkable is happening: Lithuanians are preparing for independence, with the Estonians and Latvians not far behind.

There is some evidence that more sophisticated coercion, via the economy, may be used. Already there are some problems of nondelivery and delay by centrally run enterprises in the Baltic republics.[16] This tactic of implied economic ruin can only boomerang. The Lithuanians and their Estonian and Latvian neighbors will soon enough become indignant and even more determined to secede if it continues.[17]

Similarly, efforts to build a base among the non-Lithuanian peoples (Russians and Poles, via the Unity group) or more conservative elements of the Lithuanian Party (the "loyalists" whom the Central Committee hesitatingly decided to support[18]) bear little chance of success. They too would prove counterproductive, intensifying Lithuanian resistance to Moscow and speeding up the move to independence. The popularity of the Party in Lithuania seems to have rebounded somewhat because of this kind of external pressure, as well as its cooperation with Sajudis.[19]

Ironically, one path *might* keep the Balts part of the Soviet Union: allowing the Balts to become the operational vanguard of reform. The Balts might be challenged to reform the rest of the country. The prospect of a major leadership role for them, in which they not only determine their own conditions but also assist Gorbachev in other republics and at the all-union level, just might appeal to the national pride of these peoples. Already we have seen the Congress of People's Deputies accept the Balts' demands for reassessment of the Molotov–von Ribbentrop Pact and for economic autonomy. And the pluralism evolved by Lithuania (and elsewhere) has been made all-union policy through the Central Committee's decision to eliminate Article 6 of the Soviet Constitution, the article that guarantees the Party exclusive political control of the government and other bodies.

The major difficulty with this approach is the contradiction of market-based reformist principles and the long-standing Soviet principles of equality and participation of all national groups. Gorbachev cannot hope to swing Central Asian elites, much less Russians, more firmly into action changing the society if the Balts are perceived as enjoying too much respect and influence.

Gorbachev has continually turned difficult crises to his own advantage, furthering the transformation of the Soviet Union as well. If anyone can make the Balts the champions of *perestroika* without alienating the other nationalities, he is the one. Without that, the odds are quite good that the map of the Soviet Union will be redrawn soon.

Notes

1. Published in *Izvestia* (no. 154) as translated in *The Soviet Empire: Its Nations Speak Out*, edited by Oleg Glebov and John Crowfoot (New York: Harwood Academic Publishers, 1989) p. 22.

2. The following discussion of the sources and manifestations of the Lithuanian dissident movement is taken from my *Political Justice in the Soviet Union: Lithuania, 1969–1987* (Boulder, Colo.: East European Quarterly Press/Columbia University Press, 1988).

3. Robert Sharlet, "Dissent and Repression in the Soviet Union and Eastern Europe," *International Journal* 23(4) (autumn 1978): 763–795. There did arise a new type of dissident, the "hybrid," who shared specific grievances with the nationalist, religious, and human rights dissidents. This type performed the vital function of bridging the gaps between these others. *Political Justice*, pp. 55–58.

4. S. Frederick Starr, in his "Soviet Union: A Civil Society," *Foreign Policy* 70 (spring 1988): 26–41, has analyzed the sociological and technical basis of the rise of this social formation. However, I maintain that in some of the non-Russian areas, at least, the "networking" of the dissidents was the basis of the social movement prior to the "networking" of the late 1980s in informal groups, which he discusses on p. 33.

5. This process was autonomous of developments in Moscow, whether one looks at elite conflict or all-union repressive policy. *Political Justice*, chapter 7.

6. This periodization, excluding the most recent stage of liberalization, was first presented in my paper "The Human Rights Offensive in
the USSR: The Fourth Side of Liberalization," presented to the American Political Science Association, Washington, D.C.: 3 September 1988.
The speech is analyzed on pp. 2–3.

7. V. Stanley Vardys, "Lithuanian National Politics," *Problems of
Communism* (July–August 1989): 60–64.

8. *USSR News Briefs* (Munich), 1988 (12), report 12–5.

9. The strength of Sajudis and the rejection of the old Party leadership in the upcoming elections is shown in at least one statistic: only 21
of the 350 previous members of the Lithuanian Supreme Soviet are
even running this time. Saul Girnius (RFE/RL Research Department),
"Lithuanian Supreme Soviet Elections," *This Week in the Baltic States*, 1
February 1990 (Washington, D.C.: Sovset electronic network, run by
the Center for Strategic and International Studies). At few times in
history have parliaments seen such dramatic turnover.

10. For this League role, see Vardys, "Lithuanian National Politics,"
p. 58 passim. Most of the eighteen members of the Temporary
National Council of the League listed in *USSR News Briefs*, 1988 (13),
report 13–4, were prominent dissidents included in my *Political Justice*
study.

11. *USSR News Briefs*, 1987 (15/16), report 15/16–3; (17/18), report
17/18–27; 1988 (19/20), report 19/20–4.

12. *USSR News Briefs*, 1989 (1), report 1–3; (4), report 4–7; (19/20),
report 19/20–5. The dramatic flag- and uniform-burning in June 1989,
at a rally of the Association for Lithuanian Independence (see next
note), was a tactic not endorsed by Sajudis, which prevented the August
rallies from having draft card burning by Young Lithuania. *USSR News
Briefs*, 1989 (12), report 12–5; (13/14), 13/14–5.

13. *USSR News Briefs*, 1989, varied issues. Vardys, "Lithuanian
National Politics," p. 58, notes that the League formed its own alliance
outside Sajudis, the Association for Lithuanian Independence, which
included several of these groups. Also, as one might expect, the new
groups often adopted the techniques of the dissident movement: mass
petitions, processions, hunger strikes, religious ceremonies, the use of
traditional emblems.

14. The last-named was the ruling party of interwar Lithuania from
1926 to 1939. *USSR News Briefs*, 1989 (15/16), report 15/16–8. The list is
drawn from varied issues of *USSR News Briefs*. In the upcoming
elections, the Social Democrats, Democrats, Greens, and Christian

Democrats have registered four or more candidates each. Girnius, "Lithuanian Supreme Soviet Elections."

15. Last year, there were three countermeasures against individuals associated with the League: the search of the premises of a League member in January 1989, the psychiatric detention of Antanas Kemiza in February 1989, and the trial of Stasis Zickus (who threatened public officials in the name of the League, though not himself a member). On the other hand, Party Secretary Brazauskas spoke at public ceremonies alongside League and other representatives, for example in Kaunas on February 16. *USSR News Briefs,* 1989 (2), report 2–3; 1989 (7/8), reports 7/8–13 and 7/8–6; 1989 (4), report 4–7. Also to be noted: the major *samizdat* journal *Chronicles of the Catholic Church in Lithuania* has continued underground, a reflection perhaps of the uncertainties of many dissidents despite the pluralization process.

16. Bill Keller, "Baltics Say the Kremlin Blocks Economic Shifts," *New York Times,* 11 February 1990, p. 21.

17. Already, CPSU Politburo member (and chairman of Gosplan, the state planning commission) Yuri Maslyukov publicly admitted "how residents of the [Lithuanian] republic react with irritation to outside speculation about how much their freedom will cost them in rubles or in convertible currency." Bill Keller, "Buying Time in Lithuania," *New York Times,* 13 January 1990, p. 6.

18. Paul Goble, "Plenum Condemns Lithuanian Party," *RFE/RL Daily Report,* no. 28, 8 February 1990.

19. A January 1990 poll found that 82 percent of the public supported the Party's decision to assert its independence. Esther B. Fein, "Lithuanians Cry 'Freedom' on Eve of Gorbachev's Visit," *New York Times,* 11 January 1990, p. A14. Another poll found public approval of the Party had zoomed from 17 percent to 83 percent. Alison Mitchell, "In Lithuania, a Tenuous Coalition," *Newsday* (New York), 5 February 1990.

John Jekabson

Economic Independence Is Not Enough for Lithuania, Estonia, and Latvia

John Jekabson was born in Latvia in 1941 and has lived in the United States since 1952. His journalism appears in many publications through the Pacific News Service and in such periodicals as *The Economist*. Mr. Jekabson is also the founding publisher and editor of *The Baltic News,* a unique publication that appears every three months in northern California, where he now resides.

In the following report, Mr. Jekabson offers a firsthand view of current turbulent events in Lithuania, Estonia, and Latvia — the three Baltic states whose citizens made the earliest moves toward democracy and independence from Moscow and whose continuing courage and skill have subsequently served as an inspiration for radical revolutionary movements in other Soviet republics and in Central Europe.

On January 1, 1990, a new law, passed by the Communist Party Presidium, gave economic independence to the Soviet Baltic republics of Estonia, Latvia, and Lithuania (annexed by Stalin in 1940). A year ago such a move by Moscow would have been viewed as an unprecedented step toward a free market economy and self-determination. But after the startling and historic changes in Eastern Europe in the fall of 1989, the promise of economic autonomy comes too late to halt the avalanche of pressure for complete political independence in the Baltic Republics.

With the continuing acceleration of economic collapse and social chaos throughout the Soviet system, the Balts (as the Estonians, Latvians, and Lithuanians call themselves) see the new law as irrelevant and are more determined than ever to break away from the Soviet Union.

"They want to leave the ship, which is being heavily rocked by a storm," Moscow political analyst Ilya Baranikas said of the Balts bitterly. "We are all together on a ship chartered for a democratic state, ruled by law. The trip has to be slow, with painstaking efforts by all."

"But we never signed on to that ship," retorts Marju Lauristin, leader of the Estonian Popular Front. "We were hijacked. So you can understand why we have no desire to go down with the Soviet economic collapse. In our hearts we were never part of the Soviet empire."

People in Estonia, Latvia, and Lithuania have never forgiven or forgotten how their independence was stolen by the Soviet Union in 1940 as a result of Stalin's pact with Hitler. Their anger is fueled by the memory of mass deportations, forced collectivization, and stringent cultural assimilation of the past fifty years. In a sense the whole population of almost eight million could be classified as dissidents, never having accepted the loss of their freedom.

Although Soviet leader Mikhail Gorbachev is respected and admired for his bold reforms and initiatives, he is not viewed by Balts as *their* leader, but as a foreign head of state. His dramatic visit to Lithuania in early January 1990, when he engaged in debates in the street, did nothing to dampen the Balts' single-minded drive for complete independence.

Originally the Baltic economic autonomy proposal had been anticipated as a major victory by political leaders in all three of the republics. But events in Eastern Europe, and the Soviet Union have moved at such breakneck speed that the economic package has become outdated even at its inception. The plan was formulated for two widely distinct reasons. Soviet officials in

Moscow hoped it would give the Balts enough self-rule to stop their agitation for political independence. The leaders of the democratic movements in the Baltic saw economic autonomy as a breathing space – a transition stage to full independence, which they anticipated would take five to ten years. Now both sides know their goals are unrealistic. The clamor for political independence is now so pervasive there is nothing the Kremlin can do to derail it. The "transition" concept also seems moot, since the Soviet economy is proving more anemic and unresponsive than was imagined.

The few months the new economic policy has been in effect it has consistently floundered and met bitter resistance from Moscow. The free-market experiments in the Baltics have provoked a virtual economic blockade from the Soviet side. Energy and industrial supplies to the Baltic republics have been cut, their bank accounts frozen in Moscow, and their market-pricing plans declared illegal. The central bank in Moscow insists it must approve all commitments of foreign currency, in effect giving it veto over joint commercial ventures with foreign companies. Such ventures are central to the Baltic republics' plans of developing their own sovereign economies.

Baltic officials say they have been greatly frustrated in establishing reliable contracts with suppliers in other parts of the Soviet Union, who generally remain puppets of industrial ministries in Moscow. Gasoline has virtually disappeared from service stations in the Baltics. Although there is an extensive lumber industry in the Baltics, newsprint has now become scarce because of a test of wills between Latvia and the Council of Ministers in Moscow. Latvian officials shut down a plant in the resort city of Jurmala because the air pollution from sulphur emissions had closed the beach for the last two years. The plant produces various paper products, including cellulose used to make newsprint in plants in other parts of the Soviet Union. There is currently no newsprint produced in the Baltics. In response to the plant closure, Moscow not only cut off the republic's entire supply of newsprint but also instructed paper mills throughout the Soviet Union not to sell to Latvia.

Now that Soviet consumers are losing confidence in the value of their rubles, hoarding and bartering have replaced currency more and more. The Latvian agricultural firm Adzi, for example, used five tons of bricks and fifteen tons of metal to purchase twenty tractors from a Russian enterprise. There is a joke in the Baltics that the only way to get a full tank of gasoline is to drive in with a live calf on your hood.

For the past two years there have been extensive planning sessions, seminars, and detailed published economic programs by the Popular Front movements of Estonia and Latvia and Sajudis, their Lithuanian counterpart. In these plans, Baltic economists anticipated an economic blockade by the Soviet Union if the Baltic states declared unilateral independence. Now it appears the blockade is being used by the Kremlin before independence, as a warning of what the future holds.

"We have been tied together for fifty years, whether you like it or not," Gorbachev warned the Balts during his visit to Lithuania. "Think not once, not a dozen times, but a hundred times before you decide to leave and bog down in an economic swamp."

"*We* in Estonia are not in an economic swamp, but we see it encroaching," says Estonian leader Marju Lauristin. "It is very strange to hear people in the West say, go slow. We are in a great hurry, because once the swamp engulfs us, it will be even harder to get out."

Estonia is the most forward looking of the three Baltic republics. Already the small country of 1,500,000 has more private business cooperatives than the rest of the Soviet Union combined. Young Estonians are being sent to business schools in the West where emphasis is placed on computer literacy and high technology. They see their future linked to Scandinavia and Western Europe, not the barter economy of the Soviet Union. With the current economic independence plan unable to get off the ground, and newly elected Popular Front leaders in control of the local parliaments, it is anticipated that all three of the Baltic republics will declare themselves independent within a year. All three have consistently stated that they will be "parliamentary democratic republics on the Western European model, based on the economic principles of market economy."

On my recent visit to Estonia and Latvia I could feel the euphoria and anticipation of independence everywhere I went. From flower vendors and taxi drivers to academics and Popular Front leaders, the talk was always about the national "awakening" and the prospects for freedom. Rock songs and pop music were not about love and flowers but about overcoming oppression and deportation to Siberia. People in the countryside were restoring destroyed monuments and overgrown cemeteries. Old and long hidden books and photographs were being exhibited in museums. The news media were daily exposing former Communist Party *apparatchiks* who had been part of the "stagnant" clique during the Brezhnev era, and hounding them out of office.

"I see a cosmic force behind all this," Latvian rock music composer Zigmars Liepins, thirty-four, told me. "With so many minds working for independence, it's inevitable it will come to pass." He had just produced a rock opera depicting a mythical Latvian hero driving red-garbed invaders out of the country.

Eduards Berklavs, seventy-five, the dean of Latvian politicians, was angry about articles he had seen in the Western press. "Questions are being raised about the viability of our independence," he said. "Those who question it aren't aware of our history. We were viable and prosperous independent states in the past. We had a strong currency, we exported butter, bacon, and wheat. We can always grow food enough for export. We did it before, and we'll do it again." Berklavs was a top leader of the Latvian Communist Party in the 1950s before he was purged for "nationalistic tendencies."

The Balts I met were full of self-confidence and eager to go out into the world. They were aware that their resourcefulness and political originality had confounded Soviet leaders in Moscow. Everything was being accomplished in a parliamentary step-by-step process, unlike the violent ethnic disturbances in other Soviet republics. They stressed that descriptions of "turmoil in the Baltics" in the Western press gave the world the wrong impression of their struggle. In all that "turmoil" not one person had been killed — or even injured. In fact their demonstrations were so orderly that there weren't even papers or garbage left to pick up after gatherings of 100,000. They also pointed out that they are not "ethnics" who want to "secede" but nation-states that are fighting to regain their independence. A basic trait I found was an air of aloofness, bordering on arrogance; their attitude was that, given the chance, they could succeed in a few years in establishing a functioning and workable economic system, something that Soviet methods had been unable to do in fifty years of power.

The problems that independence will bring to the Balts are immense: thousands of links with the shortage-prone Soviet economic system, a dispirited work force, a despoiled and polluted environment, and the presence of hundreds of thousands of immigrants from Russia. As always, all these problems have been analyzed, and position papers and programs issued on alternative solutions at the many conferences conducted by the Baltic republics. The Balts have concluded that "brain power," not coercion or force, will be their pathway into the Western world.

This conscious and careful approach to every problem is a value that will serve them well with the coming of independence. Other traits they have that are not always present in other Soviet republics include: a well-educated and diligent work force with a sense of purpose; a spirit of cooperation, not antagonism, with all their neighbors; productive farmlands and ample port facilities; and virtually unconditional support from an extensive Baltic exile community. On the last point, it is estimated that approximately 10 percent of the Baltic population lives in the West, mostly in the United States, Canada, and West Germany, with large contingents also in Sweden and Australia. The exiles' support for their former homelands can be compared to the support Jews throughout the world gave to the new state of Israel when it was established in 1947.

"The Soviets need not fear our departure, it will benefit them too," Janis Ruksans, forty-four, a Latvian journalist told me in Riga. "We will become a neutral demilitarized area, a buffer zone for peace on their border. In an economic sense we will produce Western goods on a Western technological level, to be exported to the Soviet Union. We are pragmatists and will be very friendly to our big brother to the east."

Ruksans and other Baltic leaders see their republics as mini-Finlands: that country is now the main source of Western goods and technology entering the USSR. "Actually we'll be even better than Finland in the long run," Ruksans added. "With our experience within the Soviet system we know much better how it operates. We will be a bridge to the Russian heartland for Western products and capital ventures."

The Baltic states were basically agricultural and food producing nations before the Soviet annexation; they expect to revert to that role after independence. That will involve getting rid of much of the industrial infrastructure built by the Soviets. In analyzing proposed joint ventures with the West, the Balts stress that they don't want anything that will bring in more labor. What they want are projects that will improve their agricultural and processing technology so as to bring that part of their economy up to a Western standard.

Their interdependence with the fragile Soviet economy is the largest obstacle to overcome. Their factories currently produce single items prescribed by Moscow. Much of the total Soviet output of washing machines, televisions, and computers is now made in the Baltic. But at the same time thousands of other common household items are not made in the Baltic at all and have to be imported. This sort of "single item" production is what was supposed to be gradually eliminated in the transition period of economic independence. A major drawback to economic self-sufficiency is that almost 90 percent of Baltic oil and raw materials has to be imported. With the advent of an economic blockade by the USSR, the Balts would have to export much of their food produce to obtain their energy needs.

"The years of Communist rule, or rather misrule, have spoiled our work ethic," Arturs Dudurs, fifty-eight, the Latvian Popular Front chairman of economic development told me. "People were paid the same no matter how they worked, or how poor their products were. As long as you met your quota, that was enough. Now we are behind Third World countries in some respects. Their work force can be taught how to do a certain job. We have to teach our workers twice, once how to forget the old ways, and then the new ways.

"It is fortunate that people who work the land still have the work ethic," he said. "They will see us through. After all, that is where our future lies."

But if the future of the Baltic lies in their land, much has to be done to escape from the enviromental nightmare of air, water, and soil pollution arising from the program of heavy industrialization of the 1950s. In the Stalin era, ecological concerns were shunted aside in the rush to build heavy industry. In a move to dilute the restive local populations with an influx of Russian workers, labor-intensive industries were built, mostly in Estonia and Latvia. The industrial wastes from these facilities have now closed most of the seacoast to swimming. In Latvia all the major rivers are polluted and unfit for drinking water or swimming. Uncontrolled stack emissions, as well as auto emissions, have fouled the air of all the major cities. Much of northern Estonia is unfit for habitation because of open shale mining operations. In the Latvian city of Ventspils, Occidental Petroleum has been allowed by the Soviet Union to build a refinery without even the most rudimentary pollution controls. As a result much of the vegetation around the cities has died, and respiratory illnesses are common, especially among young children.

The concern over the ecological disasters brewing in their midst was what originally galvanized the Baltic populations into "unofficial" environmental clubs. Many of the organizers and leaders of these clubs then went on to form the Popular Front groups that now have wrested power from discredited local Communist parties.

The other long-term damage from the imposed industrialization of the Baltics is the presence of a surplus of unskilled labor. Most of these workers are ethnic Russians. By now they make up 40 percent of the population of Estonia, and almost 50 percent of Latvia. In Lithuania, with less industrialization, they are only 20 percent of the total. In the past their influx was justified as part of "international brotherhood," since the Soviet Union was depicted as a "common home" for all its citizens.

But the Balts simply saw the Russians as colonists. The newcomers seldom bothered to learn the local language and never tried to integrate themselves in the local culture. Most lived in huge apartment blocks separate from the local population. In the past year there have been strikes by these workers in Estonia against what they claim are discriminatory voting laws. The laws stipulate that to vote a person must reside in Estonia at least five years and learn the local language. Gorbachev has listed as one of the conditions for independence that the Balts must pay the cost of relocating these Soviet workers.

"These workers are not a major problem," Janis Kalnins, thirty-three, editor of the Latvian Popular Front newspaper *Atmode* (*The Awakening*) explained. "In fact most of them support the Popular Front. I just came from a meeting with some of these Russians. They understand that in an economic sense they would be better off in independent Baltic states than in the Soviet Union. Our groups have always practiced a policy of inclusion, we have a Russian contingent in the Popular Front, just as we have a Jewish group, and even a Gypsy group. To be a Baltic citizen you don't necessarily have to be a Balt. We will guarantee equal rights for all our citizens. All we ask is that they learn our language and respect our culture."

A poll taken in Latvia in September 1989 bears out Kalnin's views. The survey found that 64 percent of the local Russians supported the Popular Front, while only 9 percent favored the Communist Party. The poll among native Latvians was a lopsided 79 percent to 3 percent in favor of the Popular Front.

"We have been ruled and invaded by foreigners for over 700 years," Estonian student Riina Leito, twenty-one, said. "We outlasted them all, and we shall survive fifty years of Soviet rule."

Tallinn, the Estonian capital, and Riga, Latvia, are both medieval cities, originally built by the Teutonic Knights who came in the thirteenth century to subjugate the Baltic tribes. The conquest was part of the last European Crusade, since the Baltic tribes were the last to accept Christianity. Today the two cities, with their narrow cobblestone streets and towering church steeples, remind visitors more of Germany than of the Soviet Union.

The Popular Front office in Riga, housed in a restored medieval guild building, is a scene of frantic activity. Volunteers of all ages are constantly coming and going. A fax machine is in operation next to a room full of small manual typewriters. There is a spirit of unity and a sense of purpose among everyone. Their dedication and unity give Balts the view that they will have no great problems with independence. Education was instilled as a valued trait during the years of independence (1918–40), when the Baltic states had one of the highest literacy rates in Europe. Now, the population is overeducated, if anything, with too many higher degrees and not enough professional and technical jobs to fill. Many Balts with degrees in engineering and science have taken jobs in Siberia and in the Arctic oil district where wages are higher. These are contract jobs, and few Balts settle willingly in other parts of the Soviet Union.

Since the organization of the Popular Front—initially in Estonia in the fall of 1988, then in the other two republics—Balts have consciously devised a strategy of including the whole of the Soviet Union in their goal of independence. Initially all three decided to coordinate goals and strategies among themselves. From that they branched out to establish support groups in all the other Soviet republics. Representatives from the Baltic Popular Fronts have gone out as advisers and teachers to help establish similar groups in Georgia, Armenia, Moldavia, and later in the Ukraine and Byelorussia. At Baltic gatherings there are always representatives from the other republics. In effect they have created a populist alternative to the Communist Party — an alternative that is expected to soundly defeat Communist candidates in multiparty elections.

The high standing of the Balts in the alternative political movement made it possible for them to mediate and hold a peace conference between Armenians and Azerbaijanis in Riga.

The Balts have been in the forefront of Gorbachev's reform movement, going much further than he originally intended. Lithuania was the first republic to drop the Communist Party monopoly clause from its constitution, followed by Latvia. In all three of the republics a multiparty system had already been established, when Gorbachev's was still at only the talking stage.

At one time the Balts considered themselves leaders of reform, not only in the Soviet Union but also throughout Eastern Europe. In the summer of 1989 they already had a free press, no censorship, and freedom of travel. I can remember people in Riga lamenting that the Czechs were too careful about everything and that nothing would ever budge the neo-Stalinists in East Germany. But that has become history, as Eastern Europe has leapfrogged with dramatic swiftness over the Balts, who many now consider too cautious.

With the potential reunification of Germany, the remaining questions of the Second World War may be settled. The Balts are conscious that they are the only nations that disappeared off the map of Europe as a result of the war, and one can sense impatience growing in their ranks.

Latvian Popular Front leader Dainis Ivans still says, "Are we really ready for this step just now? Have we prepared enough? After all we have a twofold goal. One is to get rid of our Communist rulers. That we can do. Getting out of the Soviet empire is the harder part."

Lithuanian Sajudis leader, Vytautas Landsbergis, also urges caution. "Independence has always been our goal. But it can be declared only once. We have to wait for exactly the right moment."

Both men are considered "moderates" and are in the pragmatic wing of the populist alliance. Both had advocated the transition period of economic autonomy within the Soviet federation as a prerequisite to full independence. Now that the much-heralded economic self-rule plan is floundering, more radical leaders are expected to emerge.

When the declarations of independence do come, they are sure to come as coordinated efforts by all three of the Baltic republics. That has been the mode of operation throughout the last two years. Even when one republic seems to be lagging behind on a certain issue, it has been on purpose, for ulterior tactical motives. This close alliance has served the Baltic cause well, and after independence the three countries will form a common Baltic economic union. It is expected that a common currency will be used in all three. There is even talk of a common language — English, which Popular Front leaders hope will eventually replace Russian. Most Baltic leaders are encouraging their children to learn English, and there has been a great demand for language textbooks from the West.

Last year, one of the most popular rock songs in the Baltic was a ballad titled "The Awakening of Baltia," with verses repeated in all three of the Baltic languages.

Although the will is there, the Balts have a long way to go before they can expect to produce consumer items that could compete on the world market. Presently they do make transistor radios and computers, but on a very elementary level. "We are in kindergarten when it comes to business and management skills," Viktors Graudins, thirty-two, told me in Riga. He was considered an expert on business because he had read a Dale Carnegie business manual, holding it in one hand with an English–Latvian dictionary in the other. "It was elementary. But you have to remember that for almost fifty years it was illegal to operate a business here. We just don't have those skills here." He felt strongly that folk art and handicrafts from the Baltics could find a place on the world market.

Karlis Berzins, fifty-four, was an ambulance driver who was a success — not as an ambulance driver but as an entrepreneur. I met him at his home in the Latvian town of Ogre. He made 200 rubles a month driving an ambulance, but his real job was raising tulips. The whole backyard of his house was devoted to greenhouses, constructed by him and his son with poles and clear plastic sheets. There were thousands of tulips in every stage of development. He had read brochures on horticulture and devised elaborate irrigation systems. "We make 400 rubles a day selling," he said, "and even then we cannot meet the demand." Often he drives as far as Moscow to sell his flowers. And of course all of this has to be done when he is not putting in eight hours on his "official" job. With the legalization of private property, and the right to keep his profits, Berzins's business should flourish after independence.

Even more potential from the land was illustrated to me by Aivars Ozols, forty-six, in the village of Prauliene some 150 miles from Riga. There, the hilly farmland is overgrown with weeds, with only a small portion used for potato farming. "We have no modern machinery," he said, showing me a makeshift tractor he had created from a motorcycle engine, a wagon, and an old plow. "If we had equipment, fertilizer, and seeds from the West, this would be very productive. This is good grazing land." The land had been in his family for generations and had been a profitable dairy farm before World War II. Now the roof on the 150-year-old stone barn was caved in, and there was no lumber to fix it. On one hill were six scarecrows in a semicircle, with musty old jackets flapping in the wind. They were there to keep out wild pigs and elk who came to eat from the vegetable garden. Ozols pointed to an immense shrub thicket where the pigs lived. "That was all grazing land before collectivization. But once the state took the land, there was nobody who bothered to clear out the shrubs, and over the decades the wild pigs have taken over. Now we have so many even our dogs cannot keep them away."

Of six farms formerly in the small valley, only three remain. The others were burned down when their owners were sent to Siberia in 1949 during a period of land collectivization. Now, private property is again allowed, and the former owners or their heirs have first chance to buy back their land. Ozols, who is a chemist in Riga, plans to buy back most of his family's former land and start up the dairy business. He is very pleased that his twenty-two-year-old son Raivis, just out of the Soviet army, also wants to learn about farming. "With hard work, and ingenuity, this land can prosper again," he said.

Sources of wealth, but also controversy, are the large port facilities of Tallinn and Riga. They have been greatly expanded under Soviet rule and now handle much of the imports going into Russia. No transit fees of any kind are paid to the Baltic republics. After independence these facilities would fall into the category of property for which Moscow could demand compensation. The Balts don't see it that way. "There may be a case for compensation for legitimate improvements," said Estonian journalist Jaak Roosaare, "but we would expect the Soviets to pay damages for all the pollution and long-range environmental damage caused by strip mining and the dumping of pollutants into the ground, the rivers, and the Baltic sea, making a virtual wasteland out of part of our country. If you consider all that, the Soviets would owe money to us!"

The Baltic cities of Tallinn, Riga, and Vilnius are the most Western appearing of all Soviet capitals. Many of the people dress like Westerners, often copying the latest styles from magazines, and Western TV, which can be seen in Tallinn. But in the past two years people who were dressed in US and Western European styles could actually have been from the West. There were large contingents of the "Baltic Peace Corps," young Balts from the US and Western Europe who have come to act as advisers and consultants to the independence movements. Besides their skills, the most valuable items they brought in were tape recorders, videocassettes and recorders, fax machines, and computers. Most of them were in their early twenties, just out of college, usually with higher degrees. Their knowledge of American media techniques and public relations has been extremely helpful in the initial battle against the stodgy Communist Party *apparatchiks*.

Taking a page from Republican Party campaign tactics, the Popular Fronts were advised always to be on the "attack." Thus, when a popular Latvian newsman was accused by the minister of justice of being "anti-Soviet," instead of being defensive the Popular Front organized a demonstration in front of the Ministry of Justice, denouncing the government for "intimidation of the press and censorship." In early 1989, this sort of counterattack was unknown, and the authorities were too flustered by it to clamp down on the media.

In another case, demonstrators were roughed up while being arrested. The next day a larger group showed up denouncing "police brutality" and filing a legal suit. These kinds of acts were unprecedented in the Soviet Union, and Party functionaries, fearful of being labeled "stagnants," in essence gave up, and let the Popular Fronts have a free hand.

Besides the army of youthful workers coming to help the Balts, the exile communities now have established extensive cultural and professional links in their home republics.

An international Latvian medical congress was held in Riga June 18–27, 1989. The congress was attended by some 6,000 medical workers including 150 doctors from the Latvian communities in the US and Canada. After the gathering, the Latvian Ministry of Health gave a virtual free hand to the newly established Latvian Doctors Association (LAB) to revamp the Soviet-established medical system. The committees organizing the changes are headed by doctors living in the West. The proposed changes include a medical insurance system (which was instituted in early February 1990), health information literature, better medical training, and access to new technology and supplies.

A congress of Latvian jurists, from both the West and Latvia is scheduled for Riga in the fall of 1990. Meanwhile Latvian legal experts living in the West are organizing seminars to be videotaped in the Latvian language and sent to Latvia. The seminars deal with trade and joint venture agreements. Interns in US legal firms will visit and work with Latvian jurists to familiarize them with American legal practices.

There have also been conferences for architects, boy scout leaders, and athletic coaches. In practically every sphere, exile groups from the West are eager to help with both education and material support.

Education is receiving the most attention. On an elementary level all three of the republics are obtaining books lacking in the Baltic. Many are works banned for almost fifty years for political reasons. In a campaign called Books for Latvia, one container ship of books has been sent to Riga, and another is still being collected. The books, in the Latvian language, include texts from grade school through university level. A special stress is being placed on history books from the independence period, many of which were destroyed after the Soviet takeover. Scientific and technical English-language books are also being sent.

Even more valuable than books is the exchange of students. Exile groups are covering the expenses of educating young Balts in the West. Currently, selected Estonian students are enrolled for advance degrees at the University of Toronto in this manner. A similar exchange is under way for students from Latvia at Pacific Lutheran University in Tacoma, Washington. The emphasis for all these students is on business management, computer technology, and English language.

On a similar note Baltic students are using a program called The American College Consortium Exchange with the Soviet Union. Although Balts are only 3 percent of the population of the USSR, more than half of the students from the Soviet side are from the Baltic republics. They have learned about this opportunity through the Baltic exile community and in general have a better knowledge of English than students in other parts of the Soviet Union. It isn't clear what their position will be in this program if the Baltic states become independent during the course of a school year.

Baltic academics in the West have been instrumental in setting up private specialized schools in their home countries. One, called the Estonian Institute for Human Sciences, was established in December 1988. A course offered there is "Estonian as a Second Language." This intensive course is meant for children of Estonian exiles who have never learned their parents' language. In Lithuania a new school called Vytautas Didysis University was established in the city of Kaunas in July 1989. It specializes in science taught mostly by professors from the West.

A large current project of all three Baltic exile communities is the financing of an airline service to the Baltic. Negotiations are ongoing to purchase one airplane from Scandinavia Air Service (SAS) as the initial passenger carrier of what is to be called Air Baltia.

For older Baltic exiles the movement toward independence has been both a shock and a joy. Most never expected they would live to see the Baltic republics regain independence. Already ads are appearing in the exile press for retirement homes and cottages on the Baltic Sea. In the US, inquiries are being sent to Congress to see what laws have to be changed so that retirement and social security checks can be cashed in the Baltics. Like their compatriots back home, Western Balts have analyzed and discussed the prospects for independence from all angles and feel confident about the future.

PART VIII

The Soviet Union

William M. Brinton

Gorbachev and the Revolution of 1989–90

William Brinton has practiced law in San Francisco for over thirty years. He has extensive experience in international law and with litigation in the federal courts. He is the publisher of Mercury House and a trustee of the Sierra Club Legal Defense Fund. He is also the author of a novel, *The Alaska Deception*, and the nonfiction book *A Role for the Small Press Publishing in a Global Village*.

In the following essay, Mr. Brinton reports on the rise of Mikhail Gorbachev and particularly how his actions encouraged the revolutionary process in Poland, Hungary, Czechoslovakia, and East Germany, in stark contrast to preceding rulers of the Soviet Union.

Following a succession of various leaders of the Soviet Union from Joseph Stalin to Yuri Andropov, Mikhail Gorbachev may be said to have inherited a legacy shaped by Marxist-Leninst philosophy, not to mention orthodoxy. Stalin's legacy was one of fear and lies. In the 1920s, he initiated intensive industrialization paid for from the labor of serfs who were forced into agricultural collectives. Over 30 million peasants were also forced to move into the urban areas to work in heavy industry. The serfs — those who resisted agricultural collectives were sent to Siberia or allowed to perish of starvation — were forced to deliver food for consumption by workers in the factories. In 1936, Stalin initiated a purge to eliminate *all* opposition to his ruinously destructive and failed policy of forced agricultural collectivization. During the period of this purge, an estimated 5 million people died or disappeared into the Gulag Archipelago.

In 1937, heavy industry allocated scarce resources to manufacture military equipment for an army that itself had been decimated by the Stalin purge. In 1939, Joseph Stalin and Adolf Hitler signed their infamous pact. It allowed Stalin to annex the Baltic states of Lithuania, Latvia, and Estonia as well as Moldavia, an area carved out of Romania. This pact also led to the outbreak of World War II in September 1939. Stalin died in 1953 and was buried in his palace of lies, the Kremlin.

In 1956, Nikita Khrushchev denounced Joseph Stalin in a six-hour speech to the Twentieth Congress of the Communist Party. The authenticity of its text obtained by Washington was never denied in Moscow.

Within Russia, the destruction of Stalin's personality cult began almost immediately. Its effect was devastating, particularly in France and Italy, where the orthodox had consistently denied Stalin's rule by terror. The reasons behind the demystification of Stalin seem to have been a recognition by Khrushchev, together with Molotov and others of the orthodox persuasion, that the Soviet Union could never hope to overcome its economic failures until the system by which Stalin had dominated the society had been thoroughly discredited. Khrushchev also had a political motive for his speech in 1956. Stalin's criminal past had to be exposed in order to discredit this dead monument to tyranny and the lies he left as his legacy. Stalin also left behind a nuclear weapons industry with enough missiles to destroy the planet.

In 1956, troops of the Soviet Union invaded Hungary to snuff out the fires of freedom that had surfaced there. Even now, in 1990, Hungary continues to be occupied by Warsaw Pact forces. Just twelve years after the invasion of Hungary, in 1968, Warsaw Pact forces invaded Czechoslovakia to end the Prague Spring of Alexander Dubček. It was in 1968 that Andrei Sakharov wrote his essay, *Thoughts on Progress, Peaceful Coexistence, and Intellectual Freedom*. This essay, smuggled out of the Soviet Union, was published in full by the *New York Times* on July 22, 1968. About one month later, General Secretary Leonid Brezhnev authorized the invasion of Czechoslovakia, invoking the so-called Brezhnev Doctrine. This doctrine allowed the Soviet Union to extend its military power to other socialist states whenever socialism, i.e., Communism, was threatened.

Throughout the entire post–World War II period, Poland was a member of the Warsaw Pact and ruled by a Communist Party answerable only to Moscow. However, it was not until 1981 that General Jaruzelski imposed martial law to end the threat posed by Solidarity and Lech Walesa. Four years later, Mikhail Gorbachev became general secretary of the Communist Party, succeeding Yuri Andropov, once Chairman of the KGB, and Konstantin Chernenko. Gorbachev soon announced two policies. One was *perestroika,* or restructuring of the political system within the Soviet Union and economic reform. The other policy was *glasnost,* or openness. This policy allowed more freedom to expose the lies of the past, the Stalin legacy. The Soviet press and television moved slowly but surely to expose the inherent corruption of the Communist Party. People in Poland, Czechoslovakia, East Germany, Hungary, and Romania once again began to think in terms of freedom and to question Communist rule. However, writers in these countries, such as Czeslaw Milosz and Thomas Oleszczuk from Poland — Oleszczuk wrote about dissent and repression in Lithuania — Reiner Kunze in East Germany, Tamas Aczel and George Konrad in Hungary, Václav Havel in Czechoslovakia, and Norman Manea in Romania had already helped lay the foundations of freedom in those countries. They seemed to have felt that Gorbachev would *not* use force to suppress freedom in these countries during late 1989. To have done so would have exposed *glasnost* as morally bankrupt. Gorbachev was too busy with *perestroika* to do what Brezhnev would surely have done — invade and suppress, as he did in 1968.

Gorbachev was young by Soviet standards, only fifty-four, and energetic, not identified with the gerontocracy that had preceded him — in effect, a new generation. The old guard were quite aware of the structural failures so evident to outsiders and the dismal state of the Soviet economy. They knew the degree of inefficiency, nepotism, bribery, and corruption that existed at the top, and at every level of Soviet society. The new generation seems largely urban in background, better educated, and much more sophisticated, with greater understanding of the realities of the outside world. They seem tough, self-confident, and able.

However, this new generation has had to deal with crisis after crisis, beginning with the loss of Central Europe: first Poland, then Hungary, Czechoslovakia, East Germany, and Romania. In Moscow itself, the Communist Party has undergone wrenching change, not the least of which was Lithuania's declaration of independence together with that of Latvia and Estonia. Then, Article 6 of the Soviet Constitution — all power to the Party — was repudiated, and the Communist Party Central Committee restored the concept of private property, declaring that this concept "does not contradict the modern stage in the country's economic development. . . ." These traumatic changes all occurred within weeks during early 1990, all of it carried live on television throughout the Soviet Union.

There are fifteen republics in the Soviet Union, and in six of them civil insurrection broke out within days of each other. Political pluralism and long-standing ethnic rivalries, such as that in Azerbaijan, led to violence and the use of Soviet armed forces. If the Communist Party of the Soviet Union survives long enough to deal with political pluralism, it will certainly have to live with a diffusion of political power in favor of some of the separate republics within the Soviet Union, including Azerbaijan. Unbelievably, there will have been free elections in Lithuania, Moldavia, Georgia, and the Ukraine between February 24 and May 20, 1990. Baku, the capital of Azerbaijan, is one of the centers of oil production for the Soviet Union. Siberia is another such center. Baku is thought to have almost 40 percent of the world's known oil reserves outside of the Persian Gulf. The sale of this oil represents the Soviet Union's principal source of hard currency. Without this, the Soviet Union may be unable to attract foreign investment in ways that will help its staggering economy recover from at least fifty years of hopelessly inefficient central planning.

With *perestroika* and *glasnost,* the people of the Soviet Union know all this, and they also know what has happened in Poland, East Germany, Czechoslovakia, Hungary, Romania, even Bulgaria. With the pent up demand for freedom, human rights, and more consumer goods in the stores finally surfacing all over the Soviet Union, people there will no longer be denied these fundamental rights.

On January 20, 1990, political insurgents from seventy-eight cities and some 100 political clubs met in Moscow. All of them called for more rapid democratization, particularly at the municipal level. There, the entrenched petty bureaucrats were seen as obstacles to change and answerable only to a remote Moscow. Political pluralism within the Communist hierarchy would be a stranger at the Communist Party, an uninvited guest at its Congress with 5,000 delegates elected by some 90 million members of the Party in October 1990. Television and the print media within the Soviet Union, however, have carried the image of change in Central Europe to a huge audience there. It wants the same democratic change now occurring in Poland, East Germany, Czechoslovakia, and Hungary. Almost without exception, the delegates to the meeting in Moscow complained that the Communist Party was incapable of legislating the sort of democratic change these delegates were then demanding.

Domestically, therefore, Gorbachev has serious problems, both political and economic. This fact helps him greatly in his relations with the West and foreign policy. It is no accident that Mikhail Gorbachev declined to intervene in Poland, East Germany, Czechoslovakia, Bulgaria, Hungary, and Romania, all but the latter Warsaw Pact members. Entire divisions of the Red Army continue to remain in all these countries, with the exception of Romania, although both Czechoslovakia and Hungary are pressing Moscow for their withdrawal. Poland is a case in point.

Opposition to political and economic Soviet occupation of Poland came from the working class, principally Solidarity led by Lech Walesa. Moscow was not the least bit enchanted at the thought of assuming direct responsibility for the Polish economy, by 1980 already in poor condition. In 1981, the Polish United Workers' Party decided democratization might be a way out of Poland's economic quagmire. It decided on freely elected delegates to the Congress, a freely elected Communist Central Committee, and a rejection of many members of the Politburo. Polish workers had simply decided that persons in positions of responsibility should be freely elected and then judged by their performance.

To put it mildly, all this was absolute anathema to the ruling class in Moscow. The ruling class in 1981 was a man in failing health, Leonid Brezhnev. He died in 1982. Those around him seemed to reject the idea of military action. Had they then taken military action and stamped out the working-class opposition with armed forces, the remaining workers would then have had to be persuaded to work even harder to produce, for example, more coal from the mines. The solution adopted was to impose martial law followed by the dissolution of the government.

General Wojciech Jaruzelski was selected as the representative for extension of Soviet power. This uneasy arrangement, with all its internal contradictions, lasted only a few years. General Jaruzelski attempted to destroy Solidarity using all means at his disposal under martial law. He failed, and Solidarity later went on strike at the Gdansk shipyard. This strike was finally settled on terms considered favorable to Solidarity. Then, in May and August of 1988, there were waves of serious strikes by workers identified with Solidarity. Wages and working conditions were the principal issues.

All of this and the background of some six years of deteriorating economic conditions seem to have produced a dialogue between Lech Walesa and Jaruzelski. This dialogue began sometime in 1988 and included General Kiszczak, minister of the interior, as a go-between. With intelligence reports before him, Kiszczak seems to have been quite aware of rising popular discontent and the generally explosive situation. In early 1989, the Tenth Plenum met, and one of its key members, General Florian Siwicki, minister of defense, threatened to resign, as did

General Jaruzelski and General Kiszczak, over the issue of continuing talks with Lech Walesa and probably further democratization within Poland as a whole. Political historians will no doubt be able to piece this Byzantine maneuvering into a rational picture of what actually happened.

Gorbachev clearly but plainly had a hand in settling what might have been a dispute with awkward consequences for him. He could be seen as washing his hands of all further responsibility for Poland's rapidly deteriorating economy. Gorbachev's solution was quite simple. He persuaded General Jaruzelski to allow limited free elections in June 1989. Six months later, Poland's minister of finance, Leszek Balcerowicz, announced a new, but painful, economic program.

Within less than sixty days, the Paris Club, a group of seventeen creditor nations, rescheduled $9.4 billion of Poland's debts, extending the time for payment of principal and interest over a period of fourteen years. In addition, the International Monetary Fund and the World Bank pledged an economic aid package to Poland of $1.3 billion.

In Hungary, however, the Communist Party seems to have fallen apart under Janos Kadar over the period beginning roughly in 1986. Opposition parties began to surface, such as the Alliance for Free Democrats and the Alliance of Democratic Youth. The Social Democrats and the Smallholders Party both seemed to survive the brutal Soviet invasion in 1956, albeit in somewhat decimated form. They rose again like the phoenix from the ashes.

The last free election in Hungary was in 1945. The next one will take place on March 25, 1990, although there was a referendum election in Hungary on November 26, 1989. This measure asked voters to delay the date of the presidential election, then scheduled for January 7, 1990, until there was enough time to organize the opposition parties and mount an effective campaign. The measure passed by a narrow margin. Imre Pozsgay and the Communist Party naturally opposed the referendum and adopted a policy of silence, doing no more than complain about the cost of having an election at all. Worth noting is the fact that the Communist Party changed its name to Socialist in October 1989, losing all but a small fraction of its members. They had been given a negative option. If they failed to re-register as Socialists in writing, the membership rolls would reflect the drop in members unwilling to sign up with a dis-credited party. The loss to the renamed Communist Party was quite substantial. The membership dropped from 700,000 to about 35,000 registered voters.

Balint Magyar and Miklos Haraszti are both members of the executive committee of the Alliance for Free Democrats. Both complained about electoral fraud before the election of November 26, 1989. Haraszti complained about government efforts to sabotage the election entirely by issuing false and misleading instruction leaflets to the voters. Magyar, for his part, declined to enter into a coalition with the Communist, now Socialist, Party. In an interview last November, he said: "For real change to take place in Hungary, it is necessary to separate the Communist Party from public administration and the government. A coali-tion that includes the Communist Party means that we cannot achieve this goal. It would mean a continuation of the system in which Communist Party members are tied to their governmen-tal positions or to positions in public administration . . . We are not in the same position as Solidarity in Poland. Their roots are deep in the industries, and they can react immediately to a lot of the government's behavior. This means that they could exercise permanent pressure on the government, calling strikes wherever and whenever they chose. In Hungary, we do not have the [same] means to put pressure on the government whenever we want."

In Czechoslovakia, the disintegration of the Communist Party began openly on November 17, 1989, before the comments quoted from the interview in Budapest with Balint Magyar. In Prague, Václav Havel was widely known as a writer, poet, and playwright. He was also widely known as a man willing to go to jail rather than retreat from his views as expressed in his essay, *The Power of the Powerless,* a brilliant analysis of the nature of Communist power in a post-totalitarian society. For his role in forming the Committee to Protect the Unjustly Prosecuted — VONS is the Czech acronym — he was convicted and sentenced to four years in prison, beginning in 1979. Two years earlier, Havel and many others had joined in issuing the Charter 77 Declaration, a call for freedom that was widely circulated. As a result of his activities, Havel was perhaps best known among students and intellectually autonomous writers.

It was not by coincidence that students were among the demonstrators on November 17, 1989, and the victims of police brutality. However, it was not until the students concentrated on enlisting the workers that any real progress was made. The threat of a national strike was enough to bring the Communist Party government to the bargaining table, and Civic Forum, the opposition umbrella group, became a reality with real political power. During the rest of November and on into December, the Communist Party reluctantly and even sullenly gave way to political pressure. Compromised members of the Politburo, those who had been in power ever since the Warsaw Pact invasion of 1968, such as Vasil Bilak and Miloš Jakeš were ousted. An issue of *Lidové Noviny* (People's News) that chronicled events in 1968, including more current news, identified Jakeš as a man who had denounced anti-Communist groups in 1968 financed by unidentified mass media in the West.

One after another, members of the Politburo either resigned or were replaced by lesser known Party functionaries. Finally, Marian Calfa emerged as prime minister with considerably less than a Communist majority in his government. Jiri Dienstbeir, a Civic Forum member, became foreign minister, Václac Klaus became minister of finance, and other persons, all with the approval of Civic Forum, took key positions in the government, such as minister of the interior. It is now engaged in dismantling the secret police apparatus. On January 1, 1990, Václav Havel gave his acceptance speech as president of Czechoslovakia. The revolution from below was over, and economic reform is underway. At this writing, one cannot say what form it will take.

In the Deutsche Democratische Republik (East Germany), supposedly free elections are scheduled for May 6, 1990. Whether they are genuinely free will be determined by what the Democratic Forum, the umbrella organization for opposition parties, does or fails to do. Chancellor Hans Modrow is a dedicated Communist Party member reluctant to relinquish power. Gregor Gysi is chairman of the East German Communist Party and a lawyer said to have defended anti-Communists in court; one has to ask just how independent the East German judiciary system has been during the forty years of Communist misrule and corruption. Many people somewhat older than Gysi — he is forty-two — remember the Stalin show trials of the 1930s and what passed for fair trials when Leonid Brezhnev was general secretary. As recently as the late 1970s, the labor camps of the Soviet Union were full of people whose only offense was to publicly and peacefully express opposition to the ruling class.

In the book *To Live Like Everyone* by Anatoly Marchenko, Andrei Sakharov wrote the foreword. In its opening lines, Sakharov wrote: "The words that have become this book's title were repeated to the author throughout his life. 'Live Like Everyone,' some said with concern, others with narrow-minded contempt, still others with hatred. People like Marchenko — people of immaculate honesty who are prepared to make any sacrifice in the name of moral principles — share a tragic yet happy fate. As I leaf through the pages of his life, I always picture his wife, Lara, beside him, and though prison separated them, they seemed always together."

This book was published by Henry Holt and Company in 1987, and it describes a show trial in great detail. Marchenko was, of course, convicted and sentenced to prison on the basis of perjured testimony from witnesses claiming they had heard Marchenko shouting "slanderous slogans." In fact, the state proscecutor's depositions showed the witnesses didn't even know Marchenko and had never seen or heard him say anything.

In June 1989, Mikhail Gorbachev rehabilitated Andrei Sakharov, a Nobel Laureate in 1975. Sakharov had been exiled to the closed city of Gorky for over ten years. He appeared in Moscow to take part in political change. Tragically, the gesture by Gorbachev was too late. Sakharov, in failing health after his exile, died on December 14, 1989. This anthology begins with his essay smuggled out of the Soviet Union in 1968. The *New York Times* published it in full on July 22, 1968.

The *New York Times* on January 20, 1990, reported that the Communist Party meeting in East Berlin had some problems, "internal dissent." Wolfgang Berghofer, mayor of Dresden, was expected to resign from his position as vice chairman of the Communist Party, calling for dissolution of the Party. Gregor Gysi was reported to have argued against dissolution, saying on television, "That would be a catastrophe. Structures in society would collapse as a result of that." He might become unemployed!

Up until March 15, 1990, there has been one new and surprising development after another. For example, when East Germany's Communist Prime Minister, Hans Modrow, returned from a visit to Moscow on January 31, 1990, he seems to have brought a message from Mikhail Gorbachev: reunification of the two Germanys might not be all bad, if only there were an international referendum. This idea was promptly rejected by Chancellor Helmut Kohl. Then, in mid-February 1990, a Communist Party Plenum met in Moscow to consider a draft of some rather sweeping political and economic reforms within the Soviet Union. The text of the final document emerging after the Plenum's consideration may never be published, but its results, reflecting at least some compromises, may be seen more or less as they occur. Modrow is seen now as a caretaker prime minister. When the elections take place in East Germany on June 6, 1990, Modrow will simply disappear, and reunification of the two Germanys is expected to occur by the end of 1990.

"Z" (anonymous)

To the Stalin Mausoleum

> *The most dangerous time for a*
> *bad government is when it starts*
> *to reform itself.*
> —*Alexis de Tocqueville,*
> *anent Turgot and Louis XVI*

A storm of controversy has raged around this essay since its first appearance in the January 1990 issue of *Daedalus* magazine. At a time when most of the world was applauding the success and prospects of Mikhail Gorbachev, this broadside raised serious questions about the capabilities of the Soviet political and economic system to achieve the structural reforms promised by *perestroika*. Moreover, speculation about the true identity of the anonymous author, "Z," has ranged from a member of George Bush's administration, or a high-ranking official in the Soviet government, to Martin Malia, a history professor at the University of California at Berkeley.

Whoever the author may actually be, what follows is a distinctly skeptical view of recent and future events in the Soviet Union, which we offer as a counterpoint to the successes and promises expressed elsewhere.

I

The Soviet socialist "experiment" has been the great utopian adventure of our century. For more than seventy years, to millions it has meant hope, and to other millions, horror; but for all it has spelled fascination. Nor does age seem to wither its infinite allure.

Never has this fascination been greater than since Mikhail Gorbachev launched *perestroika* in the spring of 1985: a derivative painting in the Paris manner of 1905, a Beatles' vintage rock concert, or a *Moscow News* article revealing some dark episode from the Soviet past known to the rest of the planet for decades could send tremors of expectation throughout the West if it were datelined Moscow. So conservative-to-centrist Margaret Thatcher and Hans-Dietrich Genscher have vied with the liberal-to-radical mainstream of Anglo-American Sovietology in eulogizing Gorbachev's "modernity." Even though after seventy years, the road to the putative "radiant future" of mankind no longer leads through Moscow, the road to world peace still does. And who is against world peace?

But this is not the whole explanation: Moscow is still the focus of a now septuagenarian ideological fixation. On the Right there is the hope that communism may yet repent of its evil totalitarian ways and evolve into a market democracy of sorts (into the bargain putting down the Western Left). On the Left there is the wish that the "experiment" not turn out to be a total loss (if only so as not to comfort the Western Right) and yet acquire something approximating a human face. So on all sides alleged connoisseurs of the *res sovietica* are anxiously asked: Are you optimistic or pessimistic about the chances for perestroika? Can Gorbachev succeed? Will he survive? Should we help him?

These questions, however, presuppose answers with diverse ideological intonations. To what is no doubt a majority in Western opinion, Gorbachev's reforms mean that Stalinism and the Cold War are over and that democracy is at hand in the East, bringing with it the end of global conflict for all. For a smaller but vocal group, the Cold War is indeed over and the West has

won, a victory that presages the global triumph of capitalism, the
end of communism, indeed even the "end of history."[1] A third
group, once large but now a dwindling phalanx, holds that
communism remains communism for all Gorbachev's glitter,
and that *glasnost* is simply a ploy to dupe the West into financing
perestroika until Moscow recovers the strength to resume its
inveterate expansionism.[2]

Yet the two dominant Western perspectives on Gorbachev have
one element in common: the implication that our troubles with
the East are over, that we are home free, at the "end of the
division of Europe" and on the eve of the Soviet Union's "rein-
tegration into the international order," a prospect first advanced
by Gorbachev but eventually taken up by a hesitant President
Bush. So in an odd way the perestroika pietism of the Gor-
bophiles and the free-market triumphalism of the Gorbophobes
converge in anticipation of a happy dénouement of a half-
century of postwar polarization of the world.

And, indeed, in this avalanche year of 1989 we are surely
coming to the end of a historical epoch. It is hardly so clear,
however, that we are entering a simpler, serener age: decaying
superpowers do not go quietly into the night. It is not even clear
that we are asking the right questions at all about Gorbachev.
Certainly Western Sovietology, so assiduously fostered over the
past four decades, has done nothing to prepare us for the surprises of the past four years.

Nor is the predominant Western question about Gorbachev's
chances for success the most pertinent one, or at least the first we
should ask. The real question is: Why is it that seventy years after
1917—which was to have been the ultimate revolution, the revolution to end all further need of revolutions—Gorbachev pro-
claims *urbi et orbi* that Soviet socialism urgently requires a "new
revolution," a "rebuilding" of its fundamental fabric? What is so
drastically wrong as to require such drastic action? And what,
after four and a half years of increasingly frenetic activity, has in
fact been accomplished?

The most natural way to approach this question is to focus on
personalities and policies: on Gorbachev and his "conservative"

opponents; on "perestroika," "glasnost," and "democratization." And it is this preoccupation which explains the cult of his personality in the West. But if fundamental revolution is now really on the Soviet agenda, then our focus of inquiry ought to be the *longue durée* of deep structures and abiding institutions. And these, as Gorbachev constantly reminds us, were created "sixty years ago," a euphemism for Stalin's "Year of the Great Break," 1929. For this was the beginning of the forced collectivization of agriculture through "dekulakization," together with "full steam ahead" in industry for a "First Five-Year Plan in four years," policies that created the Soviet system as it exists in its main outlines to the present day. In short, Gorbachev is calling into question the very basis of the Soviet order and the historical matrix of what until now was called "developed" or "real" socialism. Perestroika is thus not just a reform of a basically sound structure, but the manifestation of a systemic crisis of Sovietism per se.

II

It is precisely because during the past twenty-odd years mainline Western Sovietology has concentrated on the sources of Soviet "stability" as a "mature industrial society" with a potential for "pluralist development" that it has prepared us so poorly for the present crisis, not only in the Soviet Union but in communist systems everywhere.[3] Instead of taking the Soviet leadership at its ideological word — that their task was to "build socialism" — Western Sovietology has by and large foisted on Soviet reality social science categories derived from Western realities, with the result that the extraordinary, indeed surreal, Soviet experience has been rendered banal to the point of triviality.

Much of this was done in the name of refuting the alleged simplifications of the post–World War II "totalitarian model," itself deemed to be the product of the ideological passions of the Cold War. Thus, beginning in the mid-1960s successive waves of revisionists have sought to replace the totalitarian model's emphasis on ideology and politics with an emphasis on society and economics, to move from "regime studies" to "social studies," and to displace "history from above" with "history from below."[4] This reversal of the totalitarian model's priorities of explanation has yielded a Soviet Union where the political "superstructure" of the regime derives logically from its "social base" in the proletariat and a peasantry being transformed into urban workers, with a new intelligentsia emerging from both classes. This inversion of the actual roles of state and society obviously gives the Soviet world a normal, almost prosaically Western, character and a democratic cast as well.

At the cost of some simplification, it is possible to say that this social science approach (with a fair admixture of Marxism) has produced a consensus that the Soviet historical trajectory leads "from utopia to development."[5] In this perspective the key to Soviet history is presented as "modernization" through "urbanization" and "universal education"—a process carried out in brutal and costly form, to be sure, especially under Stalin, but the end result of which was the same as in the West. Often this social science reductionism holds that the Stalinist excesses perpetrated during an essentially creative Soviet industrial transformation represented only a passing phase, an "aberration," which under Brezhnev gave way to "normalcy" and "institutional pluralism" expressed through such "interest groups" as the army, industrial managers, or the Academy of Sciences.[6] Indeed, Stalinism itself has been viewed by the more thoroughgoing revisionists not as an aberration at all, but as an essentially democratic phenomenon, stemming from a "cultural revolution" from below, within the Party and the working class, and resulting in a massive "upward mobility" that produced "the Brezhnev generation." In this view the whole revolutionary process may be summed up as "terror, progress, and social mobility," with the modest overall cost in purge victims falling in the "low hundreds of thousands."[7]

A corollary to this revisionist picture is that Gorbachev's "restructuring" will be the crowning of the edifice of Soviet modernity. Thus, all that is required to humanize the Soviet Union is a measure of "reform" in the ordinary sense of reorganization: that is, a "calibrated" decentralization and a gradual debureaucratization of administrative structures, or more specifically, a reduction of the role of the central plan and the *nomenklatura,* or those administrative and managerial posts reserved for appointment by Party committees.

Such, indeed, was the expectation behind Gorbachev's early policies, as in the new Party program (now forgotten) voted at the Seventeenth Party Congress in February 1986 and expressed in his book *Perestroika and New Thinking* in the fall of the next year. This was still the expectation two years later of the main line of American Sovietology; indeed, this Sovietology to a degree reflected Soviet thinking in the Moscow social science institutes of the Academy of Sciences.[8] But the border nationalities crisis of 1988 and the unionwide economic crisis of 1989 have made these anticipations, though hardly four years old, already superannuated. As for the blatant fantasies — to use a charitable term — about democratic Stalinism, they are clearly destined for that same trashcan of history to which Trotsky once consigned the Provisional Government of 1917.

As the crisis year 1989 draws to a close, it is — or ought to be — patent that both the Soviet regime and its Western analysts are in for an agonizing reappraisal of long-standing assumptions about Soviet "stability." More precisely, the time has come to take a fresh look at the starting point of Western Sovietological analysis: namely, the two bases of the totalitarian model, ideology and politics, and at the ways in which these factors have modeled the institutions and the mentalities created by seventy years of "utopia in power."[9] For if the fact of glasnost demonstrates the Soviet capacity to return to human "normalcy," the revelations of glasnost prove incontrovertibly that for the past seven decades Russia has been anything but just another modernizing country. As we now know, both from Gorbachev's economists and from televised shots of empty shelves in Moscow stores, the Soviet Union, though clearly a failed utopia, is neither a developed nor a modern nation. It is rather something *sui generis,* a phenomenon qualitatively different from all other forms of despotism in this or previous centuries.

It is for this reason that the term *totalitarian*, coined by Mussolini with a positive connotation to designate his new order and first applied in a negative sense to Stalin's Russia by Trotsky, was taken up by Hannah Arendt to produce a general theory of perverse modernity. And she did so because the blander term *authoritarian,* serviceable, say, for a Salazar or a Chiang Kai-shek, simply would not do for the gruesome grandeur of Stalin, Hitler, or Mao. Contrary to current opinion, Jeane Kirkpatrick did not invent but simply continued this distinction, though she added the corollary that totalitarian regimes are far more permanent than authoritarian regimes, a proposition with which the struggling intellectuals of Eastern Europe thoroughly agree, since as yet no country, not even Poland or Hungary, has successfully completed its exit from communism.

The Sovietological revisionists of the West, however, find Kirkpatrick's distinction scandalous, in part because of the conflation it effects between communism and fascism (though the Soviet novelist Vasili Grossman does exactly this in his enormously popular *Fate and Life*) and in part because Stalin must be presented as an aberration from the Leninist main line of Sovietism, for if he is integral to the system, then the prospects for its democratic transformation are dim indeed. But this sanitization of the Soviet regime into mere authoritarianism, at least for the period after Stalin, is achieved only at the cost of a fundamental conceptual confusion, if not an outright caricature of the totalitarian concept. Totalitarianism does not mean that such regimes in fact exercise total control over the population; it means rather that such control is their aspiration. It does not mean they are omnipotent in performance, but instead that they are institutionally omnicompetent. It is not Soviet society that is totalitarian, but the Soviet state.

This conceptual confusion results from taking as the defining criterion of a regime the degree or quantity of repression, not its nature or quality. Thus, since Khrushchev shrank the dimensions of the Gulag and Brezhnev killed or imprisoned far fewer people than did Stalin, the Soviet regime is deemed to have evolved from totalitarianism to authoritarianism (or as some would put it, "posttotalitarianism"), say on the model of Greece under the colonels or of Pinochet's Chile. But this view neglects the central fact that the structures of the Party-state, with its central plan, its police, and its nomenklatura, have remained the same — as Gorbachev's more liberal supporters, such as Sakharov, have constantly complained. Consequently, the milder face of Sovietism after Stalin — and the quantitative change is quite real for those who live under it — simply offers us, in Adam Michnik's phrase, "totalitarianism with its teeth knocked out."[10]

Paradoxically, just as the "T word" was being expunged from Western Sovietology around 1970, it became current in Eastern Europe: Hannah Arendt was translated in *samizdat,* and Soviet intellectuals now routinely refer to the whole system, including its Leninist phase, as totalitarian, and to the Brezhnev period as classical or stable Stalinism.[11] Even more paradoxically, it is when communist totalitarianism began to unravel under Gorbachev that the inner logic of the system became most transparently clear to those who have to live under it.[12] To resort, à la Marx, to a quotation from Hegel: in matters of historical understanding "the owl of Minerva takes flight only as the shades of night are falling." It is this twilight, Eastern view of the evolution of the Soviet experiment from 1917 to Gorbachev that will be adopted here, in an effort to present a historicized update of the original, and in truth too static, totalitarian interpretation.

III

It is impossible to understand anything about Gorbachev and perestroika without taking seriously the origins of the Soviet system in a utopia. The utopia, of course, was never realized, but this is not the point. For applied utopias do not simply fail and fade away; the effort to realize them leads rather, through a perverse cunning of reason, to the creation of a monstrous antireality, or an inverted world. So the great Soviet adventure turned out to be, in the words of an early Polish observer, a grim "mistake of Columbus." This unforeseen landfall led to the creation of a new politics, a new economics, and a new Soviet man, which are at the root of the present crisis of perestroika.

The utopia in which the Soviet system originated is integral revolutionary socialism. This is not to be confused with simple egalitarianism, although this is obviously involved under so protean a label as "socialism." Nor is it to be confused with mere social democracy (a term for which both Marx and Lenin had a distinct aversion), for this is clearly compatible with a mixed economy and constitutional government. Rather, integral revolutionary socialism in the Marxist tradition means full noncapitalism. As the *Manifesto* puts it, "The theory of the Communists may be summed up in the single phrase: Abolition of private property." From this it follows that the product of private property—profit—and the means for realizing this profit—the market—must also be abolished. For property, profit, and the market dehumanize man and fetishize the fruits of his labor by transforming both into reified commodities. It was to end this scandal that the most deprived and dehumanized class, the proletariat, received the world-historical mission of bringing about the socialist revolution, whereby mankind would at last be led out of "prehistory" into genuine human existence in the oneness and unity of a classless society. And all of this is supposed to come about through the inexorable logic of history, operating through the self-enriching alienation of the class struggle. This set of beliefs—the core tenets of Marxism—has been characterized by Leszek Kolakowski as "the greatest fantasy of our century."[13]

But the logic of history does not work this way (if indeed it exists at all); and although private property and the market can be abolished, their demise will not come about automatically. Therefore, the hand of history must be forced by the creation of a special instrument, "a party of a new type," with which Lenin declared he "would overturn all Russia." Thus, utopia can be achieved only by an act of political will exercised through revolutionary coercion, in short by quasi-military means. Utopians of this ruthless temper, however, can get a chance at power only in extreme crisis, amid the collapse of all structures capable of resisting them. Such an exceptional state of affairs came about in

Russia in 1917, when under the impact of modern war, the old order unraveled with stunning rapidity to the point where Lenin's Bolsheviks simply "found power lying in the streets and picked it up." True, they enjoyed a significant measure of worker support at the time and their ranks were largely filled with former workers. But this does not mean that what they themselves called, until well into the 1920s, the October overturn (*perevorot*) was any the less a minority coup d'état staged against a background of generalized, particularly peasant, anarchy, and not a "proletarian revolution" in any meaningful sense of that term.[14]

The Bolsheviks then had to confront their utopia with reality in the form of economic collapse and civil war. Under the combined pressure of the military emergency and the logic of their ideology, between 1918 and 1920 they produced the world's first version of noncapitalism, "War Communism." Nor at the time was this viewed as an emergency expedient. For Lenin, socialism would emerge out of the fullness of capitalism; the "imperialist war" was the highest phase of capitalism; General Ludendorff's militarization of the German economy during the struggle was therefore the supreme form of capitalism and by the same token, the matrix of the new socialist order. So nationalizing the entire urban economy under the Supreme Economic Council (the ancestor of the present Soviet industrial ministries and of "Gosplan"), the Bolsheviks amplified Ludendorff's practices in Russia and abolished profit and the market. To this was added the "advanced" American method of Taylorism for the rational organization of work and an ambitious program for building power stations under the conviction that "socialism equals Soviet power plus electrification." At the same time, the Bolsheviks experimented with rural collectives, or *Sovkhozes,* and thereby adumbrated the extension of their statist model to the countryside and the entire population; and in the meantime they simply pillaged alleged "petty bourgeois kulaks" for grain under the policy of "class warfare" in the villages. In fact, during War Communism the Bolsheviks created the first rough draft of what later would be called a planned, or more accurately a command, economy.[15]

Simultaneously, Trotsky hit upon another essential component of the new system, the political commisssar. The vocation of the Party is political and ideological, not technical and professional in any of the activities necessary for the functioning of society. Since the Party was at war, the most important professional expertise at the time was military, expertise the Bolsheviks lacked, while most trained officers in the country were former members of the Imperial Army and hence unreliable. So the new people's commissar for war simply conscripted the officers he needed and flanked them with trustworthy Party monitors, such as Stalin, Kirov, Voroshilov, and Orjonikidze, all future leaders of the 1930s. In this way a dual system of administration was created in the army, but one that could easily be adapted to economic and other civilian tasks, where Party figures would supervise industrial managers, collective farm chairmen, educators, scientists, writers — indeed, everybody and everything. This is the earliest origin of the *apparat* and its nomenklatura right of appointment to all functional posts of importance in society. Dual administration thus adumbrates the end of "civil society," by which Central Europeans and Soviets mean social groups capable of self-organization independent of the state. This mode of control is the essence of the Party-state, a system wherein the functional, governmental, or "soviet," bureaucracy is monitored from behind the scenes by a parallel and unaccountable Party administration that has the real power of decision.

The period of War Communism produced a second monitoring apparatus as well, this time for "enemies" of the whole system — the Cheka, or political police. Conceived by Lenin as early as November 1917 to wage class war against those who were certain to resist the Bolsheviks' unilateral seizure of power, the Cheka was originally directed against "feudal" or "bourgeois" parties, but was soon turned against erring, "petty bourgeois" socialist parties as well as recalcitrant workers and peasants who supported them. But there was no structural reason in the system to prevent the Cheka's eventual use against enemies within

Bolshevik ranks themselves. For as the Civil War raged on, it became increasingly apparent that the Party and its leadership represented (to use Kolakowski's language again) not the "empirical proletariat," but a "metaphysical proletariat" that had the world-historical mission of leading mankind to socialism. Thus, whenever workers or peasants rejected the Party's power, as in the Kronstadt revolt of 1921, they were automatically revealed as "petty bourgeois" and disposed of *manu militari*.

And so by 1921 all the essential institutions of Sovietism had either been created or sketched in: the Party-state with its monopoly of power, or "leading role," as it is now called; the dual administration of soviet and apparat, both backed by the Cheka; the central plan and the agricultural collective; and a propaganda monopoly in the service of the dictatorship of the proletariat, with its single "correct" ideology and the cult of technological Prometheanism. It is difficult to believe that a system of such internal coherence and logic should be the passing product of military emergency, although this is now the dominant view in Western Sovietology. In any event, it is this model that, in fact, was to become the main line of Soviet development, from Stalin to the eve of perestroika. And this, as the Soviets used to say in their earlier, more ideological days, is surely "no accident."

But War Communism would become the Soviet norm only after what turned out to be the temporary retreat to the mixed economy of the New Economic Policy (NEP) in the 1920s. For War Communism, though it permitted the Bolshevik victory over the Whites, also produced one of the worst social and economic collapses of the twentieth century. In the course of the Civil War, some 15 million to 19 million people perished from war, terror, famine, and epidemic — or more than in all of World War I. By 1921 industrial production had virtually halted, money had disappeared, and organized exchange had given way to barter. To be sure, a part of this primitivization was due to six years of war; but it was due in even greater part to the ideological extravagance and incompetence of Bolshevik policy, which continued with fanatical grimness for months after the war had been won.[16]

IV

The limited return to the market under the NEP was a success in reviving the country, but not in leading it to socialism. This contradictory circumstance has given rise to endless speculation and controversy about the true nature of the system in the past, and thus about the proper tasks of perestroika in the present. The central questions are these: Is the "hard" communism of War Communism and Stalin the norm or a deviation in Soviet history? Or is the "soft" communism of the NEP this norm and therefore the model for perestroika—a perspective in which Stalinism, together with its Brezhnevite prolongation, becomes the deviation from which perestroika is the hoped-for recovery? Finally, which of these two communisms, the hard or the soft, is the legitimate heir of Lenin and October? Or to put the whole debate in one classic question, Was Stalin necessary?[17]

In strictly temporal terms there is no doubt about the answer to these questions: three years of War Communism, twenty-five of Stalin, and eighteen of Brezhnev clearly add up to the empirical norm of Soviet history, and it is the eight years of the NEP (together with bits and pieces of the Khrushchev period) that are the "aberration," or, if one prefers, the metaphysical norm of "real" Leninism; and this overwhelming preponderance of hard communism must have something to do with the logic, if not of history, then at least of the Soviet system. Yet these questions are not really about chronology; they are about essences, and through these about present attitudes and policies toward Soviet reformability.

The case for the NEP as essential Sovietism rests on the fact that Lenin inaugurated it and did so with the admission that War Communism had been an error, or at least a premature attempt at attaining socialism. In his dying months, moreover, he gave his blessings to "cooperatives" (a concept he did not flesh out) as the means for arriving at socialism. Nikolai Bukharin then developed these hints into something of a system in the mid-1920s and thereby became the true heir of Lenin. Stalin (attacked by name, moreover, in the founder's "Testament") thus rose to power only as an intriguer and a usurper.

In this view the true Leninist-Bukharinist course, which enjoyed majority support in the Party by mid-decade, drew from the horrors and errors of War Communism the lesson that the regime's first priority should be to preserve the "revolutionary alliance of workers and peasants" allegedly forged in October. To this end, the Party was to conciliate the 80 percent of the population that was peasant by orienting the "commanding heights" of state industry to meet rural consumer needs and thereby to accumulate through the market the capital for the industrial development necessary to achieve mature socialism. In this way the socialist sector, since by definition it would be the more efficient, would outcompete the private, peasant sector; the rural cooperatives would be gradually transformed into genuine collective farms; and the whole nation would thus "grow into socialism," in the sense of the full transcendence of capitalism.[18]

There are numerous objections to this view over and above the puerile fetishization of Lenin involved and the bizarre notion that the supreme achievement of October Revolution was the discovery, in 1921, of the virtues of cooperatives and the market. The first major objection is that never during the NEP and Bukharin's brief ascendancy did the Party play the economic game according to market rules: it constantly resorted to "administrative" means to manipulate both supply and demand since it feared the peasants' power over the economy, and hence the state, through their purchasing power, or more simply their freedom to grant or withhold the supply of grain. The second major objection is that the empirical evidence about the resistance of the peasants to the forced requisition of grain during War Communism, and their refusal even to market it under the NEP, especially after 1927, whenever the price ratio was unfavorable, indicates their inveterate distrust of Bolshevik arbitrariness. Never under a Bolshevik monopoly of power would they have entered collective farms voluntarily. Given these circumstances, a collision between the Party and the peasants was at some point inevitable, and the NEP was inherently unstable. Ultimately, either the Party would have to give up on integral socialism and share economic, and eventually political, power with the peasants through the market — in short, opt for mere social democracy — or it would have to crush peasant independence, and along with it the market, and march toward full socialism by coercive, "administrative" methods.

By the end of the 1920s it became imperative for the country to embark on a program of intensive industrialization and heavy capital investment, if only to replace an obsolete plant that had not been renewed since 1913. This imperative was translated into a plan and given an ideological aura as the "building of socialism." Bukharin advocated that this transition be financed in cooperation with the peasantry and through the mechanisms of the market. Still, it was necessary to raise industrial prices after 1927 in order to get the plan started at all. The response of the distrustful peasantry was immediate: a "production strike," as the regime called it, and thus also a "procurement crisis," which forced rationing on the cities at the moment the plan was launched.

The choice before the Party was clear: either follow Bukharin's policy and capitulate to the peasants, a course leading eventually to the abandonment of the Party's monopoly of power, or revert to the military methods of War Communism, but in institutional, permanent form as collective farms, or *kolkhozes*. Stalin, as General Secretary, chose the latter course as the only one compatible with maintaining the Party's monopoly of power. And in this he was thoroughly Leninist.[19]

The monopoly of power, and not any one economic program, whether hard or soft, had been the cardinal Leninist principle since 1917, indeed since *What Is To Be Done?* was written in 1902. This was the reason Lenin carried out the October coup rather than wait for elections to the Constituent Assembly, which he knew he could not win. The decision to coerce the peasantry had good Leninist precedent also: when their "production strike" of 1918 threatened the new regime with starvation, Lenin resorted to "class warfare in the villages" and then to *prodrzvyorstka,* or grain requisition. True, he later came to reconsider this decision; but he never reconsidered the Party's irrefragable right, conferred by the logic of history, to a monopoly of power.

And Stalin's decision was good Trotskyism, too. "Full speed ahead" for industrialization has always been the Left's program, as was making the peasant pay for it through a "primitive socialist accumulation of capital" carried out on their backs. To be sure, the Trotskyite Left had always paid lip service to the notion that collectivization would have to be voluntary. But this position did not derive from consulting with the peasants while theorizing on the matter; and when Stalin encountered peasant resistance, the Trotskyites supported him in the use of coercion, as indeed their whole previous record indicated they would do, for the sake of the Party and of socialism. Stalin's decision even turned out to be compatible with basic Bukharinism, for when the chips were down in 1929 Bukharin went along with the new "General Line" and served the leader devotedly for seven more years. He even penned what was considered to be the crowning achievement of "built socialism," the Stalin Constitution of 1936, proudly exhibiting the historic pen to an emigré friend in Paris the same year during his last days of freedom; for to him, as to all the others, *partinost,* or Party spirit, meant more than any economic program or policy toward the peasants.

So to answer the famous question "Was Stalin necessary?" it must be reframed in terms of a second question: Necessary for what? If one means necessary for Russia's industrialization, then the answer must be no. In strictly economic terms Bukharin's program would no doubt have done as well, if not better, at modernizing Russia, and at far less cost, both human and material — a proposition that may be advanced with a high degree of certainty by analogy with the state-guided development of Finance Minister Witte in Russia during the 1890s, or of Meiji Japan, or of post–World War II South Korea. But if one means necessary to achieve industrialization in a form compatible with preserving the Party's monopoly of power, then the answer must be yes. Only the coercive Stalinist method of institutionalized War Communism could break the ever-present peasant threat to this monopoly by extending Party control from the cities, where Lenin had left it, to the countryside and the entire population. The real choice in 1929 was to do approximately what Stalin did or to give up on utopia and the Party monopoly of power.

So the Great Break of 1929 resulted from a political, not an economic, decision, and one which for the first time established the iron primacy of politics over economics in all aspects of Soviet life. Thereby the Party became genuinely totalitarian in its policies, if not always in its performance. Private property, profit, and the market had been suppressed, or driven underground and branded as "speculation" and "corruption." "The leading role of the Party" was established in all types of social activity, a status written into law in the Constitution of 1936; this leading role was the Party's very *raison d'être,* the concrete realization of utopia in actual history.

That the man Stalin presided over this realization no doubt made it more brutal, costly, and ultimately paranoid than it otherwise might have been. But too much can be made of his warped personality and lust for power in accounting for the extraordinary events of the 1930s. Stalin's power stemmed not from the drives of his psyche, but from a set of institutions: the monopolistic, monolithic Party operating on the principle of "democratic centralization," or command from the top down, and on the myth of the historical inevitability of socialism. The Party, as an institution, cried out for personification in a Leader. Trotsky or some other ruthless Civil War commissar could well have filled Stalin's role and done the job of building socialism in his place. And this attempt had to be made at some point because the myth that socialism could be built was the *raison d'être* of the Party's leading role, the justification of its monopoly of power. But since the myth is only that, any leader acting on it would be compelled to a massive use of force and violence. Thus, in the Leninist world we have not only the Stalin-sized Mao, but a whole series of pocket Stalins, such as Ceauşescu, Kim Il Sung, and Castro. It is difficult to blame all of this on Joseph Djugashvili's psyche.

V

The building of socialism was conducted like a military operation and was carried out on two main "fronts," to use the language of the time. The first was the agricultural front. Between 1929 and 1935 some 85 percent of Russian peasant households were herded into collective farms, or kolkhozes, and transformed into state serfs, obliged to turn over to the regime a fixed quantity of produce without regard for what the annual harvest left to the producers. Peasant resistance was such that millions of so-called kulaks and their families were deported to Siberia; and in 1932 the state induced a "terror famine" to destroy peasant independence once and for all. Altogether, some 6 million to 11 million people perished in the course of collectivization, and as glasnost proceeds the higher figure seems increasingly to be the more probable.[20] At the same time, some some 30 million peasants were forced to migrate to the new industrial cities then being created under the plan—the largest and most rapid rush, or more accurately push, to urbanization in world history.

Economically the result for those who remained in the countryside was the greatest man-made disaster of the twentieth century. The rural standard of living sank far below that of 1929, indeed below that of 1913, and has never reached those levels since. Russia, which before 1914 had been a grain-exporting country, has for the past decade been obliged to import food (whereas both India and China now export it). The Russian peasantry became, and has remained, a demoralized, listless, and often alcoholic work force, suspicious of state power and unwilling to take any initiative on its own. Moreover, the cost of this operation in human lives, in slaughtered livestock, and in material loss has been exorbitant beyond calculation.

What, then, was the rationale behind the whole enterprise? Initially the Party genuinely expected that large-scale, mechanized, and collective agriculture would be more productive than small, family, or "capitalist" farming. When this proved not to be the case, the Party settled for the political advantage of state control over the peasantry: with collectivization, the last fortress of Soviet civil society was destroyed. At the same time, economically the regime was guaranteed a food supply independent of the caprices of the market, a supply for which the regime therefore did not have to pay. With this assured, they could then advance on the second, and more important, front—the Promethean development of heavy industry. Thus, the net advantage of collectivization for the regime was, as in all things, political and not economic.

On the industrial front operations were conducted with the voluntaristic conviction that "there are no fortresses that Bolsheviks cannot storm." And here the results were genuinely spectacular, at least up to a point. In such grandiose projects as the steel manufacturing city of Magnitogorsk (erected for the man of steel himself), the Dnieprostroi dam and electrification project, the Turksib railroad, and the Moscow metro, the Soviet Union gave itself the basis for a modern industrial economy that was also autarkic, depending on international capitalism for nothing but the prototypes, blueprints, and imported specialists necessary to get things started. And growth rates for the 1930s overall were quite good, but nowhere nearly so good as has long been assumed. At the time, the Soviet government gave out the figures of some 20 percent, while Western specialists generally accepted a figure of from 12 to 14 percent and these figures have been repeated in countless textbooks and journalistic accounts ever since. But later calculations by Western economists, recently confirmed by the revelations of glasnost, yield a much more modest 4 to 6 percent. And a comparable lowering of growth rates from some 15 to around 5 percent is now generally accepted for the first postwar decade. Witte in the 1890s, with far milder market methods, did much better at 8 percent, as did Meiji Japan at 6 percent, not to mention postwar Japan at 16 to 18 percent—or even Deng Xiaoping's China at 10 to 12 percent.[21]

Moreover, Stalinist growth was extremely one-sided: all that grew was heavy industry to produce capital goods, to produce more capital goods, to produce more heavy industry, to produce, after 1937, equipment for the military. The primary sector, agriculture, as we have seen, was blasted and blighted; and the tertiary, or service, sector was barely developed, as was that part of the secondary, or industrial, sector devoted to consumer goods. So Soviet modernization meant essentially a hypertrophied secondary sector producing neither for an internal market nor for export, but for itself and for the all-encompassing state, with just enough in the way of consumer goods and services to keep the population alive.

Even when, under Khrushchev, the Soviet Union became the world's "second largest economy," just behind the United States, indeed outstripping it in output of the sinews of modern industry — steel — this number two status was true only in quantitative, not qualitative, terms. Almost all Soviet products were imitative, archaic, crude, or outright defective. Almost nothing the Soviet Union produced, outside of military hardware, was competitive on the international market; and it could sell its products on the internal market only because it had a monopoly that excluded more efficient foreign competition. Even in its most successful decades, therefore, under Stalin and in the early years of Khrushchev, the Soviet Union was never a great industrial power, and still less a "modern" society. The belief that it was such a power is among the great illusions of the century, shared until recently not just by the editorialists of our major newspapers, but by economists of the prominence of John Kenneth Galbraith, and even Wassily Leontilev.[22] In reality, however, the Soviet Union in its prime was never more than a great military-industrial complex and a Party-state superpower.

VI

In still another domain Sovietism at its height represents a deviant form of modernity: the indispensable underpinning of its power by terror. A minuscule underground organization before 1917, the Party inevitably developed a conspiratorial mentality, and after it seized power as a minority of some 115,000 in a largely hostile country of 170 million, surrounded moreover by a hostile world, it added to this a state-of-siege mentality. Barely 600,000 at the end of the Civil War, and hardly more than a million at the time of the Great Break, it is this small and ever-beleaguered army that carried out the titanic "revolution from above" of the 1930s. And the enormous risks of this task enhanced the Party's sense of the precariousness of its power. Indeed, by 1932, at the worst of the collectivization drive and before the new industrial plant had begun to function, it looked as though the whole enterprise might well collapse. The sole reassurance, therefore, was a return to the terror of the Civil War period; so the political police shifted its efforts to combating "crypto-Menshevik" and "bourgeois specialist wreckers."

Matters did not stop there, however, because of another imperative of Sovietism. It is in the logic of a system where everything is nationalized, with a single, omnicompetent bureaucracy accountable to no one but itself, to secrete permanently the phenomenon of apparat ossification. The problem first appeared when the Civil War was won and the dying Lenin, misdiagnosing it as a tsarist holdover, sought a cure in the inefficacious, indeed utterly self-defeating, solution of creating parallel monitoring bureaucracies: the Workers and Peasants Inspectorate for the soviet, or state, administration and the Central Control Commission for the Party. Then Stalin, in response to the extraordinary social tensions generated by the building of socialism, developed this control mechanism on a scale commensurate with the rest of his enterprise. Beginning in the early 1930s he used periodic administrative purges of Party membership rosters to remove the incompetent or those lukewarm toward the General Line. After the great crisis of 1932–1933 had finally passed, however, he decided on a complete renewal of Party-state personnel in order to give himself the human base of the socialism he had built. And this led to the Great Terror of 1936–1938.

It would be too much to say that this was a rational political undertaking in the usual sense of that term. It did, nonetheless, have its rationale in the nature of the system and the circumstances of the day. And this rationale lay in the transition from utopia *in potentia* to its realization *in actu*. Until the mid-1930s, socialism existed only in the "radiant future," and belief in its supreme beneficence was thus easy. But after the Party's "Con-

gress of the Victors" in 1934 socialism had been declared built,
and it turned out to be nothing more than a system of inefficient
state-driven industrial expansion as an end in itself, achieved,
moreover, at appalling cost. In short, the instrumental program
of integral socialism had been carried out, but the expected
moral result had not followed; quite to the contrary, a moral
disaster of unprecedented proportions had ensued, and this fact
had somehow to be negated and denied. As Pasternak put the
matter in *Doctor Zhivago,* "Collectivization was an erroneous and
unsuccessful measure and it was impossible to admit the error.
To conceal the failure people had to be cured, by every means of
terrorism, of the habit of thinking and judging for themselves,
and forced to see what didn't exist, to assert the very opposite of
what their eyes told them."[23] So the great bloodletting of collectivization led "naturally" to the bloodletting of the Great Purges.

But there were other, more political reasons for this connection as well. Stalin and the Party leadership were clearly responsible for the perverse outcome and the costs of the First Five-Year
Plan; hence, doubts about the new system, and with them
opposition to its author, were only to be expected. Stalin, therefore, decided to make a preemptive strike against all the forces
that might menace him and the socialism he had wrought. His
person and his work as "the Lenin of today" had become one,
both in his mind and in the regime's relentless propaganda.

So in 1936 he carried out a gigantic coup d'état against the
personnel of the system over which he himself presided (somewhat as Mao would later wage the "cultural revolution" against
his own Party). Stalin reorganized the political police descended
from the old Cheka into a spanking new People's Commissariat
of Internal Affairs, or the NKVD, and brought it under his
personal control by placing at its head his creature Yezhev. With
this refurbished instrument he made a clean sweep of all potential opponents, indeed of all simple doubters, waverers, and
critics, and not just at the top, among such has-beens as Zinoviev
and Bukharin, but at every level of the Party and the state
administration. Thus by 1939 he had given himself a Party
membership, a staff of industrial managers, and a corps of

military officers that was 80 percent new, all of them products of the system built since 1929 who owed everything to it and to him personally—and who indeed would grow old together as "the Brezhnev generation."[24]

This course was no doubt not the wisest policy on what turned out to be the eve of total war; and the potential for Party disloyalty in a crisis was nowhere near so great as Stalin imagined. Still, this course does make sense as an extreme effort to render irreversible the fruits of the Great Break. And it was Leninist in its basic principle, although Leninism of a greatly intensified variety; for splitting the Party to purge deviant groups and then recruiting new loyalist cadres was a constant tactic of the founder from his break, in 1903, with the Mensheviks onward. Moreover, Stalin's action did solve the problem of bureaucratic petrification for many years. After the end of the frenetic terror of Yezhev years, 1937–1938, the repression of "enemies of the people" was routinized into a system of periodic purge and the pervasive fear of purge, backed up by the Gulag, to keep everyone constantly on his toes, a system which continued right through the war and until the leader's death in 1953. So approximately another 10 million victims were added to Stalin's score, to yield a grand total of 20 million, the conservative estimate of the American historian Robert Conquest now generally accepted, indeed amplified, by such Soviet scholars of Stalinism as Roy Medvedev.[25]

One final, momentous consequence of these extraordinary transformations was that their source, the Myth, was now transformed into the Lie, to use a term first brought to public attention by Solzhenitsyn but long current throughout Eastern Europe; for Soviet socialism as actually realized was a fraud in terms of the Myth's own standards. This Lie could be made to appear to be the truth, and the fraud concealed for a time, indeed for quite a long time, by a combination of terror and drumbeat indoctrination. Until Khrushchev's "secret speech" of 1956, millions, both within the Soviet Union and in the outside world, believed that the Myth had in fact been realized and that Stalin was its Coryphaeus. But eventually the truth would out and the fraud be exposed, and then the regime would be confronted with a terrible dilemma: namely, that Sovietism has a criminal past which is at the same time the centerpiece of Soviet achievement. But when this moment came, could the regime admit to the truth and at the same time preserve the results of the achievement? This moment has now arrived and constitutes one of the great unresolved contradictions of perestroika today. The collapse of the Lie under glasnost is destroying acceptance of the system itself, especially among the young, just as Gorbachev is trying to save it by restructuring.

Nor is this all: decades of living under the Lie have had a morally debilitating effect on the national culture and the population, among ruled and rulers alike. As de Tocqueville once put the problem, "Men are not corrupted by the exercise of power, or debased by the habit of obedience, but by the exercise of a power which they believe to be illegitimate, and by obedience to a rule they consider to be usurped and oppressive."[26] And this degradation of the "human factor," a factor Gorbachev puts at the center of his reform effort, must be contended with, both in himself and in his people, if perestroika is to succeed.

VII

The system completed by Stalin in 1939 would have four long decades of success before the bill came due for living high on the Lie for so long. To be sure, the Soviet edifice as of 1939 was still very much a jerry-built, shaky affair, and Stalin knew it, which is why he tried so desperately to avoid submitting it to the test of war by his pact with Hitler. But when, in spite of all, the test did come, the Soviet Union survived, yet not through a win on the merits of the system, at least in the first phase. Rather, survival came because the country was so huge it could afford (though not through conscious design) to lose space long enough to permit Hitler to make mistakes enough to set himself up for defeat. And at that point, the essentially military command structure of the Party-state indeed proved effective in relocating factories, mobilizing the economy, and mounting its counterattack for victory.

It was this belated victory that at last made the Soviet system impregnable. It transformed what had been since 1929, indeed since 1917, an extravagant gamble into a world-class success. This success, moreover, was attributed by the regime to the superiority of socialism and endlessly extolled as the justification for all the suffering and sacrifices of the 1930s. Thus the "Great Fatherland War" at last conferred on Soviet power a measure of the legitimacy that had hitherto eluded it. As Solzhenitsyn has argued, the victory of 1945 was a tragedy in triumph for the Russian people, for it fixed on them for decades more a regime that otherwise lacked the inner resources to endure.

The Party was now no longer a small army of occupation, molding by force from above a recalcitrant population, but instead the structural ribbing of a new Soviet imperial nation; and the Party's ranks swelled to almost 7 million at the end of the war and then upward to 19 million under Brezhnev. When to all this was added the security zone of an empire in Eastern Europe and the grandeur of great power status, Marshal Stalin towered to world-historical stature. At home he was the Father of his people, and abroad he was either the hero of the Left as the foe of American imperialism or to the Right the object of awe of such a hard-headed *realpolitiker* as Henry Kissinger, and of such an anti-Communist economist as Joseph Schumpeter. Stalin's "rational terror," in Camus's phrase, created power, and power compels universal respect.[27]

Soviet success followed Soviet success seemingly without end. Stalin acquired the atom bomb with stunning rapidity in 1949. Then Khrushchev triumphed with Sputnik and the first man in space, and frightened the world with his rockets. Brezhnev intervened at will throughout the Third World, ringed the continents with his submarines, and at last attained nuclear parity with the United States. Russia bestrode the world as a superpower. And after 1968, as the West reeled under the impact of the Vietnam disaster, Watergate, two oil shocks, and the collapse of the shah's Iran, it seemed that the "correlation of forces," as the Soviets were wont to put it, was shifting definitively "in favor of socialism."

In reality, however, the high opinion held in the West of Soviet achievement was quite wide of the modest truth. For if there was always enough accomplishment to make the world avoid looking squarely at Soviet reality, the world in fact was being hoodwinked by the assertion of efficacy and power in just one domain. This was the domain of "extensive" economic development, which operates effectively only by using great quantities of men and capital in large-scale projects (and in the Soviet case, without regard for costs). But this technique is adequate only for the simpler modern tasks such as launching heavy industry or concentrating resources for winning a war. But once institutionalized, the apparatus for extensive development becomes an impediment to the next state of econonic development, the intensive growth necessary for the refined and skilled tasks of a more complex modernity.

To put the matter another way, in the 1930s the Soviets had built a crude, but serviceable imitation of a Pittsburgh-Detroit or a Ruhr-Lorraine economy; then they rebuilt it after the war, when it was already becoming obsolete, or at least was no longer at the cutting edge of economic practices in the West; finally, after Stalin's death, they multiplied the same model seven or eight times over when genuinely advanced countries were phasing out their Garys, Birminghams, and Essens. At the same time, the West and East Asia passed by, first with an electronic, and then with a computer, revolution. And so, by the end of the 1970s, as Russia reached the peak of her international standing, domestically she was becoming a gigantic Soviet socialist rust belt.

At the same moment the country encountered still another limit to easy economic expansion: the depletion of cheap natural resources and a decline of available labor. The great expansion from the 1930s onward had been possible only because the vast Eurasian heartland offered, or seemed to offer, inexhaustible resources of raw materials; and they were used up wantonly, without regard for cost, by extravagant engineering projects, waste, and mismanagement. By 1980 these reserves were no longer abundant, and in their place ecological disaster zones had appeared, such as the shrinking Aral Sea and the dying Lake Baikal. At the same time the demographic trend turned too. The great population explosion of the late nineteenth and early twentieth centuries, which had made Russia by far the most populous nation of Europe, had offered to the Soviet experiment a demographic reservoir on which Stalin's extensive development, as well as the Gulag, had drawn without counting. The poor housing of Soviet urbanization made this reservoir shrink further still, especially in the Slavic heartland, and by Brezhnev's demise that labor reserve was gone.

A similar impasse appeared in the method of managing the Soviet economic mastodon, the Plan. It is in the logic of a system where everything is nationalized, and where the market and real prices are eschewed as "capitalist," that all production decisions should be taken by administrative fiat and implemented in a quasi-military manner through what Western analysts have come to call a command economy. In other words, economic decisions are taken for political and not economic reasons, in accordance with the policy priorities of the Party-state, and not in response to social demand (except from the military) or for reasons of production efficiency. The inevitable result is that the Plan operates through what the reform economist Gavriil Popov has recently baptized the *kommandno-administrativnaia systema,* or "command-administrative system,"where everything is run by imperious order from above and blind submission from below, a system that operates not only in industry, but in all social relationships.[28]

This method, like the strategy of extensive development, worked effectively, if not efficiently, during the early, crash phase of Soviet industrialization and the war. It still worked effectively after the war when Stalin and Khrushchev crash-programmed their way to nuclear weapons and ballistic missiles, and then when Brezhnev ploughed on to global superpower parity. But it was a method developed by, and only suitable for, such economic and technological semiliterates as Sergo Orjonikidze, the Civil War commissar who became Stalin's industrializer-in-chief during most of the 1930s; it could not be successfully adapted to the high-technological world symbolized, say, by, Andrei Sakharov. In that world it became only a stultifying hindrance, an institutionalized damper on inventive initiative and entrepreneurial innovation.

Thus, on every front the "storm and conquer" methods of bolshevism's Homeric age that had worked to build socialism eventually became a brake on the system's further development and modernization. The techniques of extensive economic growth became institutionalized and ossified in Gosplan, "Gossnab," and the specialized economic ministries, which grew in number from a handful during the 1930s to some seventy by the time Brezhnev died. By the same period the kolkhoz system had acquired hundreds of thousands of nonproductive bureaucrats. And all of this constituted a network of entrenched vested interests, comprising, according to Gorbachev, some 18 million functionaries. The command-administrative ways of the nomenklatura society, also created by Stalin's "storm" tactics, had turned against their own purpose and become a source of "stagnation," to use Gorbachev's term for the Brezhnev era. The result was that by 1979 — the same year as the great Afghan miscalculation — the growth rate of the once Promethean Soviet Union was down to about zero, and there it has stubbornly remained for the past decade.[29]

This outcome will be all the more difficult to remedy because in the mature Soviet system the economy is in fact at bottom a polity, a projection of the purposes of the Party-state and at the same time the chief means of the regime's hold over the population. This interlocking of the economy with a political structure — and of both with culture — in one overarching unity is the institutional essence of totalitarianism.

VIII

It is with this unitary and increasingly petrified socialism that all of Stalin's successors have had to contend. And they have done so in a pattern of alternating reform and retreat, for the hope of soft communism never wholly died after 1929 and would revive every time hard communism, by its very rigidity, provoked system-threatening problems.

First, Khrushchev liquidated Stalin's last chief of terror, Beria, and greatly reduced the power of the political police and the size of the Gulag, in part as a measure of self-defense by the Party against its monitors, and in part to humanize the system and make it more efficient. Khrushchev was perhaps the last ideological Leninist among Soviet leaders; he was convinced that the system, if properly managed, could produce not just power for the state, but the realization of utopia for the masses.

Even more daring than his crushing of Beria, in his secret speech at the Twentieth Party Congress of 1956, Khrushchev attacked Stalin himself for his crimes against the Party. But Khrushchev soon discovered that de-Stalinization had a logic he could not control. It delegitimized the system per se and released a flood of pent-up grievances throughout the empire; this process in turn provoked a conservative reaction among the apparat, and so Khrushchev was compelled to fight back by unleashing the creative intelligentsia against the conservatives, most notably by publishing Solzhenitsyn's *One Day in the Life of Ivan Denisovich,* which unmasked not just Stalin's person, but his camp system as well.

The ideological crisis produced by this "thaw" was compounded as Khrushchev simultaneously tampered with the institutional basis of the regime. In order to limber up the economy, he decentralized it by establishing Regional Economic Councils, or *Sovnarkhozes.* More disturbingly still, he tried to split the Party in two, making one part responsible for industry and the other for agriculture, a brutal change of role for the political and ideological functionaries of the apparat. Moreover, to break their resistance to this institutional attack on the "little Stalins," in Yevtushenko's phrase, he sought to limit all important Party mandates to fixed terms. It is this presumption even more than his foreign policy misadventures in Cuba that provoked his fall.

In October 1964 Khrushchev was deposed for "voluntarism" by the very colleagues he had made safe against the political police, by then called the KGB. And their safety was indeed the source of his vulnerability. By bringing Stalin's terror to a halt, he gave away his only leverage against the apparat and thus his own safeguard. By the same token he gave the *apparatchiki* not only security of their persons; he inadvertently gave them life tenure in their positions as well. It was to preserve this status that the Politburo decided that he and what they considered his "hare-brained" innovations had to go.[30]

The result of Khrushchev's failed reform, therefore, was the triumph of the nomenklatura rather than the Leader as the fulcrum of the system; and it is only in the late 1970s that the world learned of this new term and the privileged caste it designated.[31] Brezhnev and his allies prudently drew from Khrushchev's fate the lesson that this group's privileges must forever remain inviolate. This policy was the origin of the extra-ordinary gerontocracy, led by Brezhnev himself, Suslov, Andropov, and Chernenko, who dominated the Soviet scene in the last decade before Gorbachev and whose longevity compounded the arteriosclerosis of all other aspects of Soviet life.

Under their direction the Soviet Union experienced eighteen years of "stagnation," as the period after Khrushchev is now officially designated. First of all, de-Stalinization was halted as too dangerous to the system's stability. The late leader was never formally rehabilitated, but attacks on "the cult of personality" ceased. As for the economy, the moderate decentralizing reforms of Prime Minister Kosygin, developed from the Lieberman incentive experiments of the Khrushchev era, were smothered at birth by the noncooperation of the industrial ministries. Concurrently, the working class, secure with a minimal but universal welfare safety net and comforted by the socialist ethos of egalitarian leveling, or *uravnilovka,* developed a mentality of minimum effort for minimum reward. At a higher social level, the officially stigmatized entrepreneurial ethos expressed itself in a growing "second," or "black," economy, which was indispens-able to the functioning of the official "first" economy, a phe-nomenon that led to the "Mafiaization" of the police, industrial management, and portions of the Party, especially in the south-

ern border republics where these Mafias also had an ethnic base.[32] Finally, Andropov's reinvigorated KGB exiled or
repressed Russia's best talent, such as Solzhenitsyn, Sakharov,
and Brodsky, to mention only the Nobel Prize winners among
them; Russian culture was either driven underground into
samizdat (clandestine self-publication) or abroad into *tamizdat*
(publication in the West). In consequence, sometime around the
mid-1970s the Myth faded away almost completely among the
people, and left only a repressed awareness of the Lie, which as
yet no one dared speak of publicly.

By the turn of the 1980s, therefore, as one gerontocrat after
another was laid to rest in the Kremlin wall, a pall of gloom and
despair descended over the nation. And so, at the zenith of Soviet
power internationally, internally the system became a Eurasian-
sized Stalin mausoleum.

IX

Against the background of such a history and the
highly constraining structural logic underlying it, the task of
reform can only be Herculean. But do the system's constraints
permit the emergence of the people, and of the vision, necessary
for such a staggering task? In this question lies the whole drama,
and the dilemma, of the Gorbachev era.

Awareness that something was seriously amiss with Sovietism
first came to the surface in 1983 under Andropov. As head of the
KGB, he knew far better than his colleagues the true state of
affairs; and he took the novel step of calling on intelligentsia
specialists, especially economists and sociologists from the Academy of Sciences, to consult on possible remedies, an enterprise
in which his protégé Gorbachev was involved. This endeavor
produced the *Novosibirsk Report* by the sociologist Tatania Zaslavskaia, who argued that the Soviet system of centralized planning had become obsolete, a fetter on production, and that Soviet
society, far from being a harmonious unity, was riven by the
conflicting interests of both the ruling and the ruled—an analysis that implied the necessity of radical restructuring for sheer
survival. This document, leaked to the Western press in the once

putatively fatal year of 1984, first alerted the world to the impending end of Soviet stability.[33]

At the beginning of his general secretaryship, Gorbachev may be considered as Andropov redux, though the younger leader was driven by a much more acute sense of crisis and a correspondingly bolder willingness to experiment. His initial program of perestroika as controlled economic reform from above therefore quickly branched out in new directions under the pressure of events. *Perestroika* soon came to stand for "radical reform," then "revolutionary change"; and further policies were added to it: "new thinking," or retrenchment, in foreign relations, and "acceleration," "glasnost," and "democratization" domestically. It is in this historical sequence that its course will be examined here.

When Gorbachev first launched perestroika in April 1985, it had the relatively limited purpose of producing a rapid acceleration, or *uskorenie,* of national economic performance; and his method was similar to Andropov's: reliance on administrative action from above in consultation with intelligentsia experts and operation within the existing structures of the Plan and its attendant ministries. For *perestroika* means, literally and simply, refashioning an existing edifice, or *stroika,* the root also of the Russian term for the "building" of socialism. Thus, while he summoned Zaslavskaia and the Novosibirsk economist Abel Aganbegyan to Moscow and positions in Academy of Science think tanks, his basic approach was to jump-start the stalled Soviet productive mechanism by the classic administrative methods of exhortation and bureaucratic reorganization.

An example of the first tack was his 1986 anti-alcohol campaign. This measure backfired, however, by increasing the budget deficit through loss of sizable vodka sales, which now went to the "black" economy. An example of the second tack was the "quality control" of industrial products by state inspectors, whose power to refuse substandard goods, and hence also to lower enterprise revenues, generated insecurity among both managers and workers. In addition, Gorbachev regrouped ministries and replaced cadres on a scale not seen since Stalin. As a result of this, by the fall of 1986 strong resistance emerged among the apparat to further changes, whether of policy or of personnel.[34]

Gorbachev therefore embarked on a second policy, glasnost. In this he was advised by his chief theoretician, Alexander Yakovlev, who had become a connoisseur of modern, Western ways during a decade as ambassador to Canada, an experience that both sharpened his appreciation of Russia's backwardness and acquainted him with the contemporary television techniques required to stimulate innovation. In choosing this new course, Gorbachev was guided by two considerations. As a question of conviction, he recognized that a dynamic economy could not be built with a passive population, isolated from knowledge of the modern world, ignorant even of real conditions within the Soviet Union — a state of affairs that produced Chernobyl, for example. Glasnost was thus intended to energize the nation. Also, as a matter of political tactics, he now made an all-out wager on the "creative intelligentsia" to bring pressure for reform on the recalcitrant apparat.

To signal this change, and to give the intelligentsia assurance that they could speak up without fear, he made a dramatic telephone call to Sakharov in Gorki in December 1986 to summon him back from exile. During the next eighteen months the liberal intelligentsia, in the press and on television, began to criticize society's ills, and to fill in the "blank spots," in Gorbachev's expression, of the Soviet past, with a fervor born of the twenty years of frustration that had built up since the previous thaw under Khrushchev. They did this with all the more passion since it was only by owning up to the errors of the past that they could attack the problems it had created for the present.[35]

In the course of this glasnost explosion, both Gorbachev and his supporters radicalized as they encountered resistance from "conservative" (or more accurately, old socialist) forces under Ligachev. A note of desperation crept into the debate, and on both sides. Ligachev and his allies asserted that the liberal intelligentsia's criticism was leading the country to ruin by undermining the institutions and values that had built socialism and won the Fatherland War. Gorbachev and his supporters answered that the situation was so far gone that there was "no alternative to perestroika": to continue the policies of stagnation would lead to the rapid obsolescence of the economy, loss of superpower status, and ultimately the death of the system. As Yakovlev, in early 1989, put it more bluntly than Gorbachev himself would have dared, "We probably have no more than two to three years to prove that Leninist socialism can work."[36] Thus in 1987 and 1988, the initially self-confident campaign for perestroika of 1985 took on the air of an increasingly desperate gamble, an ever more urgent race against time; and by 1989 matters had acquired the aura of a crisis of survival, which recalled, though in different form, the disaster years of 1921, 1932, and 1941.

The flood of candor under glasnost did indeed produce the consequences of which the conservatives complained, and in a form more radical than during Khrushchev's thaw. For each new revelation about past crimes and disasters did less to stimulate the people to new effort than to desacralize the system in their eyes; it did so all the more thoroughly since the Myth was long since dead, especially among the young. Repressed awareness of the Lie poured forth in a flood progressing from the publication of Anatoli Rybakov's mild novel *Children of the Arbat* in 1986 to that of Solzhenitsyn's outright anti-Soviet *Gulag Archipelago* in 1989. In the process, not only were the long decades of Stalin and Brezhnev swept away, but the very foundations of Sovietism, the economic theories of Marx and the political practices of Lenin, were touched. By 1988 Marxism-Leninism was a shambles; and by 1989 it could be openly denounced by leading intellectuals, such as the historian Iyuri Afanasiev, as a dead weight on the mind of the nation.[37]

In the midst of the turmoil unleashed by glasnost, the system was threatened by still another danger: the nationalities crisis and the beginning of the breakup of the empire. The leadership had known from the start of perestroika that it faced an economic problem, but in its Russocentric naiveté was quite unaware it had an equally grave nationalities problem. So the mass strikes of February 1988 in Armenia over the issue of Nagorny-Karabakh came as a total surprise, a "moral Chernobyl," as one Soviet leader put it. But soon autonomist, even separatist, agitation spread to the Baltic states, then to Georgia and Azerbaijan, and by 1989 to the vital Ukraine.

These movements, moreover, everywhere assumed the form of "popular fronts," grouping all classes of the population against the Party apparat (or in the Baltic virtually taking the Party over), a pattern reminiscent of the "dual power" that existed between the original "soviets," or workers' councils, and the Provisional Government in 1917. The cause of this sudden explosion lay in the same process of desacralization that was undermining all Soviet institutions. The fiction that the Party-state was a federal "union" was perhaps the most egregious form of the Lie, for all the border "republics" had in fact been conquered by the Great Russian central region beginning in 1920, with the Baltic states and the Western Ukraine added only as recently as 1939–1944, and then only after a deal with Hitler. When the freedom to criticize released these border populations from fear, the result was a national as well as an anti-Party upsurge; for them *perestroika* came to signify "sovereignty," by which they really meant independence.

With this danger added to the other strains produced by glasnost, the old-line socialists, or conservatives, redoubled their efforts to retain control of the apparat, where the general secretary still lacked an unquestioned majority, from the Politburo down to the base. Given the constraints of Party discipline, this resistance could express itself in public only obliquely, but behind the scenes, what liberals called a bloodless civil war in fact was raging. Its most open expressions were the firing of Boris Yeltsin as Moscow Party chief in the fall of 1987 and the national-Communist, anti-Gorbachev manifesto, known as the "Nina Andreeva Letter," published in much of the press in the spring of 1988.

In response to these pressures, the general secretary moved to a third and still more revolutionary policy: democratization. First bruited in early 1987, this meant double or multiple candidacies in elections and fixed terms of office for all Party and state, or Soviet, posts. This policy was first applied to the Party by convening a Special Party Conference (in effect, a mini-Congress) in June 1988 in an effort to gain at least the majority necessary for a renewed attempt at economic reform. Yet this device, like glasnost, overshot the mark assigned to it, while at the same time it fell short of achieving its intended positive function. The conference turned out to lack the necessary majority of pro-reform delegates for a purge of apparat deadwood yet began the politicization of the hitherto quiescent Russian lower classes, since the partially televised proceedings revealed the once mono-lithic and mysterious Party to be a fallible and quarrelsome body of self-seeking interests.

Failing to revitalize the Party, Gorbachev then upped the ante of democratization by using it the following year to reanimate the hierarchy of state administrative bodies, the soviets. Taking up the 1917 slogan "all power to the soviets," he sought to give real political life to both halves of the system of dual administra-tion, in which all power, since Lenin, had belonged to the Party. Again his motives were mixed. There was first his Leninism — by no means a mere ritual invocation — which he vaunted as the "pragmatic" capacity to adapt policy rapidly to changing circum-stance and the constant willingness to risk a gamble. Then, too, democracy, like glasnost, was necessary to galvanize the popula-tion for perestroika. But above all, Gorbachev sought to give himself a structure of power parallel to the regular apparat. He sought this in part so that he could not be deposed by a Central Committee coup as Khrushchev had been in 1964 — a precedent on everyone's mind in the perestroika era — and in part to give himself an independent instrument for putting through his stalled economic programs.[38] And, as some Soviets noted, this effort to outflank the old guard by a parallel power was reminis-cent, *mutatis mutandis,* of the way Stalin had used the NKVD against the mainline Party.

This second round of democratization overshot its intended mark far more widely than the first. This became apparent during the elections in March 1989 to a Congress of People's Deputies, whose function was to create a strong executive presi-dency for Gorbachev and to elect a Supreme Soviet, or national parliament, with some measure of legislative power, unlike its rubber-stamp predecessor. An unintended result of these elections, however, was to produce a resounding defeat not just for the apparat, as Gorbachev wished, but for the Party as an institution. For the first time in seventy years, the population had the possibility of saying no to official candidates, and did so, at least in the large cities, on a major scale. As a result, the "correlation of forces" within the country changed radically: the Party which had hitherto inspired fear in the people suddenly came to fear the population, and demoralization spread throughout its ranks.

This effect was compounded at the Congress meetings, televised live for two weeks during May and June. To be sure, Gorbachev got himself elected president and thus secured a buffer against a coup by the Party. He also obtained the selection of a new Supreme Soviet — in effect, a consultative assembly, rather than a genuine legislature — which he felt confident would do his bidding. But the authoritarian way he pushed these elections through the Congress caused his popularity, already low because of the economic and ethnic problems engendered by perestroika, to reach its nadir; he, too, was desacralized and made to appear as just a bigger apparatchik. Moreover, the liberal delegates, though a minority, dominated the proceedings with a barrage of exposés of all the ills with which the country is afflicted: the poverty, the abominable health service, the rising crime rate, the ecological disasters, the economic disintegration, the KGB's "secret empire," as one deputy dared call it, and the Party corruption. The net result of the Congress was, in the words of another deputy, "the demystification of power."

As a result, Gorbachev's initially demagogic slogan "all power to the people" began to acquire some real content. The Congress first of all produced an organized Left opposition to Gorbachev in the form of the Interregional Group, led by such figures as Sakharov, Yeltsin, Afanasiev, and the economist Popov, a loyal opposition to be sure, yet one that nonetheless insisted that real perestroika was still in the future. Even more boldly, this group broke the supreme taboo of communism and demanded an end to the leading role of the Party.[39] Simultaneously, the Congress debates produced a politicalization of the Great Russian and Ukrainian populations almost as intense as that of the border nationalities. And since the Congress had come up with no concrete remedies for the ills its debates had exposed, by July the population began to take matters into its own hands. The country was swept with a wave of self-organization from below; popular fronts and embryonic trade union associations appeared in the cities of Russia and the Ukraine. Thus "civil society," as the opposition called these new formations, began to emerge for the first time since it had been suppressed in 1918; and in some areas this movement edged off into a form of "dual power," as some radicals asserted, a phenomenon of which the Kuzbas and Donbas miners' strikes in July 1989 were only the most visible and spectacular manifestations.

X

While all this was going on, what had been accomplished in the economic sphere to produce the hoped-for "acceleration" that had been perestroika's starting point? The short answer is: nothing much. Or more accurately still, those measures that were taken led to an outright deterioration of the situation.

Gorbachev's economic program has thus far consisted of two main components, both formulated in 1987.[40] The first of these is the creation of small "cooperatives," in reality private ventures, in the service sector. But the impact of this cooperative sector has been derisory, since its services are priced far above the purchasing power of the 200-ruble-per-month average wage of the majority of the population. These enterprises have therefore become the focus of popular hostility to economic reform in general, since any form of marketization is perceived by "the people" — as the miners made clear during their strike — to benefit only "speculators" and the privileged — a reaction quite in conformity with the socialist egalitarianism the regime inculcated in the population for decades. Moreover, the cooperatives are harassed by the state bureaucracy, whose monopoly they threaten, and are often either taken over by, or made to pay protection money to, various Mafias from the "black" economy.

The second component of Gorbachev's economic reform is the Law on State Enterprises, providing for "self-management" and "self-financing." If actually applied, these provisions would significantly reduce the role of Gosplan and the central ministries by using self-interest to correct the predominance of administrative directives. This reform is thus an effort to return to the spirit, if not the precise institutions, of the NEP, and to its policy of *khozraschyot*, or businesslike management and accountability under a regime of state enterprise. In other words, it is a variant of the half-measures of soft communism, put forth periodically in Soviet history from Bukharin to Eugene Varga just after World War II to Kosygin, but never really implemented because they threaten the Party apparat's "leading role." And, indeed, this time too, the Law on State Enterprises has remained a dead letter ever since it took effect in January 1988, because the silent resistance of legions of apparatchiki has kept industry operating at 90 percent on "state orders" — that is, on the old Plan.[41]

In still other domains, Gorbachev's economic perestroika has met with failure, but this time without his having really tried to produce a program. In agriculture Gorbachev has spoken repeatedly of long-term leases of land, indeed up to fifty years, for the peasantry. But this proposal bas gone nowhere, in part because of the resistance of the huge kolkhoz bureaucracy, in part because the peasantry has seen so many different agrarian reforms imposed from above that it will not trust the regime to respect leases of any duration and hence will not take up the government's half-offer.

Thus, Gorbachev is in a far more difficult position than his predecessors in communist economic reform. He no longer has the option of Lenin in 1921 at the beginning of the NEP, or of Deng Xiaoping in 1979 of reviving agricultural and artisan production rapidly by granting the 80 percent of the population that is peasant a free market. The Russian peasantry, now disproportionately aged and only 35 percent of the population, is too decimated and demoralized by over sixty years of collectivization to respond to any NEP-type initiatives. In consequence, Gorbacbev has been obliged to begin his perestroika with industry, where the transition to marketization is far more difficult than in agriculture. Here the very success of Stalin in urbanizing Russia has created a cast-iron block to progress.

Another such block is financial and monetary policy. Heavy state subsidies to hold retail prices low, to keep unprofitable factories running, to maintain full employment, and to secure the safety net in place — what some Western specialists call the social contract between regime and people — cannot be abolished without unleashing inflation and thus igniting a social explosion. But unless these subsidies are abolished, or at least reduced, the economy cannot move to real prices; and without real prices there can be no dilution of the Plan by marketization or privatization; nor can there be convertibility of the ruble to reintegrate Russia into the international order. And without movement in these directions, there can be no revival of the economy. So the alternative before Gorbachev is either economic stagnation through subsidies or social upheaval through real prices.

And perestroika faces other problems as well: the infrastructure and the capital stock created by decades of extensive development are now approaching exhaustion. In a nationally televised address in October 1989, Prime Minister Ryzhkov warned that the overburdened railway system (Russia still lives basically in the railroad age) was on the verge of collapse. The country's enormous metallurgical plant is outmoded and unprofitable. Housing and administrative buildings are in a state of disrepair often bordering on disintegration. The extraordinary number of industrial "accidents," from Chernobyl to the gas-line and train explosions of June 1989, are usually due to functional breakdown or criminal neglect. All this exhausted equipment must be restored or replaced, and much of the work force retrained and remotivated.

Then, too, the stores must be filled again. Under the present conditions of collapse and penury, available goods are either siphoned off legally by state enterprises to supply their workers, or they disappear illegally into the black economy. But short of massive imports of foreign goods, stocking the shelves is an impossible task, since decades of wasteful investments and subsidies, and of printing money to finance both, have now created an enormous budget deficit and rapid inflation — both "discovered," or admitted, by the government only in late 1988. As a result of this, a movement away from the ruble to the dollar or to barter is well under way, a phenomenon that presages the collapse of the consumer market.

Under such conditions of near breakdown, any transition to real prices, self-management, and self-financing are quite out of the question for the foreseeable future; and the old reflexes of the command-administrative system are sure to persist, if only to ensure a modicum of order. Thus, active consideration of real market reform has been postponed time and again and is now slated, more or less, for the mid-1990s. Indeed, economic perestroika of any type has been stalled since early 1988.

Overall, then, the balance sheet of more than four years of perestroika has been that the half-reforms introduced so far have unsettled the old economic structures without putting new ones in their place. And in this, perestroika resembles earlier failed halfway-house reforms in Central Europe: General Jaruzelski's reforms of self-management in 1982 and of self-financing in 1987 in Poland, and earlier still the failed, halfway New Economic Mechanism in Hungary. Yet, despite this accumulated evidence of failure, Gorbachev intends to stick to the unnatural hybrid of "market socialism," as his chief economic advisor, Leonid Abalkin, made clear in November 1989 in launching an updated plan of alleged "transition" away from statism.[42]

The current impasse of perestroika, furthermore, resembles the Soviet NEP, but in reverse. The NEP saw the progressive stifling of the surviving prerevolutionary market economy by the nascent ambitions of Party-state power. Gorbachev's perestroika has witnessed the tenacious resistance of an ailing but still massive Party-state structure to a fledgling yet corrosive market. Whereas it proved easy to move brutally from a market to a command economy, it is turning out to be inordinately difficult to make the more delicate reverse transition. Between Gorbachev and a neo-NEP stands the mountainous mass of decaying Stalinist success, whereas between Lenin and the first NEP there stood only the failed wreckage of War Communism. So Gorbachev is left with the worst of two possible worlds: an old one that refuses to die and a new one without the strength to be born.

At the same time, this failure of economic perestroika coincides with the runaway success of glasnost and the progress of democratization and popular politicalization. The result is a new kind of "scissors crisis," to appropriate a metaphor used by Trotsky during the unstable NEP to describe the upward curve of industrial prices when charted against the downward curve of agricultural prices. Similarly, under the unstable neo-NEP of perestroika, the curve of glasnost and politicalization is running alarmingly high, and that of economic restructuring is sinking catastrophically low.[43] So perestroika, like its predecessor, risks being destroyed by the widening gap of the scissors unless energetic emergency measures are taken soon.

By late fall 1989, Moscow began to hear rumors of a coup. Other rumors, more plausibly, offered speculation about an imminent state of emergency or of a mitigated form of martial law (*osoboe polozhenie*). To everyone, society seemed to be adrift in disorder. Fear of state authority had almost vanished during the summer after the Congress, and with it, so it seemed, the regime's ability to govern. When the emigré Andrei Amalrik twenty years ago published his *Will the Soviet Union Survive until 1984?* his question was met with incredulity, even derision.[44] Now it may well turn out that he was only a few years off.

In the midst of all this, what of Gorbachev, on whose person the West concentrates its attention and hopes? To the outside world, he passes for a bold and decisive leader, a mover and a shaker of major stature, especially in international affairs. When seen from Moscow, however, after his first initiative in unleashing the perestroika deluge, he has come to look more like a reactive than an active figure, a man increasingly incapable of staking out strong policy positions on the two make-or-break domestic issues of his reign, the economy and the nationalities. Instead, he appears essentially as a political tactician, fully at home only in Party maneuvering, now pruning the Politburo of conservative foes such as the former KGB chief, Chebrikov, or the Ukrainian Party boss, Shcherbitsky, as in the fall of 1989, now tacking from left to right and back again in the debates of the new Supreme Soviet. Indeed, by giving way totally and immediately to the miners' demands in July 1989, he appeared downright weak. And in all things he acts as if his economic problems could be solved by political means. Yet, since the direct road to economic perestroika is closed to him by structural blockage, this easier political route of glasnost and democratization is the only one left open to him.

Nor does he seem to be able to make up his mind whether he is head of state or head of the opposition. As one Soviet commentator put it, he is trying to be both Luther and the pope at the same time.[45] But in such a contradictory situation, for all his political prowess, he may yet turn out to be no more than the ultimate sorcerer's apprentice of Sovietism.

XI

As 1989 draws to a close, it is clear that it will enter history as the beginning of communism's terminal crisis, the year of the Second Great Break, but in the descending, not the ascending, phase of utopia in power; and this not just in Russia, but from the Baltic to the China Sea, and from Berlin to Beijing. It is also clear that perestroika and glasnost, welcome as they are in their intention, have in their application only aggravated the systemic crisis they were intended to alleviate. And they have done so because like all forms of soft communism, they go against the logic of the system they are trying to save. The internal contradiction of perestroika is that Gorbachev has been trying to promote soft communism through structures and a population programmed for hard communism. But the latter is the only variety of Sovietism that is the genuine article, for the essence of all varieties of Sovietism is Party supremacy. Thus, the instrument of Gorbachev's reform — the Party — is at the same time the basic cause of Sovietism's troubles. To adapt a diagnosis of Alexander Herzen regarding earlier revolutionaries, the Party is not the doctor; it is the disease.

And the way out of this contradiction then? As one Soviet reformer put it after the June Congress, "The country now stands at a crossroads. From here we either go the Chinese way or the Polish-Hungarian way." Although the speaker obviously wished for the latter course, the alternative he posed may well be a Hobson's choice. The Chinese way since June 1989 means relative, though now declining, market prosperity under a regime of political and military repression. Repression is certainly a possibility in Russia, but market prosperity is quite out of the question for the indefinite future. Conversely, the Polish-Hungarian way means genuine democracy, but this is being attempted in the midst of economic ruin so severe as to threaten the survival of the new constitutional order. In Russia the economic ruin is even worse than in Poland and Hungary, but real democracy, as opposed to mere democratization, is not even on the agenda. Thus, the Russian way could well combine the worst of the Chinese and the Central European scenarios: economic failure in conjunction with an inexpungeable leading role for the Party.

Indeed, all three paths of communist reform (we may leave out of consideration the frozen Albanias such as Romania, Cuba, and North Korea) seem to end in one or another type of impasse. In this way Leninist totalitarianism shows another facet of its difference from ordinary authoritarianism. As Polish radicals discovered in the early 1980s in looking for possible models of liberation, post-Franco Spain and post-Pinochet Chile could not serve as examples. For those countries were able to make the transition to democracy because they had only been political authoritarianisms, not economic, social, and ideological monoliths. And, of course, they possessed market economies, so when political tyranny was ended, civil society, which had never been destroyed, could emerge fully into the light of day. But Leninist regimes, when they enter their final decline, seem able only either to implode, as in Poland, Hungary, and East Germany, or to dig in their heels militarily to stave off implosion, as under Deng Xiaoping in 1989, or his favorite model, the General Jaruzelski of 1981.

Yet whether they implode or hang on for a last desperate stand, all that they leave behind is economic and social rubble — hardly the foundation for building a "normal" society, as the Poles call their hoped-for post-Leninist order. And the leaders of Solidarity are acutely aware of the enormous risk they are taking in assuming power under such parlous conditions. Yet they have no choice but to try, since after eight years of Jaruzelski's failed attempt at being a Polish Kádár — that is, repression followed by liberalizing economic reform — the Party was as bankrupt as the country.

XII

This grim impasse at the end of utopia in power is the logical outcome of the structures which that power had built. The whole impossible enterprise of Lenin and Stalin was sustainable only as long as the human and material resources on which the system fed retained the vitality to endure the burden of the regime, and as long as some modicum of material success undergirded the Party's monopolistic position. But when these conditions ceased to hold, beginning with Deng Xiaoping's marketization of 1979 and Solidarity's revolt of 1980, the Communist parties' will to power began to flag and their people's habit of fear began to fade. This soon made necessary, for the Soviet Party-state's survival, the recourse to the expedients of perestroika and glasnost. But these are only pale substitutes for the market and democracy, halfway measures designed to square the circle of making the vivifying forces of a resurrected civil society compatible with the Party's leading role.

But this circle cannot be squared. If marketization and privatization are the economic goals of reform in communist countries, then Party planning becomes superfluous, indeed downright parasitical. If multiple parties, elections, and the rule of law are the political goals of reform in communist countries, then the dual administration of the Party-state becomes super-numerary, indeed positively noxious.

The Party is not a party, in the normal sense of an association for contesting elections and alternating in government under the rule of law. The Party is, rather, a self-appointed society for the monopoly of power. It can tolerate normal parties only as tempo-rary expedients, satellites, or fronts when the political weather is stormy. Likewise, the dual administrative body of the Party-state is not a normal state, but a special instrument created by the Party to act as a transmission belt of its policies to the population through the nomenklatura. Such a state cannot therefore be turned into a normal polity simply by legalizing other parties, since they will not have equal access with the Party to the monopolistic facilities of the state apparatus, from its police to its press. Nor is socialist planning an alternative way to organize the economy; it is the negation of the economy, its death as a separate sphere of human activity through its subordination to politics and ideological imperatives. It is this total amalgam, this whole surreal world, that is summed up by the sacrosanct tenet of the leading role.

This role is in its essence inimical to all the professed goals of reform now echoing throughout the Soviet Union and Central Europe, whether glasnost, democratization, or multiparty elec-tions. All these reforms imply that there is a third way, a halfway house between what the ideological call socialism and capital-ism, or what the inhabitants of the East think of as Sovietism and a "normal society." But there is no third way between Leninism and the market, between bolshevism and constitutional govern-ment. Marketization and democratization lead to the revival of civil society, and such a society requires the rule of law. But civil society under the rule of law is incompatible with the preserva-tion of the lawless leading role.

At some point, therefore, the redline will be reached where reform crosses over into the liquidation of the leading role and all the structures it has created. And both Russia and Central Europe are now reaching that critical line. The false problem of how to restructure Leninism is now giving way to the real problem of how to dismantle the system, how to effect at last an exit from communism. Perestroika is not a solution, but a transition to this exit. As Milovan Djilas foresaw early in perestroika: communism is not reforming itself, it is disintegrating.[46]

XIII

As yet, the only country that has posed the problem of the exit from communism openly and as a matter of practical policy is Poland. Hungary so far has given up on communism and the leading role only verbally; and its free elections are still in the future. To be sure, changing the Party's name to "Socialist" caused membership to drop from 700,000 to 30,000; but even this rump party still controls all the institutional assets of the old Party-state and preserves the aim of maintaining some form of socialism. But Poland has already crossed the redline with a Solidarity-led government proclaiming a goal of full marketization, the phasing out of the nomenklatura, and the decommunization of the army, the police, and the public administration — in short, the end in fact, not just in law, of the leading role, indeed of the whole communist system.

But even in Poland all the structures and coercive power still remain in the Party's hands, and the Solidarity ministry is proceeding very cautiously with de-Sovietization for fear of provoking a "Kabul reaction," a bunker defense, among the 2-million-member Party. Simultaneously, the official trade union, larger than worker Solidarity, is now demagogically exploiting the socialist reflexes inbred by forty years of Sovietism to "defend the rights of workers" against the free-market policies of the Solidarity ministry. Such an attempt at destabilization should not be too difficult to promote amid the economic wreckage left behind after the Party's unexpected implosion during what were to have been the fail-safe elections of last June. (These elections were set up during the previous winter's round table negotiations with Solidarity, designed to give the Party a few more years of respite.) Under such unstable conditions, the oldest and most lucid critic of Polish communism, Stefan

Kisielewski, concludes that it will take twenty years to de-Soviet-ize the Polish mentality and Polish institutions.[47]

So as we rub our eyes in astonishment at the most stunning communist implosions of all, the November collapse of the Berlin Wall and the ensuing Prague revolt, we should not conclude that the structures it shielded for so long can be transformed by a few reform decrees. The revolutionary rapidity of events in 1989 should not breed the illusion that the exit from communism these events presage will itself be a rapid process.

And the most difficult case of all will be the Soviet Union. There, unlike Central Europe, the real problem of dismantling, not reforming, communism is not yet posed, not even by the Interregional Group of People's Deputies: Russia, after all, has had seventy, not forty-five, years of Sovietism. Also, the Soviet Party is a national institution, not an alien imposition, with deep roots in the patriotic success of World War II. Finally, this national-imperial Party has the military apparatus of a super-power. To be sure, Gorbachev is clearly retrenching from the global overextension of the Brezhnev era. True also, in the course of the Polish elections of June, the Hungarian Party reforms and the East German and Czech *Zusammenbruch* of 1989, Moscow has clearly accepted the inevitability of the Finlandization of Central Europe, or national autonomy within the Warsaw Pact, and possibly even some type of Rapallo cooperation with West Germany to revive the ruined economies of the area. Nonetheless, the Soviet military budget has not significantly decreased, nor has modernization of its arsenal ceased. And these circumstances give to the Soviet Party's leading role vertebrae that its little brothers lack.

XIV

Let us return now to the questions with which this inquiry began: Can Gorbachev succeed? Should we help him? It is now the official United States position, to quote President Bush, that Gorbachev is a "genuine reformer" and that we all "wish perestroika to succeed," a stance that implies at least moral help. But to answer these questions meaningfully, we must, as with the questions of Stalin's necessity, rephrase them first. Succeed at what? Help him to do what?

If by perestroika's success we mean producing a communist system that is economically effective and politically democratic, then the answer must be no: the empirical record of seventy years shows that the fundamental structures of the Leninist system reached an inextricable impasse at the end of the 1970s; and the mounting contradictions of perestroika indicate that the system cannot be restructured or reformed, but can only either stagnate or be dismantled and replaced by market institutions over a long period of time. In this case, any aid the West might render to the Soviet state to save or improve the existing system would be futile: on this score, Gorbachev is beyond our help. Such aid would also work against the real interests of the restive Soviet peoples and thus of international stability. Like Western credits to Eduard Gierek and the Polish Party-state in the 1970s, aid to the Soviet government would simply prolong the agony of everyone concerned.

Yet if by perestroika's success we mean effecting a transition from a Party-state and a command economy to democracy and the market, then the answer, unfortunately, must still be no. First of all, such a transition is not the aim of Gorbachev's perestroika; its aim, rather, is to salvage what can be saved of the existing system by halfway-house concessions to economic and human reality, concessions moreover that are constantly being revised as new sections of the system give way and as the regime improvises frantically in the hope that something might turn the situation around. Second, and even more important, such a transition would bring the end of the cardinal leading role and hence would amount to the self-liquidation of communism, something Gorbachev clearly does not intend to do.

Still, events are pressing toward the eventual dwindling away of the system, whatever the Soviet leadership's intentions and whoever that leader might be in the future. And here Western help could play a constructive role. First, reducing the mutual burden of armaments, if carried out with due attention to legitimate security concerns, would ease the severity of the Soviet crisis (though it would not alter its structural causes). And Gorbachev has clearly indicated his willingness to engage in arms reductions, while at the same time taking care that the Soviets' international retreat does not turn into a rout.

Second, although Western aid should not go to shoring up Soviet economic institutions in the state sector, it could be usefully applied to the piecemeal development of parallel structures in a private sector operating on market principles so as to promote economic and eventually, political pluralism. This could take the form, say, of free economic zones operating under IMF conditions in such places as the Baltic states, Armenia, or the Soviet Far East. In this case, the expectation would be that such a parallel sector, perhaps with its own convertible currency, would eventually spread across the Soviet Union.

Such a policy is, indeed, the approach that the Mazowiecki government and its finance minister, Leszek Balcerowicz, are now attempting to inaugurate in Poland. But what Gorbachev is prepared to accept for his outer empire in Central Europe (where he effectively lost control over events sometime in 1988) would be much more difficult for him to accept for the inner empire of the Soviet Union itself, since foreign investment would imperil national sovereignty. So Western investment, in joint or other enterprises in Russia, would have to be handled without triumphalism about capitalism's superiority, and with due sensitivity to Soviet national pride. The West's aim should be to encourage the change of Soviet realities, while leaving the old labels intact — in a kind of socialist-emperor-of-Japan arrangement.

Yet, however the Soviet Union edges toward its particular exit from communism, this unchartered process can only be a long and painful one. Nor will it be a unilinear or an incremental progress toward integration in some "common European house." Instead, further crises will most likely be necessary to produce further, and more real, reforms. And a last-ditch attempt to stave off ruin by curtailing destabilizing reform altogether could lead to that military reaction so feared by Moscow liberals. And who knows, in this scenario Gorbachev might be agile enough to become his own successor, or if perestroika ends in another eighteenth of Brumaire, to be his own Bonaparte. Gorbachev would be hard to replace because his international reputation is now the Soviet Union's chief capital asset; yet he could not afford to be a very tough Bonaparte, since he has become the prisoner of his foreign policy successes.

Obviously, none of these prospects is a cheering one, and none would be easy for the West to live alongside. But it is better to look realistically at the genuine options in the East as they have been molded by seventy years of failed utopia than to engage in fantasies about Gorbachev as a demiurge of instant democracy or about the end of conflict in history. Nor should we forget that communism, though a disaster in almost every creative domain, has always been supremely successful at one thing: resourcefulness and tenacity in holding on to its monopoly of power. So the Soviet world's transition to normality will be a long time coming, for the Party, though now dyed with the hues of glasnost and democratization, will cling to the bitter end, like some poisoned tunic of Nessus, around the bodies of nations it has enfolded in its embrace for so many decades.

Notes

1. Francis Fukuyama, "The End of History?" *The National Interest* (Summer 1988).

2. See, for example, Judy Stone, *The Coming Soviet Crash: Gorbachev's Desperate Pursuit of Credit in Western Financial Markets* (New York: The Free Press, 1989) — a bad title for an otherwise good book. The threat of financial crash is quite real, but until now Gorbachev has steadfastly refused to use foreign credit extensively for fear of compromising national independence.

3. See, for example, Frederic J. Fieron, Jr., ed., *Communist Studies and the Social Sciences: Essays on Methodology and Empirical Theory* (Chicago: Rand McNally, 1969); and Susan Gross Solomon, *Pluralism in the Soviet Union* (New York: St. Martin's Press, 1983). See also the social-science-oriented essays in Erik P. Hoffman and Robin F. Laird, eds., *The Soviet Polity in the Modern Era* (New York: Aldine Publishing Company, 1984). For the thesis of "stability" as the great common characteristic of the Soviet Union and the United States, see Samuel P. Huntington,

Political Order in Changing Societies (New Haven: Yale University Press, 1968).

4. See notably *Stalinism, Essays in Historical Interpretation,* ed. Robert C. Tucker (New York: Norton, 1977), especially the Introduction and contributions by S. Cohen and R. Tucker.

5. The theme of a seminal, and for the most part penetrating, essay by Richard Lowenthal, "Development versus Utopia in Communist Policy," in Chalmers Johnson, ed., *Change in Communist Systems* (Stanford, Calif.: Stanford University Press, 1970). A revised version of this essay, entitled "Beyond Totalitarianism?" in Irving Howe, ed., *1984 Revisited* (New York: Harper and Row, 1983) could still be presented as the last word on Sovietism on the eve of Gorbachev's accession to power. In the same volume see also Michael Walzer's more categorical rejection of the relevance of the totalitarian concept, in "On 'Failed Totalitarianism.'"

6. Jerry F. Hough and Merle Fainsod, *How the Soviet Union Is Governed* (Cambridge: Harvard University Press, 1979). The book in fact has kept virtually nothing of Fainsod's original *How Russia Is Ruled* (Cambridge: Harvard University Press, 1963), which offered the classic statement of the totalitarian model. For urbanization as the supposed key to Sovietism, see Moshe Lewin, *The Gorbachev Phenomenon: A Historical Interpretation* (Berkeley and Los Angeles: University of California Press, 1988).

7. See *Cultural Revolution in Russia, 1928–1931,* ed. Sheila Fitzpatrick (Bloomington, Ind.: University of Indiana Press, 1978), especially the essays by S. Fitzpatrick and J. Hough; and Sheila Fitzpatrick, *The Russian Revolution* (New York: Oxford University Press, 1982), especially 8, 157, and 159.

8. *Politics, Society and Nationality Inside Gorbachev's Russia,* ed. Seweryn Bialer (Boulder and London: Western Press, 1989).

9. The theme of Mikhail Heller and Alexander Nekrich, *Utopia in Power,* transl. Phillis B. Carlos (New York: Simon and Schuster, 1985). First published in Russian (London: Overseas Press, 1982).

10. Adam Michnik, "Towards a Civil Society: Hopes for Polish Democracy," *Times Literary Supplement* (4, 429) 19–25 February 1988: 188, 198–99.

11. See especially the essays of Pierre Hassner, Jacques Rupnik, and Aleksander Smolar in *Totalitarismes,* ed. Guy Hermet (Paris: Economica, 1984).

12. Paul Thibaud, "Réflexions sur la décomposition des communismes," *Notes de la Fondation Saint-Simon* (July 1989).

13. Leszek Koltakowski, *Main Currents of Marxism,* transl. P. S. Falla, vol. 3 (Oxford: Clarendon Press, 1978), 523.

14. For a convenient short course in revisionist history on 1917 as a proletarian revolution, see Ronald Suny, "Toward a Social History of the October Revolution," *American Historical Review* 88 (1) (February 1983).

15. See Thomas Remmington, *Building Socialism in Bolshevik Russia: Ideology and Industrial Organization, 1917–1921* (Pittsburgh: University of Pittsburgh Press, 1984); and Silvana Malle, *The Economic Organization of War Communism, 1918–1921* (New York: Cambridge University Press, 1985).

16. See Laszlo Szamuely, *First Models of the Socialist Economic Systems* (Budapest: Akademiai Kiado, 1974).

17. Alec Nove, *Was Stalin Really Necessary?* (New York: Praeger, 1965).

18. The classic statement of this position is Stephen Cohen, *Bukharin and the Bolshevik Revolution* (New York: Oxford University Press, 1980[1971]). See also Moshe Lewin, *Lenin's Last Struggle,* transl. A. M. Sheridan Smith (New York: Random House, 1970). The most sophisticated elaboration of this position is Lewin's *Russian Peasants and Soviet Power,* transl. Irene Nove and John Biggard (Evanston, Ill.: Northwestern University Press, 1968).

19. For the essentially political nature of the Great Break, see especially Alexander Gerschenkron, *Economic Backwardness in Historical Perspective* (Cambridge: Harvard University Press, 1962), passim. See also Alexander Erlich, *The Soviet Industrialization Debate, 1924–1928* (Cambridge: Harvard University Press, 1960).

20. Robert Conquest, *The Harvest of Sorrow* (New York: Oxford University Press, 1986). The best general work on the Stalin period as a whole remains Adam B. Ulam, *Stalin: the Man and his Era* (Boston: Beacon Press, 1987).

21. For the revision of Soviet growth statistics, see Abram Bergson, *The Real National Income of the Soviet Union since 1928* (Cambridge: Harvard University Press, 1961). For the comparison with Russia under Witte, see Gerschenkron, chaps. 6 and 10.

22. For example, John Kenneth Galbraith, *The New Industrial State* (Boston: Houghton Mifflin, 1967), and Wassily Leontiev, "The Decline

and Rise of Soviet Economic Science," *Foreign Affairs* 38 (January 1960): 261–72.

23. Boris Pasternak, *Doctor Zhivago,* transl. Max Hayward and Manya Harari (London: Collins and Harvil Press, 1958), 422.

24. Interpretive literature on the Great Purges is both sparse and shallow. The view expressed here draws on Heller and Nekrich; Ulam; Nicholas Werth, *Les Procès de Moscou* (Brussels: Editions Complexe, 1987); and Jonathan Haslam, "Political Opposition to Stalin and the Origins of the Terror in Russia, 1932–1936," *The Historical Journal* 29 (2) (1986): 395–418.

25. Robert Conquest, *The Great Terror* (New York: Macmillan, 1968), now being published legally in the Soviet Union. For Medvedev's most recent estimate of Purge victims, see *Argumenti i Facty* (September 1989).

26. Alexis de Tocqueville, "Introduction," in vol. 1, *De la démocratie en Amérique, Oeuvres Complètes,* 6.

27. For example, the last sections of Joseph Schumpeter, *Capitalism, Socialism and Democracy,* 3d ed. (New York: Harper and Row, 1950).

28. Gavriil Popov, *Puti perestroiki: mnenie ekonomista* (Moscow: Ekonomika, 1989) is the most recent statement of this influential critic of the Soviet economy and society.

29. The most relevant items are: *CIA Handbook of Economic Statistics* for 1987 and 1988; Robert Gates, *Revisiting Soviet Economic Performance Under Glasnost: Implications for CIA Estimates* (1988), a critique of the preceding item. On the Soviet side see especially the relatively optimistic early item of Abel Aganbegyan, *The Economic Challenge of Perestroika,* trans. Pauline M. Tifflin (Bloomington, Ind.: Indiana University Press, 1988) and his more recent and rather alarmist *Inside Perestroika, The Future of the Soviet Economy* (New York: Harper and Row, 1989). Recent Soviet estimates of their economy's performance tend to be lower than Western ones, and the most recent are the lowest of all. It is these estimates that have been followed here. For a statement of the misleading character of attempting to measure the Soviet economy at all in Western terms, see Alain Besançon, *Anatomie d'un Spectre* (Paris: Calmann-Levy, 1981). This work also effectively brings out the "surreal" nature of the Soviet world in general, a factor the dominant Western social science approach quite misses.

30. Pierre Daix, *L'Avènement de la nomenklatura: La Chute de Khrouchtchev* (Brussels: Editions Complexe, 1982).

31. Mikhail Voslensky, *Nomenklatura: the Soviet Ruling Class,* transl. Eric Mosbacher (Garden City, N.Y.: Doubleday, 1984). Published several years earlier in Russian and German, this work brought the nomenklatura's role to world attention.

32. See, for example, Konstantin Simes, *U.S.S.R.: The Corrupt Society, The Secret World of Soviet Capitalism* (New York: Simon and Schuster, 1982).

33. Tatiana Zaslavskaia, "The Novosibirsk Report," *Survey* 28 (1) (1984): 88–108. An early and perceptive Western statement of the growing contradictions of Sovietism is Seweryn Bialer's *The Soviet Paradox: External Expansion, Internal Decline* (New York: Knopf, 1986).

34. The best treatment of the beginnings of perestroika is Michel Tatu's *Gorbachev: L'U.R.S.S., va-t-elle changer?* (Paris: Le Centurion-Le Monde, 1987).

35. The most comprehensive collection of reformist intelligentsia writings was issued for the June 1988 Special Party Conference. See *Inogo ne dano,* ed. Iuri Afanasiev (Moscow: Izdatel'stvo Progress, 1988). A partial translation exists in French under the title *La Seule Issue* (Paris: Alban Michel, 1989). For the geneology of the submerged tradition of soft communism from the 1920s on, see Moshe Lewin, *Political Undercurrents in Soviet Economic Debates: From Bukharin to the Modern Reformers* (Princeton, N.J.: Princeton University Press, 1974).

36. Quoted in *Le Monde,* 20 December 1988.

37. Quoted in *Russkaia Mysl'* (*La pensée russe*) (Paris), 4 August 1989.

38. Igor Kliamkin, *Moscow News,* 15 April 1989.

39. Sakharov's speech at the Congress launching his idea was reproduced in *The New York Review of Books,* 17 August 1989, 25–26.

40. The best discussion of the background to Gorbachev's economic reforms and the development of his early programs is Ed. H. Hewett, *Reforming the Soviet Economy* (Washington, D.C.: The Brookings Institution, 1987). On the Soviet side see Tatiana Zaslavskaia, in *A Voice of Reform: Essays by Tatiana Zaslavskaia,* ed. Murray Yanovitch (Armonk, N.Y.: M. E. Sharpe, 1989) and especially Nikolai Shmelyov and Vladimir Popov's *Na perelome (At the Breaking Point)* (Moscow: Ekonomika, 1989).

41. The most informed, penetrating, and realistic study of economic perestroika's record to date is Anders Aslund, *Gorbachev's Struggle for Economic Reform* (Ithaca, N.Y.: Cornell University Press, 1989).

42. The best general treatments to date of the Gorbachev era overall are: Alec Nove, *Glasnost in Action: Cultural Renaissance in Russia* (Boston:

Unwin Hyman, 1989), which is moderately pessimistic; and Walter Laqueur, *The Long Road to Freedom: Russia and Glasnost* (New York: Scribners, 1989), which is distinctly pessimistic. A strong statement of the internal contradictions of Gorbachevism is Vladimir Bukovsky's "Who Resists Gorbachev?" *Washington Quarterly* (Winter 1989).

43. The scissors metaphor was applied to Gorbachev by the historian Sergio Romano, Italian ambassador to Moscow during the last four years. It will be the theme of his forthcoming book, in Italian, on perestroika.

44. Andrei Amalrik, *Will the Soviet Union Survive Until 1984?* (New York: Harper and Row, 1970).

45. Andranik Migranyan, *Literaturnaia Gazeta,* 16 August 1989.

46. Milovan Djilas and George Urban, "Djilas on Gorbachev," *Encounter* 71 (September-October 1987): 3–19.

47. For an example of his thought, see Stefan Kisielewski, *Polen-Oder die Herrschaft der Dilletanten: Sozialisinus und Wirtschaftspraxis* (Zurich: Edition Interform, 1978).

Mikhail Gorbachev

Address to the Soviet Communist Party Central Committee's Plenary Meeting, February 5, 1990

Mikhail Gorbachev was born on March 2, 1931, in the village of Privolnoye in Stavropol territory, a vast grain and sheep-rearing center north of the Caucasus mountains. Gorbachev comes from peasant stock: his grandfather founded a collective farm, and his father was an agricultural machine operator who fought at the front in World War II.

After graduating from the Faculty of Law at Moscow State University in 1955, Gorbachev returned to Stavropol and became active in the Young Communist League. Rising in the territory's Party power structure, he gained extensive local experience in the fields of health and social welfare, science, education, agriculture, and industry.

In 1978 he was elected secretary of the Central Committee, and two years later was elevated to the Politburo. In 1984 he was elected general secretary of the Communist Party, subsequently beginning a series of initiatives in the fields of domestic social and economic policy and international affairs that have been characterized by his calls for *glasnost* (openness) and *perestroika* (revolutionary transformation or restructuring).

The following is the full text of Gorbachev's historic speech of February 5, 1990, calling for the repeal of Article Six of the Soviet Constitution (which had guaranteed the political dictatorship of the Communist Party) and for the advent of democratic political pluralism in the Soviet Union.

Comrades, I think you will agree that we have gathered for a very important plenary meeting, a meeting which Communists and all society have been waiting for with immense interest and impatience.

The Central Committee has received thousands of letters with suggestions and wishes from Party members and non-Party people, from Party organisations and committees, from work collectives, factory workers and farmers, intellectuals, scientists, veterans and youth.

Telegrams continue to pour in. You, too, have seen rallies and meetings at which the most vital problems were discussed often from various positions, in an acute and interested way. Their participants also wanted to make their viewpoint known to the Party Central Committee.

All this combined is a phenomenon that reflects profound changes that have already occurred and are occurring in our society along the tracks of *perestroika* and in conditions of democratisation and *glasnost*. The main thing that now worries Communists and all citizens of the country is the fate of *perestroika*, the fate of the country and the role of the Soviet Communist Party at the current, probably most crucial, stage of revolutionary transformation.

Society wants to know the Party's position, and this determines the entire significance of our plenum. During preparations for the meeting we were faced once again with the question of when to hold the 28th Party Congress. In December last year the Central Committee considered it necessary to bring forward the convocation of the Congress by six months. But the course of developments is so fast that it is necessary to review this issue again.

Having assessed the entire situation and examined petitions from Communists and Party organisations, the Politburo submits the following proposal for your consideration: to hold the 28th Communist Party Congress late in June–early in July this year. We are convinced that the proposal will be approved at this plenum.

The Congress should be preceded, in our view, with a full report-and-election campaign in all links of the Party with a broad debate on the platform and the draft new rules of the Soviet Communist Party. Overdue personnel issues will be resolved and new elected Party bodies will be formed during the reports and elections. This will create a totally different situation for holding the Congress.

At this plenum we are to adopt the Central Committee's draft platform for the Congress. In a month or, better, three weeks from now — not later — we will probably have to gather again for a plenary meeting to consider the draft new rules and have them published for public discussion. Preparations for the Congress are entering the decisive stage. One should clearly understand why it is necessary to bring forward the Party Congress and what its main objective is, as we see it.

The Soviet Communist Party initiated *perestroika* and generated its concept and policy. Profound revolutionary changes encompassing all spheres of life and all sections of the population have been launched on this basis in the country. This has paved the way for renewing society and tapping socialism's potential. The Party has succeeded in expressing in theory and policy the country's acute needs and realities of present-day world development.

Rapid changes, unusual in scope and originality, are taking place within the framework of *perestroika*. This makes ever new demands on state and public institutes and, of course, on the Soviet Communist Party. As a matter of fact, we have approached the moment when the Party should enrich its policy with due account for changes that have already occurred during *perestroika* and problems that have recently emerged. Any delay threatens a lag and the loss of the initiative, which would, in turn, inevitably affect the Party itself and the future of its revolutionary undertakings.

By raising the question in this way, the Politburo does not intend to dramatise the situation and impart a tragic character to these decisions. We should at last understand well at what time we live and what tasks we are handling, and ensure the draft platform gives a fresh impetus to our struggle. Let us work hard on the document at this plenary meeting.

Of no less importance is the understanding of the fact — which is the other aspect of the problem that also demands the bringing forward of the Congress — is that the Party will be able to fulfill the mission of political vanguard only if it drastically restructures itself, masters the art of political work in the present-day conditions and succeeds in cooperating with all forces committed to *perestroika*.

The crux of the Party's renewal is the need to get rid of everything that tied it to the authoritarian-bureaucratic system, a system that left its mark not only on methods of work and interrelationships within the Party, but also on ideology, ways of thinking and notions of socialism.

The platform says: our ideal is a humane, democratic socialism. Expressing the interests of the working class and all working people and relying on the great legacy of Marx, Engels and Lenin, the Soviet Communist Party is creatively developing socialist ideals to match present-day realities and with due account for the entire experience of the twentieth century.

The platform states clearly what we should abandon. We should abandon the ideological dogmatism that became ingrained during past decades, outdated stereotypes in domestic policy and outmoded views on the world revolutionary process and world development as a whole.

We should abandon everything that led to the isolation of socialist countries from the mainstream of world civilisation. We should abandon the understanding of progress as a permanent confrontation with a socially different world. We are giving up the notion of building socialism on an earlier construed pattern which serves as a rigid framework for the ingenious creativity of the masses. Much has been said about the decisive role of the masses, but this truly determining force of socialist development has actually been neglected.

The Party's renewal presupposes a fundamental change in its relations with state and economic bodies and the abandonment of the practice of commanding them and substituting for their functions. The Party in a renewing society can exist and play its role as vanguard only as a democratically recognised force. This means that its status should not be imposed through constitutional endorsement.

The Soviet Communist Party, it goes without saying, intends to struggle for the status of the ruling party. But it will do so strictly within the framework of the democratic process by giving up any legal and political advantages, offering its programme and defending it in discussions, cooperating with other social and political forces, always working amidst the masses, living by their interests and their needs.

The extensive democratisation currently under way in our society is being accompanied by mounting political pluralism. Various social and political organisations and movements emerge. This process may lead at a certain stage to the establishment of parties.

The Soviet Communist Party is prepared to act with due account for these new circumstances, cooperate and conduct a dialogue with all organisations committed to the Soviet Constitution and the social system endorsed in this Constitution. At the same time we openly state that at this crucial period the Soviet Communist Party is able to play the consolidating, integrating role and ensure progress of *perestroika* for the benefit of the entire nation.

The Party's renewal presupposes its thorough, comprehensive democratisation and rethinking the principle of democratic centralism with emphasis on democratism and power of the Party masses. This will help consolidate the CPSU as an integrated organisation and raise its prestige among the people. An important step forward in this respect should be taken during the report and election campaign in the run-up to the Congress and the election of delegates to the Congress. We regard as correct numerous demands by Party members that the decisive role in these elections belongs to Communists and primary Party organisations.

Comrades, what do we proceed from and what realities do we bear in mind when formulating the tasks for the period ahead? If we are to speak in the broadest terms, both vast opportunities for movement forward and real dangers simultaneously are typical of the present state of society. In fact, they exist side by side.

Opportunities are available because the restructuring processes keep developing, freeing the enormous energies of the people. So far, the most important result of *perestroika* – the platform also states this – has been the emancipation of society, thanks to which millions of Soviet people have gained civic dignity and are taking the running of the affairs of the state into their own hands.

This tendency will grow, and the pledge of the success of the work launched by the Party is ultimately in this tendency. In this there is no cause for panic. The process of forming new economic and political structures is under way. This also creates a favourable atmosphere for people's active involvement, for speeding up and deepening restructuring processes in all areas of life.

At the same time, in moving along the path of *perestroika*, we saw that the crisis that battered the country was immeasurably deeper and more serious than we expected. Much of what is happening is explained by this. Problems and contradictions that have been piling up within the social organism for decades, have come out into the open. Regrettably, we could not escape miscalculations and mistakes during *perestroika* and this, too, has complicated the situation. Social tension and anxiety are typical of it now. Elements of apathy and disappointment have emerged. Such is the contradictory but real situation.

There is the danger, and the Party should be mindful of this, that adventurists will try to exploit the arisen difficulties and speculate on real problems and the working people's dissatisfaction. The signs of this danger are obvious, including in recent days. Some perplexity, sentiments of defeatism and liquidation make themselves felt. This is just as dangerous for the Party as for the whole of society. We have already heard some allege that we have adopted an overly steep course, threatening the very foundations of the socialist system, and that there is no way out of the difficulties except a return to the former order. Others, on the contrary, allege that reforms aiming to bring out the potential of the socialist system are doomed to failure and the country can be rescued only through capitalisation.

We might not speak about this if these were only abstract theoretical disputes or debates in political circles. But such destructive judgements, penetrating into society, befuddle quite a few people, adversely affect the political atmosphere and stop people from seeing the restructuring process in the right perspective.

We should see that the crystallisation of both the conservative and the left-radical tendencies has accelerated lately. This is why, Comrades, we vitally need now, and I want to emphasise this one more time, a platform of the Party Central Committee that can give clear political guidelines and consolidate all the wholesome forces of society around the goals and tasks of revolutionary transformations.

I want to call your attention to the fact that the pivot of the proposed platform is the approach to solving immediate and strategic tasks of Soviet society along the lines of renewing socialism. We remain committed to the choice made in October 1917, the socialist idea. But we move away from its dogmatic interpretation, refuse to sacrifice the people's real interests for schematic constructions. We set the task to translate into life step-by-step the principle of social justice without the slightest illusions of a speedy miracle. We intend to do this by rejecting the prejudices of the past and various ideological taboos, using everything valuable that is available in other societies, in their economies and social sphere, political life, the organisation of production and everyday life, science and technology, culture and intellectual creativity.

Perhaps, you have noticed the peculiar construction of the platform. It seemed to us to be of fundamental importance to show even in the arrangement of the material that the citizen and his well-being are put in the centre of the Party's policy from now on and forever, that advances along the socialist path should be measured primarily by this criterion.

The platform begins by setting out the political and socio-economic rights of the Soviet citizen, freedoms of the individual. I think that Comrades have also noticed that, after human rights in the draft, the need is stressed to adopt a range of measures to enrich the spiritual world of people, to raise society's educational and cultural level. Unfortunately, this factor has been in the background for some time now and has been regarded as almost a balance for industrial growth figures.

We had to pay for this by seriously lagging behind and we will be paying for it for a long time. We were nearly one of the last to realise that, in the age of information science, the most expensive assets are knowledge, breadth of mental outlook and creative imagination. To make up for lost time it is necessary today not to spare resources on science, education, culture and the arts — everything that elevates man and at the same time multiplies labour productivity.

Along with long-term matters, the draft platform puts forward urgent tasks connected with the modern situation in the country. This has paramount importance. We hoped to surmount the peak of the crisis in 1989, but recent events have shown that there has been no change for the better.

The recently published results of economic performance of the past year revealed once again the contradictory nature of processes in the economy. On the one hand, a number of indices posted slight growth despite considerable losses caused by strikes, ethnic conflicts, lax discipline and mismanagement. More foodstuffs and consumer goods have been produced.

On the other hand, we can see further disruption of the consumer market, a growth in shortages and queues, and a fall in the purchasing power of the ruble. The situation is worsened by the activity of shadow economy dealers and criminal elements. People are especially dissatisfied with the food situation. The question should be posed squarely. We worked out an innovative agrarian policy and voted for it at the March plenary meeting. We assess it as progressive and pointing to real ways out of food crisis. The main outcome of the plenum was that it lifted all restrictions on the use of diverse forms of land tenure. This conclusion was drawn on the basis of experience of many collectives. Several regions managed to blunt the acuteness of the situation at the food market.

Nevertheless, on the scale of the country, no fundamental improvement has taken place. The reason is that people in many localities are still in the sway of old attitudes and methods of management. Yes, there are shortages of resources and technology. Yes, social transformations must be conducted on a different scale and at different rates. All this is true. But primary importance should be assigned to restructuring relations of production in the village. And the crux of the matter now is the position of our cadre at the centre and localities. This is a political rather than an economic question. All obstacles should be removed in the way of the farmer; he should be given a free hand. This is how the draft platform poses the problem.

Food is only part of the problem of normalising the consumer market. The draft stresses the importance of a range of measures to improve finances and monetary circulation, and to strengthen the purchasing power of the ruble as an urgent task for the next two years.

True, we had a discussion on whether it is expedient to go into so much detail on these problems. After all, we are speaking about a Party platform, political orientation points. Is there a need to repeat what is contained in the government programme considered by the Congress of People's Deputies? Matters of principle absorbed these issues. However, they are so acute that people may be unsatisfied not to find certain specifics. Therefore, it seems quite in order to change opinions and take a more definite stand on this score.

I think that until now we have lacked resolve, and this should be overcome. This, particularly, concerns the main missing link that caused the entire economic reform to stall — the pricing system. It is necessary to speed up the solution of this problem. The Party continues to stand on the principled position: price reform should not affect the standard of living, especially that of low-income strata.

We can no longer reconcile ourselves with the glaring manifestations of mismanagement. Can we expect any results from credits that draw ridiculously low interest? Our interest is found nowhere in the world. It is such that no one cares to return credits because this interest does not change much, after all. This explains why neither credit nor ruble works. This won't do at all.

Is it permissible that commodity material stocks in the economy are rising by billions of rubles every year? Figures of 200 and 240 billion rubles for excessive stocks at enterprises are already being cited.

At a time when the country is rumbling, there is a shortage of resources. Moreover there is a shortage of basic goods on the market. This means that a mechanism is again lacking that would stimulate enterprises to have as many resources as they need and to get rid of the surplus.

Can we count on the success of economic reform if unfinished construction projects are flourishing? We remember with what stubbornness, worthy of better application, representatives of the state planning committee proved during the discussion of the draft plan for 1990 that no further cuts in capital construction could be made. In the last year alone, unfinished projects over and above norm increased by 20 billion rubles and absorbed four-fifths of the national income increment. And all this as the market of building materials is experiencing huge hunger, and trade orders, even by the most conservative count, are not satisfied by three billion rubles. But this involves direct goods exchange and monetary resources held by the population.

I could continue this list of unused possibilities with examples from the field of resource saving, storage and reprocessing, utilisation of secondary waste, etc. There the scale of losses is even more staggering. Such a situation simply cannot continue any longer.

We can get rid of these old ailments of our economy only by moving ahead, by introducing cost-accounting relations as part of the economic reform. All attempts to spur on somehow through commands were doomed long ago, Comrades. They have not worked for decades. They certainly would not work today. All echelons of economic management and all labour collectives should have specific plans of action in these areas of work.

Comrades, our society is concerned, no less than with the situation in the economy, with a number of complex problems that arose in the inter-ethnic field, which affect the future of the Soviet federation. In working on the draft of the document that we are now discussing, we drew on the platform on inter-ethnic issues that was adopted at the September 1989 plenum.

We think that the platform on inter-ethnic issues can serve as a departure for transforming our federation. At the same time, we tried to take into account recent developments. The pre-Congress platform points to the possibility of and the need for the further development of the treaty principle of the Soviet federation. This would involve the creation of legal conditions that would open the possibility for the existence of diverse forms of federative ties.

We stand for the diversity of modes of ethnic life in an integral and united Soviet state. We all have lately had the opportunity to think seriously about the state of affairs and developments in the sphere of ethnic relations. Searches for ways to use the potential of the federation better have been accompanied by developments that have alarmed the country and that must be given due assessments.

I think the Party and society are coming to understand, although with much difficulty and with clashes of opinion, that one must act in a well-balanced and responsible way in this sphere. People are becoming more and more aware of where separatist nationalistic, especially extremist, slogans may lead and what they can entail for people, nationalities and the whole country.

We must display principled approaches in opposing nationalism, chauvinism and separatism and, at the same time, understand that ethnic problems are no fantasy; they are real and are waiting to be solved by *perestroika*. The sooner decisions are taken to delimit the competence of the union and that of republics, to actually strengthen their political and economic independence, to broaden the rights of ethnic autonomies and to achieve the harmonious development of all languages and cultures, the sooner people will see the enormous advantages of the new Soviet federation.

Separatists, chauvinists and nationalists of all kinds understand this well and are trying to use the growth of people's national self-consciousness for their selfish aims. They evidently want to deliver a preventive strike at *perestroika*, which threatens to thwart their far-reaching plans. This has been patently manifest in the recent developments in Azerbaijan and Armenia. I don't think I should describe in detail the history of the conflict, which is rooted in the distant past.

I would like to draw your attention to the principled aspect of the problem. The conflict is centred round Nagorno-Karabakh.

Serious problems accumulated in the economic and cultural development of this autonomous region, and the Central Committee and the government took major measures to solve them. There appeared hope that this tough knot could be solved and the situation could be improved, but such prospects did not suit certain forces in both republics and in Nagorno-Karabakh itself.

Those for whom *perestroika* is a thorn in the side and who are afraid of democratisation and *glasnost*, ignore laws. I am speaking about representatives of the shadow economy, a veritable mafia that is fanning the flames of ethnic strife and putting pressure on state bodies under the slogans of national revival.

The conduct of the authorities and Party bodies in both republics, which yielded one position after another under pressure, does them no credit. Unfortunately, many representatives of the intelligentsia in Azerbaijan and Armenia failed to assess the situation correctly, to find the real causes of the conflict and to exert a positive influence on developments. Meanwhile, corrupted anti-*perestroika* forces managed to take the lead and direct misled people's actions into the destructive channel.

I should say that there has been perhaps no other issue in the past two years that has been given so much attention in Moscow. The initial position of the centre was that the Nagorno-Karabakh conflict should be settled in a way that would leave no winners and no losers. Otherwise, new flare-ups of hostility and violence, new victims and losses would be inevitable. We continued to adhere to this position at the height of the conflict. And still we failed to check the aggravation of the situation.

Late last year, in a difficult situation, the supreme bodies of power in both republics took decisions that aggravated the situation still more. The republics found themselves on the brink of all-out war. Armed groups from both sides began clashing; they began to seize weapons and attack troops and law-enforcement bodies and tightened the blockade of railways and roads.

Baku became the scene of brutal pogroms. If the state of emergency had not been introduced in Nagorno-Karabakh, in some border areas and then in Baku, the blood of not dozens but thousands upon thousands of people would have been shed.

The tasks of this plenum do not include a complete analysis of what happened, but it must be said already that there are no easy explanations and easy decisions in this respect.

The main lesson is that all issues connected with the development of nations and ethnic relations must be resolved on the road of *perestroika*, the renewal of society and democratic dialogue. Attempts to use force and methods of terror intimidate the people, and pressure by the authorities directly leads to chaos with all the ensuing consequences. Everything must be done to rule out the possibility of such developments in any part of the country.

The great and responsible role played by Party, local government and state bodies, our cadres and the intelligentsia, has become more obvious now. It must be clear that those who depart from principled positions, follow in the wake of obsolete sentiments or fall under the influence of nationalist passions will find themselves outside political life. It is not only the principled stance of our cadres that matters. Of no less importance is the ability to resolve practical problems that worry people.

We know how hard and painful *perestroika* processes are in these two republics. This is one of the reasons why nationalist forces have succeeded in winning over the people. This is what we ought to consider here. The centre has apparently failed to use all its capacities and authority to influence the course of *perestroika* in the republics more effectively and to support its followers. I have already said that a greater tragedy was prevented thanks to resolute actions. The safety of several thousand people was jeopardised—this was the main motive of the decisions taken.

The key fact is that nationalist, anti-Soviet groups openly encroached on the constitutional system, strove for power and sought to establish a dictatorship—not a democracy—by naked force and through militant nationalism. This was in fact a coup attempt—nothing more, nothing less. All structures, above all military ones, had been prepared for that. And the flirtation of some political forces with this wing of the Azerbaijani Popular Front only reveals their own goals.

We express condolences to all Armenians, Azerbaijanis, Russians and people of other nationalities, who lost dear ones or suffered themselves during those tragic days. The Party and the Soviet government will do everything possible to alleviate the plight of the refugees and help them return to normal life.

Soldiers and officers of the Soviet army and Interior Ministry troops displayed a lofty sense of responsibility before the people, courage and restraint, and thus averted the escalation of bloodshed, saved thousands of lives and created conditions for defusing the situation in the region.

It is now up to the peoples of the two republics and their Party and state leaders. Their actions will determine how soon normal life will be restored and the state of emergency lifted. Surely, everything must be done to resolve as soon as possible the

problems of Nagorno-Karabakh — urgent, primary ones — and
those problems that have emerged around it — given strict
observance of constitutional principles, including Azerbaijan's
integrity.

Comrades, the logic of the struggle for *perestroika* has led to new
major decisions. The USSR Supreme Soviet will soon adopt
laws on ownership, on land, on local self-government and local
economy, on the tax system, on the delineation of the competence of the union as a whole and of the constituent republics,
and other fundamental legislative acts.

The second stage of political reform has been launched,
encompassing the formation of governing bodies at republican
and local levels. Real outlines of a new Soviet federation begin to
emerge. As a matter of fact, new forms of our entire political,
economic and public life are taking shape, together with a new
system of bodies of power, characterised by profound democratisation and the development of self-governing principles.

Indeed, society is acquiring a new quality. But the processes
that the Party consciously activated, which will undoubtedly
bring forth positive results, have not been insured, as we already
see, against manifestations of instability, weakened management
and centrifugal tendencies. The effect is making itself felt on
society, causing misunderstanding of these phenomena and anxiety by the people.

At present, from the viewpoint of strategic tasks and in view of
current realities, it is necessary to realign forces in the upper
echelons of power in order to give more dynamism to *perestroika*
processes and ensure their irreversibility more firmly. At the
same time it is necessary to restrain destructive trends and erect
obstacles in the way of everything that complicates and hinders
the renewal of society.

At issue are processes in the economy and in inter-ethnic
relations affecting people's security, order and discipline. It
should be added that this question is already widely debated.
People welcome what has been done to enhance the role of

legislative bodies and divide the functions of party and state bodies. At the same time, they express clear dissatisfaction with the lack of decisive actions where they are needed.

The question has been raised to form an institute of presidency with all necessary powers to implement the policy of *perestroika*. The draft platform naturally speaks about this concisely, stressing the need to act without delay. I think this idea deserves discussion by this plenum. We do not have the right to allow the development of *perestroika* and the implementation of the plans associated with it to be put in peril.

I will not dwell now on other issues of political and legal reform, which are laid down, in a concentrated but full way, in the draft platform. They were formulated in line with the decisions of the nineteenth Party Conference and, certainly, take account of the experience gained by our society over the time that has passed since then.

Democratisation and creating a law-based state and a self-governing socialist society remain the principal directions of our development.

Comrades, naturally the draft platform speaks about the international aspect of *perestroika*, about the modern world outlook that defines our foreign policy strategy. The Soviet Union's foreign policy based on new thinking was given a strong impetus at the twenty-seventh Party Congress. It became increasingly broad and concrete as the nature of contacts with the outside world changed and was translated into life. Its fundamental principles were set out at the United Nations late in 1988. The new foreign policy is legislatively sealed on behalf of the whole people in the documents of the Congress of People's Deputies and the Supreme Soviet.

The draft platform formulates the tasks in all directions of international activity at present and in future. As the twenty-eighth congress is approaching, we reaffirm our innovative and truly restructuring foreign policy. It drew wide response and gained recognition all over the world, and it has already brought about a considerable improvement in the international climate. This policy meets our internal requirements, strengthens the international positions of the soviet State, raises its prestige, favours forming civilised relations all over the world, and brings humanity closer to a peaceful period in its development.

The all-important thing for us now is to push forward the negotiating disarmament process, deepen dialogue and mutual understanding on crucial sections of international development, and facilitate in every way efforts to expand and strengthen the ground covered in building a common European home. It is important to upgrade within its framework allied relations with Eastern European countries, which really need this. This approach meets with understanding and response on the part of their new leaders.

The draft platform also formulates the CPSU's principled approaches to issues of security and defence, and points to the need to work toward a military reform. I want to dwell now on one or two aspects of this issue.

We intend to pursue the line of disarmament in future, mindful of the current situation and within the framework of negotiations. In realistically evaluating the international situation, we take into account both the positive elements of its development and the existing dangers. The situation in the world did improve in recent years, but the danger of war is still preserved. The doctrines and concepts of the United States and NATO, which are far from being defensive, remain in force. Their armies and military budgets also exist.

This is why we need well-trained and well-equipped armed forces. Certainly, they need improvement and restructuring. But there should be a more responsible approach to changing the principle of their staffing and their construction as a whole in the context of changes in the world situation.

Some questions have arisen in view of the ongoing and possible reductions in troops and armaments. Specifically, apprehensions are expressed about whether this does not weaken the country's defence capability. Evidently additional explanations are necessary, to show that the reduction and reorganisation of the armed forces is being carried out strictly in conformity with the principle of reasonable sufficiency for defence, reliable defence.

Some social problems have arisen, especially those of housing provision to servicemen and persons who retired or were transferred to the reserve, and their employment. The defence ministry alone cannot cope with them. The government passed several decisions that took the heat out of the issue, but evidently much still has to be done to rid officers and their families of the feeling, which has emerged lately, that they lack social protection. These decisions should be implemented. It is also necessary to draft and endorse a special programme of social security for servicemen and members of their families and for officers and warrant officers in reserve service.

One more serious issue: it concerns mass media coverage of life in the army and the navy. It should be truthful and respectful to the Soviet army, to officers' and soldiers' military service. We cannot agree with anti-army propaganda. Our people will not allow this. The functioning of our army should be the subject of democratic discussion in society.

Comrades, at the beginning of my speech I set out the reasoning regarding recomprehension of the Party's role in society at the present stage of its development, in conditions of *perestroika*, the division of functions between Party, state and economic bodies. Evidently, there was the need to record the Central Committee's stance on this all-important issue.

But, in principled terms, we cannot bypass in the platform those aspects of the Party's renewal that are related to its internal restructuring. Without this it cannot realise its potential to be the vanguard political force in present-day conditions. The draft contains several proposals on this score. Certainly, all that concerns the Party's inner life should be presented in detail in the rules. But since at issue is the new role of the CPSU, we included basic provisions also in the platform.

Comrades, I want to say one more time that the pivotal idea of restructuring the Party itself is in asserting the power of Party masses. In this connection, we are to recomprehend, among others, the role of primary organisations in what concerns admission to the Party and quitting it, using membership dues, and implementing the tasks related to the new role of the Party as the political vanguard.

The role of district and city organisations should be revised and their rights should be considerably broadened. We should change the system of forming Party bodies at all levels. We need a new, effective election mechanism, which should also be sealed in the rules. We agreed that proposals on this issue, after their discussion in the commission for Party issues, will be submitted to members of the Central Committee, participants in the plenum. The future rules should definitely say that all elective bodies, from top to bottom, must be under control of and accountable to Communists and that the apparatus must be under the control of and accountable to elective bodies.

We have long been concerned by the fact that the inner life of the Party and its functioning do not give Party members the opportunity to participate regularly in the formation of its policy. Much has been said about it, but still we have no mechanism to translate this idea into reality. This is one of the problems that has to be discussed before the Congress during the work on the new rules.

So far I would say that the influence of Communists on the work of upper bodies, including the Central Committee, in a decisive measure will depend on their ability to send their representatives, those whom they trust, real leaders and active supporters of *perestroika*. We should call for the vigorous representation of the most active advanced workers and farmers, who are well known in the Party, in all elective bodies of the Party, including the Central Committee.

Glasnost in the work of the Party's leadership, including the Central Committee and bodies elected by it, should be ensured on a larger scale than before. Then Communists will know everything and will be able to make conscientious judgements, conclusions and proposals. We are also increasing Communists' real participation in the formation of the policy by giving Party bodies the possibility to develop their own platforms on various problems of social development in the context of one or another region. Communists should be given the opportunity actually to participate in the drafting of these documents, in their discussion and adoption.

Of course, these are not all problems of Party democracy. I have set forth some considerations and would like them to be thoroughly discussed before the Congress.

The draft platform includes a proposal on changing the structure of the upper Party bodies. The meaning of this proposal is not just to rename them and thus show our readiness for renewal. They are intended to strengthen the factor of democratism in the Party leadership and simultaneously to create the best conditions for its activity as a working collective.

One may ask, why reduce the Central Committee? Let us discuss it. We proceeded from the need to turn the Central Committee into a body working on a permanent basis.

We should also depart from the principle of electing to the Central Committee mainly people holding certain posts. This principle was actually an expression of the Party-and-state system of power in the country.

We think these changes will help strengthen the Central Committee's ties with Party organisations, because these ties will be maintained not through the apparatus but mainly through elected members of the Central Committee. In addition, almost all of them will take part in the work of a Central Committee commission, actually becoming politicians of the Party-wide rank.

It would be appropriate to speak here also about the central Party apparatus. It is clear that the change of the Party's role should entail changes in the qualitative composition of the apparatus. It should become an assistant of the Central Committee and work strictly under its control. The experience of the Central Committee's work in the past few years has revealed the need to give the Central Committee co-optation rights which, naturally, should be limited by the rules. There is also a proposal to abandon the practice of electing candidate members of the Central Committee.

I will not speak about other issues raised in the draft platform. The Politburo hopes that by joint efforts we will work out a document that will give answers to all questions vital to Communists and all Soviet people and that *perestroika* in the country will thus receive a new, powerful, positive impetus.

Translated by Tass

"*During the decades of distortion and stagnation, such a critical mass of explosive material has accumulated that further delay could have resulted in a shock of enormous strength . . . Today we can see this clearly in the examples of the countries of Eastern Europe.*"

— *Vadim A. Medvedev, Ideology Secretary,*
USSR Communist Party, February 7, 1990

PART **IX**

Commentary

William M. Brinton

The Role of Media in a Telerevolution

Here Mr. Brinton presents a McLuhanesque analysis of how television and other media played a crucial role in the revolution of Central Europe in 1989.

I

Televised images of violence and change played a central, political role in what has been described as a revolution from below, stirring the deepest impulses of freedom of the spirit after forty years of force and lies under Communism. One Soviet citizen in Moscow, having viewed the televised scenes of violence and change in Prague and Bucharest, said: "I watched that with the greatest compassion. It is inevitable that all people claim their right to a decent life, freedom" (reported in the *New York Times*).

Television reached out and touched a Central European audience of millions. Mesmerized crowds of workers, shoppers, and commuters in Prague saw televised in storefront windows the violence of Czech army units beating demonstrators marching peacefully on November 17, 1989. Films of this bloody confrontation were obtained by students and hastily made into videotapes. Copies were sent all over Czechoslovakia, and an estimated 600,000 people saw televised violence within hours of the time it occurred.

The visual image of Romanian dictator Nicolae Ceauşescu lying dead after his trial was seen in Romania, Austria, and both

Germanys. In Czechoslovakia, viewers in mid-November saw live coverage of some 500,000 demonstrators on Letna Plain demanding democracy and saw Václav Havel addressing huge crowds in Wenceslas Square.

In East Germany, some 85 percent of the population saw the images of change from West German television's live coverage of police violence in Leipzig and Dresden. Even Yugoslavian television could be seen in part of Romania, and Hungarian television picked up live coverage of demonstrations elsewhere and sent visual images into Transylvania for the benefit of the two million Hungarians forced to live in Romania by the Treaty of Trianon in 1920. It was Yugoslavian television that reported the slaughter of thousands there by the Romanian army after December 15, 1989, and the beginning of violence at Timisoara. Inaccurate as this summary may be, the medium was still the message.

On January 1, 1990, Václav Havel, newly elected president of Czechoslovakia, told the nation on television that for forty years they had heard lies from the Communists. In fact, the revolution from below that had elected him president a week earlier was based to a significant degree on the use of the new political medium, television.

The visual images of violence and change in Central Europe were dramatically different in their impact on people there from anything experienced in the past history of man. With the single exception of violence at Tiananmen Square in Beijing, even governments have decided, metaphorically speaking, that it is useless to "shoot the television film crew. Its message has already been seen 10,000 miles away." The Voice of America and Radio Free Europe will still broadcast its message of freedom.

To a lesser but still significant extent in the success of this revolution from below was the use of the printed word in books written by Central European authors published as part of a literary tradition that seems to exist only in Europe. This tradition began with the moral obligation to dissent where human rights suffered from oppression and where people were humiliated and exploited. Indeed, writers such as Andrei Sakharov, a Nobel Laureate in 1975, Václav Havel, Josef Škvorecký, Reiner

Kunze, Christa Wolf, Christoph Hein, Czeslaw Milosz, a Nobel Laureate in 1980, Thomas Oleszczuk, Miklos Haraszti, Tamas Aczel, George Konrad, and Norman Manea helped create the conditions that led to revolutionary change. Reiner Kunze, an East German, wrote *Die wunderbaren Jahre* in 1976, published in English as *The Wonderful Years* in 1977, and Miklos Haraszti, a Hungarian, wrote *The Velvet Prison: Artists under State Socialism,* in 1989. Czeslaw Milosz wrote *The Captive Mind* in 1981, the year martial law was declared in Poland by the Communist government. In 1984, an East German writer, Christa Wolf wrote *Patterns of Childhood,* and Christoph Hein, also an East German, wrote *The Distant Lover,* in 1989, a novel that mirrors the self-imposed alienation of East Germans.

Václav Havel, in prison under Communism from 1979 to 1984, wrote *Letters to Olga,* his wife. Then, in 1984 he wrote *The Power of the Powerless: Citizens against the State in Central Eastern Europe.* He was arrested again for this use of a much older medium, but the medium was still the message. In 1960, Tamas Aczel wrote *The Revolt of the Mind,* soon after the Soviet Union's invasion of Hungary in 1956. In 1969, Norman Manea, then living in Romania, wrote *Noaptea pe Latura Lungă,* a child's view of the concentration camp and life in postwar Romania. Manea himself, born in 1936, spent four years in a concentration camp in the Ukraine from 1941 to 1945. In the early years of liberalization in Romania, he also wrote articles in *Povestea Vorbii,* an avant-garde magazine that was suppressed after six issues. Josef Škvorecký wrote *The Engineer of Human Souls* in 1984, and Thomas Oleszczuk, himself Polish, wrote *Political Justice in the USSR: Dissent and Repression in Lithuania, 1967 to 1987.* These and other writers may fairly be said to have helped lay the foundations of revolutions by other means, namely, without violence. Their books had been read and discussed by hundreds of thousands of people over the years, and television reached out and touched many more throughout all of Europe, many of them familiar with these writers.

II

In 1964, Marshall McLuhan wrote his seminal book about communications, *Understanding Media*. Many remember his aphorism, "the medium is the message." By this he meant that the way we acquire information affects us more than the information itself. McLuhan also believed that television shaped the reactions of people in ways they hardly suspected. "There is," McLuhan wrote, "a basic principle that distinguishes a hot medium like radio [or books or newspapers] from a cool one like the telephone, or a hot medium like film from a cool one like television. A hot medium is one that extends one single sense [hearing in combination with the mind's reaction to what is heard, e.g., data] in 'high definition.' High definition is the state of being well filled with data." Television, he said, was a cool medium that was "high in participation and completion" by the viewer, e.g., individual decisions to join and support others in demonstrations for democracy. "Hot media are, therefore, low in participation, and cool media are high in participation." The telephone is cool "or one of low definition, because the ear is given a meager amount of information."

Contemporary scholars analyzing McLuhan begin with the Homeric odes of some 2,500 years ago. Of these the best known are *The Iliad* and *The Odyssey*. These poems had to be recited with a cue, so that when one man left off, another began. This custom continued until the time of the pseudo-Platonic dialogue *Hipparchus,* about 600 years after Homer. During this period, the Homeric odes created a *rhythm of thought and culture,* and Greek culture breathed, i.e., acted according to its rhythms. At each recitation, and they are thought to have been performed throughout Greece, crowds gathered to hear what had been memorized by the actors and performed before audiences. Those who participated as the audience heard expressions of the "collective mind," the complex of elements in an individual that feels, perceives, thinks, and reasons. What they heard was absorbed, remembered, and acted upon. Hubris—overweening pride or arrogance—became part of the cultural lexicon, as did catharsis — purification of emotions, such as pity or fear, by action. Aristotle and Sophocles developed these rhythms both philosophically and as drama.

Drama was what people saw during the revolutions in Central Europe in 1989. Within an environment of nonviolent change as shown on television, what viewers saw in their living rooms was a *rhythm of thought* played out by the actors on camera. The actual spectators acted on cue from the actors in the drama. A chant was their response.

Descriptions of the demonstrations in Czechoslovakia shown on television make a remarkable point. Huge crowds in Wenceslas Square responded on cue from the players in the drama, just as they must have done at a recitation of *The Iliad* in Homer's time some 2,500 years ago. A *rhythm of thought* moved a huge audience to participate by responding only to speech in 1989. Václav Klaus, an economist, addressed a huge crowd. With respect to the demands submitted to the government by Civic Forum, he said: "If he [Prime Minister Ladislav Ademec] doesn't respond adequately, they [Civic Forum] will call for the resignation of the government." As if on cue, the crowd chanted, "Resignation, resignation." When Klaus said that if the prime minister was unwilling "to ensure free elections" and paused, with one voice, the crowd cried "Free elections, free elections." Several days later, the crowd gathered again in Wenceslas Square on a bitterly cold day. A proposal to recall some of the Communists who had compromised themselves in the Federal Assembly was read from the same balcony. As each name was read aloud, the huge crowd repeated the names in a sort of rhythm, "Jakěs, Jakěs," or "Bilak, Bilak" with boos and jeers. The crowd had been cued by speech, just as they were by actors in a play by Homer. It was all eerily similar to what an audience somewhere in Greece must have done 2,500 years earlier in responding to speech on cue, or even one actor responding on cue from another to continue the drama later developed by Sophocles.

Television is of comparatively recent origin, while widespread use of radio dates from the early 1930s. Until the late 1940s, it was the only electronic communications media available to a mass audience worldwide. Radio, McLuhan observed, was quite different in its impact from television. "Although the medium is the message, the controls [limitations imposed on the new media, radio, by newspaper and advertising interests, when the British Broadcasting Company was first incorporated] go beyond programming. The restraints are always directed to the 'content,' which is always another medium." Clearly, content limitations lead to censorship, or even worse self-censorship, and both radio and television tend to rely more on entertainment as a strategy of neutrality, thereby avoiding controversy. This strategy ensures maximum pervasiveness for any medium whatever, even the book or textbook. The pervasive nature of state-controlled radio, or access to it, exists today in altogether too many countries.

In the 1930s, radio was the only electronic medium available. "That Hitler came into political existence at all," McLuhan wrote, "was directly owing to radio and public address systems." In this respect, at least, television is different from radio. Television combined with radio now allows perceptions to occur at two different levels. They can be sensed as data — radio or the press, both hot — and either reinforced or defused by television, a cool medium that invites viewers to participate in the thought processes of the message seen as a visual image and heard.

Lithuanians, for example, knew two highly significant facts, one from the televised image of Mikhail Gorbachev's impassioned address to the Central Committee in Moscow on December 25, 1989. There, he said: "Isn't it clear that if we cross this line [independence for Lithuania], we will be deliberately heading toward the disintegration of the Soviet Union?" Gorbachev was talking to his domestic opponents, but for the benefit of Lithuanian viewers who became more aware of the depth of opposition to Gorbachev and what he had to do to create a climate of understanding in Lithuania. The other significant fact occurred some five months earlier, and it was reported only by Radio Moscow, *Pravda,* and *Izvestia.* At that time, Gorbachev was reported as summarily dismissing the views of his two principal hard-line opponents, Nicolai Ryzhkov and Yegor Ligachev. Gorbachev was reported as saying: "Surely, it is not necessary to panic when revolutionary processes become a reality. It was *we* who produced them with *our* policy. Didn't *we* understand this when *we* discussed all this?" This seems a brilliant way of inviting his private audience to share the public consequences of "revolutionary processes."

Lithuanian viewers who saw the televised image of his December 25 address almost instantaneously participated in Gorbachev's thought processes by combining data obtained earlier with the visual image of *agreement* with his opposition. They sensed intuitively that Gorbachev had addressed local, political concerns, not his Lithuanian audience. It had, after all, made a dramatic gamble by declaring its independence from Moscow. Some nine days after his televised address, their intuition was reinforced. A delegation of the Lithuanian Communist Party visiting Gorbachev in Moscow was told there would be "unprecedented changes in the democratization of the Party." He was right.

On February 7, Article 6 of the Soviet Constitution was repudiated at a meeting of the Central Committee of the Communist Party. Article 6 read:

> The leading and guiding force of Soviet society and the nucleus of its political system, of all state organizations and public organizations, is the Communist Party of the Soviet Union. The Communist Party of the Soviet Union exists for the people and serves the people.
>
> The Communist Party, armed with Marxism Leninism, determines the general perspectives of the development of society and the course of the domestic and foreign policy of the Union of Soviet Socialist Republics, directs the great constructive work of the Soviet people, and imparts a planned, systematic and theoretically substantiated character to their struggle for the victory of Communism.

> All Party organizations shall function within the
> framework of the Constitution of the Union of
> Soviet Socialist Republics.

In mid-February 1990, the Communist Party Central Committee *restored* the concept of private property, a concept that had
never really existed after 1917. Because so many Russians still
cultivated the land, the adoption of this new concept had to be
seen as approved by familiar authority. Television throughout the
Soviet Union carried the message of *private property.* There can be
little doubt that Mikhail Gorbachev has learned how to control
both hot and cool media.

Parallel developments have been occurring almost too rapidly.
Secessionist movements are now underway in Latvia and Estonia.
In Azerbaijan, Moldavia, the Ukraine, and Georgia, there will
have been free elections for what amounts to the local legislative
body of a state. Gorbachev knows that he may be presiding over
the liquidation of the Soviet empire. A combination of radio and
television has produced a Frankenstein for a once-monolithic
Communism with its revelations of truth from the palace of lies
in Moscow.

Although Marshall McLuhan might disagree, this combination of radio, newspapers, and television may be considered as a
mixed medium, inviting participation within a revolutionary
environment by listeners, readers, and viewers, particularly those
in Central Europe and the Baltic states.

Use of state-controlled television (and radio) for political ends
has a long history. That "Great Communicator," Ronald Reagan,
with his soothing, almost laxative themes, used television to
great effect in explaining away any problems during his eight
years in office. Earlier, Franklin D. Roosevelt had used radio to
equally great effect in his fireside talks. Earlier still, the press had
had a field day with silent Calvin Coolidge. According to Marshall McLuhan, "the hot press medium found Cal very cool and
rejoiced in his lack of image, since it compelled the participation
of the press in filling in an image of him for the public." Were
Theodore Roosevelt alive today, however, he would certainly use

television as his "bully pulpit," just as the late Ayatollah Kho-meini did in Iran for his sermons to the Shiites. Nicolae Ceauşescu used television only days before his departure for Iran to extol the virtues of "scientific socialism." He also used it for an orchestrated rally of the people after his return to Bucharest. His audience, however, had seen the televised violence there and jeered him while his speech was being carried live. Ceauşescu was then seen as being vulnerable, and four days later he was dead.

During the days of Brezhnev, state-controlled television in the Soviet Union became a palace of lies, much of it admitted during 1989, such as the invasion of Hungary in 1956 — it was all a mistake — and the suppression of dissent during the Prague Spring of 1968. Dissent was punished by jail, exile, the Gulag Archipelago or commitment to a state psychiatric institution. In satellite states, dissent was punished in very much the same way.

In the new era of *glasnost*, state-controlled television showed tens of thousands of mourners filing by the bier of that great human rights activist, Andrei Sakharov, in Moscow. Were his ten years of exile in Gorky for this Nobel Laureate in 1975 all based on state-controlled lies? In the United States and elsewhere in Europe, people saw the visual image of mourning for Sakharov. Within this context of death, there seems to be no opportunity for participation, but in the highly developed situation of revolu-tion, one can expect to see the full variety of human expression and exploration by its individual participants, all as visual images from a remote location.

Television viewers, many of them conditioned by the televised violence of the war in Vietnam, shared the same feelings as the students, intellectuals, trade unionists, and just ordinary people of Leipzig, Dresden, and Prague. Their level of emotional involvement, increased so instantaneously by television, moved them to share the feelings of those victims of violence and, even more significantly to participate in revolutionary change them-selves. Revolution from below was another, new rhythm, and television was the flickering fire around which crowds gathered to see the collective consciousness.

Perhaps never before has this cool medium been used with greater emotional impact than in Bucharest. The gruesome televised bodies of Nicolae Ceauşescu and his wife, Elena, were very high definition. They were dead, executed after a military trial. The visual image of death was enough, even though its repetitive use had a political purpose. The Romanian Council of National Salvation needed repetition to induce the hated Securitate, Ceauşescu's paramilitary secret police, to turn themselves in. State-controlled Romanian television, converted to Free Romanian Television on December 21, was on the air almost continuously from the time demonstrations began in Timisoara on December 15, 1989. The Securitate stormed the building in Bucharest to silence television, but failed. The visual images were supplementd by the shooting during one or more fire fights just outside the building itself. One exhausted worker in the Free Romanian Television studio put it succinctly: "We knew we had to stay on the air. If television falls, the revolution falls. That's for certain."

Television knows no international borders. Visual images of revolution with high definition reached most of Europe and the United States. Viewers saw the formation and defense of revolutions, stirring the long-held impulse of human beings everywhere for freedom from tyranny and lies. It was not by accident that the police in both East Germany and Czechoslovakia were ordered to halt the use of violence. Those who issued this order knew or sensed the impact on them of more violence to suppress dissent. The pace of change, already astonishing, might have accelerated. In Poland, change took almost eight years because of the imposition of martial law in 1981, thereby controlling the use of radio and television. In Hungary, Czechoslovakia, East Germany, and Romania, change took only months or even weeks. With Mikhail Gorbachev's visit to Lithuania, democratic change may take less than a week.

What might happen next can only be speculation. However, the palace of lies, state-controlled television within the Soviet Union and the Warsaw Pact countries, may lose some of its political effect. The truth will replace lies. The business of organizing opposition parties, selecting candidates to run for office in free elections, and rebuilding staggering economies is hardly the emotional grist for the mills of television. These Communist monopolies have publicly apologized for the invasion of Hungary in 1956 and suppressing the Prague Spring of 1968, admitting they were incorrect from a Communist Party perspective, as was Afghanistan. Were they justified at the time, or was the justification formulated within the walls of the palace of lies? Television historians may address this question soon, but one thing seems certain. The revolutions we have seen are truly telerevolutions, not only visual images of extraordinarily high definition, but also high in terms of the collective consciousness.

III

The phrase *palace of lies* is used by design. Gustav Husak lived in Hradcany Castle in Prague, Janos Kadar lived in a palace in Budapest, and Nicolae Ceauşescu lived in a number of palaces in Bucharest, most of them connected by secret tunnels. Erich Honecker lived in a securely guarded palace-like compound, Wandlitz, in East Berlin. All of these four Party leaders are either deposed or dead, and one of them, Honecker, will go on trial for the corruption disclosed by a combination of the press, radio, and television. He diverted Party funds and appropriated them for his own use to live like a king. Such corruption on a massive scale was a cynical betrayal of those oppressed by the Communist Party in the guise of egalitarianism. Václav Havel knows the nature of symbolism well. He will continue to live in his modest apartment in Prague, not Hradcany Castle, the palace of lies used by his Communist predecessors.

In the Soviet Union's pre-Gorbachev era, the Kremlin was not the only palace of lies. In Leningrad, Yuri Solovyov was expelled from the Communist Party for using his influence to buy a Mercedes Benz at a deep discount. In the Ukrainian city of Chernigov, the local Party leadership was ousted after disclosure that a car on its way to a New Year's Eve celebration carried a load of scarce, expensive food. In the Siberian city of Tyumen, Gennadi Bogomyakov and his entire Communist Party entourage resigned after another Party official wrote a letter saying that Bogomyakov had ruled like a "feudal lord" and blocked *perestroika* at every opportunity. The local newspaper reported this, and all these incidents were also covered on state-controlled television. As time passes, there will be other instances of Communist Party corruption similar to those found at Wandlitz near Berlin and also shown on television. Mikhail Gorbachev seems a past master at the use of television to expose the kind of scandal that may lead to democratic reforms.

The establishment of democracy in Central Europe, even within the Soviet Union itself, is a process that may take time. However, there can be little doubt that television will accelerate the pace of change.

IV

In the United States, the Constitution was not ratified by Congress until 1779, years after General Cornwallis surrendered to General Washington at Yorktown. Its first ten amendments, our Bill of Rights, were not ratified by Congress until 1791. The Bill of Rights guaranteed freedom of speech, the press, and religion, as well as freedom from unreasonable search and seizure by representatives of the government, freedom from "cruel and unusual punishment," and trial by jury. The original thirteen colonies, then states, did not have any of the structural problems that newly free Central European states must face after forty years of Communism. Free elections are only the beginning of a long process, and democracy needs to be extended into every area of society, the economic as well as the political.

One thing seems certain. Television seems destined to continue as the medium of choice by all concerned. We all live in the postindustrial Information Age, and television, together with many other ways of acquiring information electronically, seems certain to stimulate more movement toward democratic institutions, such as free elections within a multiparty enviroment.

William M. Brinton

The Helsinki Final Act and Other International Covenants Supporting Freedom and Human Rights

In this final essay, Mr. Brinton discusses the importance of the Helsinki Final Act of 1975 and other legal covenants in the future integration of Western, Central, and Eastern Europe.

The struggle to obtain human rights and freedoms in Lithuania, Poland, East Germany, Czechoslovakia, Hungary, and Romania has been expressed in one treaty and four covenants over the past forty-two years. They include chapter I, article 2, of the United Nations Charter ratified by the United States in 1948, the International Covenant on Civil and Political Rights (1966), the International Covenant on Economic, Social, and Cultural Rights (1966), and the Universal Declaration of Human Rights (1948). These were all signed — or supported — by the United States, but never ratified by the Senate of the United States. They originated, however, in the General Assembly of the United Nations.

Article 8 of the Universal Declaration of Human Rights is broader than the Eighth Amendment to the United States Constitution: "Excessive bail shall not be required, nor excessive fines imposed, nor *cruel and unusual punishment inflicted.*" Article 8 states: "No one shall be subjected to torture, or to cruel, inhuman or degrading treatment or punishment." In *Trop v. Dulles,* 78 S. Ct. 590 (1958), Chief Justice Warren noted that "the exact scope of the constitutional phrase *'cruel and unusual'* has not been detailed by this court. But the basic policy reflected in these [italicized] words is firmly established in the Anglo-American tradition of criminal justice. The phrase in our Constitution was taken directly from the English Declaration of Rights of 1688, and the principle it represents can be traced back to the Magna Carta [of 1215]."

In a case decided thirty years later, *Thompson v. Oklahoma*, 108 S. Ct. 2687 (1988), the Supreme Court said in a footnote: "We have previously recognized the relevance of the views of the international community in determining whether a punishment is *cruel and unusual*, citing *Trop v. Dulles*. The court specifically mentioned Article 6 (5) of the International Covenant on Civil and Political Rights. There can be little doubt that some European and African legislative enactments have been construed in a manner consistent with precedents set by the United States Supreme Court.

Unfortunately, the United States Senate, although requested to give its advice and consent to several of these international covenants, has not done so. In messages sent to the Senate by Presidents Johnson and Reagan, they asked for a declaration that these covenants would not be self-executing. Thus Congress would have to enact laws incorporating their substantive provisions. Procrastination is the thief of time. The United States, after forty years, recently ratified the Genocide Convention in 1988.

In Europe, work proceeded expeditiously on what is now known as the European Convention on Human Rights. In 1949, the Council of Europe drafted this convention. It was perhaps less extensive in the rights it guaranteed than it might have been, but much stronger in enforcing those rights. Article 10 (1), for example, provides that "Everyone has the right to freedom of expression. This right shall include freedom to hold opinions and to receive and impart information and ideas without interference by public authority and regardless of frontiers." The European Convention on Human Rights also established the European Court of Human Rights in Strasbourg, France.

Presented as a draft in 1949, the European Convention on Human Rights became effective in November 1953. It has been ratified by all twenty-one members of the Council of Europe. Except for Malta and Cyprus, all of them have accepted the right of individuals within their jurisdictions to bring complaints against them to the European Court of Human Rights in Strasbourg as applicants, or to petition for the redress of grievances.

From its inception, this court has heard and determined cases involving challenges to the actions of executive public officials, national legislatures, and various supreme courts of member states. In *Sunday Times v. United Kingdom,* for example, it found an opinion of the House of Lords — a contempt order against the newspaper — inconsistent with the provisions of Article 10; *Case of Silver and Others* invalidated censorship of convicts' letters by a prison official; in *Lingens v. Austria*, a criminal libel action was set aside on appeal to the Vienna Court of Appeals. In perhaps one of the most prominent cases involving racial discrimination, *The East African Asians Case,* this matter was resolved at the Commission level. At the urging of Prime Minister Harold Wilson, Parliament enacted the Commonwealth Immigrants Act of 1969. This law was blatantly discriminatory on its face and literally made stateless persons out of U.K. nationals living in Kenya, Tanzania, and Uganda. They could not return to England without fear of imprisonment, and they were fearful of remaining where they were with Great Britain's threat to revoke their passports.

The applicants challenged this law on the basis that it was in violation of Article 3 of the European Convention on Human Rights. Article 3 stated in part: "No one shall be subjected to torture or to inhuman or degrading treatment or punishment." The European Commission decided that "a special importance should be attached to discrimination based on race [as constituting] a special form of affront to human dignity . . . [and] therefore . . . capable of constituting degrading treatment." For various reasons, the challenge in this case, which the Wilson government accepted rather than appeal to the European Court of Human Rights, was not made under the provisions of Article 13. It provides that "The enjoyment of the rights and freedoms set forth in this Convention shall be secured without discrimination on any ground such as sex, race, color, language, religion, political or other opinion, national or social origin, association with a national minority, property, birth or other status."

Ironically, minorities in the United States may now have to live with more, not less, discrimination after some recent decisions by the conservative majority of the Rehnquist Court. Moreover, Europeans, particularly those living in newly free Poland, Czechoslovakia, and Hungary, may enjoy more political, civil, and other rights than Americans even with the rights guaranteed by the First through Tenth Amendments to the Constitution. If, as most people expect, Poland, Czechoslovakia, and Hungary become members of the European Economic Community (EEC) before December 31, 1992, they will have to adhere to the European Convention on Human Rights. It seems long past due for the Senate give its advice and consent to the International Covenant on Civil and Political Rights as well as the International Covenant on Economic, Social, and Cultural Rights.

Taken as a whole, these international covenants guarantee freedom of speech, the press, and religion, as well as the freedom of association and the right to petition for the redress of grievances. On January 7, 1977, Václav Havel and numerous other Czechoslovakian writers signed the Charter 77 Declaration. It was a call for civil and human rights to be respected in Czechoslovakia. It specifically referred to the International Covenant on Civil and Political Rights and the International Covenant on Economic, Social, and Cultural Rights, noting that "Their publication . . . [in the Czechoslovak Register of Laws No. 120 of 13 October 1976] serves as a powerful reminder of the extent to which basic human rights in our country exist, regrettably, on paper alone."

Last, but certainly not least, the Charter 77 Declaration referred specifically to the Helsinki Final Act of 1975. The Conference on Security and Co-operation in Europe opened at Helsinki in 1973, continued at Geneva, and was concluded at Helsinki on August 1, 1975. Thirty-five countries, including the United States and the Soviet Union, signed the Helsinki Final Act. Other countries signing included the Finland, the United Kingdom, France, the Federal Republic of Germany, the German Democratic Republic, Poland, Czechoslovakia, Hungary, Bulgaria, Romania, Turkey, Malta, Yugoslavia, Switzerland, Italy, Spain, Portugal, the Netherlands, Denmark, Sweden, and Norway. The Final Act has no legally binding effect, but it did provide for follow-up meetings. These meetings are referred to as the CSCE Review Process or the Helsinki Review Process.

The first of the Review Processes occurred in Belgrade, Yugoslavia and ended on March 8, 1977, with a Concluding Statement adopted by consensus. By agreement among those present in Belgrade, the next follow-up meeting was held in Madrid and ended on September 9, 1983. Secretary of State, George Schultz, inter alia, adressed the meeting. In part, he stated: "The Helsinki process was launched with great hopes ten years ago. It was born at what seemed to be an encouraging moment in East-West relations: the United States and the Soviet Union had just reached the first agreements on strategic arms limitations. Broad vistas of economic cooperation appeared open. Progress seemed possible on human rights . . . The Helsinki Final Act is an eloquent statement of aspirations to which the United States gladly subscribed, because we subscribe to every one of its principles. It affirms the most fundamental human rights: liberty of thought, conscience, and faith; the exercise of civil and political rights; the rights of minorities. It calls for a freer flow of information, ideas and people; greater scope for the press, cultural and educational exchange. . . . And it reaffirms the basic principles of relations between states: nonintervention, sovereign equality, self-determination, territorial integrity, and the inviolability of frontiers other than through peaceful means."

Parties to the convention included Poland — it imposed martial law six years later; East Germany — it was not until 1989 that its Communist Party was ousted; Czechoslovakia — it was not until

1990 that free elections were held there for the first time since 1948; Hungary—no free elections until March 25, 1990; and Romania—no elections of any kind, only the iron rule of Nicolae Ceauşescu for twenty-eight years. It was the lip service paid to these solemn covenants that finally led to the revolution from below in all of them signing the Helsinki Final Act.

When the dust settles in these once-Communist-ruled countries, the governments formed may have to prepare for the next meeting of the thirty-five countries signing the Helsinki Final Act. It is scheduled to take place in Helsinki, beginning in March 1992, nine months before the European Economic Community becomes a single market of some 340 million people. In one of his speeches, Mikhail Gorbachev mentioned a "Helsinki 2." This comment has caused some speculation that the next Helsinki Review may occur in 1990, instead of 1992. With the reunification of the two Germanys quite likely to occur before the end of this year—1990—the next meeting may take place quite soon. It is not just Gorbachev who seems concerned about a neutral Germany with NATO playing a political, not military, role in a reunified Germany. Others, who remember World Wars I and II, have expressed some misgivings.

The Helsinki Final Act addresses issues of collective security, human rights, civil and political rights, as well as economic and cultural rights and the protection of the environment. There is speculation that Gorbachev may suggest that the meeting be held in 1991, instead of 1992. With elections in the Federal Republic of Germany in December 1990, Gorbachev may have to consider his options if peaceful reunification of the two Germanys were to occur in 1991. A ranking Social Democratic member of the Bundestag's Foreign Affairs Committee, Karsten Voigt, has already addressed this issue in his speech in Washington. Then early this year, Social Democrat Oskar LaFontaine, from the Saar, emerged as Christian Democrat Helmut Kohl's leading opponent for chancellor of the Federal Republic of Germany in the December 1990 elections. He has a popular program. LaFontaine wants to keep the East Germans at home by reducing benefits they receive as refugees from East Germany. West Germans resent being taxed to pay these benefits as well as to pay the construction cost of new affordable housing for refugees. The West German elections should attract worldwide media attention. There can be no doubt at all that the media — print, radio, and television — around the world will report the proceedings in Helsinki.

In the Central Europe of 1990 and beyond, the Helsinki Final Act of 1975, signed by thirty-five states, may well serve as a framework for settling disputes between its parties.

The Concluding Statement at Madrid affirmed the intention of the parties to convene "a Conference on Confidence- and Security-Building Measures on Disarmament in Europe." The first stage of this conference was scheduled to begin in Stockholm on January 17, 1984. A report of its proceedings may be obtained from the State Department in Washington. It was not until 1989 that the follow-up meeting in Vienna meeting noted "the adoption of the Stockholm Document [as] a politically significant achievement."

The third follow-up meeting of states who were parties to the Helsinki Final Act was held in Vienna, Austria, ending on January 19, 1989. Less than ten months later, Poland, East Germany, Czechoslovakia, Hungary, Bulgaria, and Romania had "revolutions from below" and to a greater or lesser degree had terminated the role of the Communist Party after forty years.

It is immediately apparent that all of these countries are members of the Warsaw Pact, an agreement with the Soviet Union to allow it to maintain units of the Red Army in each of these countries. Such units were used in 1956 to invade Hungary and in 1968 to invade Czechoslovakia. The Concluding Statement of the Vienna Meeting in 1989 was quite long and contained no express mention of these invasions. In Annex II, some of the states with representatives present acknowledged that "it is their armed forces which bear most immediately on the essential security relationship in Europe, in particular, as they are signatories of the Treaties of Brussels (1948), Washington (1949) or

Warsaw (1955), and accordingly are members of the North Atlantic Alliance (NATO) or parties to the Warsaw Treaty or Pact."

The appearance on the scene of Mikhail Gorbachev in 1985 seems to have made a significant difference, particularly with his policy of *glasnost*. The Russian translation of this word is "openness." However, the Czech equivalent is *hlasitost*, or "loudness." The Czechs simply use the Russian word in reporting Gorbachev's actions, speculating that it really means publicity, not openness. In any event, the media in Moscow have reported that the invasions of 1956 and 1968 were all mistakes made by Gorbachev's predecessors, one of them being Leonid Brezhnev. It was this general secretary who formulated the so-called Brezhnev Doctrine justifying the invasion of Czechoslovakia in 1968.

Prior to World War II, this country was one of the six or seven most highly advanced, industrialized countries in the world. Since the 1948 Communist occupation, Czechoslovakia's economic decline has been gradual but visible. As to the prevailing atmosphere there, one French writer described it as a "cultural cemetery" in 1980. It was in 1977, however, that the Charter 77 Declaration was issued by Václav Havel and many other intellectually autonomous writers and activists. The Charter 77 Declaration, inter alia, cited the Helsinki Final Act as the basis for this declaration in support of human rights. Havel also wrote the essay "The Power of the Powerless" in this anthology, and other Czech writers either used the underground press, issuing *samizdat* newspapers or writing books beginning around 1982. Many of these books were published in the West for fear of prosecution for writing material subversive of the state. A Helsinki Watch Committee was formed in Prague and elsewhere in Central Europe. As Charter 77, the Czech human rights group wrote in 1985, in the Prague Challenge: "For forty years no war has been fought on European soil, yet Europe is not a continent at peace. Quite the contrary, as the foremost arena of the friction between two power blocs, it is the focus of constant tension posing a threat to the entire world."

Thirteen years later, Václav Havel took a very significant step in the direction of peace. His foreign minister, Jiri Dienstbeir, announced that, effective immediately, Czezhoslovakia would no longer export arms. According to the International Peace Institute in Stockholm, Sweden, the Czech arms industry was among the top seven in the entire world in terms of total weapons exports in 1988. The Soviet Union, the United States, West Germany, and Brazil were also among the top seven.

From this move toward a more peaceful world, it seems quite clear that both Václav Havel and Jiri Dienstbeir believe in the principles of the Helsinki Final Act. In issuing the Charter 77 Declaration in 1977, they both cited the Helsinki Final Act as one of the international conventions on which those signing the Declaation relied. It seems equally clear to the new Havel administration that the rationale behind NATO and the Warsaw Pact has become obsolete. New ideas and new thinking will simply have to replace both. Dienstbeir also observed that the reunification of the two Germanys was not something "we have to be afraid of." Neither President George Bush nor Secretary of State James Baker have yet acknowledged this fact of international life, even though the United States was one of the signatory countries of the Helsinki Final Act.

The next follow-up meeting of those countries is scheduled to be held in Helsinki beginning on March 24, 1992. Those states meeting in Vienna could not really have anticipated the changes that occurred in late 1989 and 1990 or the astonishing pace of revolutionary change. Accordingly, the meeting in Helsinki will have a new agenda with a few anticipated additions. One of them will clearly be the European Economic Community (EEC) and how it will treat the newly free countries of Central Europe. The EEC will be fully operational by December 31, 1992. Poland, Czechoslovakia, and Hungary will, by then, have applied for membership in the EEC, and their applications will in all likelihood be granted. The EEC and the Helsinki Final Act, with their similar objectives, must necessarily exist side-by-side, and it would be a serious mistake for the EEC to superimpose its policies on the Conference on Security and Co-operation in

Europe (CSCE), the umbrella organization of states signing the Helsinki Final Act. The EEC and CSCE will have many interests in common.

At the Vienna meeting, Section 24 of the Concluding Statement dealt with the environment, noting as follows: "Recognizing the need for preventive action, the participating States will strengthen their cooperation and intensify efforts aimed at protecting and improving the environment, bearing in mind the need to maintain and restore the ecological balance in air, water and soil. They will do this by, *inter alia*, developing their internal legislation and international commitments, and by applying the best available means, taking into account levels of development as well as economic and technical constraints. They underline the importance of the Regional Strategy for Environmental Protection and Rational Use of Natural Resources in EEC Member Countries Covering the Period Up to the Year 2000 and beyond. They welcome, and will take due account of, the report of World Commission on Environment and Development and the Environmental Perspective to the year 2000 and beyond, as well as the work already undertaken within the competent international fora, in particular within the framework of the 1979 Convention on Long-Range Transboundary Air Pollution. . . . " The fora (forums) mentioned include the International Court of Justice and the European Court of Justice in Luxembourg.

The Vienna Concluding Statement also dealt with Questions Relating to Security in Europe. Section 3 was as follows: "In this context, they confirm that they will respect each other's right freely to choose and develop their political, social, economic and cultural systems as well as their right to determine their laws, regulations, practices and policies. In exercizing these rights, they will insure that their laws, regulations, practices and policies conform with their obligations under international law and are brought into harmony with the provisions of the Declaration on Principles and other CSCE commitments." One of these commitments appeared in Article V of the Helsinki Final Act fifteen years earlier. "The participating States will settle disputes among them by peaceful means in such a manner as not to endanger international peace and security, and justice."

Does this mean that the Soviet Union will voluntarily agree to adjust the boundaries of Poland, as well as those of Lithuania, Latvia, and Estonia, as a matter of "justice"? A brief history of this dispute seems appropriate. On August 23, 1939, German Foreign Minister Joachim von Ribbentrop signed a nonaggression pact with Joseph Stalin. Von Ribbentrop signed on behalf of the absent Adolf Hitler. This pact led to the outbreak of World War II on September 1, 1939, with the invasion of Poland by armed forces of the Third Reich. However, a *secret* protocol was also signed at the same time and became effective immediately. This secret protocol allowed Stalin to annex Finland, Lithuania, Estonia, and Latvia. Lithuania had been assigned to Germany as being within its sphere of influence. However, on September 28, 1939, von Ribbentrop agreed with Stalin to cede Lithuania to the Soviet Union in exchange for a slice of Poland for the Germans. Stalin did not wait very long to activate this secret protocol. On June 15, 1940, the Red Army marched into Lithuania and annexed it together with Estonia and Latvia. During the winter of 1939–40, Finnish armed forces and guerrilla units successfully resisted the units of the Red Army, and in 1941 Germany invaded the Soviet Union. Stalin had other problems, even though he never hesitated to supply Germany with raw materials used to continue its war against Great Britain, France, and Poland. It seems impossible to find any act so cynical as that of Joseph Stalin, particularly when he belatedly asked for military assistance from the United States after it joined the war on December 7, 1941.

There is some speculation that Mikhail Gorbachev may request that the countries who are parties to the Helsinki Final Act advance the date of the next follow-up meeting to 1991, instead of 1992. He is just as aware of Stalin's actions in 1939 and 1940 as any other country's leaders. On January 15, 1990, he addressed a group of some 2,500 environmentalists in Moscow, offering a positive program to halt and even reverse the environmental degradation of the Soviet Union, Poland, East Germany, Hungary, and Czechoslovakia. The text of his address seems certain to attract the interest of EEC member states. Gorbachev mentioned the disaster at Chernobyl in 1985 as an example of what might go wrong, and even mentioned on-site inspection within the Soviet Union of other threats to the environment. Currently, the Soviet Friendship oil pipeline terminates within Czechoslovakia. There are two plants there, an oil refinery and a chemical-steel complex. The combination is devastating, and this area of Czechoslovakia, not far from Prague, is considered the most polluted area in the world. Sulphur emissions into the atmosphere and toxic waste dumped into the Danube River have created an environmental nightmare for those who live there. Václav Havel's speech on January 1, 1990, mentioned this legacy of pollution bequeathed by the Communist Party of Czecho-slovakia.

Last, but not least, is the future political role of the NATO and Warsaw Pact forces. This dispute seems certain to be part of the agenda for the follow-up meeting of 1992 in Helsinki, particularly if there is reunification of the two Germanys. To discuss collective security at all, there must be an enemy. Both Western Europe and the Soviet Union remember World War II and Hitler's Third Reich. No country wants to see a powerful and reunified Germany emerge as a military power again. While West Germany seems firmly committed to its membership within the EEC, NATO and the Warsaw Pact forces may be considered useful in a political, not military, role. They may be used to police Germany to prevent it ever again from becoming a military threat to all of Europe. Thus, Central Europe in 1990 and beyond will continue to engage the attention it has gotten in the media during the peaceful revolution beginning in 1989. The year 1990 may be considered an exciting and eventful period in history, but the *beyond* will mark a new, postrevolutionary period for historians.

Epilogue

Václav Havel

Address to the United States Congress, February 1990

We've chosen to end our book with the complete text of the address given on February 22, 1990 by Václav Havel, now the president of Czechoslovakia, to a joint session of the United States Congress. In this eloquent speech, Mr. Havel has once again best expressed the intelligence, decency, courage, and hope for the future that have characterized the revolution he and others have led in Central Europe.

My advisers advised me to speak on this important occasion in Czech. I don't know why. Perhaps they wanted you to enjoy the sweet sounds of my mother tongue.

The last time they arrested me, on October 27 of last year, I didn't know whether it was for two days or two years.

Exactly one month later, when the rock musician Michael Kocab told me that I would probably be proposed as a presidential candidate, I thought it was one of his usual jokes.

On December 10, 1989, when my actor friend Jiri Bartoska, in the name of the Civic Forum, nominated me as a candidate for president of the republic, I thought it was out of the question that the parliament we had inherited from the previous regime would elect me.

Nineteen days later, when I was unanimously elected president of my country, I had no idea that in two months I would be speaking before this famous and powerful assembly and that what I would say would be heard by millions of people who had never heard of me and that hundreds of politicians and political scientists would study every word I said.

When they arrested me on October 27, I was living in a country ruled by the most conservative Communist government in Europe, and our society slumbered beneath the pall of a totalitarian system. Today, less than four months later, I am speaking to you as the representative of a country that has set out on the road to democracy, a country where there is complete freedom of speech, that is getting ready for free elections, and that wants to create a prosperous market economy and its own foreign policy.

It is all very extraordinary.

But I have not come here to speak for myself or about my feelings or merely to talk about my own country. I have used this small example of something I know well to illustrate something general and important.

We are living in very extraordinary times. The human face of the world is changing so rapidly that none of the familiar political speedometers are adequate.

We playwrights, who have to cram a whole human life or an entire historical era in a two-hour play, can scarcely understand this rapidity ourselves. And if it gives us trouble, think of the trouble it must give political scientists, who spend their whole lives studying the realm of the probable — and have even less experience with the realm of the improbable than we playwrights.

Let me try to explain why I think the velocity of the changes in my country, in Central and Eastern Europe, and of course in the Soviet Union itself, has made such a significant impression on the face of the world today, and why it concerns the fate of us all, including you Americans. I would like to look at this first from the political point of view and then from a point of view that we might call philosophical.

Twice in this century the world has been threatened by catastrophe; twice this catastrophe was born in Europe; and twice you Americans, along with others, were called upon to save Europe, the whole world, and yourselves. The first rescue mis-

sion—among other things—provided significant help to us
Czechs and Slovaks.

Thanks to the great support of your president, Wilson, our
first president, Tomáš Garrigue Masaryk, was able to found our
modern independent state. He founded it, as you know, on the
same principles on which the United States of America was
founded, as Masaryk's manuscripts held by the Library of Congress testify.

In the meantime, the United States made enormous strides. It
became the most powerful nation on Earth, and it understood
the responsibility that flowed from this. Proof of this are the
hundreds of thousands of your young citizens who gave their
lives for the liberation of Europe and the graves of American
airmen and soldiers on Czechoslovak soil.

But something else was happening as well: the Soviet Union
appeared, grew, and transformed the enormous sacrifices of its
people suffering under totalitarian rule into a strength that, after
World War II, made it the second most powerful nation in the
world. It was a country that rightly gave people nightmares,
because no one knew what would occur to its rulers next and
what country they would decide to conquer and drag into their
"sphere of influence," as it is called in political language.

All of this taught us to see the world in bipolar terms, as two
enormous forces, one a defender of freedom, the other a source
of nightmares. Europe became the point of friction between
these two powers, and thus it turned into a single enormous
arsenal divided into two parts. In this process, one half of the
arsenal became part of that nightmarish power, while the other—
the free part—bordering on the ocean and having no wish to be
driven into it, was compelled, together with you, to build a
system to which we probably owe the fact that we still exist.

So you may have contributed to the salvation of us Europeans,
of the world, and thus of yourselves for a third time: you have
helped us survive until today—without a hot war this time but
merely a cold one.

And now what is happening is happening: the totalitarian
system in the Soviet Union and in most of its satellites is

breaking down, and our nations are looking for a way to democracy and independence. The first act in this remarkable drama began when Mr. Gorbachev and those around him who were faced with the sad reality of their country initiated their policy of *perestroika*. Obviously they had no idea either what they were setting in motion or how rapidly events would unfold. We knew a lot about the enormous number of growing problems that slumbered beneath the honeyed, unchanging mask of socialism. But I don't think any of us knew how little it would take for these problems to manifest themselves in all their enormity and for the longings of these nations to emerge in all their strength. The mask fell away so rapidly that, in the flood of work, we have literally no time to be astonished.

What does this all mean for the world in the long run? Obviously a number of things. This is, I am firmly convinced, a historically irreversible process, and as a result Europe will begin again to seek its own identity without being compelled to be a divided armory any longer. Perhaps this will create the hope that sooner or later your boys will no longer have to stand on guard for freedom in Europe, or come to our rescue, because Europe will at last be able to stand guard over itself. But that is still not the most important thing: the main thing is, it seems to me, that these revolutionary changes will enable us to escape from the rather antiquated straitjacket of this bipolar view of the world and to enter at last into an era of multipolarity. That is, into an era in which all of us — large and small, former slaves and former masters — will be able to create what your great President Lincoln called "the family of man." Can you imagine what a relief this would be to that part of the world that for some reason is called the Third World, even though it is the largest?

I don't think it's appropriate simply to generalize, so let me be specific:

First, as you certainly know, most of the big wars and other conflagrations over the centuries have traditionally begun and ended on the territory of modern Czechoslovakia, or were somehow related to that area. Let the Second World War stand as the most recent example. This is understandable: whether we like it or not, we are located in the very heart of Europe, and, thanks to this, we have no view of the sea and no real navy. I mention this because political stability in our country has traditionally been important for the whole of Europe. This is still true today. Our Government of National Understanding, our present Federal Assembly, the other bodies of the state, and I myself will personally guarantee this stability until we hold free elections, planned for June. We understand the terribly complex reasons, domestic political reasons above all, why the Soviet Union cannot withdraw its troops from our territory as quickly as they arrived in 1968. We understand that the arsenals built there over the past twenty years cannot be dismantled and removed overnight. Nevertheless, in our bilateral negotiations with the Soviet Union, we would like to have as many Soviet units as possible moved out of our country before the elections, in the interest of political stability. The more successful our negotiations, the more those who are elected in our places will be able to guarantee political stability in our country even after the elections.

Second, I often hear the question: How can the United States of America help us today? My reply is as paradoxical as the whole of my life has been: You can help us most of all if you help the Soviet Union on its irreversible, but immensely complicated, road to democracy. It is far more complicated than the road open to its former European satellites. You yourselves know best how to support, as rapidly as possible, the nonviolent evolution of this enormous, multinational body politic toward democracy and autonomy for all of its peoples. Therefore, it is not fitting for me to offer you any advice. I can only say that the sooner, the more quickly, and the more peacefully the Soviet Union begins to move along the road toward genuine political pluralism, respect for the rights of nations to their own integrity and to a working— that is a market—economy, the better it will be, not just for the Czechs and Slovaks, but for the whole world. And the sooner you yourselves will be able to reduce the burden of the military budget borne by the American people. To put it metaphorically, the millions you give to the East today will soon return to you in the form of billions in savings.

Third, it is not true that the Czech writer Václav Havel wishes to dissolve the Warsaw Pact tomorrow and then NATO the day after that, as some eager journalists have written. Václav Havel merely thinks what he has said here, that for another hundred years, American soldiers shouldn't have to be separated from their mothers just because Europe is incapable of being a guarantor of world peace, which it ought to be, in order to make some amends, at least, for having given the world two world wars. Sooner or later Europe must recover and come into its own and decide for itself how many of whose soldiers it needs, so that its own security and all the wider implications of that security may radiate peace into the whole world. Václav Havel cannot make decisions about things that are not proper for him to decide. He is merely putting in a good word for genuine peace, and for achieving it quickly.

Fourth, Czechoslovakia thinks that the planned summit conference of countries participating in the Helsinki process should take place soon and that, in addition to what it wants to accomplish, it should aim to hold the so-called Helsinki II conference earlier than 1992, as originally planned. Above all, we feel it could be far more significant than seemed possible before. We think that Helsinki II should become something equivalent to the European peace conference that has not yet been held — one that would finally put a formal end to the Second World War and all its unhappy consequences. Such a conference would officially bring a future democratic Germany, in the process of unifying itself, into a new pan-European structure that could decide about its own security system. This system would naturally require some connection with that part of the globe we might label the "Helsinki" part, stretching westward from Vladivostok all the way to Alaska. The borders of the European states, which, by the way, should become gradually less important, should finally be guaranteed legally by a common, regular treaty. It should be more than obvious that the basis for such a treaty would have to be general respect for human rights, genuine political pluralism, and genuinely free elections.

Fifth, naturally we welcome the initiative of President Bush, which was essentially accepted by Mr. Gorbachev as well, according to which the number of American and Soviet troops in Europe should be radically reduced. It is a magnificent shot in the arm for the Vienna disarmament talks and creates favorable conditions not only for our own efforts to achieve the quickest possible departure of Soviet troops from Czechoslovakia but also indirectly for our own intention to make considerable cuts in the Czechoslovak army, which is disproportionately large in relation to our population. If Czechoslovakia were forced to defend itself against anyone, which we hope will not happen, then it would be capable of doing so with a considerably smaller army, because this time — after not just decades but centuries — its defense would be supported by the common and indivisible will of both its peoples and its leadership. Our freedom, our independence, and our newborn democracy have been purchased at great cost, and we shall not surrender them. For the sake of order, I should add that whatever steps we take are not intended to complicate the Vienna disarmament talks but, on the contrary, to facilitate them.

Sixth, Czechoslovakia is returning to Europe. In the general interest and its own interest as well, it wants to coordinate this return — both politically and economically — with the other returnees, which means, above all, with its neighbors the Poles and the Hungarians. We are doing what we can to coordinate these returns. And at the same time, we are doing what we can so that Europe will be capable of really accepting us, its wayward children. Which means that it may open itself to us and may begin to transform its structures — which are formally European but de facto Western European — in that direction, but in such a way that it will not be to its detriment but rather to its advantage.

Seventh, I have already said this in our parliament, and I would like to repeat it here in this Congress, which is architecturally far more attractive: for many years, Czechoslovakia — as someone's meaningless satellite — has refused to face up honestly to its coresponsibility for the world. It has a lot to make up for. If I dwell on this and so many important things, it is only because I feel—along with my fellow citizens—a sense of culpability for our former reprehensible passivity and a rather ordinary sense of indebtedness.

Eighth, we are of course delighted that your country is so readily lending its support to our fresh efforts to renew democracy. Both our peoples were deeply moved by the generous offers made a few days ago in Prague at the Charles University, one of the oldest in Europe, by your secretary of state, Mr. James Baker. We are ready to sit down and talk about them.

Ladies and gentlemen, I have been president for only two months and I haven't attended any schools for presidents. My only school was life itself. Therefore I don't want to burden you any longer with my political thoughts, but instead I will move on to an area that is more familiar to me, to what I would call the philosophical aspect of those changes that still concern everyone, although they are taking place in our corner of the world.

As long as people are people, democracy in the full sense of the word will always be no more than an ideal; one may approach it as one would a horizon, in ways that may be better or worse, but it can never be fully attained. In this sense you too are merely approaching democracy. You have thousands of problems of all kinds, as other countries do. But you have one great advantage: you have been approaching democracy uninterruptedly for more than 200 years, and your journey toward the horizon has never been disrupted by a totalitarian system. Czechs and Slovaks, despite their humanistic traditions that go back to the first millennium, have approached democracy for a mere twenty years, between the two world wars, and now for the 3½ months since November 17 of last year.

The advantage that you have over us is obvious at once.

The Communist type of totalitarian system has left both our nations, Czechs and Slovaks—as it has all the nations of the Soviet Union and the other countries the Soviet Union subjugated in its time—a legacy of countless dead, an infinite spectrum of human suffering, profound economic decline, and above all enormous human humiliation. It has brought us horrors that fortunately you have not known.

At the same time, unintentionally, of course, it has given us something positive: a special capacity to look, from time to time, somewhat further than someone who has not undergone this bitter experience. A person who cannot move and live a somewhat normal life because he is pinned under a boulder has more time to think about his hopes than someone who is not trapped that way.

What I am trying to say is this: we must all learn many things from you, from how to educate our offspring and how to elect our representatives all the way to how to organize our economic life so that it will lead to prosperity and not to poverty. But it doesn't have to be merely assistance from the well educated, the powerful, and the wealthy to someone who has nothing and therefore has nothing to offer in return.

We too can offer something to you: our experience and the knowledge that has come from it.

This is a subject for books, many of which have already been written and many of which have yet to be written. I shall therefore limit myself to a single idea.

The specific experience I'm talking about has given me one great certainty: Consciousness precedes Being, and not the other way around, as Marxists claim.

For this reason, the salvation of this human world lies nowhere else than in the human heart, in the human power to reflect, in human meekness, and in human responsibility.

• Without a global revolution in the sphere of human consciousness, nothing will change for the better in the sphere of our Being as humans; and the catastrophe toward which this world is headed, be it ecological, social, demographic, or a general breakdown of civilization, will be unavoidable. If we are no longer threatened by world war, or by the danger that the absurd mountains of accumulated nuclear weapons might blow up the world, this does not mean that we have definitively won. We are in fact far from the final victory.

We are still a long way from that "family of man"; in fact, we seem to be receding from the ideal rather than drawing closer to it. Interests of all kinds — personal, selfish, state, national, group, and, if you like, company interests — still considerably outweigh genuinely common and global interests. We are still under the sway of the destructive and vain belief that man is the pinnacle of creation, not just a part of it, and that therefore everything is permitted. There are still many who say they are concerned not for themselves but for the cause, while they are demonstrably out for themselves and not for the cause at all. We are still destroying the planet that was entrusted to us and its environment. We still close our eyes to the growing social, ethnic, and cultural conflicts in the world. From time to time we say that the anonymous megamachinery we have created for ourselves no longer serves us, but rather has enslaved us, yet we still fail to do anything about it.

In other words, we still don't know how to put morality ahead of politics, science, and economics. We are still incapable of understanding that the only genuine backbone of all our actions — if they are to be moral — is responsibility. Responsibility to something higher than my family, my country, my company, my success. Responsibility to the order of Being, where all our actions are indelibly recorded, and where, and only where, they will be properly judged.

The interpreter or mediator between us and this higher authority is what is traditionally referred to as human conscience.

If I subordinate my political behavior to this imperative mediated to me by my conscience, I can't go far wrong. If on the contrary I were not guided by this voice, not even ten presidential schools with 2,000 of the best political scientists in the world could help me.

This is why I ultimately decided — after resisting for a long time — to accept the burden of political responsibility.

I am not the first, nor will I be the last, intellectual to do this. On the contrary, my feeling is that there will be more and more of them all the time. If the hope of the world lies in human consciousness, then it is obvious that intellectuals cannot go on forever avoiding their share of responsibility for the world and hiding their distaste for politics under an alleged need to be independent.

It is easy to have independence in your program and then leave others to carry that program out. If everyone thought that way, pretty soon no one would be independent.

I think that you Americans should understand this way of thinking. Wasn't it the best minds of your country, people you could call intellectuals, who wrote your famous Declaration of Independence, your Bill of Rights, and your Constitution and who—above all—took upon themselves the practical responsibility for putting them into practice? The worker from Branik in Prague that your president referred to in his State of the Union message this year is far from being the only person in Czechoslovakia, let alone in the world, to be inspired by those great documents. They inspire us all. They inspire us despite the fact that they are over 200 years old. They inspire us to be citizens.

When Thomas Jefferson wrote, "Governments are instituted among Men deriving their just Powers from the Consent of the Governed," it was a simple and important act of the human spirit.

What gave meaning to that act, however, was the fact that the author backed it up with his life. It was not just his words, it was his deeds as well.

I will end where I began: history has accelerated. I believe that, once again, it will be the human mind that will notice this acceleration, give it a name, and transform those words into deeds.